Studies in Funerary Archaeolog

The Archaeology of Cremation

Burned human remains in funerary studies

edited by
Tim Thompson

 OXBOW | books
Oxford & Philadelphia

First published in the United Kingdom in 2015. Reprinted in 2021 by
OXBOW BOOKS
The Old Music Hall, 106–108 Cowley Road, Oxford OX4 1JE

and in the United States by
OXBOW BOOKS
1950 Lawrence Road, Havertown, PA 19083

Paperback Edition: ISBN 978-1-78297-848-0
Digital Edition: ISBN 978-1-78297-849-7

A CIP record for this book is available from the British Library

Library of Congress Cataloging-in-Publication Data

The archaeology of cremation : burned human remains in funerary studies / edited by Tim Thompson.
       pages cm. -- (Studies in funerary archaeology ; vol. 8)
   Includes bibliographical references.
   ISBN 978-1-78297-848-0 (paperback) -- ISBN 978-1-78297-849-7 (digital) 1. Human remains (Archaeology) 2. Cremation--History--To 1500. 3. Cremation--Social aspects--History--To 1500. 4. Funeral rites and ceremonies, Ancient. 5. Death--Social aspects--History--To 1500. 6. Social archaeology. 7. Excavations (Archaeology) 8. Archaeology--Methodology. I. Thompson, Timothy James Upton.
   CC79.5.H85A83 2015
   930.1--dc23

                             2015008202

Printed in the United Kingdom by Severn

For a complete list of Oxbow titles, please contact:

UNITED KINGDOM
Oxbow Books
Telephone (01865) 241249
Email: oxbow@oxbowbooks.com
www.oxbowbooks.com

UNITED STATES OF AMERICA
Oxbow Books
Telephone (610) 853 9131, Fax (610) 853-9146
Email: queries@casemateacademic.com
www.casemateacademic.com/oxbow

Oxbow Books is part of the Casemate Group

Front cover: Light and Water © Michael Bosanko
Back cover: A large trunk of charred wood found in the tomb 250, residue of the funeral pyre (photo courtesy of Dr Michele Guirguis)

Contents

List of contributors

ETHEL ALLUE
Institut de Paleoecologia Humana i Evolució
Social (IPHES), Àrea de Prehistoria
Universitat Rovira i Virgili, Tarragona, Spain

VANESSA CAMPANACHO
Department of Archaeology
Faculty of Arts and Humanities
University of Sheffield, United Kingdom

JENNY CATAROCHE
Public Health Directorate
Health and Social Services
States of Guernsey

CLAUDIA GARRIDO-VARAS
International Committee of the Red Cross (ICRC)
Geneva, Switzerland

DAVID GONÇALVES
Research Centre for Anthropology and Health (CIAS),
University of Coimbra
Calçada Martim de Freitas
Coimbra 3000-456, Portugal

REBECCA GOWLAND
Department of Archaeology
Durham University
South Road, Durham, DH1 3LE, United Kingdom

MICHELE GUIRGUIS
Dipartimento di Storia, Scienze dell'Uomo e della
Formazione
Università di Sassari

LISE HARVIG
Laboratory of Biological Anthropology
Department of Forensic Medicine
Faculty of Health Sciences, University of
Copenhagen, Frederik V's vej 11
DK 2100 Copenhagen, Denmark

MARISOL INTRIAGO-LEIVA
Unidad Especial de Identificación Forense
Servicio Médico Legal
Santiago, Chile

RUI MATALOTO
Municipality of Redondo
Praça da República
7170-011 Redondo, Portugal

GIAMPAOLO PIGA
Scienze Politiche
Scienze della Comunicazione e Ingegneria
dell'Informazione
Università di Sassari

FILIPA CORTESÃO SILVA
Research Centre for Anthropology and Health (CIAS)
University of Coimbra
Calçada Martim de Freitas
Coimbra 3000-456, Portugal

KIRSTY E. SQUIRES
Faculty of Computing, Engineering and Science
Staffordshire University, Science Centre
Leek Road, Stoke-on-Trent
ST4 2DF, United Kingdom

TIM THOMPSON
School of Science & Engineering,
Teesside University, Borough Road
Middlesbrough, TS1 3BA, United Kingdom

DOUGLAS H. UBELAKER
Smithsonian Institution
Washington, D.C.

PRISCILLA FERREIRA ULGUIM
School of Science & Engineering
Teesside University, Borough Road
Middlesbrough, TS1 3BA, United Kingdom

Foreword

Jacqueline I. McKinley

I was requested by the editor to provide a personal view of how the study of cremated remains has evolved within the UK over the course of my experience within the subject. Much has changed generally within the ever widening investigation of human bone from archaeological sites within the last three decades. There has been a massive expansion in the number of people engaged therein, of establishments at which they can study and undertake research, and of areas of analysis and the angles of approach. That complementary diversity enriches our understanding of past populations, the influences on their lives, affects on their bodies and their treatment of the dead, and further facets of these themes continue to emerge over time. The variety of terms with which those working in the field describe themselves - palaeopathologist, physical anthropologist, osteoarchaeologist, biological anthropologist, forensic anthropologist, bioarchaeologist - illustrates the varied approaches, backgrounds and areas of interest that currently abound. The last 10–15 years in particular have seen a marked increase of interest in, and study of, cremated bone and the mortuary rite of cremation in the UK. Such was not always the case.

Many early British antiquarians dismissed cremated remains as valueless "... nothing but Ashes, or burnt Cinders ..." (seventeenth century quotation; Jessup 1974, 139). A more enlightened approach in the late nineteenth and early twentieth centuries saw some archaeologists presenting good descriptions of graves and potential pyre sites, but recording was erratic and details of the formation processes, and particularly the relevance of the cremated bone itself, were frequently overlooked or misunderstood. As recently as the early 1960s cremated remains were being discarded on some sites and neither they nor the context were being considered in detail, with a tendency to describe all deposits as "cremations" ... a source of much frustration given the wealth of material that was excavated over these years.

Thirty years or so ago, when I first began working with cremated remains, this "always the bridesmaid never the bride" subject aroused little enthusiasm amongst most of those working with human remains from archaeological sites in the British Isles; though a few, such as Calvin Wells, Leonard Wilkinson and T. S. Spence had made some serious sorties into the subject in the 1960s–70s. At this time, most UK practitioners styled themselves "palaeopathologists" (something I have never dared do), and the fragmentary and altered state of cremated remains, together with the commonly observed incomplete recovery of all the bone from the pyre site for burial, rendered them of apparently limited value for such studies.

My own first encounter with cremated remains left a similarly inauspicious impression – wet sieving samples from a Bronze Age barrow cemetery in cold water in an Orcadian bothy in November 1979 thinking "... who on earth is going to be able to do anything with this lot? ..."; the remains were, as I recall, poorly preserved and heavily comminuted (thanks to heavy acid soils). Excavation of a Bronze Age cemetery in north Wales the following year provided the source material for my undergraduate dissertation and set the course for the future, igniting a plethora of queries about this multi-faceted mortuary rite to which, at the time, there appeared to be limited satisfactory answers. Many contemporaneous archaeological excavation reports (which is where most references to the material and the rite did and still do appear) written in the UK seemed to display a lack of understanding of the cremation process and its effects on bone, the influence of the burial environment was not fully appreciated, and the possible existence of a variety of cremation-related deposits was rarely considered. I recall, on commencing the analysis of the approximately 2400 burial remains from the Anglo-Saxon cemetery at Spong Hill, Norfolk in the mid-1980s, being told by the then osteological advisor to the funding body that "... there will be no pathology ..." (see Chapter 7 of the monograph publication which features, amongst other conditions, a rare example of a calcified lymph node indicative of tuberculosis).

Elsewhere in Europe, particularly in Germany, Poland and Sweden, cremated remains from sites had been routinely examined from a much earlier date (see Lange *et al.* 1987). Analytical techniques were being developed and the nature of cremated bone was being explored both in Europe and the US (associated with the development of forensic anthropology; see Doug Uberlaker's excellent review, Chapter 9). Calvin Wells had enhanced his understanding of the cremation process by visiting his local crematorium in the 1960s–70s (one of several crematoria I subsequently made observations at); whilst in the US, Baby and Binford had considered the differing effects of burning "green" and "dry" bone. The area of enquiry was followed in subsequent decades by Pointeck in Poland, Pat Shipman and co-workers in the US, and Holden, Phakey and Clement in Australia, amongst others, all of who considered the effects of temperature and oxygen supply on the macroscopic (colour, fragmentation) and microscopic appearance of the bone (see Thompson, Chapter 1). Histological examination of cremated bone in the 1970s and subsequently by Herrmann and other colleagues in Germany and the Netherlands provided insights into the heat-induced structural and chemical changes to the bone, and considered the application of microscopic ageing and sexing techniques to cremated bone. Per Holck's 1980's holistic review of Norwegian cremated remains included chapters on thermo-technology and "grades of cremation", including the potential efficiency of different fuels. Recognising the intrinsic problems of sexing cremated individuals, in the 1970s–80s Gejvall, Van Vark and Wahl developed metric methods aimed at assisting in the process: limited bone recovery render some measurements more applicable than others and variable shrinkage presents another potential problem. A major break-through recently has been the development of a reliable radiocarbon technique for use on cremated remains (Lanting *et al.* 2001), releasing a massive, previously untapped resource and allowing routine analysis of samples from deposits devoid of datable artefactual material, enabling the bone and the mortuary rite to be placed in it's correct temporal phase.

There has been a growing interest in the mortuary rite and recognition of its complexity. Much of the recent research in academic institutions has focused on microscopic changes, confirming and/or enhancing via advanced or newly developed techniques the observations of earlier researchers (e.g. see Thompson and Squires, Chapters 1 and 7). The scope of enquiry, both in universities and the wider archaeological community (in which I include myself), has broadened, however, with observations in modern crematoria (e.g. see Gonçalves *et al.* Chapter 4), experimental work in laboratories and numerous experimental pyre cremations enhancing the understanding of how cremation works and what may be expected to survive at the end of the process. This information has fed-back into the contextual data and enabled a wider appreciation of the various parts of the rite which continues to be explored, together with the potential symbolic relevance of what was being undertaken at different stages of the rite.

It is this broader view of the mortuary rite that I find particularly fascinating. I believe much remains to be revealed of this often under-estimated rite, much of which can be accessed only via formation processes. Archaeologists undertaking the excavation of cremation-related features/deposits need to appreciate that they are dealing with the physical remains of a multifaceted rite from which much can be deduced. Not all deposits containing cremated bone will represent the remains of a burial, and bone from a single cremation may be distributed between several deposit types including small *memento mori*. Improvements over the last few decades in excavation and post-excavation procedures, with greater consistency and objectivity in approach, are providing better quality site recording to assist in interpretation; some recently applied techniques being of particular assistance where the soil acidity results in destruction of much of the trabecular bone (see Harvig, Chapter 3). In other words, context is vital, both in an archaeological and forensic setting (see Garrido-Varas and Intriago-Levia, Chapter 10). Adoption, by both excavators and osteologist, of a common (or at least commensurate) terminology, excavation methodology and analytical methods, will allow comparison of data across broader geographic and temporal areas.

Publications such as this, devoted exclusively to cremated/burnt human remains, their context and/or the mortuary rite, are rare. There are some holistic period/geographic volumes such as that by Holck (Norway), Sigvallius or Artelius and Svanbery (Sweden), bibliographic reviews such as that by Lange *et al.*, and the excellent, largely forensic oriented 2008 publication by Schmit and Symes. The 1997 *Cremation Studies in Archaeology* presents papers from a further rarity, a symposium (in Amsterdam) dedicated to the subject, with contributors from six European countries (although there were no UK contributions). More often, however, papers on some aspect of the subject form one or two contributions within broader themed works such as *The Oxford Handbook of the Archaeology of Death and Burial* (2013: Tarlow and Nilsson Stutz (eds)), which features three contributions on cremation amongst its 44 chapters, including my own most recent offering on excavation, analysis and interpretation of cremation-related deposits.

By far the largest body of publication comprises the thousands of individual site excavation reports written world-wide, featuring specialist cremated bone reports which, certainly in recent decades, often include important revelatory discussion on pyre technology and aspects of the cremation ritual, setting the data in its broader temporal/geographic context. Such publications include site monographs, though more often – at least in the UK – the reports appear in national or local county journals. Sadly, many seem to languish un-noticed by the academic world despite the wealth of information they now often contain. Hopefully, with the growth of on-line publishing this valuable source of data and discussion will become more widely accessible to us all (though we may simply end-up with just too much to read!).

The subject matter of this volume crosses national borders, drawing together papers from a wide geographic sphere, illustrating many broad similarities and some intriguing differences in various aspect of the mortuary rite. An example of the latter is provided by Piga and Guierguis (Chapter 5), where the unusual formation processes demonstrated in several of the *busta* excavated within the seventh–sixth century BC Sardinian necropolis *Monte Sirai* indicate the presence of the unmanipulated *in situ* remains of a corpse cremated in a prone position, and intriguing indications of partial burning, the formation process of which is as yet unknown. Ulguim's paper on fifteenth–seventeenth century AD Brazilian cremation cemeteries (Chapter 8) represents a rare example of being able to compare the archaeological remains with fascinating contemporaneous written accounts of the cremation rite. The volume features both archaeological and forensic data, demonstrating how the same analytic techniques inform both areas of application, and presenting recent research results in the light of previously gathered evidence. There will undoubtedly be much more to follow.

Wessex Archaeology, Salisbury. Summer 2014

References

Most of the references are to be found elsewhere in the volume in the contributions by Thompson, Squires and Ubelaker, and in an attempt to minimise the bibliography in a short foreword the reader is referred to these three chapters; only publications not cited elsewhere are included here.

Artelius, T. and Svanberg, F. (eds) 2005. *Dealing with the Dead: Archaeological Perspectives on Prehistoric Scandinavian Burial Ritual*. Stockholm: National Heritage Board Sweden.
Jessup, R. 1974. *Curiosities of British Archaeology*. Colchester: Phillimore.
Lange, M., Schutkowski, H., Hummel, S. and Herrmann, B. 1987. *A Bibliography on Cremations*. PACT 19. Göttingen: University of Göttingen.

Lanting, J. N., Aerts-Bijma, A. T. and van der Plicht, J. 2001. Dating of cremated bones. *Radiocarbon* 43(2), 249–54.

Pointeck, J. 1976. The process of cremation and its influence on the morphology of bones in the light of results of experimental research. *Archaeologia Polski* 21, 254–80.

Sigvallius, B. 1994. *Funeral Pyres: Iron Age Cremations in North Spånga.* Thesis and Papers in Osteology 1. Stockholm: Stockholm University.

Smits, E., Iregren, E. and Drusini, A. G. (eds) 1997. *Cremation Studies in Archaeology.* Saonara: Logos Edizioni.

Wahl, J. 1982. Leichenbrändun ter suehungen tin Uberbluck uber die Bearbeitungens und Aussage-Möglichkerten von Brandgräber. *Praehistorische Zeitschrift* 57(1), 1–125.

Acknowledgements

Many people have contributed to the drawing together of this volume. This book is the product of many conversations and discussions and of a collective desire to push the field of cremation studies forward. My first foray into the study of cremation and burned bone happened during my MSc in the Department of Archaeological Science at Bradford (supervised by Rob Janaway and Bob Pastor) and then continued and developed during my PhD work at the University of Sheffield (under Professors Andrew Chamberlain and Martin Evison). This early work was focussed on the difficulties associated with identifying victims of mass fatalities incidents, and from there expanded into cremation practices more broadly. Since then, I've been fortunate enough to work on material from a broad range of contexts and periods, although I would never describe myself as an archaeologist. My 'period', such as it is, is the modern one (the always moving last 70 years of forensic interest), but really my experience focusses on the development of new techniques and the refinement of methodologies which help others to better answer the questions that interest them.

Whether they realise it or not many people have influenced my work in this area. Pamela Mayne Correia (University of Alberta, Canada) has written work that I will always refer to and which has been largely the inspiration for mine. Dr Steven Symes (Mercyhurst University) and Dr Douglas Ubelaker (the Smithsonian) have also been tremendously influential, and working with them always reminds me of my excitement for this subject. Currently, much of my work has been with Dr Meez Islam (Teesside University), and I am grateful to him for his expert advice and willingness to try new ideas and approaches just to see if they work. I have also immensely enjoyed working with Dr David Gonçalves and our Portuguese colleagues and I have learned a lot from them all. Likewise GP with his unusual sites in beautiful parts of Italy. Thanks too, to the many people who have set me countless burned bone challenges over the years which have sent me off in many interesting and unexpected directions.

With regard to this volume, I would like the thank Oxbow Books and Clare Litt and Julie Gardiner for their help and guidance, the authors for sharing their work and results, and the peer reviewers who gave their time and comments freely – including but not limited to, Sarah Ellingham (Teesside University), David Errickson (Teesside University), Roxana Ferllini, Gillian Fowler (University of Lincoln), Dr Rebecca Gowland (Durham University), Dr Andrew Millard (Durham University), Dr John Robb (University of Cambridge), Gaynor Western (Ossa Freelance).

Overall though, this is the product of my long-standing interest and fascination with the study of cremated and burned material, and as such, with the study of people.

Chapter 1

Fire and the body: Fire and the people

Tim Thompson

Introduction

For many years, the study of cremated bone has been seen as less important and worthwhile than the study of unburned human remains. Williams (2008), in the excellent Schmidt and Symes edited volume *The Analysis of Burned Human Remains*, has argued that human remains from cremation contexts were viewed as being peripheral to other less fragmented bodies, such as unburned remains, mummies and bog bodies. He concluded that "cremation is assumed to be 'poor' archaeological data" (*ibid.,* 240), and that there has been an over-emphasis on the destructive nature of cremation. The reasons for this marginalisation focussed on the perceived lack of information that this material can present combined with the challenging nature of actually analysing it. Unfortunately this defeatist view within archaeology fails to recognise the "rich evidence provided by the artefacts, contexts, monuments and landscapes" (*ibid.*) associated with the act and process of cremation. We must remember that "context is all important: burned human remains do not just simply occur in a vacuum but are, rather, mostly the result of human agency" (Thompson 2009, 296). Cremation is therefore not simply burning a body – there are myriad stages, technologies and actions involved, which can vary between communities and across time, resulting in a practice that can be a dominant or exceptional rite. The study of cremation therefore "offers insights into life and the living" (Kong 2012, 416). In addition, this lack of focus on burned remains means that our understanding of the nature of heat-induced change of bone itself is still lacking. This complex situation demands that the topic requires its own theoretical framework, beyond simple reference to the burial of unburned bodies – an *archaeology of cremation*. This book demonstrates that the study of cremation and its associated material culture is well underway, and combined with new intellectual frameworks, is offering interesting and innovative interpretations of the past.

Our ability to provide full and rounded interpretations of cremations from the past relies upon the quality and quantity of our research – and we can see that this underpinning research has undergone thematic changes over the past few decades. Table 1.1 displays the general thematic trends in this area. As can be seen, initial case studies and isolated preliminary studies developed into more thorough experimental work, although arguably at the expense of the surrounding funerary context. This is perhaps understandable since so little has been fully understood about heat-induced changes in the skeleton. Over the past few years, the majority of publications have focussed on the increasingly analytical study of bone microstructure, with the incorporation of progressively more complex methodologies to further understand the physical and chemical changes to the bone itself and relate these back to the process of burning (Table 1.1). Yet subsequent use of this information to interpret archaeological contexts is rare. That is not to say that it is not happening, as will be explored further below. Nonetheless, we are still largely in the situation where we understand the heat-induced changes in bone in much greater detail and depth, and have a larger portfolio of tools to study this material, but have advanced our understand of the importance and significance of the act of cremation by only a little.

In the October of 2009, archaeologists at Cardiff University hosted the 'Ancient Cremations Workshop: Ancient Cremation – reigniting the debate' conference. This marked the first time that such a conference had been held focussing solely on the

Table 1.1: General themes of research with burned bone.

Approx. time frame	Pre-1980s	1980s	Mid-1990s to mid-2000s	Mid-2000s onwards
General Research Themes	Isolated and preliminary studies	Actualistic experimental studies	The nature of heat-induced change	Increasingly microscopic analysis of heat-induced change
			Implications of heat-induced change for practice	Review commentaries
Typical Publications	Baby, 1954; Wells, 1960; Bindford, 1963; Gejvall, 1969; Van Vark, 1974; 1975	Thurman and Willmore, 1981; Gilchrist and Mytum, 1986; Buikstra and Swegle, 1989; Spenneman and Colley, 1989	Holden et al. 1995a; 1995b; Christensen, 2002; Rogers and Daniels 2002; Hiller et al. 2003; Koon et al. 2003	Piga et al. 2008; Thompson et al. 2009; Rogers et al. 2010; Beckett et al. 2011; Harbeck et al. 2011; Lebon et al. 2011; Thompson et al. 2013
			Herrmann and Bennett, 1999; de Gruchy and Rogers, 2002; Thompson, 2002; 2004; Pope and Smith, 2004	Thompson, 2009; Ubelaker, 2009; Gonçalves, 2012

Table 1.2: Cremated bone terminology (adapted from Thompson 2009).

Term	Definition
Cremation	The act and process of burning a body as part of a funerary rite; a ritualised event
Cremated bone	The bone that remains, usually having undergone some form of heat-induced alteration, after a cremation
Burned bone	Bone that has been heated or burned, but not necessarily as part of a funerary rite
Incineration	The act of burning
Calcined bone	Bone that has progressed through all stages of heat-induced transformation (Mayne Correia 1997; Thompson 2004) resulting in structural change, a loss of organic material and a white colouration
Cremains	Generally an American term to describe cremated human remains
Pyrolysis	The transformation of a compound by heat

study and interpretation of cremated bone and cremation contexts. It was a useful event for galvanising those interested in this area – indeed, some of those present and giving papers in Cardiff have also contributed to this volume. In the years since that workshop there has been an increase in the work undertaken on cremated material and as a result the discipline more widely is seeing the potential value of these remains. As such, the cremated remains and associated material from a range of new areas and contexts are being studied. These are very positive developments for the study of ancient cremations, but it was still felt that a single volume was needed to draw together current thought on their study of cremations and their contribution to our understanding of the funerary context, and past societies more broadly.

At this stage, it is worth just defining the terms that are used within the study of cremated bone, as the misuse of some terms has and can cause problems when discussing interpretations of archaeological contexts (Symes *et al.* 2008; Thompson 2009). Table 1.2 presents definitions of the key terms and phrases used within the cremation literature. As can be seen, there are subtle but important differences between these terms which are particularly significant when attempting to interpret the funerary context. With these in mind, it is important to consider the physical changes to the body as a result of burning, before we can consider the wider social implications of the rite.

Fire and the body

The body undergoes significant change when it is exposed to fire; this is what makes the study of cremated remains so challenging, but is also likely why cremation has been used as a funerary rite for thousands of years. Since it is not possible to fully interpret a scene of burning or cremation without reference to the transformation the burning causes to the body, a summary of these changes is presented below. Readers who require greater detail are directed to the likes of Fairgrieve (2008) or Schmidt and Symes (2008).

Damage to the body is largely the result of proximity to the fire. Thus since the soft tissues are the most external and superficial of the bodily tissues, they will be exposed to the heat of the fire and will change first. The initial change that is undergone by the soft tissues (and the hard tissues too, see below) is dehydration as the water contained within the body is lost. In the soft tissues, this causes shrinkage and contraction which result in the splitting and tearing of the organs and thus exposure of the deeper tissues. Burns are often described by their severity, with a first degree burn involving the epidermis, second degree burns going deeper into the dermal layer, third degree burns involving all layers of the skin and some subcutaneous structures, and fourth degree burns extending deep to the muscle and bone. Hair and nails will also be affected, and will tend to melt and deform. The internal organs will shrink considerably due to their high moisture content.

Blood will also be affected by the process of burning. This happens in two ways. First, the heat of the fire causes physical destruction of the contents of the blood, such as the red blood cells. But the products of the fire will also cause changes in the blood. A common example is the release of carbon monoxide from the fire which is breathed into the body and then binds preferentially with the red blood cells instead of oxygen. This in turn can cause characteristic colour change in the soft tissues.

Once the soft tissues are severely compromised, the fire can begin to alter the underlying skeleton. Symes *et al.* (2008) provide a detailed description of the order in which the skeleton would be exposed and damaged. They note that areas with thin soft tissue coverage will exhibit heat-induced changes first. Thus for example, the skeletal elements associated with the back of the hands, the knees, heels, and face will be damaged before the shafts of the long bones, the inner pelvis and the palms of the hands. One should also note that the body will adopt the "pugilistic attitude" when burned which will provide further protection for some anatomical regions. This sort of information, which is based on the examination of modern burning cases and examples from modern crematoria, allow one to interpret the position of the body in relation to the fire when only the bones remain. This is particularly helpful in identifying examples of "non-standard" body positioning or handling.

Microscopically the skeleton will also undergo significant change, and it is in this area that much of the recent burned bone research has focussed (see Table 1.1). In her important review of 1997, Mayne Correia described four stages of heat-induced degradation in bone. These stages are *Dehydration* (the loss of the water from the bone), *Decomposition* (the loss of the organic components of the bone), *Inversion* (the alteration of the inorganic structure), and *Fusion* (the coalescing of the inorganic crystals in the bone). Later, Thompson (2004) slightly modified the detail of these stages, but crucially termed them "heat-induced transformation" rather than "degradation". This was important as the original term implied that as burning continues the usefulness of the bone for study decreases. Recent research has shown that this is not the case, but rather it simply becomes more difficult to glean useful information from this material. Further, while it is useful for our understanding to use these four categories, the heat-induced changes that occur within them are rather more complicated, and several stages can be exhibited on the same bone simultaneously. Thompson (2005) has divided the range of heat-induced changes seen in bone into primary- and secondary-level changes. Prior to 2000 (Table 1.1), the bulk of the work on burned and cremated bone focussed on so-called secondary-level changes. These include colour change, propagation of fractures and changes to the mechanical strength of the bone. This is easy to understand since these changes are easy to see and record, and do not require advanced methods for study. However as has been noted (Thompson 2005; 2009), these changes do not actually explain what is occurring within the bone as it is burned. Rather they are the manifestation of other, more fundamental, changes. Thompson (2005) has shown that these more fundamental, or primary-level changes, are the removal of the organic component and the modification to the inorganic crystal component. All other changes (that is, the more visible and popular secondary-level changes) derive from this.

The most obvious change to occur to bone as it is burned is in colour, and this has been repeatedly used in the interpretation of cremation and burned bone contexts. The general trend regarding heat-induced colour change is for the bone to alter from its natural colour of creamy white, through dark greys and black and then if burning continues, to travel through light greys and finally resulting in white bone with occasional light blue patches (Asmussen 2009; Gejvall 1969; Gilchrist and Mytum 1986; Heglar 1984; Lyman 1994; Mayne Correia 1997; Nicholson 1993; Quatrehomme *et al.* 1998; Shipman *et al.* 1984; Sillen and Hoering, 1993; Stiner *et al.* 1995). An argument has been made that colour is related to the temperature of the fire, and there are a number of publications that explicitly make this link, although some with more conviction than others (for example: Chandler 1987; Grévin *et al.* 1998; Parker 1985; Shipman *et al.* 1984). Yet this is not entirely the case. Colour is actually related to the combustion of the carbon within the bone (Buikstra and Swegle 1989; Mayne Correia 1997) and this in turn is influenced by a range of variables (such as duration, oxygen levels, clothing, presence of accelerants, etc.) of which temperature is but one. Not all colours found on burned bone are related to the combustion of carbon-rich compounds either. Although the presence of browns has been associated with the presence of haemoglobin, other colours such as greens, yellows and pinks have been linked to trace metals and various contaminants from the burial and funerary contexts (Amadasi *et al.* 2014; Dunlop 1978; Gejvall 1969; Gilchrist and Mytum 1986). Further, the removal of the organic component (and therefore the changes in colour) can even occur in bone buried under a source of fire (Asmussen 2009; Bennett 1999; Stiner *et al.* 1995), although clearly the protection of the surrounding soil matrix means that the loss of the organic matter is not as great as if the bones were directly in the fire (Bennett 1999).

The presence of heat-induced fractures has also been used to interpret cremation contexts. Early work (Baby 1954; Binford 1963; Buikstra and Swegle 1989; Gonçalves *et al.* 2011; Kennedy 1996; Thurman and Willmore 1981) suggested that bone burned with soft tissue present produced U-shaped fractures along the long axis of the bone, while bone burned dry resulted in linear fractures in a grid-like pattern. With the U-shaped fracture, the concave surface generally forms on the side with the soft tissues remaining (Symes *et al.* 2008). This rule has held true for a number of years, although recent work by Gonçalves *et al.* (2011) has noted that U-shaped fractures can also appear in bone that was burned without the surrounding soft tissues. Their suggestion is that it might not be the soft tissue *per se* that results in the U-shaped fractures, but rather the collagen contained within the bone which can survive after the decomposition of the external soft tissues. The longitudinal fractures are likely running along lines of weakness present in the diaphysis (Turner-Walker and Parry 1995). In cremation studies, the examination of fracturing is common since it feeds into our interpretation of the number of individuals involved in the cremation, and their age and sex. Waterhouse (2013) for example, notes that younger bone responds differently when burned. A number of publications have noted relationships between fragment size and weight and demographic variables (Bass and Jantz 2004; Malinowski and Porawski 1969; McKinley 1993; Murad 1998; Gonçalves *et al.* 2013; Warren and Maples 1997). However, care must be taken since fragmentation of the weak burned bone due to burial may be misinterpreted as being the result of heat-induced fracturing, and this may affect subsequent funerary interpretations (Drusini *et al.* 1997).

The other crucial change to occur to bone when heated is the recrystalisation of the inorganic phase (Hummel *et al.* 1988). Although still not fully understood, current research suggests that as burning intensity increases so does the extent of crystal change. This is exhibited as increasing crystal size, increasing crystalline organisation, and decreasing crystal strain within the bone (Thompson *et al.* 2011; 2013). Interpreting these changes within the archaeological record can be problematic, since similar crystal changes occur due to diagenesis and the two signals are difficult to separate with current approaches (Thompson *et al.* 2011; 2013). Nonetheless, workers have used these crystal-based methods to differentiate burned from unburned archaeological bone (Squires *et al.* 2011; Stiner *et al.* 1995; Van Strydonck *et al.* 2013). This whole process of crystal fusion results in the heat-induced shrinkage that many researchers record (Thompson 2005). Generally, two levels of shrinkage can be seen, with the lower amounts corresponding to lower intensity burning events. High intensity burning events can result in shrinkage of up to 25% (*ibid.*).

The impact of these heat-induced changes can also influence how archaeologists recover and subsequently handle burned and cremated bony remains. Mayne Correia and Beattie (2002) provide some useful suggestions, but the key issue to address is the inherent weakness and instability of the bone and its tendency to fragment further during transport, handling and analysis.

Although much of the discussion focusses on the bones of the skeleton, the dentition will also exhibit heat-induced change. Unfortunately they are referenced far less in the interpretation of cremation contexts, and significantly less research has examined this hard tissue. This is despite their clear and well-recorded potential for providing useful and pertinent information on identity and lifestyles (see for example Bowers 2011). The work that has been undertaken suggests that similar colour changes to bone occur (Chandler 1987; Harsanyi 1976; Sandholzer *et al.* 2013; Shipman *et al.* 1984), as do increases in crystal thickness (Sandholzer *et al.* 2014). Heat-induced shrinkage is also an issue to consider when analysing cremated dentition (Sandholzer *et al.* 2013). A key consideration with the study of the dentition is their increased fragility following burning and the associated handling methods that are required (Bowers 2011). In modern contexts, dental restorations can survive cremations and thus still provide some identification potential (*ibid.*).

A great deal of the work currently being published tends to be heavily methodological. However, through a combination of these methods with a greater and more overt incorporation of the archaeological context, a deeper understanding of past funerary practices can be gained.

Fire and the people

Cremated bone is not an uncommon find during archaeological excavations. Indeed, in excess of some 10,000 cremation burials have been excavated in Britain during the last century (McKinley 1998). However, it must be remembered that cremation (as a funerary rite) is a process of which the actual burning is just one part (Table 1.2; and a point also made by Oestigaard 2000), and not all cremation rites are the same in all contexts. For example, in some cultures the human remains will be burned and then buried, and some will be burned, moved and deposited elsewhere; some remains can be scattered and some stored in containers. A challenge for archaeologists is to distinguish between these variations. Ultimately though, people whether in the past or present, do things for a reason. Thus cremation is not simply a random process – it has meaning and purpose.

Interpreting that meaning and purpose is problematic since there is often very little remaining from this process. The human remains may be incomplete and will undoubtedly be accompanied by fragmented, tiny pieces of the pyre, ritualistic artefacts may or may not be present, and naturally the actions of the mourners do not leave a record. Some associated activities such as scattering the ashes on land or in water, or the breaking of bones prior to burning (Hadders 2013; Kong 2012; McKinley 2006) will also not be detectable in the archaeological record. Some of this is also true for inhumations, however with cremation the fact that the process involves such a destructive component (the fire) and that the burning may not occur in the same location as the deposition, create additional challenges. The difficulties with this material have led to a delay in the full discussion of cremation as a funerary rite in its own terms. However, there are isolated classic early studies such as the paper by Baby (1954) who examined the cremated remains and practices of the Hopewell people, Binford's (1963) study of three Late Archaic cremation sites in Michigan and the reports of McKinley (2000) including Spong Hill (McKinley 1994) (see Table 1.1 for other examples). Despite this general lack of enthusiasm for burned remains, it can be seen that archaeological interpretations have been made. Examination of the literature reveals that a number of themes can be seen in how such events have been viewed. Largely, these themes are: commenting on whether burned remains represent a genuine cremation; the transformation of a person from one state to another; cremation as a representation of a change in belief system, and; as a celebration or spectacle associated with special people or events.

One of the primary challenges for the archaeologist is to determine whether a set of burned remains actually represents a cremation. In the archaeological context, this may mean attempting to identify if the bone was burned as a result of being in the fire or simply close to a fire (Asmussen 2009), bearing in mind that the latter may also occur post-depositionally (Asmussen 2009; Berna *et al.* 2012; Stiner *et al.* 1995). In the modern context, it is regularly noted that burned remains can also be a product of an accident, crime or mass disaster incident. Interestingly we very rarely allow for the same possibilities in the past. Scott *et al.* (2010) in their study of burned remains from the Lapita period on the Pacific Islands consider this as a possibility for the isolated burned remains excavated in 2005. They ultimately decide against it despite the limited evidence for the practice of cremation in this period and region and noting that it is "impossible to say why this individual was cremated while the other individuals excavated from the burial ground were not" (2010; 907 – although they use other contextual evidence to support this decision). In this example, as in others, the determination of cremation is often concluded through comparison with inhumations. Within this particular theme, the burned material is often found as a surprise. This was the case with the material Scott *et al.* (2010) examined, and also the remains discussed in Kutterer *et al.* (2012) from the Neolithic period in south-east Arabia. This would be a particularly important example since they would represent the earliest such material in this region. The discovery of remains from the Neolithic period in Spain has produced questions of intent, although here there was uncertainty as to whether the bone had been heated at low temperatures (Bosch *et al.* 2011). In this Spanish example, the heating was not part of a cremation event, but rather cooking and this highlights the multiple associations of fire with skeletal material in the archaeological record, and thus the difficulties in determining a cremation event from any other heating or burning event. Further, faunal remains (which can form part of a cremation assemblage) may have been burned as a fuel source, as part of normal cooking practices or as part of other group economic strategies (Asmussen 2009; Berna *et al.* 2012; Bond 1996; Gilchrist and Mytum 1986; Lyman 1994; Roberts *et al.* 2002; Schiegl *et al.* 2003; Worley 2005).

A classic interpretation of the cremation rite is that it allows the transformation of the person from one state to another. Put simply, the argument is that "cremation is transformation. It is a medium of change and transmutation" (Oestigaard 1999), and one that is a highly visible and powerful agent of transformation and purification that requires technical knowledge and resources to control successfully (Downes 1999; Green 2002). Within this framework, we can see three forms of transformation – technological, social and ritual (Oestigaard 1999). The technological transformation emphasises the physical processes involved in cremation ritual itself – the location of the pyre, the collection of the remains, the use of the urn, and the subsequent burial. The urn in this context is particularly important, yet often over-looked since it is an "ideologically transformed multi-vocal container with several functions" (*ibid.*, 351). Two types of urn are often noted, the first being a container specifically created for the cremation with a primary function of being an urn, the second being a container of some other material before later being appropriated as a cremation urn (Oestigaard 1999). Note that there are times when the material of the urn is also of significance (such as with copper in India; Oestigaard 2000). The social transformation focusses on commemoration. In his article on cremation in modern Sweden, Williams notes that the cremated body can also be transformed through the "subsequent display, translation and incorporation of ashes into a range of landscapes and materialities [which] can serve as technologies of remembrance" (2011, 113). Thus the cremated body is transformed to better allow for a more communal remembrance which slightly removes the individual from the immediate familial world while embedding it within the broader physical and thus historical and cultural landscape. In this way the social order and relationships within a society can also be emphasised (Oestigaard 1999). Note as well that it has been recorded that cremated remains have been separated and placed in multiple locations (André *et al.* 2013). The third framework is that of ritual transformation. A key aspect of this process is to demonstrate how the physical being can be treated while allowing for the recreation or resurrection of the social being (Hadders 2013). It is a form of dialogue between the living and the dead (Oestigaard 1999). Thus while the act of burning can "free the soul from the deceased body" (Hadders 2013, 204), the subsequent plight of that soul may vary from culture to culture. It may be that cremation in this context may allow for rebirth, or provide a safe journey to heaven or another place, or allow the soul to become a benign ancestor rather than a haunting spirit (Hadders 2013). In this way, it has been argued that the act of cremation, possibly more so than the act of inhumation, is a way of making the dead rest (Downes 1999). Perhaps this is partly because the process of inhumation hides the transformation of the remains and therefore permits considerable uncertainty regarding the fate of the corpse.

This transformative approach can also have a non-religious and entirely pragmatic origin too. For example, Kutterer *et al.* (2012) note that cremation allows for the body to be converted into something inert and transportable within nomadic tribes, Kong (2012) discusses the use of cremation as a means of saving space, and Hadders (2013) uses the example of modern Norway to show the establishment of cremation for notions of hygiene and order in a secular society.

Another interpretation of the use of cremation concerns changes to religious practice. In this regard, the discovery of cremations is used to suggest that religious practices have changed or been replaced. In this context, it is important not to forget the importance of the fire itself in the cremation process (Oestigaard 1999), for example it can be seen as dangerous, yet also allows for cooking, warmth and for warding off danger (both literal and spiritual). This suggests an intriguing duality to the perception of fire. Topp (1973) discussed the changing symbolism that fire holds from the pre-Christian era through to the modern day. He essentially argues that before the onset of Christianity, fire had positive associations with the deities and spirituality – fire was a direct symbol of the gods. Green (2002) makes a similar point for Ancient Greece and Roman Europe. With the establishment and subsequent development of Christianity, fire became increasingly associated not with God, but with punishment (Topp 1973). Hadders (2013) shows how fire can be associated with negative themes in one religion (Christianity) but positive themes in another (Hinduism) within the same period of time. The feelings of negativity towards fire within the funerary context are clearly waning. The Cremation Association of North America reports that in recent years there has been a substantial increase in the popularity of cremation over inhumation throughout all regions of the United States (Murad 1998; Warren and Shultz 2002). Cremation also accounted for 72% of funerary practices in England in 1998 (de Gruchy and Rogers 2002).

A final point to note is what Hadders argues about Hinduism, in that it is a "vast conglomerate of traditions, beliefs and ritual practices" (2013, 204). If we accept this principle, perhaps we need to apply this similarly to beliefs in the past, and recognise that some beliefs may be vast enough to incorporate both cremation and inhumation simultaneously. Indeed there are archaeological sites with both. Further, within Christianity there has been an increasing flexibility and liberalisation of the cremation funerary rite over time (Parsons 2012), just as there is increasing flexibility as to the deposition of cremation ashes (see Williams' (2011) discussion of modern Sweden). One could therefore argue that this may be true of religious practices in the past, the result of which could also be simultaneous cremation and inhumation rites, or variations to approaches to the cremation rite, within a single belief system. Indeed Kong (2012) notes how in modern Asian cultures, increased uptake of cremation coincides with periods of economic growth. Thus the appearance of cremations in one location may not necessarily represent an influx of new religious beliefs – we may just have an overly simplistic and limiting view of religion in the past.

Another common view of cremation is that it is used as a form of display, which could be to celebrate a particular individual or event. In this interpretation it is assumed that cremation involves more effort, resources and skill than a burial (it is also more visible and spectacular) and therefore is reserved for special people. This argument is essentially one focussed on 'investment' or economics. Although not necessarily the case, this can be viewed as being entirely in keeping with the way in which Oestigaard's (1999) transformation framework can differentiate and distinguish between individuals. McKinley has previously argued that cremation is not as previously felt, a 'poor relation' to burial (2006, 81). It involves significant investment of resources, effort and time. One of the forms of evidence often associated with the idea of cremation as a spectacle or celebration of an important individual is the type of wood used in the pyre. Thus the high proportion of a given taxa in the cremation assemblage may indicate that it had been specially selected for the event – for example, pine for its smell or heather for its flammability, or because the tree species held spiritual significance (Deforce and Haneca 2012; Moskal-del Hoyo 2012). Certain species could also be avoided for similar reasons, such as larch which in some groups is avoided for child cremations because of the noise it makes when burned (Moskal-del Hoyo 2012). However, the selection of wood for the pyre could also be a consequence of whatever species grew locally. It may also be that some of the charcoal recovered with the remains derives from previous cremations performed on the same pyre locations or from wooden artefacts placed with the burning body (Deforce and Haneca 2012). A thorough palaeoecological study of the surviving charcoal compared with evidence from the surrounding locale (Moskal-del Hoyo 2012) or standard household refuse (Deforce and Haneca 2012) can help answer this question. It is also worth noting that there may well be a selection bias at work with regard to the samples of charcoal chosen for analysis, either by the archaeologist or simply as a result of what has survived (Moskal-del Hoyo 2012). The presence of animal remains within cremation material is also a sign of investment in this rite, whether the animals are an offering in themselves or are remnant of feeding alongside the pyre (Bond and Worley 2006). Their presence has likely been underestimated over the years.

Within the forensic context, the use of fire is an effective means of disposing of a body in order to destroy evidence or make identification more difficult. Although never discussed, we do need to assume that this occurred in the past too. Further and also associated with the notion of *spectacle*, there is clear symbolism to this use of fire in acts of self-immolation. While an uncommon form of suicide (Hahn *et al.* 2014; Leth and Hart-Madsen 1997; Shkrum and Johnston 1992; Sukhai *et al.* 2002) – it accounted for just 1% of suicides in Ontario, Canada during the late 1980s (Shkrum and Johnston 1992), 1.8% in South Yorkshire between 1985 and 1991 (Cooper and Milroy 1994) 9.9% of all suicides in Durban, South Africa during the five-year retrospective study of Sukhai *et al.* (2002), and 0.9% of all burn injuries in the US between 1999 and 2008 (Hahn *et al.* 2014). As a self-inflicted act, it may be the result of delirious, typical or reactive behaviour (Kamolz 2013), but regardless as a method of suicide or protest is also extremely dramatic and visible. If the intent is indeed suicide, then one could argue that this is a funerary practice, although it is unlikely that it would be detectable within the archaeological record.

The Archaeology of Cremation

Despite the use of these key themes to interpret the presence of cremated material in the archaeological context, the skeletal remains are still largely viewed in isolation – that is, as the bony material itself and separated from the wider archaeological contexts and discussions. The aim of this book is to present a series of examples where the burned human material has been studied in great analytical detail, but yet is still embedded in the archaeological and interpretive context. This approach is the only way to ensure that discussions of cremations lead to discussions of people, their lives and their beliefs.

'The Archaeology of Cremation: burned human remains in funerary studies' has drawn together contributions from eight different contexts spread through time and across the world. The book is arranged chronologically simply to provide some structure – but could also be categorised by location. It would not be appropriate to place the chapters together by scientific method, since these are merely a means to an end and in general, the modern burned bone literature tends to focus on method and technique at the expense of interpretation (see Table 1.1). The first archaeological discussion examines a previously poorly studied set of cremations from a Neolithic site in Guernsey. Here Jenny Cataroche and Rebecca Gowland discuss the challenges of reinterpreting sites from early excavations and demonstrate the information available to archaeologists from a thorough osteological and colour analysis of burned bone. Following this, Lise Harvig applies an innovative CT imaging method to cremation urns to help explore changes in funerary practices between the Bronze and Iron Ages in Denmark. David Gonçalves continues his detailed work on the use of cremation weight measures (here with Vanessa Campanacho, Tim Thompson and Rui Mataloto) to provide a full interpretation of funerary practice at the Iron Age site of Tera in Portugal. Giampaolo Piga, Michele Guirguis and Ethel Allue turn their attention to the complex Monte Sirai site in Sardinia, Italy and apply advanced analytical methods to interpret the conditions of cremation and the remaining pyre debris. Filipa Silva investigates the practice of cremation in the Roman site of Augusta Emerita in Spain which is closely associated with retired veteran soldiers. Kirsty Squires also uses advanced methods of microstructural analysis (although combined with a detailed histological analysis), to provide an understanding of the relationship between funerary practice and demographic and social identities in Anglo-Saxon England. A rare discussion of cremation in South America is given by Priscilla Ferreira Ulguim where she combines a range of analytical methods in an attempt to understand funerary practice in Brazil. Douglas Ubelaker brings us into the modern context, where he uses forensic examples to discuss how the study of modern burnings (here in the US) can allow for a more nuanced understanding of cremation in the past. Finally, Claudia Garrido-Varas and Marisol Intriago-Leiva provide another modern example (this time from Chile) to detail how burning at the time of death can be distinguished from burning sometime afterwards – a common problem within the archaeological context – and how this allows for a different interpretation of the context of death.

This collection of studies draws together and range of expertise, analytical methods and techniques, and discussion of funerary practice in a way which will allow us all to better appreciate the significance and potential of this challenging form of human remains.

References

Amadasi, A., Merli, D., Brandone, A. and Cattaneo, C. 2014. Chromatic variation of soot coiling: a possible marker for gunshot wounds in burnt bone. *Journal of Forensic Sciences* 59, doi:10.1111/1556-4029.12300.

André, A., Leahy, R. and Rottier, S. 2013. Cremated human remains deposited in two phases: evidence from the necropolis of the Tuileries site (Lyon, France: 2nd Century AD). *International Journal of Osteoarchaeology* DOI: 10.1002/oa.2317.

Asmussen, B. 2009. Intentional or incidental thermal modification? Analysing site occupation via burned bone. *Journal of Archaeological Science* 36, 528–36.

Baby, R. S. 1954. Hopewell cremation practices. *The Ohio Historical Society Paper in Archaeology* 1, 1–7. Columbus OH: Ohio Historical Society.

Beckett, S., Rogers, K. D. and Clement, J. G. 2011. Inter-species variation in bone mineral behaviour upon hearing. *Journal of Forensic Sciences* 56, 571–9.

Bennett, J. L. 1999. Thermal alteration of buried bone. *Journal of Archaeological Science* 26, 1–8.

Berna, F., Goldberg, P., Horwitz, L. K., Brink, J., Holt, S., Bamford, M. and Chazan, M. 2012. Microstratigraphic evidence of in situ fire in the Acheulean strata of Wonderwerk Cave, Northern Cape province, South Africa. *Proceedings of the National Academy of Science* 109, e1215–e1220.

Binford, L. R. 1963. An analysis of cremations from three Michigan sites. *Wisconsin Archaeologist* 44, 98–110.

Bond, J. M. 1996. Burnt offerings: animal bone in Anglo-Saxon cremations. *World Archaeology* 28, 76–8.

Bond, J. and Worley. F. L. 2006. Companions in death: the roles of animals in Anglo-Saxon and Viking cremation rituals in Britain. In: Gowland, R. L. and Knusel, C. (eds), *Social Archaeology of Funerary Remains*, 89–98. Oxford: Oxbow Books.

Bosch, P., Alemán, I., Moreno-Castilla, C. and Botella, M. 2011. Boiled versus unboiled: a study of Neolithic and contemporary human bones. *Journal of Archaeological Science* 38, 2561–70.

Bowers, C. M. 2011. *Forensic Dental Evidence: An Investigator's Handbook* (2nd ed.). New York: Academic Press.

Buikstra, J. E. and Swegle, M. 1989. Bone modification due to burning: experimental evidence. In: Bonnichern, R. and Sorg, M. H. (eds), *Peopling of the Americas*, 247–58. Oronoo: Center for the Studies of the First Americans.

Chandler, N. P. 1987. Cremated teeth. *Archaeology Today* August, 41–5.

Christensen, A. M. 2002. Experiments in the combustibility of the human body. *Journal of Forensic Sciences* 47, 466–70.

Cooper, P. N. and Milroy, C. M. 1994. Violent suicide in South Yorkshire, England. *Journal of Forensic Sciences* 39, 657–67.

Deforce, K. and Haneca, K. 2012. Ashes to ashes: fuelwood selection in Roman cremation rituals in northern Gaul. *Journal of Archaeological Science* 39, 1338–48.

De Gruchy, S. and Rogers, T. L. 2002. Identifying chop marks on cremated bone: a preliminary study. *Journal of Forensic Sciences* 47, 933–43.

Downes, J. 1999. Cremation: a spectacle and a journey. In: Downes, J. and Pollard, T. (eds), *The Loved Body's Corruption: Archaeological Contributions to the Study of Human Mortality*, 19–29. Glasgow: Cruithne Press.

Drusini, A. G., Ranzato, C., Onisto, N. and Rippa Bonati, M. 1997. Anthropological study of cremated bones from Northern Italy (9th century B.C.–3rd century A.D.). In: Smits, E., Iregren, E. and Drusini, A. G. (eds), *Cremation Studies in Archaeology – Proceedings of the Symposium, Amsterdam, 26–27 October 1995*, 51–72. Saonara: Logos Edizioni.

Dunlop, J. M. 1978. Traffic light discoloration in cremated bones. *Medicine, Science and the Law* 18, 163–73.

Fairgrieve, S. I. 2008. *Forensic Cremation: Recovery and Analysis*. Boca Raton, FL: CRC Press.

Gejvall, N.-G. 1969 Cremations. In: Brothwell, D. and Higgs, E. (eds) *Science in Archaeology* (2nd ed.), 468–79. London: Thames and Hudson.

Gilchrist, R. and Mytum, H. C. 1986. Experimental archaeology and burnt animal bone from archaeological sites. *Circaea* 4, 29–38.

Gonçalves, D. 2012. The micro-analysis of human burned bones: some remarks. *Cadernos do GEEvH* 1, 32–40.

Gonçalves, D., Thompson, T. J. U. and Cunha, E. 2011. Implications of heat-induced changes in bone on the interpretation of funerary behaviour and practice. *Journal of Archaeological Science* 38, 1308–13.

Gonçalves, D., Cuhna, E. and Thompson, T. J. U. 2013. Weight references for burned human skeletal remains from Portuguese samples. *Journal of Forensic Sciences* doi: 10.1111/1556-4029.12167.

Green, M. A. 2002. *Dying for the Gods: Human Sacrifices in Iron Age and Roman Europe*. Stroud: Tempus.

Grévin, G., Bailet, P., Quatrehomme, G. and Ollier, A. 1998. Anatomical reconstruction of fragments of burned human bones: a necessary means for forensic identification. *Forensic Science International* 96, 129–34.

Hadders, H. 2013. Cremation in Norway: regulation, changes and challenges. *Mortality* 18, 195–213.

Hahn, A. P., Jochai, D., Caufield-Noll, C. P., Hunt, C. A., Allen, L. E., Rios, R. and Cordts, G. A. 2014. Self-inflicted burns: a systematic review of the literature. *Journal of Burn Care and Research* 35, 102–19.

Harbeck, M., Schleuder, R., Schneider, J., Wiechmann, I., Schmahl, W. W. and Grupe, G. 2011. Research potential and limitations of trace analyses of cremated remains. *Forensic Science International* 204, 191–200.

Harsányi, L. 1975. Scanning electron microscopic investigation of thermal damage of the teeth. *Acta Morphologica Academy of Science Hungary* 23, 271–81.

Heglar, R. 1984. Burned remains. In: Rathburn, T. and Buikstra, J. E. (eds), *Human Identification: Case Studies in Forensic Anthropology*, 148–58. Springfield IL: Charles C. Thomas.

Herrmann, N. P. and Bennett, J. L. 1999. The differentiation of traumatic and heat-related fractures in burned bone. *Journal of Forensic Sciences* 44, 461–9.

Hiller, J. C., Thompson, T. J. U., Evison, M. P., Chamberlain, A. T. and Wess, T. J. 2003. Bone mineral change during experimental heating: an X-ray scattering investigation. *Biomaterials* 24, 5091–7.

Holden, J. L., Phakey, P. P. and Clement, J. G. 1995a. Scanning electron microscope observations of incinerated human femoral bone: a case study. *Forensic Science International* 74, 17–28.

Holden, J. L., Phakey, P. P. and Clement, J. G. 1995b. Scanning electron microscope observations of heat-treated human bone. *Forensic Science International* 74, 29–45.

Hummel, S., Schutkowski, H. and Herrmann, B. 1988. Advances in cremation research. *Actes des 3èmes Journées Anthropologiques Notes et Monographies Techniques* 24, 177–94.

Kamolz, L.-P. 2013. Attempted suicide by self-immolation is a powerful predictive variable for survival of burn injuries. *Journal of Burn Care and Research* 34, e271.

Kennedy, K. A. R. 1996. The wrong urn: commingling of cremains in mortuary practices. *Journal of Forensic Sciences* 41, 689–92.

Kong, L. 2012. No place, new places: death and its rituals in urban Asia. *Urban Studies* 49, 415–33.

Koon, H. E. C., Nicholson, R. A. and Collins, M. J. 2003. A practical approach to the identification of low temperature heated bone using TEM. *Journal of Archaeological Science* 30, 1393–9.

Kutterer, A. U., Doppler, S., Uerpmann, M. and Uerpmann, H-P. 2012. Neolithic cremation in south-east Arabia: archaeological and anthropological observations at FAY-NE10 in the Emirate of Sharjah (UAE). *Arabian Archaeology and Epigraphy* 23, 125–44.

Lebon, M., Reiche, I., Bahain, J.-J., Chadefaux, C., Moigne, A.-M., Fröhlich, F., Sémah, F., Schwarcz, H. P. and Falguères, C. 2010. New parameters for the characterization of diagenetic alterations and heat-induced changes of fossil bone mineral using Fourier transform infrared spectrometry. *Journal of Archaeological Science* 37, 2265–76.

Leth, P. and Hart-Madsen, M. 1997. Suicide by self-incineration. *American Journal of Forensic Medicine and Pathology* 18, 113–18.

Lyman, R. L. 1994. *Vertebrate Taphonomy*. Cambridge: Cambridge University Press.

Malinowski, A. and Porawski R. 1969. Identifikationsmöglichkeiten menschlicher brandknochen mit besonder berücksichtigung ihres gewichts. *Zacchia* 5, 1–19.

Mayne Correia, P. M. 1997. Fire modification of bone: a review of the literature. In: Haglund, W. D. and Sorg, M. H. (eds), *Forensic Taphonomy: The Post-Mortem Fate of Human Remains*, 275–293. Boca Raton FL: CRC Press.

Mayne Correia, P. and Beattie, O. 2002. A critical look at methods for recovering, evaluating, and interpreting cremated human remains. In: Haglund, W. D. and Sorg, M. H. (eds), *Advances in Forensic Taphonomy: Method, Theory, and Archaeological Perspectives*, 435–50. Boca Raton FL: CRC Press.

McKinley, J. 1993. Bone fragment size and weights of bone from British cremations and the implications for the interpretation of archaeological cremations. *International Journal of Osteoarchaeology* 3, 283–7.

McKinley, J. I. 1994. *The Anglo-Saxon Cemetery at Spong Hill, North Elmham. Part VIII: The Cremations*. East Dereham: East Anglian Archaeology 69.

McKinley, J. I. 1998. Archaeological manifestations of cremation. *The Archaeologist* 33, 18–20.

McKinley, J. I. 2000. The analysis of cremated bone. In: Cox, M. and Mays, S. (eds) Human osteology: in archaeology and forensic science. Greenwich Medical Media Ltd: GB. pp403–421.

McKinley, J. I. 2006. Cremation... the cheap option. In: Gowland, R. L. and Knusel, C. (eds), *Social Archaeology of Funerary Remains*, 81–8. Oxford: Oxbow Books.

Moskal-del Hoyo, M. 2012. The use of wood in funerary pyres: random gathering or special selection of species? Case study of three necropolises from Poland. *Journal of Archaeological Science* 39, 3386–95.

Murad, T. A. 1998. The growing popularity of cremation versus inhumation: some forensic implications. In: Reichs, K. (ed.), Forensic Osteology: Advances in the Identification of Human Remains, 86–105. Springfield, IL: Charles C. Thomas.

Nicholson, R. A. 1993. A morphological investigation of burnt animal bone and an evaluation of its utility in archaeology. *Journal of Archaeological Science* 20, 411–28.

Oestigaard, T. 1999. Cremations as transformations: when the duel cultural hypothesis was cremated and carried away in urns. *European Journal of Archaeology* 2, 345–64.

Oestigaard, T. 2000. The Deceased's Life Cycle Rituals in Nepal: Present Cremation Burials for the Interpretations of the Past. Oxford: British Archaeological Report S853.

Parker, S. 1985. An experimental and comparative study of cremation techniques. Unpublished MA Thesis: University of Sheffield.

Parsons, B. 2012. Identifying key changes: the progress of cremation and its influence on music at funerals in England, 1874–2010. *Mortality* 17, 130–44.

Piga, G.. Malgosa, A., Thompson, T. J. U., Mazzarello, V. and Enzo, S. 2008. A new calibration of the XRD technique for the study of archaeological burned human remains. *Journal of Archaeological Science* 35, 2171–8.

Pope, E. J. and Smith, O. B. C. 2004. Identification of traumatic injury in burned cranial bone: an experimental approach. *Journal of Forensic Sciences* 49, 1–10.

Quatrehomme, G., Bolla, M., Muller, M., Rocca, J.-P., Grévin, G., Bailet, P. and Ollier, A. 1998 Experimental single controlled study of burned bones: contribution of scanning electron microscopy. *Journal of Forensic Sciences* 43, 417–22.

Roberts, S. J., Smith, C. I., Millard, A. and Collins, M. J. 2002. The taphonomy of cooked bone: characterizing boiling and its physio-chemical effects. *Archaeometry* 44, 485–94.

Rogers, K. D., Beckett, S., Kuhn, S., Chamberlain, A. and Clement, J. 2010. Contrasting the crystallinity indicators of heated and diagenetically altered bone mineral. *Palaeogeography, Palaeoclimatology, Palaeoecology* 296, 125–9.

Rogers, K. D. and Daniels, P. 2002. An X-ray diffraction study of the effects of heat treatment on bone mineral microstructure. *Biomaterials* 23, 2577–85.

Sandholzer, M. A., Sui, T., Korsunsky, A. M., Walmsley, A. D., Lumley, P. J. and Landini, G. 2014. X-ray scattering evaluation of ultrastructural changes in human dental tissues with thermal treatment. *Journal of Forensic Sciences* doi: 10.1111/1556-4029.12400.

Sandholzer, M. A., Walmsey, A. D., Lumley, P. J. and Landini, G. 2013. Radiologic evaluation of heat-induced shrinkage and shape preservation of human teeth using micro-CT. *Journal of Forensic Radiology and Imaging* 1, 107–11.

Schiegl, S., Goldberg, P., Pfretzschner, H-U. and Conard, N.J. 2003. Paleolithic burnt bone horizons from the Swabian Jura: distinguishing between in situ fireplaces and dumping areas. *Geoarchaeology* 18, 541–65.

Scott, R. M., Buckley, H. R., Spriggs, M., Valentin, F. and Bedford, S. 2010. Identification of the first reported Lapita cremation in the Pacific Islands using archaeological, forensic and contemporary burning evidence. *Journal of Archaeological Science* 37, 901–9.

Shipman, P., Foster, G. and Schoeinger, M. 1984. Burnt bones and teeth: an experimental study of color, morphology, crystal structure and shrinkage. *Journal of Archaeological Science* 11, 307–25.

Shkrum, M. J. and Johnston, K. A. 1992. Fire and suicide: a three-year study of self-immolation deaths. *Journal of Forensic Sciences* 37, 208–21.

Sillen, A. and Hoering, T. 1993. Chemical characterization of burnt bones from Swartkrans. In: Brain, C. K. (ed.), *Swartkrans: a Cave's Chronicle of Early Man*, 243–9. Cape: Transvaal Museum Monograph 8.

Spennemann, D. H. R. and Colley, S. M. 1989. Fire in a pit: the effects of burning on faunal remains. *Archaeozoologia* 3, 51–64.

Squires, K. E., Thompson, T. J. U., Islam, M., and Chamberlain, A. 2011. The application of histomorphometry and Fourier Transform Infrared Spectroscopy to the analysis of early Anglo-Saxon burned bone. *Journal of Archaeological Science* 38, 2399–409.

Stiner, M. C., Kuhn, S. L., Weiner, S. and Bar-Yosef, O. 1995. Differential burning, recrystallization, and fragmentation of archaeological bone. *Journal of Archaeological Science* 22, 223–37.

Sukhai, A., Harris, C., Moorad, R. G. R. and Dada, M. A. 2002. Suicide by self-immolation in Durban, South Africa: a five-year retrospective review. *American Journal of Forensic Medicine and Pathology* 23, 295–8.

Symes, S. A., Rainwater, C. W., Chapman, E. N., Gipson, D. R. and Piper, A. L. 2008. Patterned thermal destruction of human remains in a forensic setting. In: Schmidt, C. W. and Symes, S. A. (eds), *The Analysis of Burned Human Remains*, 15–54. New York: Academic Press.

Thompson, T. J. U. 2002. The assessment of sex in cremated individuals: some cautionary notes. *Canadian Society of Forensic Science Journal* 35, 49–56.

Thompson, T. J. U. 2004. Recent advances in the study of burned bone and their implications for forensic anthropology. *Forensic Science International* 146S, S203–5.

Thompson, T. J. U. 2005 Heat-induced dimensional changes in bone and their consequences for forensic anthropology. *Journal of Forensic Sciences* 50, 1008–15.

Thompson, T. J. U. 2009. Burned human remains. In: Blau, S. and Ubelaker, D. (eds), *Handbook of Forensic Anthropology and Archaeology*, 295–303. Walnut Creek CA: Left Coast Press.

Thompson, T. J. U., Gauthier, M. and Islam, M. 2009. The application of a new method of Fourier Transform Infrared Spectroscopy to the analysis of burned bone. *Journal of Archaeological Science* 36, 910–14.

Thompson, T. J. U., Islam, M. and Bonniere, M. 2013. A new statistical approach for determining the crystallinity of heat-altered bone mineral from FTIR spectra. *Journal of Archaeological Science* 40, 416–22.

Thompson, T. J. U., Islam, M., Piduru, K. and Marcel, A. 2011. An investigation into the internal and external variables acting on crystallinity index using Fourier Transform Infrared Spectroscopy on unaltered and burned bone. *Palaeogeography, Palaeoclimatology, Palaeoecology* 299, 168–74.

Thurman, M. D. and Willmore, L. J. 1981. A replicative cremation experiment. *North American Archaeologist* 2, 275–83.

Topp, D. O. 1973. Fire as a symbol and as a weapon of death. *Medicine, Science and the Law* 13, 79–86.

Turner-Walker, G. and Parry, T. V. 1995. The tensile strength of archaeological bone. *Journal of Archaeological Science* 22, 185–91.

Ubelaker, D. H. 2009. The forensic evaluation of burned skeletal remains: a synthesis. *Forensic Science International* 183, 1–5.

Van Strydonck, M., Decq, L., Van den Brande, T., Boudin, M., Ramis, D., Borms, H. and de Mulder, G. 2013. The Protohistoric 'Quicklime Burials' from the Balearic Islands: cremation or inhumation. *International Journal of Osteoarchaeology* DOI: 10.1002/oa.2307.

Van Vark, G. N. 1974. The investigation of human cremated skeletal material by multivariate statistical methods I. Methodology. *Ossa* 1, 63–95.

Van Vark, G. N. 1975. The investigation of human cremated skeletal material by multivariate statistical methods II. Measures. *Ossa* 2, 47–68.

Warren, M. W. and Maples, W. R. 1997. The anthropometry of contemporary commercial cremation. *Journal of Forensic Sciences* 42, 417–23.

Warren, M. W. and Schultz, J. J. 2002. Post-cremation taphonomy and artifact preservation. *Journal of Forensic Sciences* 47, 656–659.

Waterhouse, K. 2013. The effect of victim age on burnt bone fragmentation: implications for remains recovery. *Forensic Science International* 231, 409.e1–409.e7.

Wells, C. 1960. A study of cremation. *Antiquity* 34, 29–37.

Williams, H. 2008. Towards an archaeology of cremation. In: Schmidt, C. W. and Symes, S. A. (eds), *The Analysis of Burned Human Remains*, 239–69. New York: Academic Press.

Williams, H. 2011. Cremation and present pasts: a contemporary archaeology of Swedish memory groves. *Mortality* 16, 113–30.

Worley, F. 2005. Taphonomic influences on cremation burial deposits: implications for interpretation. In: O'Conner, T. (ed.), *Biosphere to lithosphere: new studies in vertebrate taphonomy*. Proceedings of the 9th ICAZ Conference. Oxford: Oxbow Books.

Chapter 2

Flesh, fire, and funerary remains from the Neolithic site of La Varde, Guernsey: Investigations past and present

Jenny Cataroche and Rebecca Gowland

Introduction

The Neolithic was a time of significant social, economic and technological change (Smith and Brickley 2009, 9) characterised ultimately by the abandonment of mobile hunter-gatherer subsistence strategies and the adoption of agrarian systems based on the cultivation of cereal crops and the rearing of domestic animals (Scarre 2007, 8). In addition to agriculture, other elements of the Neolithic "package" included ceramics, new lithic technologies, increased sedentism and altered types of ritual and ideological beliefs (Smith and Brickley 2009, 9; Cunliffe 2001, 151). One manifestation of the latter, particularly ubiquitous throughout western Europe, was monumental funerary architecture, often in the form of tombs containing multiple inhumations. For the Neolithic: "the dead seem to be more visible than the living" (Thomas 1991, 127). The distinctive funerary practices of the Neolithic indicated a new response to the need to dispose of the dead (Cunliffe 2001, 198) and, in all probability, new social functions for the dead in the sphere of the living.

Neolithic funerary monuments have, for many centuries, been a source of great interest and the subject of countless investigations as to their design, typology, orientation, method of construction and more. Surprisingly, however, the occupants of the tombs and the funerary contexts in which they were deposited, have been comparatively neglected (Fowler 2001; Wysocki and Whittle 2000, 591; Beckett and Robb 2006, 57; Chambon 2003, 5). The Channel Islands, situated off the coast of Normandy, are no exception. Though the archipelago boasts a rich and tangible Neolithic history, with dense concentrations of megalithic tombs in several of the islands, much of the surviving skeletal material from the period has never been studied using modern osteological methods. The tombs themselves, meanwhile, have received considerable scholarly attention (e.g. Hibbs 1985; Kinnes 1988; Kinnes and Hibbs 1988; Patton 1995; De Pomerai 1997; Bukach 2003; Le Conte 2005; Cassen *et al.* forthcoming).

The poor taphonomic condition of the bones – frequently commingled, disarticulated, fragmentary and few in number – along with the past failure of archaeologists to realise the value of human remains have been cited as likely explanations for the disregard of Neolithic skeletal assemblages (Wysocki and Whittle 2000, 591). The fact that many Neolithic collections were recovered during the nineteenth century (Smith and Brickley 2009, 15) and are currently curated in settings where they fall under the radar of the academic community is likely to have been another contributing factor to this neglect.

The conceptualisation of the Neolithic as a generalised entity in which all components of the "package" were adopted wholesale by different cultures has been roundly critiqued in recent years (Jones 2005). With regard to burial, recent reconsiderations of Neolithic assemblages have demonstrated that there was no uniform, homogeneous, funerary rite (Fowler 2000). Research has demonstrated a range of regional and localised idiosyncrasies, with regard to the treatment and manipulation of the bodies of those interred within the funerary monuments. A variety of arrangements, including articulated primary interments, reconstituted burials, disarticulated partial skeletons, disarticulated and dissembled skeletal elements, and burning are just some of these treatments. At some sites, defleshing appears to have occurred prior to admittance to the tomb, while at others the process of decomposition occurred *in situ*. The incorporation and retention of some or all of the remaining skeletal elements and in what manner is subject to a great deal of variation (Thomas 1991) and it has been argued that the tombs in which bones have been discovered should not be viewed simply as "repositories for the dead", but rather as foci for transformation in which human bone was employed as a resource to establish relations between members of the living and between the living and the dead. (Jones 2005, 213).

Here we present the findings of an osteological investigation, carried out in 2009, of human bones excavated in the 19th century from the Neolithic site of La Varde, Guernsey. The application of cutting-edge techniques developed within the forensic and archaeological contexts to an assemblage excavated by antiquarians aimed to shed light on the specific regional funerary rites and to glean information concerning the identity of the occupants (e.g. sex and age). The osteological analysis was supplemented with an examination of the primary documentary sources from the original excavations to furnish additional information about the context of their deposition. The results of the investigation have added to the growing number of studies that give due consideration to the subjects of Neolithic burial monuments themselves.

The funerary context

La Varde is a large passage grave (measuring approximately 10 m in length, 3.6 m at its widest point, and 2.1 m in height beneath the westernmost capstone), which is located in the north of the island of Guernsey in the western portion of L'Ancresse

Common (Kendrick 1928, 104) (Fig. 2.1). Internally there is only one feature; a lateral chamber or 'recess' at the north-west end (Patton 1995, 41; Kendrick 1928, 104). Externally there is a covering mound of turf and sand, reconstructed in the early 20th century (Fig. 2.2). A plan of the tomb is shown in Figure 2.3.

Radiocarbon values in the range 4100–3900 cal BC were recently obtained for human bone from another Guernsey passage grave, Le Déhus (Schulting *et al.* 2010,

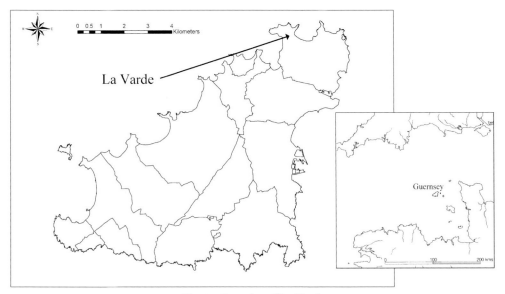

Fig. 2.1: Location of La Varde.

Fig. 2.2: La Varde in 2013.

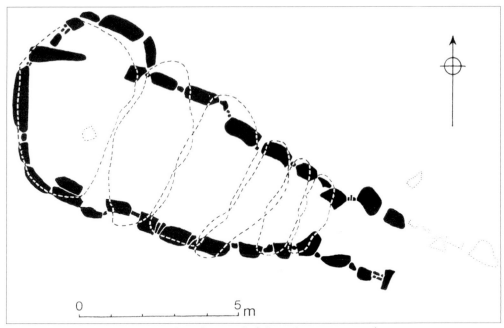

Fig. 2.3: Plan of La Varde (after Johnston 1981, 108).

160), and it is reasonable to suppose that the bones from La Varde are of a similar period, with construction of the monument dating, probably, to the second half of the 5th millennium BC (Patton 1995, 43).

Having lain concealed beneath a deep layer of blown sand for hundreds of years, La Varde was rediscovered by soldiers in 1811 and subsequently subjected to limited investigation. Twenty-six years later, in 1837, the site was excavated by the antiquarian and natural historian Frederick Corbin Lukis. Lukis thoroughly examined and recorded the tomb and, in so doing, established a method of investigation which he would apply at numerous other sites during the course of several years following. Large quantities of finds, including many human bones, were recovered during the excavation, and all of these were taken to Lukis' own museum in St Peter Port, Guernsey for storage and display. These finds were eventually incorporated into the collections of Guernsey Museum, where they have since remained.

By modern standards Lukis' excavation and recording of La Varde is woefully inadequate, however, it is only fair to judge the investigation by the standards of the day. Compared with many of his contemporaries Lukis was a meticulous and conscientious investigator. In making clear plans and section drawings as well as a written description of each site he examined, Lukis adopted a scientific methodology more typical of the 20th century. Lukis became a character of considerable renown, both in the Channel Islands and further afield, and was remembered for his progressive outlook and willingness to engage in key intellectual debates of the era (Sebire 2005, 27).

Methods of analysis

The sources of data that have resulted from the 1837 examination of La Varde consist of the human bones and other finds recovered from the tomb plus an archive of written documents, attributable to Lukis, which detail how the excavation was conducted and what was found. The skeletal sample comprises two large storage boxes of non-accessioned bones, all disarticulated and fragmentary, plus a small amount of accessioned bone, including a few pieces which are on permanent display in Guernsey Museum. The total weight of bone is approximately 15 kg and most of this shows colour change consistent with burning. The archive consists of one journal article (Lukis 1845) and five unpublished manuscripts (DXV 2, GMAG 7632.36, GMAG 7492 10th Oct. 1838, GMAG 7492 15th Jan. 1839 and GMAG 7453). The relevant documentary sources were located using an electronic search of Guernsey Museum's Lukis Archive and were then transcribed, read and reviewed.

In preparation for study, the bones and bone fragments of the skeletal sample were dry-brushed with a toothbrush and, where necessary, lightly probed with a wooden cocktail stick to remove loose soil. They were then separated into 'identifiable' and 'non-identifiable' groups, the 'identifiable' subset being further divided into six anatomical categories (after Scheuer and Black 2000, v): cranium, thorax, pectoral girdle, upper limb, pelvic girdle, and lower limb. A bone or bone fragment was generally only considered to be fully identifiable if the element and laterality could be determined. In a very few cases, however, this stringent criterion was relaxed so as to permit the inclusion of fragments not fully identified, but which were otherwise significant by virtue of their displaying taphonomic or pathological features.

A limited attempt was made to re-associate (or "refit") broken fragments of the same bone, and a numbering system was implemented where each anatomical category was allocated a batch of numbers sufficient to cover the quantity of bones/fragments in that category. Identifiable bones were marked, or bagged, with a number from the relevant batch. A quantity of spare numbers was also apportioned to each batch to "future-proof" the system against the possibility of more bones from the site coming to light at a later date.

A database comprising 14 information fields was generated and observations concerning each identifiable bone or bone fragment inputted. These fields allowed for standard observations to be made on completeness, preservation, age, sex, pathology and non-metric traits. Adult sex was assigned, where possible, using cranial features (Acsádi and Nemeskéri 1970; Buikstra and Ubelaker 1994); metrics (Bass 1995); sacral morphology (Anderson 1962); and greater sciatic notch form (Buikstra and Ubelaker 1994). Non-adult age was estimated from dental development/eruption and epiphyseal fusion or non-fusion in comparison to known standards (Anderson 1963; Scheuer and Black 2000; Ubelaker 1989). Adult ages were estimated from dental attrition (Brothwell 1981); sacral fusion and medial clavicle fusion (Scheuer and Black 2000), and pubic symphyseal morphology (Brooks and Suchey 1990). A total of 28 non-metric traits were assessed (Buikstra and Ubelaker 1994; Brothwell 1981; Saunders and Rainey 2008). An additional field allowed for the recording of taphonomic factors (e.g. animal gnawing, weathering), which were considered as potentially useful for the interpretation of the funerary rites.

It was clear from the outset that some of the bones had undergone heat-induced changes. Colour change is a significant factor to consider when interpreting burned human skeletal remains as it may be linked to the intensity of burning. Colour change was quantified by comparing each identified bone/fragment to a colour index. The index used in this study was created through rudimentary adaptation of the scale produced by Munro *et al.* (2007, 94). Munro's original scale is a simple colour bar. To adapt it numbers in the range 1–30 were applied to each separate colour segment of the bar. This permitted scores of between 1–30 to be assigned to bones/fragments showing any colour change. The highest attributable score was noted in cases where multiple colours were present, while those with no signs of heat-induced change were scored 0.

Findings from the archive

The documentary sources reveal that the excavation of La Varde began on 31 August 1837 and was carried out by F. C. Lukis, two of his teenage sons and a labourer (GMAG 7453). Access to the tomb was initially by way of a shaft sunk beneath the second capstone from the west (GMAG 7453; GMAG 7632.36). Once inside the tomb in this central position, the excavators hollowed out a working space in which they could stand underneath the capstone. Figure 2.4 illustrates that from here they projected their first trench to find the northern and southern limits of the tomb (points A and B) before returning to the central point and extending a second trench at right angles to the first, which is to say east across the long axis of the passage to point 2. Deposits from the northeast, then southeast portions of the tomb – marked 4 and 3 respectively – were removed, and finally, the west–east trench was extended west to find the back of the tomb (point 5). This allowed deposits in the northwest and southwest corners (areas 6 and 7) to be accessed and excavated. Unlike in modern excavations where deposits are removed horizontally in layers, Lukis and his team removed the chamber fill in vertical or oblique slices, working outwards from their central starting points (GMAG 7632.36). The greater part of the tomb contents were passed through a sieve to ensure maximum recovery of finds (GMAG 7453). The sieving of the tomb's contents illustrates one way in which Lukis' excavation technique was progressive for its time.

All documents agree that pottery, limpet shells and human bones, both burnt and unburnt, were found in abundance within the tomb, yet the finer stratigraphic detail of the various accounts differs according to when they were written. An early description and sketch of the chamber fill, made at the time of excavation, was later revised by Lukis in light of his experience at other sites (Lukis 1845, 150). The final version (Fig. 2.5) describes a sequence which can be summarised as consisting, from top to bottom, of loam, white sand, brown sand, animal bones with stone and two

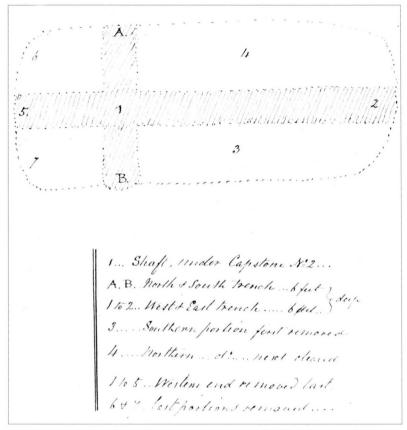

Fig. 2.4: Sketch showing the position of the 1837 excavation trenches (GMAG 7453 Collectanea Antiqua Vol. V, 9).

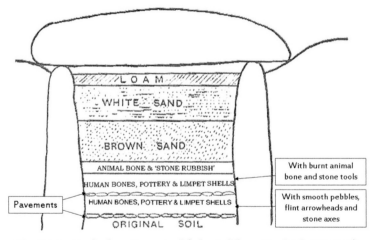

Fig. 2.5: La Varde deposits revised (adapted from Kendrick 1928, 109).

layers containing human bones, pottery and limpet shells. These strata all rested on a paved floor atop the original ground surface. The double layer of human remains, which contained both burnt and unburnt bones, is said to have been divided by a second floor, so that the burial deposits occurred in tiers, with the skeletal material having been placed on a succession of pavements, one above the other.

Lukis asserted that "upwards of 30 distinct skeletons" were excavated (GMAG 7632.36), and added that the remains were principally those of adults, with only one child present, aged approximately 12 years (GMAG 7632.36). He noted that the teeth of some individuals were considerably worn (GMAG 7492 Jan. 15th 1839), but gave little other information about the physical characteristics of the bones. One important point was made about their preservation. Whereas the burnt human bones were found, on removal, to be quite robust, the unburnt ones were noted as being extremely fragile (GMAG 7632.36; GMAG 7492 Oct. 10th 1838) and some so decomposed that they crumbled quickly to a powder upon excavation (GMAG 7632.36). In an effort to prevent bone loss, "warm size" (i.e. varnish) was applied to some of the unburnt bones as soon as they were exposed to the air (GMAG 7492 Oct. 10th 1838). In one source we are told that this treatment "was found to answer well" (GMAG 7492 Oct. 10th 1838) but it is not clear from the accounts what proportion of the sample was treated in this way. During the 2009 assessment only nine bone fragments from the surviving sample were found to be varnished, from which one can surmise that either it was not as successful an intervention as claimed, or that it was a remedy applied to very few bones.

In terms of spatial distribution, the human remains seem to have been confined to the chamber of the monument, there being no mention in any account of bones having been recovered from the passage. All sources remark upon the arrangement of bones into discrete groups or piles, though, again, details in earlier accounts differ from those in later ones. In notes made at the time of the excavation we learn that each "skeleton" appeared to have been buried "in a small narrow pit just capable of holding it, the bones being thrown in indiscriminately without any relation to the cardinal points or position of the corpse" (GMAG 7632.36). In the journal article published eight years later, and in another undated source, the pits get no mention, but instead Lukis provides a description and accompanying illustration (Fig. 2.6) of "distinct heaps" of bones found clustered with pottery deposits – typically a single urn – and surrounded by a ring of rolled, black, pebbles (GMAG 7453; Lukis 1845). Both burnt and unburnt skeletal material was said to have been found organised in this way (Lukis 1845; GMAG 7453).

The bones depicted in Lukis' illustration (Fig. 2.6) are not nearly numerous enough to constitute an entire skeleton, and the two arrangements described, namely burials in pits versus pot-bone-pebble clusters, are considerably different. Nevertheless, they have two points in common. Firstly the burials in the tomb appear to have been disarticulated (whether this happened once they were in the tomb or beforehand) and secondly bones seem to have been arranged so that individual burials, whether real or reconstituted, were demarcated one from another. When Lukis wrote of 30 individual "skeletons" we have to presume he was merely attempting to quantify the number of individuals represented by the mass of bones he had encountered, possibly by counting up easily recognisable elements such as skulls.

Additional details from the archive sources include the observations that the burnt human bones were encountered in the middle of the chamber and somewhat to the north of a median line running east to west (GMAG 7632.36); that "bones and skulls" were found lodged between orthostats: "as in the recesses of a catacomb" (GMAG 7453); that the mass of human skeletal remains from the centre of the tomb had lain in a greater state of "confusion" – Lukis' own term – than material found near the edges (GMAG 7453); and that several pottery vessels, some of them associated with burnt remains, had been blackened by fire in a similar manner to the bones (GMAG 7632.36; GMAG 7492 Oct. 10th 1838; GMAG 7453).

Fig. 2.6: Arrangement of artefacts at La Varde (after Lukis 1845, 148).

Lukis believed that the burnt human bones had been broken by force prior to their deposition (GMAG 7632.36). He gives no reason for this interpretation but may simply have assumed human action if he was unaware that bone will fracture naturally when burnt. Similarly he felt sure that the flesh of all individuals had been removed, either by burning or some other means, prior to their deposition in the tomb (GMAG 7453). Again there is no authority for this claim which possibly just reflects a popular assumption of the time.

The layered pavements were taken as an indication that the monument was in use over an extended period (GMAG 7453), and differences in the shapes of the ceramic vessels in the tomb, which are said to have "denoted an improvement in their manufacture", were cited in further support of this assertion (Lukis 1845). At the time of writing no more recent analysis of the surviving pottery from the site has been performed, making it impossible to comment on the validity, or otherwise, of this observation.

Quantities of yellow clay were found mixed among the lowest level of human bones and it was suggested that this material was introduced, along with the second pavement, to evenly cover the first layer of remains and make space for a new deposit (GMAG 7453). The limpet shells, which were found in great numbers, may have served a similar function, though Lukis speculated that, if deposited with their flesh inside, these could have been intended primarily as a food offering for the dead (DXV 2).

Whether by accident or design, the limpet shells were certainly important in another way: they reduced the destructive power of the acidic local soil. With an average pH in the region of 4.5 (Andrew Casebow pers. comm.), Guernsey soil is hostile to skeletal material and, over time, completely destroys bone. At La Varde, the alkaline shells created a more neutral pH in the immediate vicinity of the human bones, without which it is unlikely that any skeletal material would have survived.

Findings from the skeletal assemblage

Condition, demographic profile and representation

The skeletal assemblage was found to contain 2416 human bones or bone fragments, of which 1452 could be identified to element and 368 to element and side. Out of the fully identified subset 14 bones or bone fragments were attributable to non-adults (defined here as less than 18 years) and the remaining 354 to adults.

Surface preservation of the bones was assessed using Brickley and McKinley's (2004) seven point scale, which ranges from 0 ("surface morphology clearly visible with fresh appearance to bone and no modifications") to 5+ ("heavy erosion across whole surface ... extensive penetrating erosion resulting in modification of profile"). Just over 90% of the sample that could be assessed for this indicator scored either grade 0 or grade 1 indicating a good level of preservation overall. By contrast, completeness within the sample, i.e. the extent to which parts of individual elements were present or missing, was poor; 48% of the identified subset consisted of fragments (where less than one-quarter of the whole bone was present), 30% were partial (one-quarter to three-quarters of the bone present) and only 22% were complete (more than three-quarters of the bone present). No convincing cutmarks were observed in the sample

Fig. 2.7: Bone number 264 showing animal gnawing.

and no bones/fragments were found to be bleached or otherwise weathered. An isolated case of animal gnawing (possibly rodent) was identified on one rib fragment (Fig. 2.7).

The minimum number of individuals (MNI) represented by the sample was calculated as nine: six adults and three non-adults. Sex determination, which was possible for nine bones, confirmed the presence of both sexes, with at least one female and two males. Three distinct ages were observed among the non-adult bones (one of 3–5 years, represented by four bones/fragments; one of 7–9 years, also represented by four bones/fragments; and one of 9–19 years, represented by three partial bones/fragments).[1] Assessment of age-related fusion and degeneration in the adult bones revealed a spread of ages that included one individual aged 18–27 years and individuals in each of the categories, 'middle aged' (e.g. 25–45 years, represented by at least six bones/fragments) and 'older aged' (e.g. 45+ years, represented by at least one fragment).

All anatomical regions were represented in the sample and, with the exception of the hyoid, coccyx, triquetal and intermediate cuneiform, all skeletal elements featured within the count. Nonetheless, when representation indices were calculated for 15 skeletal elements by dividing MNI obtained from each specified element by the greatest MNI for the assemblage (after Smith and Brickley 2009, 72), considerable variation was observed. Whereas mandibles, clavicles and femora were jointly the most representative elements, each one giving an MNI of six, no single element was 100% representative and several elements, including patellae and calcanea, reached only 11% of their expected total (see Fig. 2.8).

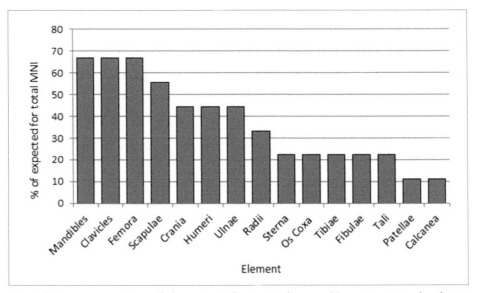

Fig. 2.8: Relative representation of elements in the La Varde assemblage. Crania in this figure are represented by frontal and occipital fragments. Where percentage representation differed between left and right sides of a paired bone the greater of the two values is shown.

Pathology and non-metric traits

The poorly preserved and disarticulated nature of the La Varde collection inhibited the identification of specific pathological conditions. There were no complete, articulated skeletons from which to gauge the pattern and distribution of pathological lesions within individual skeletons. Nevertheless, it was at least possible to comment on which broad categories of disease were in evidence. We know that spinal joint disease was present in the burial population because indicators of this affliction, namely vertebral osteophytosis, Schmorl's nodes and osteoarthritis, were recorded in seven vertebrae. Similarly, at least one individual is likely to have been affected by appendicular joint degeneration for this manifested as porosity in the glenoid cavity of a scapula.

Dental pathologies were observed in the form of calculus and periodontal disease and an enamel defect was noted, but in a loose tooth of unsecure provenance. One neoplasm was found on the endocranial surface of a probable frontal bone fragment and tentative differential diagnoses of osteoma or frontalis hyperostosis interna are offered in respect of this lesion. Trauma was seen to affect one lumbar vertebra in the sample. This took the form of spondylolysis – a type of stress fracture that usually affects the 5th lumbar vertebra, in which the ventral and dorsal parts of the bone become disunited. This condition may occur through repeated forward bending with simultaneous extension at the knees (Aufderheide and Rodriguez-Martin 1998, 63). Bilateral depressions which may have developed as a complication of spondylolisthesis (a condition associated with spondylolysis where the ventral part of a non-united 5th lumbar vertebra, having lost the anchoring effect of its dorsal anatomy, slips out of the normal position), were noted on the superior posterior aspects of the ala of a near-complete sacrum. A final example of pathology consisted of abnormal fusion in a complex of two vertebrae from the lower spine, either L5 and S1 or S1 and S2, most probably the former pair. This may be an example of a congenital border shift which resulted in sacralisation or lumbarisation or could, alternatively, be the outcome of trauma.

Non-metric traits are non-pathological variations in form, seen at various landmarks around the skeleton in a minority of individuals. These can take many forms, for example additional sutures, bony processes or differences in the number, size or arrangement of joint facets or foramina. In the La Varde assemblage observed non-metric traits included lambdoid ossicles, glenoid fossa extensions and a posterior atlas bridge. Additionally, two adult proximal row foot phalanges, the only two such bones in the assemblage, were noteworthy for being unusually symmetrical in form; a fact which made siding extremely difficult.

Colour change

When bones are burnt, changes occur both in their visual characteristics and their histological composition (Correia 1997, 276). One of the most readily detectable visual changes is colour which is known, from experimental research, to progress from the normal cream/buff colour, to brown/black, through taupe and hues of blue/

grey to white (Munro *et al.* 2007, 94; McKinley 2000, 405) as the organic component of the bone matrix is gradually destroyed (Correia 1997, 276). Of the 359 bones/ bone fragments that were assessed for colour change – nine fragments could not be assessed on account of their being heavily varnished – 352, that is to say 98% of the identified sample, showed evidence of having been burnt, whereas only seven were scored as unburnt. Visual inspection suggested that a comparable proportion of the non-identified subset was also burnt.

Black, taupe and grey were the most frequently observed shades (see Fig. 2.9) and these correspond to burning events of medium intensity, where intensity is the term used to describe the effects of temperature, time, or a combination of the two.

Very few of the burnt bones/fragments were oxidised to white and none showed evidence of the shrinkage, deformation or curved, U-shaped fissuring that typically signal the high intensity burning of fleshed bodies (McKinley 2000, 405, though see Goncalves *et al.* 2011). Detectable fractures were in all cases linear, and transverse splintering was noted in several of the larger fragments (see, for example, Fig. 2.10). These are features typically seen in cases where 'dry' bones have been burnt subsequent to the total, or near-total, decomposition of the soft tissues (Baby 1954; Binford 1963; Goncalves *et al.* 2011). Rather than indicating standard cremation, this evidence argues in favour of one or more burning events, in which the bones of deceased individuals were burnt post-mortem and once decomposition was at a very advanced stage.

The colour of the burnt bones was, in many cases, highly uneven and several fragments displayed a range of colours within a very small area. The pathological bone complex from the lower spine, described above (Fig. 2.11) illustrates this point particularly well for it is made up of two fragments which, when rejoined and viewed in the posterior aspect, exhibit markedly different colours side by side.

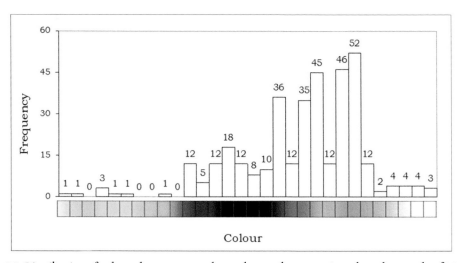

Fig. 2.9: Distribution of colour change among burnt bones shown against the colour scale of Munro et al. 2007.

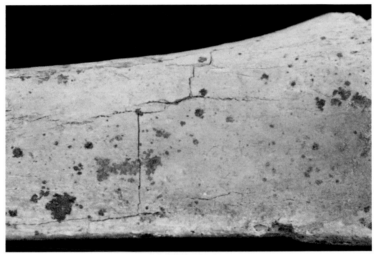

Fig. 2.10: Linear fractures and transverse splintering denoting "dry burning" in the distal metaphysis of a right humerus (lateral view).

1cm

Fig. 2.11: Bone complex No. 188, a pathological lower spine, showing contrasting colours in joining fragments.

Since both fragments are burnt, albeit to differing degrees, a scenario that could account for the observed colour contrast would involve the whole complex having split in two during an initial burning event, with the larger fragment (pictured left) rolling out of, or being removed from, the fire, while the smaller fragment (pictured right) remained in the fire where it was subjected to longer and/or hotter burning. Alternatively the bone may have been fragmented and separated through disturbance prior to burning.

Discussion

With a systematic inventory and comprehensive analysis of the La Varde skeletal assemblage complete, it was possible, for the first time, to compare the 19th century observations of F. C. Lukis to empirical data gleaned from analysis of the bones. With regard to the incidence of burning, both data sources are in agreement; it was noted during the excavation that both burnt and unburnt human bones were present in the tomb, and this fact is confirmed by the skeletal sample. As for the numbers of individuals represented, the sources differ. The first difference concerns the relative proportions of non-adult and adult remains in the burial population and the absolute number of non-adults. Whereas Lukis claimed that the human remains belonged principally to adults and contained only one child, aged approximately 12 years, analysis of the sample using modern osteological methods has revealed non-adult and adult remains in the ratio 1:3, with at least three children present, two of those certainly under 10 years of age.

The second and more significant discrepancy concerns the total number of individuals represented. Compared to the 30 or more skeletons recalled by Lukis, to which must be added a "considerable quantity" of bone said to have been removed in the 1811 investigation, the skeletal assemblage shows a marked deficit, the minimum number being only nine. Although MNI is a crude measure which often underestimates the actual number of individuals, the overall amount of bone available for study is nevertheless grossly inconsistent with the large quantity so often referred to in the excavation accounts.

In view of how long ago the excavation took place, it would be reasonable to argue that some material has simply been lost or misplaced since its discovery. In beginning his longest and fullest excavation account (GMAG 7453), Lukis recalls going to great lengths to recover and preserve artefacts that were ungraciously removed from the tomb in 1811 and it must be assumed that he treated the finds from the 1837 excavation with the same degree of concern, if not more. Nevertheless, as those familiar with old collections will attest, the reorganisation, movement, and repackaging of finds over time, together with the loaning of subsamples for display or specialist analysis, makes the loss of artefacts not uncommon. Hence there is every possibility that some unburnt bones have gone astray in the 170 or so years since their excavation.

Another plausible explanation is that the proportion of bone showing extremely poor preservation was greater than suggested in the written accounts with the result that some could not be saved, disintegrating either at the point of excavation or sometime thereafter. In this scenario, one would expect larger losses among the unburnt subset because burnt bones are conferred a degree of protection against the destructive effects of acid soil erosion, due to the structural changes in their mineral component, hydroxyapatite, which occur upon heating (Mays 1998, 209). Consequently there would be a reduction in the overall quantity of human bone and an increase in the proportion of burnt bone relative to unburnt bone. When re-evaluated as merely the surviving osseous material from La Varde, the analysed sample accords well with the expected pattern; the number of individuals represented is low and the vast majority is, by necessity, burnt.

Whilst we are in no position to shed doubt on Lukis' original estimation of 30 or more individuals with one aged about 12 years, these observations are likely to have been restricted to the unburnt assemblage, now almost totally absent, which presumably was less fragmentary prior to excavation and the bones more easily recognisable. In the absence of a trained osteologist, it is likely that the fragmentary burnt bone – i.e. the material that survives today – was unrecognisable and thus disregarded in the original assessment. The archival evidence is vague in this regard.

The burial population of La Varde

Consideration of the skeletal material in conjunction with the excavation accounts suggests that at least some of the original deposit was totally destroyed by the acidic soil matrix in which it became buried, whereas a smaller subset survived in a relatively well-preserved state on account of its being burnt. In so far as this physical characteristic is concerned, the sample is broadly consistent with other assemblages of Neolithic date, and is comparable to sites such as San Sébastien II and La Haute Suane, both in the Var region of southern France, where differing funerary treatments are thought to have caused a dichotomy in the survival of burnt versus unburnt human remains (Chambon 2003, 207, 213).

A review of 137 British and Irish Neolithic assemblages by Beckett and Robb (2006, 59) revealed relatively low MNIs (usually less than 50) for most sites and no striking age or sex bias in who was selected for burial. With regard to these broad demographic parameters, La Varde appears to be typical. Information relating to population health is unfortunately limited by the nature of the surviving skeletal remains. Roberts and Cox (2003) provide a survey of skeletal pathology during all major archaeological periods, and found that every category of disease (congenital, dental, trauma, joint, infectious, metabolic/endocrine and neoplastic) was represented in Neolithic collections. In the La Varde assemblage five of these categories were potentially evident. Joint disease and trauma share an activity-related aetiology and any significant and sustained change in activity affecting a whole population is likely to be reflected in a shift in the pattern and prevalence of these types of conditions in the skeletal remains of group members. Among Neolithic skeletal material osteoarthritis is frequently reported (Smith and Brickley 2009, 127) and this may reflect the labour requirements of an agricultural economy such as land clearance or the grinding of cereals to make flour. Sixteen bones in the La Varde assemblage, including seven vertebrae and one scapula, show lesions that are most consistent with joint disease or trauma. Although these do not necessarily correspond to sixteen individuals (some or all may derive from the same person), they do confirm the presence of joint disease among the Neolithic inhabitants of Guernsey. This may signal the arduous demands of an agrarian lifestyle in the same way as larger samples have more conclusively demonstrated. The complex and multiple aetiologies of these conditions, however, prevent any firm conclusions being drawn.

Funerary practice at La Varde

Neolithic funerary tradition is characterised by a wide array of rites taking place at various locations in the landscape, including barrows, causewayed enclosures and, most notably, chambered tombs and mortuary houses (Beckett and Robb 2006, 57). In contrast with later periods, burial in the Neolithic was predominantly collective and evidence abounds for the ceremonial manipulation of bones via mixing and sorting, which resulted in the total or partial loss of skeletal integrity for most subjects (Thomas 1991; Scarre 2007). Research suggests that within closed monuments such as passage graves, burial assemblages both in Britain (Beckett and Robb 2006, 57) and north-west France (Scarre pers. comm.) were most commonly – though not exclusively – formed through the serial introduction of complete, fleshed, primary inhumations, which were left to decompose inside the tomb, each new addition disturbing earlier burials so that the degree of disarticulation of deposited remains increased over time. Frequently the funerary programme was elaborated. At sites such as Hazleton North in Gloucestershire the conspicuous absence of certain skeletal elements suggests the removal of bones (Scarre 2007, 80), whilst at others (Knowe of Yarso, Orkney, for example), the addition of isolated bones would seem to be indicated by the excess of certain elements (Scarre 2007, 51).

Fowler (2000) discusses a number of examples where the skeletons of individuals had been disassembled and then reassembled in approximate anatomic order and cases where elements from one individual had been substituted into the body of another (e.g. skulls with mandibles from different individuals). Whereas the arrangement of remains may have been partly practical, designed simply to make space for new interments, the degree of effort expended in the cause often implies a deeper level of significance. As a result of ethnographic studies such as Hertz's (1960) work relating to Borneo, it has been suggested that the spatial manipulation of bones during this period may have been a metaphor for the changing state of the person: a way of confirming and coming to terms with the transition of an individual from the realm of the living to the realm of the dead (Smith and Brickley 2009, 61). In many societies, the period during which a corpse is decomposing is an uncertain time in which a person is neither alive nor fully dead, and it is only at the point of full skeletonisation that remains become "clean" or non-threatening/polluting (Smith and Brickley 2009, 61). With this in mind, the arrangement of bones within Neolithic tombs could be considered a way of charting or managing the progress of the deceased from one state to another, and evidence of burning, mechanical defleshing or excarnation, which are not infrequently noted in Neolithic contexts, may be viewed as processes aimed at shortening the unstable liminal period and accelerating the dead to the point of continued existence in the afterlife.

Whether this process of skeletonisation occurred within the tomb, or external to it is a matter of debate and is likely to have been the subject of regional variations. At least at some sites, individuals were cremated prior to interment within the tomb, while at others archaeologists appear to have identified what have been interpreted as "excarnation" areas, again implying post-defleshing interment (Smith and Brickley 2009, 42). At other sites the presence of primary inhumations within the tomb indicates that the process of decomposition occurred here.

At La Varde, the site archive alludes to discrete burials, either in pits or demarcated by pebbles but there is no sense that these were articulated and primary in nature. There does seem to have been an attempt to keep certain groups of bones separate from other deposits, but regrettably due to the nature of how and when the tomb was excavated, it is not possible to test through analysis Lukis' belief that grouped bones were from a single person as against multiple individuals.

We certainly have evidence of remains having been burned and we know from the dry-burning pattern seen on the cortical surfaces of the bones from La Varde that burning was not of the recently dead but rather of bodies in an advanced state of decomposition, either with very little or no flesh left to fuel the burning process. Possibly burning was performed to remove the last vestiges of soft tissue from the bones, perhaps as a treatment aimed at hastening the remains through their liminal state to a more desirable end condition. Alternatively, if no flesh remained at all, the burning may have served some other unknown ceremonial or transformative purpose.

The presence of burnt remains is nothing unusual for Neolithic funerary practices, however the fact that this burning was conducted on remains largely or totally devoid of flesh is exceptional and does warrant further consideration. Unfortunately no other reports of Neolithic assemblages which have identified burning have made the distinction between whether the bodies were burnt fleshed or without flesh and so comparisons are difficult.

The absence of fire damage to the tomb itself, along with the lack of charcoal among the recovered finds, could be taken to suggest that burning was probably conducted external to the tomb rather than inside it. Equally though, it could be that burning did occur within the tomb, after which all traces of the burning event, save for the burnt bones themselves, were removed through thorough cleaning.

Conclusions about the types of burial practice(s) responsible for the formation of commingled samples are often drawn from the presence or absence of small bones of the hands and feet, the idea being that these elements, once severely decomposed, are the most likely to be separated when a body is moved and are consequently unlikely to feature on sites where the dominant rite was for redisposition (i.e. secondary burial) of bodies previously left to decompose elsewhere (Andrews and Bello 2006; Beckett and Robb 2006, 60). Another indicator of secondary burial is evidence for exposure, and signs of bleaching or scavenger damage are often sought in order to determine whether remains might have been left open to the elements before being gathered up and transferred to a new location.

A thorough examination of the La Varde sample with regard to these factors revealed only one case of scavenging and this was consistent with gnawing by an animal such as a rodent which most likely took place inside the tomb. Small bones like carpals and phalanges were proportionally well represented. This fact, in conjunction with a lack of appreciable weathering, is suggestive of primary burial practice in which there was no opportunity for small bones to be lost in transit from one place to another. One could argue, on the strength of this finding, that it is more likely that burning took place within, not outwith, the tomb as burning events conducted elsewhere would provide exactly the sort of opportunity that might have caused small bones to become lost. The absence of cutmarks means that there is no affirmative evidence that systematic dismemberment or defleshing had taken place at this site.

The differences in skeletal element representation in the La Varde sample discussed above, namely the paucity of bones like patellae when compared with femora, or mandibles (see Fig. 2.8) may be signs of intentional modification by human action where certain bones had been favoured over others either for omission from, or particular inclusion in the tomb deposits. Unfortunately it is very difficult to disentangle the effects of natural differential decomposition of bones from human intervention (Beckett and Robb 2006, 68), and this, compounded by the relatively low rate of full identification of fragments from the La Varde assemblage and the overall level of survival of the remains, means that further resolution on the subject is unlikely to be achieved.

In consideration of all the available evidence, the most logical conclusion is that the bones of some of the eventual burial subjects of La Varde (or, for that matter, some bones from all burial subjects) were first allowed to decompose in an interim location (possibly also the tomb) then at some later point subjected to fire. Once the burning episode was complete bone fragments were collected up, taking care to include small elements, and positioned in their final locations. Fire damage to some of the pots found associated with the burnt bones may be a result of the initial firing of the vessels, but could equally be a sign that these artefacts were an important part of the burning process and that they went with the human remains to the fire. The same could be said for animal bones, a handful of which, all showing colour change, were identified during the re-analysis among the surviving human bones.

The reported presence of many unburnt bones in the tomb, and the occurrence of the same in the skeletal sample, albeit in very small numbers, proves that not all bones were subject to the same treatment. Sadly, the very poor rate of survival of this unburnt subset makes it impossible to gauge what sort of treatment they might have received other than stating the obvious: they were not subjected to fire.

The human remains were distributed around the chamber in a considered manner, with bones coming to rest in paved layers, and grouped into discrete piles, burnt ones centrally and towards the north. While details such as the significance of placing burnt bones in the northern half of the burial space – if, in fact, this was a real trend – are beyond recovery, Lukis' belief that pavements were installed as a practical space-creating measure is one still advanced by modern-day archaeologists to explain similar divisions at other sites, and is likely to be correct.

Conclusions

When viewed in isolation, the small, fragmentary and disparate assemblages of skeletal material, that are so often all that survive from Neolithic sites, seem to have little to offer in terms of our overall interpretation of Neolithic funerary tradition. By pooling data from several sites, however, even the most unpromising samples can offer new and valuable insights into the lives and deaths of people in this remote and fascinating period. The analysis performed here has shown that the burial population of La Varde contained at least nine individuals, most of whose bones were subjected to burning, and probably many more whose unburnt remains, seen by Lukis in the 19th century, do not survive to the present day. These individuals suffered a number of pathological conditions, ranging from dental disease and joint disease to trauma and neoplastic growths. Both males and females, non-adults and adults were represented in the surviving skeletal assemblage and this suggests that, whatever the programme of funerary events might have entailed here, sex and age posed no barrier to potential involvement in tomb-based rituals.[2]

At least two alternative forms of treatment were applied to human remains at the site, and, once inside the tomb, there ensued a protracted period of contact with the exterior, in which bones were manipulated according to the beliefs of living relatives of the dead or community members.

Whereas all bones were apparently left to decompose naturally in the first instance, and some, perhaps even the majority, may represent a series of straightforward primary burials that became commingled with time, others were certainly subjected to secondary rites which involved episodes of burning. In addition to the general questions of why individuals might have been afforded the rite of tomb burial in the first place, and what activities external to the tomb might have initiated or completed the funerary programme, the choice to burn or not to burn remains raises the further question of why certain types of treatment were apportioned, and on what basis.

Complete skeletonisation of human remains takes anything from a few months for unburied remains (Whittle *et al.* 2007, 132) to 3–5 years for those interred in the ground (Wysocki *et al.* 2007, 69). Because we know bones were burned when they were well on their way to being skeletonised, we can also say that, at a minimum, the period of contact with the bones must have lasted for several months. Recent developments in the study of burned human remains have advanced the analysis of the remains recovered from such sites and added an additional valuable layer of knowledge with regards to the funerary rites. Further discrimination between the burning of fleshed and unfleshed human remains at other Neolithic sites would provide useful comparanda, but has not yet been recorded.

The integration of data from documentary sources with the findings from a primary analysis of skeletal material was advantageous in this study, not only because it allowed a fuller picture to be attained of funerary activity at the particular site under consideration, but also because it highlighted the potential for misinterpretation of other sites where documentary sources may be scant or non-existent and conclusions have to be drawn solely from surviving skeletal material. Without the information derived from the Lukis archive, it would have been necessary to conclude that a minimum of nine people were represented by remains in the chamber. Given the details contained in the excavation reports it has been possible to more than triple this estimate and, were equivalent evidence available for all sites, the same alterations might likewise be necessary and achievable.

The La Varde assemblage has also proved to be a good example of a sample that required techniques and knowledge developed both in forensic science and archaeology to be applied together in order to glean maximum information from the available material. The successful application of these techniques also required a "home-grown" methodology which combined aspects from these two ordinarily quite separate fields and a willingness to tackle unpromising and difficult burnt material. The reward has been a unique observation on the timing at which burning of bones from this site took place relative to their decomposition.

Notes

1 One fragment in the last group, a small piece of a distal femoral epiphysis, accounts for the broad age range of the category as it could only be said to be from a child who was younger than the age at which this epiphysis fuses (14–19 years), but at a more advanced stage of development than a 9–11 year old individual from a reference collection consulted for comparison.

2 It could be argued that the lack of infants is significant, however infant bones have been noted by the authors among the as yet un-catalogued remains from Le Déhus, the tomb of comparable date cited above, and their absence from the La Varde material may simply be the result of chance.

References

Andrews, P. and Bello, S. 2006. Pattern in human burial practice. In: Gowland, R. and Knusel, C. (eds), *The Social Archaeology of Funerary Remains*, 14–29. Oxford: Oxbow Books.

Aufderheide, A. C. and Rodriguez-Martin, C. 1998. *The Cambridge Encyclopaedia of Human Paleopathology.* Cambridge: Cambridge University Press.

Baby, R. S. 1954. Hopewell cremation practices. *Ohio Historical Society Papers in Archaeology* 1, 1–7. Columbus OH: Ohio Historical Society.

Beckett, J. and Robb, J. 2006. Neolithic burial taphonomy, ritual and interpretation in Britain and Ireland: a review. In: Gowland, R. and Knusel, C. (eds), *The Social Archaeology of Funerary Remains*, 57–80. Oxford: Oxbow Books.

Binford, L. R. 1963. An analysis of cremations from three Michigan sites. *Wisconsin Archaeology* 44(2), 98–110.

Brickley, M. and McKinley, J. (eds). 2004. *Guidelines to the Standards for Recording Human Remains.* Reading: Institute of Field Archaeologists Paper 7.

Bukach, D. 2003. Exploring identity and place: an analysis of the provenance of passage grave stones on Guernsey and Jersey in the Middle Neolithic. *Oxford Journal of Archaeology* 22(1), 23–33.

Cassen, S., Grimaud, V., de Jersey, P. and Lescop, L. 2015 (forthcoming). The recording and representation of Neolithic engravings in the Déhus passage grave (Vale, Guernsey). *Proceedings of the Prehistoric Society.*

Chambon, P. 2003. *Les Morts dans les Sépultures Collectives Néolithiques en France: du cadaver aux restes ultimes.* Paris: CNRS.

Correia, P. M. M. 1997. Fire modification of bone: a review of the literature. In: Haglund, W. D. and Sorg, M. H. (eds), *Forensic Taphonomy: The Postmortem Fate of Human Remains*, 275–86. Boca Raton FL: CLC Press.

Cunliffe, B. W. 2001. *Facing the Ocean: The Atlantic and its Peoples 8000 BC–AD 1500.* Oxford: Oxford University Press.

De Pomerai, M. R. 1997. Neolithic engineering: the use of stone in Guernsey passage graves. *Transactions of La Société Guernesiaise* XXIV, 284–9.

Fowler, C. 2001. Personhood and social relations in the British Neolithic with a study from the Isle of Man. *Journal of Material Culture* 6, 137–63.

Gonçalves, D., Thompson, T. J. U. and Cunha, E. 2011. Implication of heat-induced changes in bone on the interpretation of funerary behaviour and practice. *Journal of Archaeological Science* 38, 1308–13.

Hibbs, J. 1985. Little Mr Stonehenge. *Bulletin of La Société Jersiaise* 24(1), 49–74.

Johnston, P. 1981. *The Archaeology of the Channel Islands.* Chichester: Phillimore.

Jones, A. 2005. Lives in fragments? Personhood and the European Neolithic. *Journal of Social Archaeology* 5, 193–224.

Kendrick, T. D. 1928. *The Archaeology of the Channel Islands: Vol.1 The Bailiwick of Guernsey.* London: Methuen.

Kinnes, I. 1988. Megaliths in action: some aspects of the Neolithic period in the Channel Islands. *Archaeological Journal* 145, 13–59.

Kinnes, I. A. and Hibbs, J. *The Dolmens of Jersey.* Jersey: La Haule Books.

Le Conte, D. 2005. The Orientation of megalithic tombs in Guernsey: an astronomical connection? *Transactions of La Société Guernesiaise* XXV(V), 889–906.

Lukis, F. C. 1845. Observations on the primeval antiquities of the Channel Islands. *Archaeological Journal* 1, 142–51.

Mays, S. 2005. Palaeopathological study of Hallux Valgus. *American Journal of Physical Anthropology* 126, 139–49.

McKinley, J. 2000. The analysis of cremated bone. In: Cox, M. and Mays, S. (eds, *Human Osteology in Archaeology and Forensic Science*, 403–21. Cambridge: Cambridge University Press.

Munro, L. E., Longstaffe, F. J. and White. C. D. 2007. Burning and boiling of modern deer bone: Effects on crystallinity and oxygen isotope composition of bioapatite phosphate. *Palaeogeography, Palaeoclimatology, Palaeoecology* 249, 90–102.

Patton, M. 1995. Neolithic Communities of the Channel Islands. Oxford: British Archaeological Report 240.

Roberts, C. and Cox, M. 2003. *Health and Disease in Britain, From Prehistory to the Present Day.* Stroud: Sutton.

Rogers, J. 1990. The human skeletal material. In: Saville, A. *Hazleton North: The Excavation of a Neolithic Long Cairn of the Cotswold Severn Group*, 182–98. London: English Heritage.

Scarre, C. 2007. *The Megalithic Monuments of Britain and Ireland* (2nd edn). London: London, Thames and Hudson.

Scheuer, L. and Black, S. 2000. *Developmental Juvenile Osteology.* London: Academic Press.

Schulting, R. J., Sebire, H. and Robb, J. E. 2010. On the road to Paradis. New insights from AMS dates and stable isotopes at Le Déhus, Guernsey, and the Channel Islands Middle Neolithic. *Oxford Journal of Archaeology* 29(2), 149–73.

Sebire, H. 2005. *The Archaeology and Early History of the Channel Islands.* Stroud: Tempus.

Smith, M. and Brickley, M. 2009. *People of the Long Barrows: Life, Death and Burial in the Earlier Neolithic.* Stroud: History Press.

Taylor, A. 2001. *Burial Practices in Early England.* Stroud: Tempus.

Thomas, J. 1991. *Rethinking the Neolithic.* Cambridge: Cambridge University Press.

Thomas, J. 1999. *Understanding the Neolithic.* Cambridge: Cambridge University Press.

Whittle, A., Barclay, A., Bayliss, A., McFadyen, L., Schulting, R. and Wysocki, M. 2007. *Building for the Dead: Events, Processes And Changing Worldviews from the Thirty-eighth to the Thirty-fourth Centuries cal BC in Southern Britain. Cambridge Archaeological Journal* 17 (supplement s1), 123–47.

Wysocki, M. and Whittle, A. 2000. Diversity, lifestyles and rites: new biological and archaeological evidence from British Earlier Neolithic mortuary assemblages. *Antiquity* 74, 591–601.

Wysocki, M., Bayliss, A. and Whittle, A. 2007. Serious mortality: the date of the Fussell's Lodge long barrow. In: Whittle, A., Barclay, A., Bayliss, A., McFadyen, L., Schulting, R. and Wysocki, M. 2007. *Building for the Dead: Events, Processes And Changing Worldviews from the Thirty-eighth to the Thirty-fourth Centuries cal BC in Southern Britain. Cambridge Archaeological Journal* 17 (supplement s1), 65–84.

Original Unpublished Archive Sources

GMAG = Guernsey Museum and Art Gallery

GMAG 7632:36. Notes by ? F. C. Lukis. Undated. Guernsey Museum.

GMAG 7492. F. C. Lukis to Lt. Col. H. Smith. 10th October 1838 (Grange). Guernsey Museum.

GMAG 7492. F. C. Lukis to Lt. Col. H. Smith. 15th January 1839 (Guernsey). Guernsey Museum.

GMAG 7453. Lukis, F. C. 1850. *Collectanea Antiqua, Vol. V.* Guernsey Museum.

DXV 2. Anonymous manuscript, 'Notes on excavation of Cromlech at Lancresse', labelled DXV 2 (Guernsey Museum).

Chapter 3

Past cremation practices
from a bioarchaeological perspective

How new methods and techniques revealed conceptual changes in cremation practices during the late Bronze Age and early Iron Age in Denmark

Lise Harvig

Introduction

In modern secularised Europe, we tend to think of cremation as a particular event in an individual funeral ceremony, with the only purpose being to reduce the corpse to ashes before the post-cremation burial. When interpreting past pastoral societies resembling our own, we have often interpreted cremation in a similar way – a uniform concept involving the process of burning a corpse before burial. Accordingly, cremation osteology has primarily focussed on demographical manifestations within grave contexts, i.e. on sexing and ageing of the buried individuals, and on recording pathological changes of the cremated remains. However, ethnographical analogies and recent developments within cremation archaeology have taught us that past cremation ceremonies may differ very much from our own perceptions of what a funeral is. We have learned that a variety of traditions may be embraced by past cremation practices, in different tempi, comprising very different social meanings. Hence, in modern cremation archaeology we are now looking at 1) pre-cremation phenomena such as defleshing before cremation (by natural or mechanical means) or parting of the body, 2) cremation processes involving burning of the body, parts of the body or several bodies (as either fresh bodies, green or dry bones) and 3) post-cremation rituals involving sorting of the cremated human remains with the purpose of disposing of these (or a selection of these) in either a grave or in a variety of non-mortuary contexts (for Scandinavian examples see Kaliff 1992; 1997; Artelius 1999; Arcini 2005; Arcini and Svanberg 2005; Gansum 2004; Wickholm 2008; Goldhahn 2012). All these ways of handling cremated human remains in past mortuary ceremonies are central for understanding the given societies' relation to and concepts of death. However, we face several challenges in understanding and describing these rituals in further detail (Fig. 3.1). Because the archaeological material discussed here does not exhibit evidence of either pre-cremation treatment of the human remains or of collective pyres or burials, this chapter will primarily focus on osteological evidence of the actual cremation process and of post-cremation rituals involving the cremated human remains.

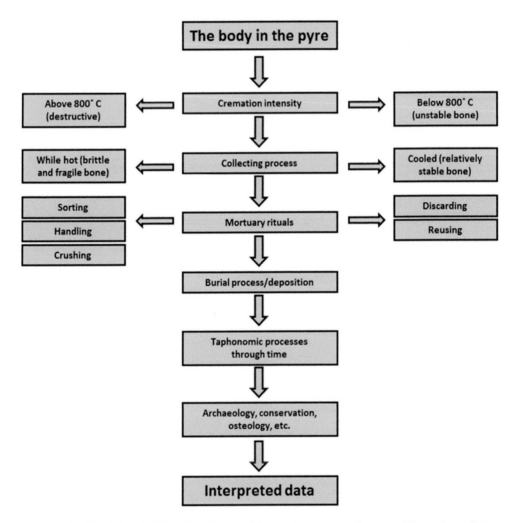

Fig. 3.1: A simplified sketch of the degrading and fracturing process of cremated bone through time, from the point of cremation until the time of analysis. The interpreted data depend on which type of event occurs during the process.

We have several ways of approaching this problem osteologically, and some of these are discussed in further detail in this chapter, primarily focussing on the southern Scandinavian archaeological record of cremation during the transition period between the Bronze and Iron Ages:

1) Modern technological invention may help us to approach the cremated human remains from new perspectives. CT scanning of prehistoric cremation urns is one way of visualising and extracting digital data from cremated human remains *in situ*, i.e. as close as possible to the prehistoric event when the cremated human remains were placed in the urn.

2) Macroscopically, cremated human remains may exhibit distinctive signs of their individual journeys before their final deposit. Nevertheless, we need to separate these from various taphonomic processes that may result in similar patterns.

First, we need to acknowledge the various types of events that can occur in the process (Fig. 3.1), and then we need to accept the difficulties in separating them. Moreover, we need to remember that absence of evidence is not evidence of absence. That such "absence" may even be calculable will be exemplified in this chapter.

First and foremost, the temperature or cremation intensity in the pyre decides the primary basis for our interpretation, either by reducing the cremated human remains to calcined, skewed and deformed fragments of the human skeleton (temperatures above 800°C) or by producing unstable bone with differing chemical resistance (temperatures below 800°C). Secondly, the eventual collection process from the cremation pyre will cause further fragmentation, depending on, for example, whether the cremated remains were still hot (brittle) or cool (relatively stable). As such, any mortuary rituals involving the cremated human remains will cause further fragmentation and wear due to handling and may also reduce the quantity of the sample because of ritual selection of the bone for various purposes. Then, at some point, the final deposition of the cremated remains takes place. Subsequently, they are subjected to further taphonomic processes during the time of lying in the ground and during modern analyses. Lastly, they form the basis for our interpretations.

Because archaeological contexts with cremated human remains, i.e. their final depositions, are the primary basis for our understanding of past cremation ceremonies, we need to use a theoretical-archaeological, osteological and critical taphonomic approach. Practically, we need to "read" the individual biographies of the cremation-related deposits and the associated cremated human remains. But how do we distinguish individual events in cremation-related mortuary rituals and ceremonies, and how can we propose or reject events that occurred prior to the final deposition of particular cremated human remains?

Using the archaeological record from seven recently excavated grave sites, containing 137 graves, from the Fraugde region on the island of Funen, Denmark, we have been able to discuss these issues more thoroughly.

The funerary context

Based on the 1000 year-long archaeological record of cremation during the late Bronze Age and early Iron Age on northern Funen in Denmark, we have been able to discuss changes in ritual practices during the period, applying the above mentioned approaches (see also methods section). During the entire period, between c. 1100 BC and 1 BC (Table 3.1), cremation practices were the norm in southern Scandinavia. For several reasons, amongst others the unfortunate Hallstatt plateau in the calibrated radiocarbon curve between 800 and 400 BC (Plicht 2004), preventing precise dating during the entire transition period in question, and limited resources within the research field, little has been investigated with regard to particular similarities and differences within cremation practices during the transition between the late Bronze Age and early Iron Age (see however Lindahl Jensen 20004; Arcini 2005; Arcini and Svanberg 2005). Cremation practices of the two periods have therefore generally been considered relatively uniform and unilinear, exhibiting little evidence of conceptual change over time (Jensen 2002; 2003).

Table 3.1: Chronological overview of the southern Scandinavian time periods mentioned in the text.

Early Bronze Age	Late Bronze Age	Pre-Roman Iron Age	Roman Iron Age
c. 1700–1100 BC	c. 1100–500 BC	c. 500–1 BC	c. AD 1–400

Although this may be the case to some extent, there are particular indications of gradual conceptual change within the mortuary beliefs during the transition period in local Danish regions. However, this is only evident when the deposited cremated human remains are studied in further detail (see also Harvig *et al.* 2014).

A variety of different grave types are known archaeologically from the late Bronze Age and early Iron Age in Scandinavia. Typologically, these are primarily categorized as following (German categorisation in brackets): urn graves (*urnengräber*), bone layer graves (*knochenlagergräber*), urn cremation pits (*urnenbrandgruben*) and cremation pits (*brandgrubengräber*). Although they all represent cremation graves or at least cremation-related deposits associated with grave sites, their characteristics are stringently differentiated and their function varies similarly (see also Bechert 1980; Harvig *et al.* 2014). Furthermore, there seems to be a chronological development in the use of certain grave types in southern Scandinavia (see Harvig *et al.* 2014).

The Fraugde area on northern Funen, Denmark

Although prehistoric burial practices varied markedly both regionally and chronologically in southern Scandinavia, cremation practices dominated exclusively on the island of Funen from the onset of the late Bronze Age, around 1100 BC, until the beginning of the late Roman Iron Age, around AD 400. In the parish of "Fraugde", seven continuous cremation grave sites from the late Bronze Age and early Iron Age have been excavated recently (for location see Fig. 3.2). The area is thoroughly investigated by archaeologists because of its current status as one of the most important industrial areas near the third largest Danish city of Odense. In the 350 ha development area, Tietgen Byen, Odense City Museums has conducted extensive excavations and uncovered a regular cultural landscape from the late Bronze Age and early Iron Age (Runge 2010; 2012; 2013). Both grave sites and settlements in the area exhibit cultural continuity from the earliest Bronze Age until and including the early pre-Roman Iron Age (see Runge 2012, 113, 132ff.). The settlements were primarily small and consisted of one or two contemporary farms (Runge 2012, 122ff.). In some cases, defined separations of grave sites and settlements were marked in the landscape by rows of cooking pits (Runge 2010, 83ff.). Over time, the settlements moved gradually within the resource area. The resource areas contained settlements and grave sites as well as gathering areas and in one case a large production area. Within Tietgen Byen, six to seven resource areas can be defined, separated by natural boundaries, such as streams and water ways (see Runge 2010; Harvig et al. 2014).

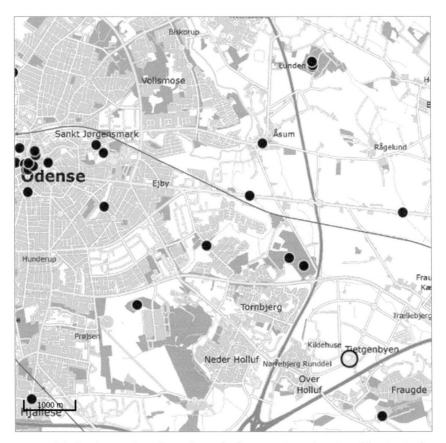

Figure 3.2: Map of the local area, where the circle marks the approximate location of the sites in the Fraugde region in the southeastern outskirts of Odense city. Protected ancient monuments in the same area are indicated by the black dots.

The cremated remains

The late Bronze Age and pre-Roman Iron Age cremation graves from the seven grave sites in the Fraugde parish were predominantly found in flat graves. The graves were located in clearly defined areas of the landscape, and each site contained graves accumulated over centuries. Despite intense cultivation of the land and modern disturbances, the sites comprised 137 graves (Runge 2010, 102ff; Harvig *et al.* 2014). However, cremated human remains were preserved in only 96 (71%) of these graves, exhibiting an unusual chronological distribution. From the two late Bronze Age sites, 56 of 59 graves (95%) contained cremated bone, whereas this was the case in only 40 of 78 graves (51%) from the pre-Roman Iron Age sites. This was not only a question of poor preservation of the individual grave contexts; all grave sites contained both poorly preserved graves and intact graves. Moreover, no particular grave types were significantly less well preserved than others. The graves therefore represent the general preservation state of those found on modern excavations on heavily cultivated lands, typical of the Danish regions. This implies urns were rarely preserved *in toto* and often broken. Graves were often truncated, so that the original extent of the cuts and the level of the original surface could not be recognised.

Chronologically, the sites mostly cover the transition period between the late Bronze Age and the early pre-Roman Iron Age, but a few cremation graves from the early Bronze Age were present on the oldest of the sites. The grave sites seemingly all represent the common rite of burying the dead in the late Bronze Age and the early Iron Age on Funen. However, similar sites are found in many areas of southern Scandinavia, particularly in southern Sweden, northern Jutland, on Bornholm and on Zealand (Fig. 3.3). The graves in the Fraugde region exhibited no exceptional wealth or status based on the limited amount of finds in the graves, which is in sharp contrast to more wealthy sites known in the region (see Thrane 1984). Hence, the graves reflect the "norm" for the low status lineages. All graves with preserved cremated bone formed the primary material for the osteological analyses discussed in this chapter.

Because of marked variation in preservation of the individual grave contexts, the material was difficult to approach using standard osteological methods, which produce limited comparable data in such circumstances. Many graves contained only a few grams of cremated bone, despite being undisturbed. Conversely, some graves were heavily disturbed but still contained fairly high amounts of cremated bone and large diagnostic bone fragments. We therefore needed to apply methods that were not solely dependent on the total amount of cremated remains in the graves, and that did not focus exclusively on "measurable" data, such as weight and volume of the remains. It was evident that the most informative approach for understanding the funerary practices and the differences in the quantities of burned bone present would be one that focussed on elucidating the nature of primary and secondary fracturing processes. Note that in this chapter, a grave is defined as a place for a burial, whereas a burial refers to a place for (or the evidence of placing) one or more dead bodies in a grave (the act of burial) (see also Ericsson and Runcis 1995).

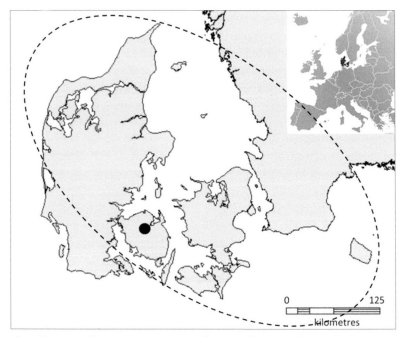

Fig. 3.3. Burial traditions similar to the ones seen in the Fraugde region during the late Bronze Age and early Iron Age are found in several areas in southern Scandinavia, particularly within the area denoted by the dotted line.

Methods of analysis

The many graves from the Fraugde region were analysed according to standard osteological principles regarding primary colouration (see also Kühl 1994; Mäder 2002; Grosskopf 2004; Walker *et al.* 2008), skeletal representation, and dehydration and fracture patterns of the cremated remains (see for example Thurman and Willmore 1981, 280; Buikstra and Swegle 1989, 253; Holck 2001; Fairgrieve 2008; Asmussen 2009; Musgrave *et al.* 2010; Gonçalves 2011). Exploratory CT scans were also taken where possible of urns and their contents *in toto* as well as post-excavation in some cases. These methods are described in further detail in the following section.

Computed Tomography (CT) scanning

In recent years, Computed Tomography (CT) has proved useful in many different types of osteological and archaeological analyses (Tout *et al.* 1980; Ryan and Milner 2006; Lynnerup *et al.* 1997; Lynnerup 2008; 2010). CT is in principle the same as digital x-ray, only performed in 3D (Hsieh 2002). CT was applied to the few intact cremation urns from the late Bronze Age sites (see Harvig *et al.* 2012) to quantify and identify bone fragments. However, CT was also used for sampled cremated remains after excavation (see Harvig and Lynnerup 2013). CT of prehistoric cremation urns and cremated remains has several obvious advantages. First, the shape of the urn as well as the bone fragments and their location are preserved digitally, making them easy to view in 3D. Furthermore, many detailed osteological observations can be made without any post-processing of the images. As such, ageing and sexing of the cremated remains are more accurate when combining CT images with cremated remains after excavation (Harvig *et al.* 2012). CT was also relevant for samples that had already been cleaned because these could be measured digitally to compare post-excavation volumes with manually measured volumes (Harvig and Lynnerup 2013).

Several computer programs allow post-processing of CT data. At the Laboratory of Biological Anthropology in Copenhagen, we currently use a software package (MIMICS®) from Materialise®, Belgium (www.materialise.be). After import of the CT data, the images can be edited digitally. To visualise certain structures, a colour-coding is applied "over" the single grey-scale pixels. This involves a process of identifying single structures on the single slice images and then following these through on the adjacent slices. After delineation (segmentation) of the single structures, they can be extracted and used as a basis for a 3D rendering (Fig. 3.4). Once structures have been

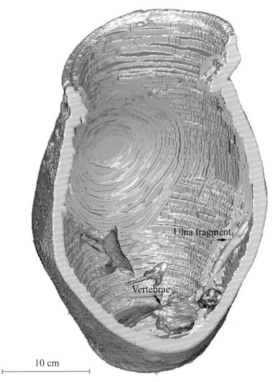

Ulna fragment

Vertebrae

10 cm

Fig. 3.4a: Post-processing of CT data represented by visualized segmentations from two Danish urns dated to the late Bronze Age: the vessel and certain bone fragments within the fill of the urn. All segmentations are dimensionally stable (see also Harvig et al. 2012).

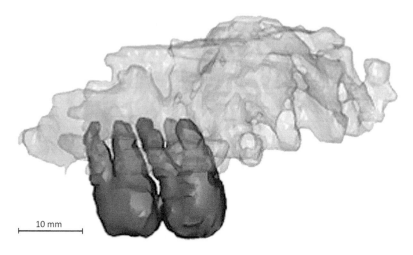

10 mm

Fig. 3.4b: Post-processing of CT data represented by visualized segmentations from two Danish urns dated to the late Bronze Age: a mandibular fragment. All segmentations are dimensionally stable (see also Harvig et al. *2012).*

segmented and visualised, they are dimensionally stable and can then be measured and assessed morphologically (see also Harvig *et al.* 2012; Harvig and Lynnerup 2013).

Macroscopic analyses of cremated remains

Macroscopic analyses of the cremated bone was also undertaken to assess fragmentation patterns and wear of the remains. As mentioned in the introduction, we aimed to distinguish original fragmentation patterns (induced in the past) from fragmentation induced during modern handling of the sample. This is significantly less complex when we can identify which type of archaeological deposition we are analysing (Fig. 3.5). Here, the purely osteological approach is not sufficient, because the archaeological interpretation of the analysed context is crucial for understanding the nature of the deposit, and hence the biographies of the cremated human remains contained within it.

Because we rarely find undisturbed cremation pyres (1) in the Danish archaeological record (see however Thrane 2004, 227, 237, 242, 275), these are not categorised as actual depositions here. Accordingly, primary depositions (2) refer to the first deposition of cremated remains or pyre remains after deliberate sorting of the remains from the cremation pyre. This could for example be a cremation urn or any other type of primary deposition. The typical Iron Age "cremation pit", containing extensive, but sorted remains of the cremation pyre, falls under this category. The cremation pit is not to be confused with an undisturbed cremation pyre or *in situ* pyre remains (e.g. the Roman *bustum* graves) (see Bechert 1980). Final depositions

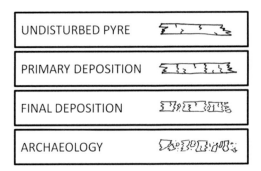

UNDISTURBED PYRE	
PRIMARY DEPOSITION	
FINAL DEPOSITION	
ARCHAEOLOGY	

Fig. 3.5: A simplified sketch of the fracturing process of cremated bone through prehistoric and modern handling processes. Whereas levels 2 and 3 involve handling in the past, which we are only able to document indirectly, level 4 represent modern handling, which should ideally always be documented in detail.

(3) refer to where the cremated remains were found during excavation. This could easily be the same context as the primary deposition, but not necessarily. Lastly, modern analyses (4) refers to the many steps in the archaeological process from excavation over cleaning and to the osteological analysis, which all involve further handling and hence, fragmentation of the cremated remains.

By studying traits of the preserved skeletal material, such as wear patterns and post-cremation fragmentation patterns (i.e. whether fractures, that are not induced during cremation, are fresh or worn), in combination with methods commonly used in cremation osteology (colouration, dehydration and fracture patterns and skeletal representation), it is in fact possible to compare characteristics of cremation graves and pinpoint similarities and differences in cremation-related rituals statistically (see Harvig *et al.* 2014). Most often, fragments from the same deposited context will exhibit similar characteristics in fragmentation and wear, despite the quantity of bone preserved, i.e. even if the context has been disturbed or ploughed through. These data therefore enable us to compare cremated human remains without being exclusively dependent on taphonomic processes that occurred prior to the archaeological investigation.

Characteristic of human remains analysed after cremation in modern crematoria (where temperatures usually reach 800°C and oxygen supply is sufficient) is that they consist of many large and diagnostic bone fragments. Already upon removal of these from the furnace, the first post-cremation fragmentation occurs. Because trabecular structures are markedly more fragile than are long bone structures, these are the first to dissolve and disintegrate. If a sample has been subject to much handling already in the past, it will therefore not only exhibit more fractures and/or wear, but also markedly fewer fragile skeletal elements, e.g. trabecular structures.

Because post-cremation fracturing of cremated human bone often occurs along dehydration fractures and fissures, there are few characteristic macroscopic differences between these and cremation-induced fractures. Therefore such fractures should ideally always be analysed in combination with evidence of wear caused by handling, primary and secondary colouration of the bone, skeletal representation and general fragment sizes, to gain a characteristic registration of the complete sample.

Applying this in practice can be straightforward, particularly for heavily burnt calcined fragments because of their chemical stability (see also Figs 3.1 and 3.6). One example could be a primary Stone Age cremation burial covered in ochre. In this case, ochre staining may reveal the biography of single bone fragments in the grave: For example, if the surface of a fracture on a specific bone fragment is equally stained by ochre as is the bone cortex, the particular fracture occurred before the ochre was applied to the grave, or shortly after. Similarly, staining of fracture surfaces can occur in cremation burials containing pyre remains, where the staining may be black or grey from ash or charcoal. Post-cremation fractures with sharp edges (i.e. seemingly fresh) exhibiting little secondary colouration from the surrounding context have thus occurred recently, e.g. after burial, during excavation or during modern handling. Conversely, fractures with heavily worn edges exhibiting secondary colouration from the surroundings, similar to that of the bone cortex, must have occurred in

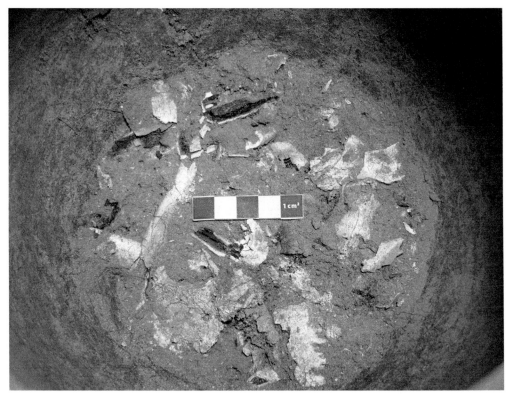

Fig. 3.6: Example of diaphysal and trabecular structures during microexcavation of a Danish urn burial dated to the late Bronze Age. Note the variation in cremation intensity. Both fragments with little chemical stability due to "low" cremation intensity (below c. 800°C) and almost completely calcined fragments are represented. The white and calcined fragments survive microexcavation far better than do the less heat altered fragments. Conversely, most of these were heavily reduced during microexcavation. Had the urn not been CT scanned and emptied by an osteoarchaeologist, the overall cremation intensity (based on the cleaned fragments after microexcavation) and the degree of fragmentation would both have been markedly overestimated. Photograph: Lise Harvig.

the past, before deposition in the final context. Note that such colouration will be less significant if the bones have been subjected to flotation or have been intensely washed. Therefore all modern handling is extremely important to document before the osteological analysis.

Recording of these fracture types may not necessarily be a meritorious task to undertake but once the different types of fractures are recognised, they are clearly separable within samples. Because a sample will often exhibit fractures that occurred both during the cremation process in the past, and during modern handling, it may often be relevant to make an overall registration of whether there were generally many worn fractures in a sample, and whether many fragile elements were still present. Significant variation within types of samples will then be evident in statistical analyses.

Discussion

How CT scanning improved our understanding of the cremated remains

As already mentioned, CT scanning of cremation urns *in toto* has many advantages. It first and foremost facilitates a contextual discussion by enabling the possibility of studying bone material *in situ*. Each link in the process, from the actual cremation in the past until the analysis of the cremated remains in the present, is represented by the preservation of the remains at a given point in time (Fig. 3.1). Many of the earliest stages in the process are practically unknown to the archaeologist, but through CT scanning we may be able to reconstruct possible scenarios as early as the stage of collecting the cremated remains for burial since bone fragments are more complete (see also Anderson and Fell 1995; Minozzi *et al*. 2010; Harvig *et al*. 2012). In the following section, some of the primary results we gained from CT scanning cremation urns and cremated remains after excavation are discussed.

Whole body cremation and burial in the late Bronze Age

Based on CT images of the urns from the late Bronze Age, we reconstructed the volume of the cremated remains digitally *in situ* using different calculation methods such as stereology. This enabled a compromised estimation of an original weight of the cremated remains at the time they were placed in the urn (see Harvig and Lynnerup 2013 and Table 3.2) that could then be compared to post-excavation weight. We were hereby able to demonstrate that the CT scanned urns from the late Bronze Age had seemingly contained the remains of almost entire human bodies, and that under-representation in these graves was primarily due to post-burial taphonomic processes in the ground and during micro-excavation of the fill (Harvig *et al*. 2012; Harvig and Lynnerup 2013). This was confirmed by skeletal representation for these samples, in that these graves usually contained elements of the entire skeleton, i.e. skull, torso, extremities, feet and hands (see also Harvig *et al*. 2014). It further corroborates with interpretations of the graves of the period as being individual and

Table 3.2: Differences between the post-excavation cremation weight and the estimated original cremation weight based on the CT scans of four Late Bronze Age cremation urns from the Fraugde region, northern Funen, Denmark (see also Harvig and Lynnerup 2013).

Urn	Post-excavation cremation weight (g)	CT estimated original cremation weight (g)
PP	1410	2370
PS	850	2130
PT	1000	2180
PZ	1150	1930

personal graves, symbolically similar to the gendered inhumation burials of the early Bronze Age in Scandinavia (see for example Sørensen and Rebay 2008; Harvig in press). This clearly indicates that post-cremation weights are generally under-estimated in osteoarchaeology, and that many cases of under-representation of archaeologically recovered human remains may primarily be ascribed to taphonomic processes, e.g. in the soil and during modern handling of the samples (such as micro-excavation and cleaning).

Over-estimation of fragmentation
A comparison of the osteological data gained from CT scanning of the late Bronze Age cremation urns and the osteological analyses of the cremated remains after micro-excavation of the urn fill also confirmed that a massive bone loss occurred during micro-excavation, resulting in marked over-estimation of fragmentation for the cleaned post-excavation samples (see Harvig *et al.* 2012; Fig. 3.6).

Over-estimation of cremation intensity
Because white calcined fragments survive micro-excavation far better than less heat-altered fragments (Fig. 3.6), samples available after micro-excavation also contained markedly fewer fragments affected by low cremation intensity than had originally been present, as seen on the CT images. Post-excavation estimations of cremation intensity (e.g. temperature) were therefore systematically biased.

Evidence of post-cremation rituals
Regarding ritual aspects of cremation practice, both fragmentation patterns and placement of the cremated remains in the urn are relevant when emptying an urn after CT scanning. For example, any evidence of longitudinal splitting of cremated remains during micro-excavation is crucial to avoid uncritical interpretations of, for example, defleshing prior to the cremation process or cremation of already dry bone, which is thought to result in similar characteristic longitudinal fractures (see for example

Whyte 2001, 439). Our results however conversely implied that the interpretation of these is highly ambiguous, and that these are more likely to occur arbitrarily during heating when the bone collagen contracts and degenerates, which has also been confirmed in other studies (Gonçalves 2011). Accordingly, longitudinal fracturing is not further discussed for the material from the Fraugde region.

Also ritual crushing of the cremated remains before insertion in the urn or grave is a commonly discussed topic in Scandinavia (Tkocz and Jensen 1984, 194; Sigvallius 1994; Kaliff 1992; 1997; Hornstrup 1999, 104; Frisberg 2005, 150). However, on the basis of our CT scans it was apparent that most bone fragments broke along dehydration fractures and fissures during micro-excavation. Furthermore, when characteristics in fragmentation were studied thoroughly, it was noted that the fracture surfaces were generally fresh and exhibited no evidence of wear or secondary colouration (Fig. 3.5), which would be expected if the bones were crushed deliberately already in the past.

How the simple macroscopic analyses improved our understanding of the cremated remains

The simple macroscopic analyses of bone fracture patterns within individual grave contexts were essential for the following interpretation of the seven sites in the Fraugde region, particularly in combination with the chronological development of the cremation-related rituals. Though the typical late Bronze Age urn burials may very likely represent entire cremated individuals, this was however clearly opposite for the early Iron Age cremation pits. Not only did these remains exhibit lower cremation intensity than did the remains in the Bronze Age burials, they also exhibited other distinctive osteological characteristics. Lack of anatomical regions, extreme fragmentation, heavy wear, as well as overall characteristics of the cremated remains, suggested that the bones from the late Iron Age cremation pits had been handled before deposition. Whether the observed fragmentation had occurred during staking of the pyre while burning, clearing of the pyre, sorting of or otherwise handling of the cremated remains after the cremation process is uncertain, but they clearly did not represent post-depositional taphonomic processes alone, and the graves could clearly not be categorised as neither undisturbed pyres, nor primary depositions (Fig. 3.5). The amount of cremated remains found in the cremation pits and their representation thus suggested that these were clearly not representative of entire skeletons. The pyre debris in the cremation pits had clearly been sorted, and during this sorting process, the majority of the cremated remains had been sorted out, as also suggested for similar Swedish graves (Arcini 2005). This leaves us with interpretations of the cremation pits as "graves" for the sorted pyre remains, but according to the previously mentioned definition not actual burials (Ericsson and Runcis 1995; Harvig *et al.* 2014, Harvig in press).

Contextual interpretations of the sites

Our overall interpretation of the seven grave sites from the Fraugde region on northern Funen has revealed particular changes in the mortuary rituals between the two periods, i.e. between the late Bronze Age and the early Iron Age: The late Bronze Age urn burials and bone layer graves often represented individual post-cremation burials of almost entire cremated human bodies. Examples of low representation of the cremated remains within this period (described through weight or representation of skeletal elements) could often be ascribed to poor preservation of the particular burial contexts. Moreover, most fragments were affected by high cremation intensity, i.e. calcined.

Conversely, the early Iron Age cremation pits often represented extremely few and heavily fragmented remains of the human skeleton, despite preservation of the individual grave contexts. Cremation intensity was also generally registered as lower for these remains than for the late Bronze Age remains (Table 3.3).

If we further elaborate on the overall symbolic expressions of the graves of the two periods, as preserved in the archaeological record, we see a clear difference between 1) the gendered, individual and personal burials in the late Bronze Age containing personal grave goods, resembling the inhumation practice of the early Bronze Age, and 2) the more impersonal and egalitarian graves of the early Iron Age containing extent remains of the cremation pyre including the pyre goods (see also Table 3.4). There seems to have been a fundamental difference between the two periods regarding the "reconstruction" of the post-cremation individual. Seemingly, this reflects a fundamental change in the mortuary beliefs: In the late Bronze Age, the cremation pyre was one of several events in the mortuary transformation process, and collection of all of the body fragments and careful deposition was obviously important, as was

Table 3.3: General trends for the three primary grave types represented in the Fraugde region (see also Harvig et al. 2014). Abbreviations: Late Bronze Age (LBA) and Pre-Roman Iron Age (PRIA).

	Urn grave	Urn cremation pit	Cremation pit
Primary period	LBA	LBA/PRIA	PRIA
Artefacts	Grave goods	Grave goods	Pyre goods
Degree of fragmentation	Low	Medium	High
Cremation intensity	High	Mixed	Medium
Representation	Whole body representation	Whole body representation	Few recognisable elements
Wear characteristics	Little wear	Little wear	Worn
Sample characteriatics	Many fragile element preserved	Many fragile element preserved	Primarily solid fragments preserved
Secondary colouration	From soil	From soil/ashes	From ashes and charcoal

Table 3.4: There seems to have been a fundamental difference between the two periods regarding the "reconstruction" of the post-cremation individual as illustrated in this table by the differences in grave characteristics, handling of artefacts, skeletal representation, catalysts for transformation, and elements of commemoration.

	LBA	PRIA
Grave characteristics	Personal expression	Extensive pyre remains
Artefacts	Grave goods	Pyre goods
Skeletal representation	Entire human bodies	Random human remains
Transformation	The burial	The cremation pyre
Commemoration	The individual and the burial	The cremation pyre and the grave

the cremation process. In contrast, the cremation pyre was seemingly the primary locus of transformation in the early Iron Age, and deposition of the majority of the cremated human remains may have taken on another form such as scattering or curation above ground. It may be that the cremation pyre itself was central, and the remains of the entire scene were disposed of and commemorated as such, in a variety of contexts on or near the actual cremation sites (see Harvig *et al.* 2014. and Harvig in press). We do in fact have little knowledge on the precise ritual actions, except for those pyre remains that were deliberately earthened in the cremation pits during the first centuries of the Scandinavian Iron Age.

Conclusions

By using CT scans of cremation urns prior to micro-excavation and by applying simple new macroscopic analytical methods, we have been able to pinpoint significant variations between the late Bronze Age burials and early Iron Age graves in a local region. It was indeed useful to let the same burials undergo different types of analyses, when possible. For example, the late Bronze Age urns were not only CT scanned and analysed digitally, they were also excavated and analysed according to standard osteological principles accompanied by more thorough macroscopic analyses of fragmentation patterns. Combined with the archaeological evidence, this resulted in detailed observations on the individual journeys of the cremated remains, revealing that in the late Bronze Age, all human remains of the cremation pyre representing the dead body were collected shortly after the cremation process and carefully placed in the cremation urns along with personal artefacts of the deceased, which were then buried as such – a tradition clearly resembling the inhumation practice of the preceding period, where the deceased were buried in personal graves with individual characteristics reflecting their social status.

Conversely, in the early Iron Age, the human remains of the cremation pyre were not collected and neither were the burned personal artefacts of the deceased. Instead the remains of the cremation pyre were collected and buried in a pit. A tradition clearly separate from the individual characteristics of the Bronze Age burial traditions, reflecting a fundamental conceptual change in cremation practices during the transition period between the late Bronze Age and the early Iron Age in southern Scandinavia.

References

Anderson, T. and Fell, C. 1995. Analysis of Roman cremation vessels by Computerized Tomography. *Journal of Archaeological Science* 22, 609–17.

Arcini, K. 2005. Pyre sites before our eyes. In: Artelius, T. and F. Svanberg 2005 (eds), *Dealing with the Dead. Archaeological Perspectives on Prehistoric Scandinavian Burial Ritual*, 63–72. Ödeshög: Riksantikvarieämbetet, Arkeologiska undersökningar skrifter 65.

Arcini, C. and Svanberg, F. 2005. Den yngre bronsålderns brandgravsmiljöer. In: Lagerås, P. and Strömberg, B. (eds), *Bronsåldersbygd. 2300-500 f.Kr. Skånska spar - arkeologi längs Västkustbanan*, 284–365. Lund, Riksantikvarieämbetet.

Artelius, T. 1999. Den döde vid dörren - reflektioner rundt förfäderskult utifrån fyns av människoben i två halländska långhus från järnålder. In: Artelius, T., Englund, E. and Ersgård L. (eds), *Kring västsvenska hus: boendets organisation och symbolik i förhistorisk tid*, 73–85. Göteborg: Göteborgs Universitet.

Asmussen, B. 2009. Intentional or incidental thermal modification? Analysing site occupation via burned bone. *Journal of Archaeological Science* 36, 528–36.

Bechert, T. 1980. Zur Terminologie provinzialrömischer Brandgräber. *Archäologisches Korrespondenzblatt* 10, 253–258.

Buikstra, J. E. and Swegle, M. 1989. Bone modification due to burning: experimental evidence. In: Bonnichsen, R. and Sorg, M. H. (eds), *Bone Modification*, 247–58. Maine: Peopling of the Americas Publications.

Ericsson, A. and Runcis, J. 1995. Gravar utan begravningar. Teoretisk diskussion påkallad av en arkeologisk undersökning inom RAÄ 40 vid Skalunda i Sköldinge socken, Södermanland. In: *Teoretiska perspektiv på gravundersökningar i Södermanland*, 31–40. Stockholm: Riksantikvarieämbetet. Arkeologiska undersögningar skrifter 8.

Fairgrieve, S. I. 2008. *Forensic Cremation: Recovery and Analysis*. Boca Raton FL: CRC Press.

Frisberg, K. H. 2005. Where are the dead? Empty graves from early Iron Age Uppland. In: Artelius, T. and F. Svanberg 2005 (eds), *Dealing with the Dead. Archaeological Perspectives on Prehistoric Scandinavian Burial Ritual*, 143–158. Ödeshög: Riksantikvarieämbetet, Arkeologiska undersökningar skrifter 65.

Gansum, T. 2004: Role of the bones - from iron to steel. *Norwegian Archaeological Review* 37(1), 41–57.

Goldhahn, J. 2012: On war and memory and the memory of war - the Middle Bronze age burial from Hvidegården on Zealand in Denmark revisited. In: Berge, R., Jasinski, M. E. and Sognnes, K. (eds), *N-TAG TEN. Proceedings of the 10th Nordic TAG conference at Stiklestad, Norway 2009*, 237–50. Oxford: British Archaeological Report S2399.

Gonçalves, D. 2011. Cremains. The value of quantitative analysis for the bioanthropological research of burned human skeletal remains. PhD thesis. University of Coimbra. Faculty of Science and Technology.

Gonçalves, D., Thompson, T. J. U. and Cunha, E. 2011. Implications of heat-induced changes in bone on the interpretation of funerary behaviour and practice. *Journal of Archaeological Science* 38, 1308–13.

Grosskopf, B. 2004. Leichenbrand. Biologisches und kulturhistorisches Quellenmaterial zur Rekonstruktion vor- und frühgeschichtlicher Populationen und ihrer funeralpraktiken. Dissertation. Doktor Phiplosophiae. Leipzig.

Harvig, L. in press. Land of the cremated dead – On cremation practices in late Bronze Age and early Iron Age Denmark. In: Williams, H., Cerezo-Roman, J. and Wessmann, A. (eds). *Cremation in European Archaeology*. Cambridge: Cambridge University Press.

Harvig, L. and Lynnerup, N. 2010. Antropologiske analyser: gravplads fra bronzealderen. In: Runge, M. (ed.), *Kildehuse II. Gravpladser fra yngre bronzealder og vikingetid i Odense Sydøst*, 58–64. Odense: Fynske Studier 23, Odense Bys Museer.

Harvig, L. and Lynnerup, N. 2013. On the effective volume of prehistoric cremains – a comparative study of cremated bone volume measured manually and assessed by Computed Tomography. *Journal of Archaeological Science* 40, 2713–22.

Harvig, L., Lynnerup, N. and Amsgaard Ebsen, J. 2012. Computed Tomography and Computed Radiography of late Bronze Age cremation urns from Denmark: an interdisciplinary attempt to develop methods applied in bioarchaeological cremation research. *Archeometry* 54, 369–87.

Harvig, L., Runge, M. and Borre Lundø, M. 2014. Typology and function of late Bronze Age and early Iron Age cremation graves – a microregional case study. *Danish Journal of Archaeology*. DOI: 10.1080/21662282.2014.942980.

Holck, P. 2001. Spesifikke problemer knyttet til brente ben. *Nordisk Rettsmedisin* 2001(3/4), 60–4.

Hornstrup, K. M. 1999. Brandgrave fra yngre bronzealder. Muligheder og Perspektiver. *Kuml* 1999, 99–145.

Hsieh, J. 2002. *Computed Tomography. Principles, Design, Artefacts, and Recent Advances*. Bellingham WA: SPIE.

Jensen, J. 2002. *Danmarks Oldtid. Bronzealder 2.000–500 f.Kr.* København: Gyldendal.

Jensen, J. 2003. *Danmarks Oldtid. Ældre Jernalder 500 f.Kr.-400e.Kr.* København: Gyldendal.

Lindahl Jensen, B. 2004: En grav är en grav är en grav!? Nya perspektiv på bronsålderns graver genom tvärvetenskpliga metoder. In: Guðmundsson, G. (ed.). *Current Issues in Nordic Archaeology. Proceedings of the 21st Conference of Nordic Archaeologists, 6–9 September 2001, Akueyri, Iceland*, 33–5. Reykjavik: Society of Icelandic Archaeologists.

Kaliff, A. 1992. *Brandgravskick och föreställningsvärld. En religionsarkeologisk diskussion*. Uppsala: Occasional Papers in Archaeology 4.

Kaliff, A. 1997. *Grav och kultplats. Eskatologiska förestallningar under yngre bronsålder och äldre järnålder i Östergötland, Aun*. Uppsala: Uppsala University.

Kühl, I. 1994. *Leichenbrandanalysen einiger Brandgräberfelder von der Bronze- bis zur Fränkischen Zeit aus dem Kreis Wesel, Niederrhein*. Aesch: Anthropologische Beiträge 5.

Lynnerup, N. 2008. Computed Tomography Scanning and three-dimensional visualization of mummies and bog bodies. In: Mays, S. and Pinhasi, R. (eds), *Advances in Human Palaeopathology*, 101–20. Chichester: Wiley

Lynnerup, N. 2010. Medical imaging of mummies and bog bodies. *Gerontology* 56(5), 441–8.

Lynnerup, N., Hjalgrim, H., Rindal Nielsen, L., Gregersen, H. and Thuesen, I. 1997. Non-invasive archaeology of skeletal material by CT-scanning and three-dimensional reconstruction. *International Journal of Osteoarchaeology* 7, 91–4.

Minozzi, S., Giuffra, V., Bagnoli, J., Paribeni, E., Giustini, D., Caramella, D. and Fornaciari, G. 2010. An investigation of Etruscan cremations by Computed Tomography (CT). *Antiquity* 84, 195–201.

Musgrave, J., Prag, A. J. N. W., Neave, R., Fox, R. L. and White, H. 2010. The occupants of Tomb II at Vergina. Why Arrhidaios and Eurydice must be excluded. *International Journal of Medical Sciences* 7(6), 1–15.

Mäder, A. 2002. *Die spätbronzezeitlichen und spätlatènezeitlichen Brandstellen und Brandbestattungen in Elgg*. Zürich: Züricher Archäologie 7.

Plicht, J. van der. 2004. Radicarbon, the calibration curve and Scythian chronology. In: Scott, E. M, Alekseev, A. Y. and Zaitseva, G. (eds), *Impact of the Environment on Human Migration in Eurasia. Proceedings of the NATO Advanced Research Workshop, St. Petersburg, 15-18 November 2003*, 45–61. Dordrecht: Klewer Academic.

Runge, M. 2010. *Kildehuse II. Gravpladser fra yngre bronzealder og vikingetid i Odense Sydøst*. Odense: Fynske Studier 23.

Runge, M. 2012. Yngre bronzealders bebyggelse indenfor et 350 hektar stort undersøgelsesområde sydøst for Odense. In: Boddum, S., Mikkelsen, M. and Terkildsen, N. (eds), *Bebyggelsen i yngre bronzealders kulturlandskab. Report from the seminar: "Bebyggelsen i yngre bronzealders lokale kulturlandskab" held in Holstebro, March 10th, 2011*, Vol. 2, 113–139. Viborg: Viborg Museum.

Runge, M. 2013. Yngre bronzealders dødekult indenfor et 350 hektar stort undersøgelsesområde sydøst for Odense. In: Boddum, S., Mikkelsen, M. and Terkildsen, N. (eds), *Dødekulten i yngre bronzealders kulturlandskab. Report from the seminar: "Dødekulten i yngre bronzealders lokale kulturlandskab" held in Viborg, March 8th, 2012*, Vol. 3, 9–24. Viborg: Viborg Museum.

Ryan, T. M. and Milner, G. R. 2006. Osteological applications of high-resolution computed tomography: a prehistoric arrow injury. *Journal of Archaeological Science* 33, 871–9.

Sigvallius, B. 1994. *Funeral Pyres. Iron Age Cremations in North Spånga*. Stockholm: Stockholm University.

Sørensen, M. L. S. and Rebay, K. 2008. From substantial bodies to the substance of bodies: analysis of the transition from inhumation to cremation during the Middle Bronze Age in Europe. In: Robb, J. and Boric, D. (eds), *Past Bodies*, 59–68. Oxford: Oxbow Books.

Thrane, H. 1984. *Lusehøj ved Voldtofte - en sydvestfynsk storhøj fra yngre broncealder*. Odense: Fynske Studier 13.

Thrane, H. 2004. *Fyns Yngre Broncealdergrave*. Odense: Odense Bys Museer i kommission hos Syddansk Universitetsforlag.

Thurman, M. D. and Willmore, L. J. 1981. A replicative cremation experiment. *North American Archaeologist* 2(4), 275–83.

Tkocz, I. and Jensen, K. R. 1984. Antropologisk undersøgelse af det brændte knoglemateriale fra Lusehøj. In: Thrane, H. (ed.), *Lusehøj ved Voldtofte*, 194–205. Odense: Fynske Studier 13.

Tout, R. E., Gilboy, W. B. and Clark, A. J. 1980. The use of computerized X-ray tomography for the non-destructive examination of archaeological objects. In: *Proceedings of the 18th international symposium on archaeometry and archaeological prospection, Bonn, 14-17 March 1978*, 608–16. Köln: Rhineland-Verlag.

Walker, P. L., Miller, K. W. P. and Richman, R. 2008. Time, temperature, and oxygen availability: an experimental study of the effects of environmental conditions on the color and organic content of cremated bone. In: Schmidt, C. W. and Symes S. A. (eds), *The Analysis of Burned Human Remains*, 129–35. London: Academic.

Wangen, V. 2009. *Gravfeltet på Gunnarstorp i Sarpsborg, Østfold. Et monument over dødsriter og kultutøvelse i yngre bronsealder og eldste jernalder*. Oslo: Norske Oldfunn 27. Kulturhistorisk Museum. Universitetet i Oslo.

Whyte, T. R. 2001. Distinguishing remains of human cremations from burned animal bones. *Journal of Field Archaeology* 28(3/4), 437–48.

Wickholm, A. 2008. Reuse in Finnish cemeteries under level ground - examples of collective memory. In: Fahlander, F. and Østigaard, T. (eds). *The Materiality of Death. Bodies, Burials, Beliefs*, 89–97. Oxford: British Archaeological Report S1768.

Chapter 4

The weight of the matter

Examining the potential of skeletal weight for the
bioarchaeological analysis of cremation at the Iron Age
necropolis of Tera (Portugal)

*David Gonçalves, Vanessa Campanacho, Tim Thompson
and Rui Mataloto*

Introduction

Cremation was a very popular practice among many past populations and, not infrequently, it was their only funerary custom. If this alone is not enough to advocate for the importance of cremated bones to bioarchaeology, then their tendency to preserve better than unburned bones in some specific inhumation environments making them the only available biological document of these past populations should make it a done deal (Mays 1998). Their importance for the biological knowledge of past populations as well as for their mortuary practices is thus unmistakable.

The main problem that bioanthropologists face whenever they come across burned bones is without a doubt the one presented by heat-induced changes. Fire is not an innocuous element – it changes the structure and the appearance of bone (Shipman *et al.* 1984; Buikstra and Swegle 1989; Mayne-Correia 1997; Thompson 2004; 2005; Walker *et al.* 2008; Gonçalves *et al.* 2011). Therefore, lack of reliability regarding bioanthropological inspection is a peril always present when dealing with burned bones and is often used as a justification – some may say it is an excuse – to avoid more comprehensive analyses. On the other hand, the amount of reliable data retrieved from burned human skeletal remains is often so little that one may feel tempted to add some less consistent information – an attempt to sugar the pill. The trick here is to find a balance between both postures – nihilism and megalomania.

A good example of one analytical approach that may enclose such peril is the one related to skeletal weight. This imaginative approach resulted mainly from the bioanthropologists inability to retrieve reliable information from burned skeletons by using the more conventional and well-established methods that are usually applied to unburned skeletons. In order to bypass this setback, skeletal weight has been at the spotlight of more than a few researches in the last decades (Malinowski and Porawski, 1969; Herrmann, 1976; McKinley, 1993; Warren and Maples, 1997; Duday *et al.* 2000; Bass and Jantz, 2004; Richier, 2005; Chirachariyavej *et al.* 2006; Lenorzer, 2006; May, 2011; Van Deest *et al.* 2011; Gonçalves, 2012; Gonçalves *et al.* 2013a), mainly because its analytical value is not impaired by taphonomic-related fragmentation – bone weight most probably remains somewhat the same whatever the degree of fragmentation affecting the skeleton. In one way or another, these have then focused on its potential regarding the estimation of the biological profile from unknown remains and on the identification of some of the details that are related to the funerary practice itself. For the more sceptical eye, this may sound too ambitious but under some circumstances, the proclaimed potential of skeletal weights may turn out to be valid. In order to achieve that, the limitations and problems of adopting the skeletal weight approach must necessarily be acknowledged.

The present chapter proposes to explore and to discuss the validity of the weight approach for the bioarchaeological analysis of burned skeletal human remains. The analysis of archaeological urned cremations from the Iron Age necropolis of Tera – a recently excavated site located in the Alentejo province of Portugal – under the light of reference data obtained from modern cremations obtained by Gonçalves (2012) will allow for the discussion of those procedures in an attempt to pinpoint the most helpful practices for bioarchaeological research.

The funerary context

The Tera necropolis is located near Pavia (Mora, Alentejo, Portugal) in a region with a rather flat but slightly undulated topography delimited to the south by the deep valley of Ribeira da Tera (Fig. 4.1). It was crossed by an apparently important natural pathway linking inland Alentejo to the banks of the Tagus. It was firstly identified in the mid-nineties (2003) and initially subject to excavation following an intervention targeting the Tera menhir alignment, where Iron Age ceramics were also found (Rocha 2003). A large cairn composed of small to medium stones was then found beneath the menhirs. Subsequently, a second intervention has been ongoing since 2006 aiming at the excavation of this cairn. We believe that the current uncovered area must represent about half of the original burial ground which extended westward.

It should be noted that no evidences clearly link the menhirs to the necropolis – we do not know if both were part of the same structure or not – although some data seem to indicate that they were put up during the formation of this burial ground instead of preceding it (for a review, see Mataloto 2013). However, it is also unclear if the menhirs are more ancient than the cairn itself and therefore constitute a case of recycling of pre-existing materials. Two cists and several structures of rectangular outline were present underneath the cairn but only some of them contained funerary depositions.

Fig. 4.1: Overview and location of the Tera necropolis in the south-west Iberian Peninsula.

The cremated remains

The funerary practice was composed of cremation in *ustrinum* – a combustion structure where one or more cremations may have taken place followed by the collection of the remains for subsequent relocation onto a secondary place. The location of the funerary pyre or pyres was not clear although a fairly large area composed of very dark and compact sediment was found at the southern border of the necropolis and may have been the result of such combustion structures. Another stratum composed of very dark, clayish and compact sediment was located at the south-east border and sealed small pits inside which adornment artefacts and minuscule bone fragments were present. This unit was interpreted not as a burial structure but, due to the small size of the bone fragments, as either the destination of some of the residues resulting from the cleansing of the *ustrinum* or as one of the *ustrina*.

Until now, 39 possible burials have been recorded but only some of them have been confirmed as this analysis is still underway. The burials were clearly concentrated at the centre of the cairn. Only one cist contained an urn. The necropolis was mainly

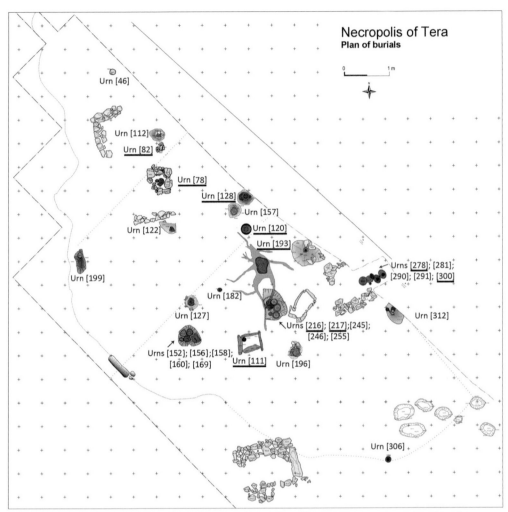

Fig. 4.2: General plan of the burials at the Tera necropolis. The cremation urns analysed in this paper are underlined.

composed of urned burials in small pits, often lined with stone blocks and sometimes associated with artefacts. In several cases, some of the pyre residues, comprising ashes and cremated remains were also deposited in the pit. As a rule, these pits included a single urn but assemblages of several urns were present occasionally (Fig. 4.2). Some of the urns that are already excavated and will be addressed in this paper are presented in Figure 4.3.

The urns are wheel-made and of medium size, and a few of these vessels are made of grayish ceramics and have morphologies similar to those found in other funerary contexts of the south-west part of the Iberian Peninsula, such as Medellín in Spain (Lorrio 2008) or Torre de Palma in Portugal (Langley *et al.* 2007).

Fig. 4.3: From top left to bottom right: Field photos of urns [78], [82], [111], [120], [128], [193], [216], [217], [278] and [300].

The artefacts associated with the burials were usually few in number and often composed of plates placed on top of the urns and small *unguentaria*, sometimes of biconical shape. A richer assemblage was found in urn [278]: two ceramic *unguentaria*, of the *alabastron* type (Fig. 4.4, 10–11) and similar in shape to one documented in the Medellín necropolis, probably of the late seventh century BC, that was distributed widely as a result of Phoenician trade (Lorrio 2008); two rings; and another undetermined artefact, apparently all made of silver (Fig. 4.4, 7–9). One of the rings has a plain rim while the other is decorated with a central collet – unrecovered – which was supported on four small volutes (Fig. 4.4, 7). The latter ring thus presents similarities with one from the Favela Nova necropolis (Ourique, Portugal) from the mid-sixth–mid-fifth century BC (Dias and Coelho 1983).

Other artefacts have been found both inside the urns and in their surroundings. A heart-shaped bracelet was found in urn [217] (Fig. 4.4, 6). In addition, three fibulae of the Alcores type were found inside urns, two of them in urn [216] (Fig. 4.4, 1, 4 and 5). The distribution of the Alcores fibulae seems to have been particularly centered in southern Iberia although the archaeological record includes fewer than three dozen of these artefacts to date. This kind of artefact was in use mainly between the seventh and the late sixth centuries BC, although it has also been documented for the fifth century BC (Ruiz Delgado 1989; Jiménez Ávila 2002). The Alcores fibulae were not associated with any other dating elements, including those indicating a utilisation of the necropolis during the fifth century BC. Another partially preserved fibula, probably of the Acebuchal or Bencarrón types, seems to corroborate the chronology indicated by the Alcores fibulae since its use referred mainly to the seventh to late sixth centuries BC.

A polychrome glass *amphoriskos* (Fig. 4.4, 12) of Mediterranean Group I, form 2 (Harden 1981), and a few turquoise collar beads with blue and white "eyes" are clearly of a foreign character and thus demonstrate that this population participated in the regional distribution circuit of these widely spread pieces. No other materials were associated with the glass *amphoriskos* thus preventing a more precise dating, but glass imports of this kind were more usual during the fifth century BC, which was also characterised by a scarcity of collar beads that only became more abundant afterwards (Jiménez Ávila 1999).

A folded iron blade was found together with a falcated knife blade. The latter thus formed part of a spear and was associated with urn [312] and a rhomboid plate belt buckle with three forks (Cerdeño DIII3/DIII5; Lorrio B3B3/B4B6; Carratiermes B6) (Fig. 4, 3). A similar belt buckle was found in a small pit. It is single-forked (Cerdeño CII or CIII; Lorrio B1D1 or Carratiermes B2a) (Fig. 4, 2) besides portions of two others of undetermined type. Both these elements and the fibulae mark the introduction of a new style of dressing during the sixth and fifth centuries BC, which possibly remained in fashion until a later date in Celtiberia (Jiménez Ávila 2003; Argente *et al.* 2000; Lorrio 1997). In summary, the available data suggest that the Tera necropolis was probably formed and utilised during the mid-sixth century and the mid-fifth centuries BC.

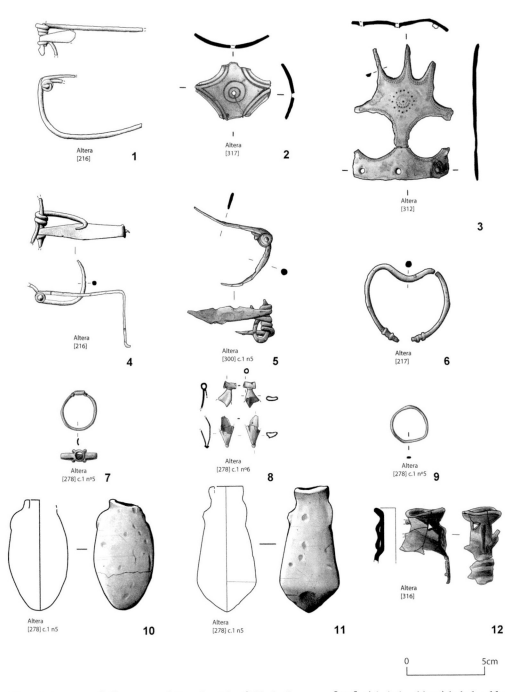

Fig. 4.4: Grave goods from several Tera burials: 1) fibula from urn [216]; 2) belt-buckle; 3) belt-buckle from urn [312]; 4) fibula from urn [216]; 5) fibula from urn [300]; 6) heart-shaped bracelet from urn [217]; 7) silver ring from urn [278]; 8) undetermined silver artefact from urn [278]; 9) silver ring from urn [278]; 10) ceramic unguentarium; 11) ceramic unguentarium; 12) polychrome glass amphoriskos.

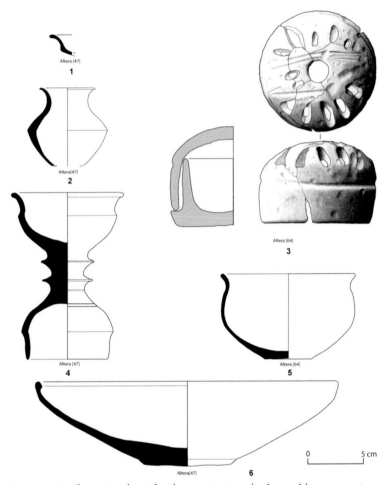

Fig. 4.5: Votive ceramics from Tera burials: 1) ceramic rim; 2) oil vessel/unguentarium; 3) incensory; 4) calix; 5) ceramic vessel; 6) ceramic plate.

Far from being a mere set of burials, the necropolis most probably was a worship space where libations took place in reverence of the ancestors who, for some authors, were possibly represented by the monoliths (Mataloto 2013). An incense burner (Fig. 4.5, 3), a chalice (Fig. 4.5, 4) and other ceramic artefacts (Fig. 4.5, 1, 2, 5 and 6) are suggestive of utilisation of the burial ground that went way beyond simple funeral rites.

Ancestor worship and memory construction are most often inseparable in burial grounds. This seems to be especially true for the Tera necropolis due to its location at the centre of a space previously occupied by several megalithic monuments, not to mention its own megalithic feature based on the menhirs and the cairn.

Methods of analysis

Method limitations

As we know, cremation is a very destructive procedure, but it is not the only one. Most archaeological cremations face a varied set of other post-depositional destructive agents that lead to additional fragmentation. As a result, it is no wonder that weight analysis of archaeological cremains, used to infer some parameters regarding funerary practice and the sex of an individual, encompasses a few assumptions that can be considered to be something of a leap of faith. One of these assumptions regards species identification through skeletal remains. All cremations will be partly composed of very small fragments for which an anatomical identification is truly impossible. Species identification relies then on other than macroscopic methods – DNA, bone histology, human albumin and possibly lattice parameters of bone mineral crystals (Cattaneo et al. 1994; Brown et al. 1995; Sweet and Sweet 1995; Williams et al. 2004; Wurmb-Schwark et al. 2004; Ye et al. 2004; Cuijpers et al. 2006; Cattaneo et al. 2009; Harbeck et al. 2011; Beckett et al. 2011; Gonçalves, 2012; Greenwood et al. 2013) although this latter assumption has been disputed (Piga et al. 2013). Besides having its own problems, these are not feasibly applied to each fragment. Therefore, and as far as we know, some of the fragments may not even be human. Nonetheless, most researchers will take into account the fraction of undetermined bone fragments as corresponding to human skeletal remains alone. This may be correct for an important part of the cremation but it may not always be the case. Some of the undetermined bone fragments may belong to fauna and thus interfere with weight assessment of human cremains. Therefore, this may be only an approximation and not the true human skeletal weight. Although sparse, some faunal remains were indeed found in cremations from Tera.

Another assumption is that cremation weight corresponds only to bone. In a few cases skeletal remains may have been picked from the cremation bed, cleaned and placed inside a container and, therefore, that assumption is somewhat true. This was probably the case for Tera since charcoals and ashes were rarely found inside the urns. In many other necropolises however, the remains were buried along with pyre residues and, therefore, may have some dirt, metal or other substances aggregated with them. A fastidious cleansing may be able to remove much of this from the bone fragments but it is impossible to do it successfully for all of them. This is partly so because a cremation may easily hold thousands of bone fragments and comprehensively cleaning all and each one of them would be a too lengthy and thus impracticable procedure. On the other hand, dirt often fills the most inner sections of bone where access is very limited – this is especially true for trabecular bone. In addition, dirt sometimes acts as adhesive for bone about to break into numerous pieces and it may be more useful to leave it alone rather than to remove it. There is no simple guideline on how to deal with each bone fragment and particular decisions must be taken according to each case.

Furthermore, the use of *ustrina* for multiple cremations may also have led to the misrepresentation of each cremated individual. The inefficient cleansing of the *ustrinum* would probably result on the neglect of some of the skeletal remains which, in turn, would then commingle with the ensuing cremations (Duday *et al.* 2000; Lenorzer 2006). On the other hand, the relocation of bones from the *ustrinum* to a secondary location may not have been complete, either deliberately or not. Both situations would then also distort the individual cremains weight.

These four variables – possible presence of fauna, inefficient cleansing of the bones and of the *ustrina* and incomplete relocation of the skeletal remains – therefore interfere with the weight of the cremains preventing a completely direct comparison with references obtained from modern cremations. This means that weight analysis focuses more on cremation weight and less on true skeletal weight. In addition, various researches have demonstrated that weight of cremains is very variable because of sex, age and body mass differences along with other factors (Malinowski and Porawski 1969; McKinley 1993; Warren and Maples 1997; Bass and Jantz 2004; Chirachariyavej *et al.* 2006; May 2011; Van Deest *et al.* 2011; Gonçalves *et al.* 2013a). For sure, the comparison of modern and archaeological populations is also far from ideal. All of this means that reference values can only be used as rough indicators of the expected cremains weights and not as completely comparable references.

This is even more so because reference values refer to calcined – or completely cremated – cremains while archaeological cremations often present a more varied palette of differentially burned remains. Some may indeed be calcined but others may be merely pre-calcined and thus not have experienced such a considerable heat-induced weight loss which is positively correlated with increasing temperature (Grupe and Hummel 1991; Person *et al.* 1996; Hiller *et al.* 2003; Enzo *et al.* 2007; Munro *et al.* 2007). Although most of it occurs at temperatures under 400°C, gradual weight loss continues to occur at increasing temperatures after that marker (Grupe and Hummel 1991; Person *et al.* 1996; Hiller *et al.* 2003; Munro *et al.* 2007). Therefore, non-calcined cremains or incompletely calcined archaeological cremations may not be entirely comparable with reference values obtained on modern cremations. In summary, using skeletal weights to make inferences about the biological profile and funerary practice of past populations is not straightforward.

Method potential

As mentioned above, the use of cremation weight to draw bioarchaeological inferences has one main advantage – fragmentation does not seem to interfere with its analysis. Weight stays pretty much the same whether the skeleton fragments into 200 or 2000 pieces. This is, therefore, one analytical target that is always at our disposal contrasting with the one focusing on the anatomical features of the skeleton, for which preservation is critical for any inference. However, cremation weight will only be truly informative in very specific situations and when focusing in adult individuals for which more reliable references are available.[1] (McKinley 1993; Warren and Maples 1997; Bass and Jantz 2004; Chirachariyavej *et al.* 2006; Van Deest *et al.* 2011; Gonçalves *et al.* 2013a).

From the parameters that can reportedly be accessed through skeletal weight, three are intimately related and interdependent – minimum number of individuals (MNI), skeleton completeness and sex of the individual. This means that the chances of being able to determine each one of them increases if the other two are known. For example, the likelihood of assessing reliably the sex of the individual will improve if the roughly complete skeleton of only one individual was buried. Regrettably, the sad truth is that such an ideal scenario is seldom presented.

Minimum number of individuals
In the case of the estimation of the MNI, the conventional procedure is based on the detection of repeated and of incompatible skeletal elements with regard to parameters such as age and sex (Ubelaker 1974; Duday *et al.* 2000; Lenorzer 2006). This is still the best way of estimating the MNI in cremains, but skeletal weights have been used for this purpose as well (Sonek 1992; Van Deest *et al.* 2011; Duday *et al.* 2000; Lenorzer 2006) and it is good practice to cross-check such analysis with the weight of the skeletal remains because skeletal fragmentation may impede the detection of more than one individual. Skeletal weight may then be useful in this very specific case. In order to do that, the weight of the cremains can be compared against documented weight references for adults that act as cut-off points – if it is larger than the heaviest cremains reported for a single individual, then this is a good indication of the presence of more than one individual. The opposite is not valid though. Cremains that are lighter than the lightest documented cremains do not forcibly refer to a single individual because the commingled remains of several partial individuals may indeed be present. Of course, and like any other technique based on cut-off points, this should be used conservatively and values that are close to the cut-off point must be interpreted carefully. If weight is the only analytical target available to the bioanthropologist, it is important to estimate MNI first, and then proceed to the estimation of skeleton completeness and eventually to the sex of the individual, because it may interfere with the assessment of the latter two parameters.

The comparison of the cremains weight can be carried out using several references for adults. The problem here is that the variation in the mean weight of cremains reported by the different researches is quite large and is significantly dependent of age, sex and geographic origin (Malinowski and Porawski 1969; McKinley 1993; Warren and Maples 1997; Bass and Jantz 2004; Chirachariyavej *et al.* 2006; May, 2011; Van Deest *et al.* 2011; Gonçalves *et al.* 2013a), so the selection is not straightforward. Choosing comparative references according to age-at-death seems to be quite unfeasible due to the problem of estimating this parameter in adults – it can seldom be done accurately enough in cremains to allow for such procedure, although some authors have presented their results according to age groups (Bass and Jantz 2004; Gonçalves *et al.* 2013a). Of course, if age-at-death is known through some other source, then the selection of comparative reference values should take this variable into account. However, all references from modern populations are based on samples composed of individuals that were quite old and thus do not exactly reflect the skeletal weight of the entire population. To stress again, weight references are forcibly only approximate and not completely comparable. As for sex, the chances of estimating it precisely are much better than for the exact age and a selection of skeletal weight references according to this parameter should also be carried out whenever possible. In forensic cases, one would probably use reference values from a population that is as close as possible to that for the individual being analysed. In archaeological cases though, it is not possible to establish such parallels in terms of population affinities so this kind of criterion has little validity.

Besides age, sex and population affinities, other variables should also be paid attention to. Among all available references, only McKinley (1993) and Gonçalves *et al.* (2013a) took two different kinds of weighting. McKinley (1993) chose to document the total weight of cremains and the weight of cremains after 2 mm sieving in order to discard the smallest fragments. Many of these refer to the coffin or other non-osseous residues and its exclusion from skeletal weight allegedly better replicates an archaeological cremation for which some post-depositional destruction can theoretically also be expected. However, the fact is that, although this makes sense, we have no experimental confirmation that this is truly so.

Gonçalves *et al.* (2013a) found a significantly different weight between the cremains of individuals cremated immediately after death (cadavers) and those of dry skeletons of individuals previously inhumed and thus free of soft tissues at the time of cremation (skeletons). The latter presented lighter cremains and, although no clear reason for this was reported, it seems prudent to choose comparative reference values according to the pre-cremation condition of the remains. Gonçalves *et al.* (2013a) give such references according to this criterion but all other researches were carried out on cadavers and values for skeletons were thus not provided. In contrast, if the archaeological cremation under analysis resulted from the burning of a cadaver, the selection of the corresponding reference weights turns out to be more challenging because of the larger number of alternatives (Table 4.1).

After the selection of the weight references for comparison, the detection of more than one individual in an archaeological cremation would then be done by comparing it with the heaviest documented modern cremation. As already stated, if the archaeological cremation happens to be heavier than the latter, then this could be an indication that more than one individual is present. The reliability of such estimation is all the more certain if that difference is quite large.

As a result, if the individual is a male or of undetermined sex, its weight could be compared with the one from the heaviest documented male from Tennessee at 5379 g (Bass and Jantz 2004). This value is considerably higher than the heaviest one recorded for a European individual – 4571 g (Gonçalves *et al.* 2013a). The sieved weight (after removal of the <2 mm fraction) of the latter was 3805 g which seems to be much more realistic for an archaeological cremation. However, these values from Gonçalves *et al.* (2013a) were actually outliers. The second heaviest male weighed merely

Table 4.1: Results for the weight of burned skeletons from females and males cremated at modern crematoria.

Authors	Combustion			Females					Males				
	g	Temp.°C	Duration	g	n	Age	Min.	Max.	g	n	Age	Min.	Max.
Malinowski and Porawski	–	±1000	–	1540	–	45–65	–	–	2004	–	45–65	–	–
Herrmann	1767	–	–	1700	226	76.2	970	2620	1842	167	72.8	970	2630
McKinley: no. 2 mm fraction	1626	–	–	1272	6	81.6	1002	1758	1862	9	77.3	1385	2423
McKinley – with 2 mm fraction	2016	–	–	1616	6	81.6	1227	2216	2284	9	77.3	1753	3011
Sonek (in Bass and Jantz)	2348**	–	–	1875	63	75.7	–	–	2801	76	64.1	–	–
Warren and Maples	2893	> 830º	73–207'	1840	40	74.1	876	2750	2893	51	66.3	1887	3784
Bass and Jantz	2858**	871–982º	120–180'	2350	155	70.7	1050	4000	3379	151	62.8	1865	5379
Chirachariyavej et al.	2400	850–1200º	60–90'	2120	55	73.3	–	–	2680	55	63.5	–	–
van Deest et al.	2737	871–927º	120'	2238	363	76.1	1057	4309	3233	365	71.4	1701	4990
Cadavers: sieved weight*	2095			1652	51	74.5	923	2420	2442	65	68.6	1487	3805***
Cadavers: overall weight*	2681			2115	51	74.5	1281	3237	3037	65	68.6	1902	4571***
Skeletons: sieved weight*	1674			1441	39	72.6	688	2263	1967	49	67.3	1245	2644
Skeletons: overall weight*	2030			1804	39	72.6	857	2883	2314	49	67.3	1389	3160

*From Gonçalves (2012); **Calculated from the data provided by Bass and Jantz (2004); ***These values were outliers; the second heaviest male weighted 3805 g (overall weight) and 3287 g (sieved weight)

3867 g with a sieved weight of 3287 g. In the case of a female, the heaviest documented cremation – 4309 g – is from California (Van Deest *et al.* 2011). Again, this is much higher than the heaviest European female cremation – 3237 g with a sieved weight of 2420 g (Gonçalves *et al.* 2013a).

Of course, the selection of references is a prerogative of each researcher. In our view, the benefit of using the references from Bass and Jantz (2004) for males and for individuals of undetermined sex and from Van Deest *et al.* (2011) for females is that it allows for a more conservative, yet possibly less perceptive, approach. It raises the bar so high that the sensitivity regarding the detection of more than one individual in a cremation is quite low. However, its reliability is higher since the eventual detection of more than one individual is based on rather solid grounds. On the other hand, using the references for sieved weights from McKinley (1993) and Gonçalves *et al.* (2013a) allows for a more realistic, yet not quite as reliable, approach. These references are probably more similar to the actual weight of ancient cremations since many of these did not include the residues of a casket nor the smallest skeletal fragments. Its sensitivity is thus theoretically better but reliability is certainly not as good.

It is also important to keep in mind that the detection of a MNI larger than two does not necessarily means that we are in the presence of a genuine double or multiple burial. Incomplete cleansing of the ustrinum may have caused the presence of intrusive bones from another individual that had been cremated previously (Duday *et al.* 2000; Lenorzer 2006).

Skeleton completeness
One question that bioanthropologists aim to see answered regards the completeness of the skeletal assemblage in order to determine if it represents an entire or a partial adult skeleton. Skeletal weights have helped in assessing this question in the past (e.g. McKinley 1994; Duday *et al.* 2000) and may be the only way to achieve it, particularly when fragmentation is severe. As for the estimation of the MNI, this parameter should preferentially be used along with the conventional inventory of each element composing the skeleton. However, skeletal weight seems to be better than the skeletal inventory at detecting skeleton incompleteness because heavy fragmentation usually impedes comprehensive anatomical identification.

For assessing skeleton completeness, it is the referenced minimum skeletal weight that is relevant. If cremains weight is considerably less than expected, this is an indication that the skeleton is incomplete. This approach can also be used even if the burial contains more than one individual but it is important that it is assessed only if the number of individuals is known. On the other hand, if it is well inside the range of variation for skeletal weight, this does not necessarily mean that the skeleton or skeletons are just about complete.

Besides incomplete recovery from the pyre, skeleton incompleteness may also be the result of poor post-depositional preservation. At Tera, until now the recorded weight of the cremains ranged from 1.5 g to 2555.4 g and there are no reasons to believe that differential post-depositional preservation alone could account for such disparity, especially because all burials were urned. Un-urned burials are possibly more susceptible to differential preservation since no barriers against the surrounding environment are present in these cases, thus limiting the destructive action of, for instance, anthropic, animal, vegetal, climacteric and chemical agents. No matter the context, it is reasonable to first try to assess the overall cremains preservation in any given site and only then decide if the analysis of skeleton completeness can be carried out without bias caused by differential post-depositional preservation, as was the case for Tera.

As seen in the estimation of MNI, the assessment of skeletal completeness is more accurate if the sex of the cremated individual is known since we can then choose the comparative reference according to this parameter. For the total weight of a cremation from an individual of unknown sex, the comparison should be done with the lightest reference available. This presently corresponds to a female cremated immediately after death with 876 g (Warren and Maples 1997). Curiously, cremains did not present smaller sieved weights in either the samples of McKinley (1993) and Gonçalves *et al.* (2013a). In the case of the cremation of skeletons previously inhumed, the smallest weight was recorded for a Portuguese female with 857 g and a sieved weight of 688 g (Gonçalves *et al.* 2013a). The previous references should thus also be used when the cremation involved a female.

In the case of a male cadaver, the lightest reference is from Herrmann (1976) with 970 g, but this value is much lower than for any other research. Therefore, this was possibly an outlier. The documented case of an individual weighting 1701 g seems to be the more reliable reference for the lightest total weight of a male cremation (Van Deest *et al.* 2011). As for the reference for the sieved weight of a male cremation, the value is of 1385 g (McKinley 1993). If the cremation resulted from the processing of a previously inhumed skeleton, the comparable reference for males is of 1389 g for total weight and of 1245 g for the sieved weight (Gonçalves *et al.* 2013a).

A more difficult task is to pinpoint the underlying reasons for an eventual incomplete skeletal representation which may either have been deliberate or unintended. In the first case, the intentional recollection of only part of the skeleton may have been related to some sort of specific funerary practice but this is not easy to prove. In our view, it is not conceivable to do it independently for each cremation. Only the analysis of several cremations from the same context may eventually allow for the detection of some enlightening pattern regarding this issue.

Sex determination
Malinowski and Porawski (1969) seem to have been the first to suggest the use of cremains weight to discriminate females from males after finding a mean difference of 464 g between the sexes on a Polish sample. This assumption was denied by Herrmann (1976) who found no such considerable difference after replicating the

research. However, all other similar investigations carried out since then have indeed confirmed that sexual differences are present in cremains weight (McKinley 1993; Warren and Maples 1997; Bass and Jant, 2004; Chirachariyavej *et al.* 2006; May 2011; Van Deest *et al.* 2011; Gonçalves *et al.* 2013a). This means that there is clearly a potential in weight analysis for sex determination. However, its application to archaeological contexts seems to be somewhat feeble. In order to estimate sex using such a parameter, one would need to be sure that the cremains belong to only one rather complete individual and this is often impossible to assess confidently. As a result, sex is certainly the hardest of the three interdependent parameters to determine by using weight and, if conditions are met to allow this, it should be left until last.

Ideally, the results from the weight analysis should be cross-checked with the data resulting from the observation of bone sex diagnostic features to see if it is compatible or not with the sex estimation. Any incompatibility that is found may, in turn, provide information about the other parameters. For example, if the weight of a female cremation is larger than expected then this could mean that more than one individual is present in the burial; if the weight is smaller than expected then the skeleton may be incompletely present in the burial.

If conditions are somehow met to attempt sex determination using solely cremains weight, then the references to be used as sex-discriminating cut-off points should follow the guidelines mentioned above for MNI and for skeleton completeness. Therefore, it seems sensible that weight references be selected according to the pre-cremation condition of the remains – cadavers or skeletons. In the latter case, the references from Gonçalves (2012) proposed a mean value of 1674 g for sieved weight and of 2030 g for total cremation weight considering the overall sample – composed of both females and males.

As for cadavers, the mean values for total cremation weight ranged between 2348 g and 2893 g (Sonek 1992; Bass and Jantz 2004; Warren and Maples 1997; Chirachariyavej *et al.* 2006; Van Deest *et al.* 2011; Gonçalves *et al.* 2013a).[2] For sieved weight, Gonçalves (2012) obtained a mean sex-pooled skeletal weight of 2095 g. Of course and like any other quantitative data, these reference cut-off points should be used conservatively and paying attention to the minimum and maximum documented weights. Therefore, we believe that sex determination can only be reasonably obtained for very feminine or very masculine individuals.

Skeletal representation
Another proclaimed contribution of cremains weight for bioarchaeology is related to the retrieval of the skeletal remains from the extinguished pyre for subsequent relocation onto a secondary place. Basically, the goal here is to detect if any preferential selection or neglect of specific skeletal parts occurred during this retrieval. Such assessment often cannot be carried out comprehensively by doing a skeletal inventory because fragmentation is usually quite large and the fraction of anatomically identified bone fragments is thus very substantial – in fact, this

can easily represent more than 50% of total skeletal weight as was seen for the cremations of Tera. This means that the inventory would only be partially completed and therefore unable to provide a trustworthy portrait of skeletal representation. In contrast, fragmentation does not interfere too much with cremains weight so it has been used instead (McKinley 1995; Duday *et al.* 2000; Blaizot and Georgeon 2005; Richier, 2005; Lenorzer 2006; André *et al.* 2013).

The premise is quite simple: the weight of each skeletal part has a known proportion in relation to total skeletal weight and considerable deviation from that proportion indicates that the skeletal representation is therefore unusual. Theoretically, this premise is equally valid for double or multiple burials comprising adult individuals. The most well-known skeletal weight references are the ones from Lowrance and Latimer (1957) although others have been published as well (e.g.: Ingalls 1931; Silva *et al.* 2009). That research was carried out on a sample of 105 Asian unburned skeletons and enabled the determination that the skull represents about 20.4% of total skeletal weight, while the trunk represents 17.0%, the upper limbs represents 17.6% and the lower limbs have a proportion of 45.0%.[3] The other studies found similar proportions and André *et al.* (2013) used the findings of Trotter and Peterson (1962) regarding the differential mass loss between skeletal elements of the same skeleton burned at similar temperatures to conclude that heat-induced differential weight loss does not significantly alter those references. Their calibration by using the results of Trotter and Peterson (1962) determined that the proportions of the skeletal parts end up being the following: skull with 20.7%; trunk with 16.5%; upper limbs with 17.8%; and lower limbs with 45.0%. The data from modern cremations obtained by Malinowski and Porawski (1969) could be used for the estimation of skeletal proportions in burned skeletons as was done by Lenorzer (2006).[4] However, as mentioned above, instead of referring to samples of skeletons, the samples actually varied according to each bone thus not providing direct estimates.

The values from Lowrance and Latimer (1957) have been used by authors such as Duday *et al.* (2000) and Richier (2005) to compare against archaeological cremations and look for unusual skeletal representations. In summary, if the proportions of each skeletal part found in these cremations were within specific intervals based on the normal mean proportions, the cremation would then be classified as having normal skeletal representation. Unusual skeletal representation would be attributed to cremations in which the proportion of one or more skeletal part was outside that very same interval.

The procedure described above seems to have some problems though. To begin with, the reference values from unburned skeletons are not always adequate to cremains because the fraction of anatomically identified bone fragments (identification rate) can be very large. For instance, if only 50% of bone fragments are indeed determined, we should expect the reference values to be quite inflated thus causing most cremations to be classified as unusual. In addition, the anatomical identification of bone fragments is not equally successful for every skeletal part. Skull and trunk fragments are much more easily identified than limbs fragments (Duday *et al.* 2000; Gonçalves 2012). This means that besides being inflated, the reference values from unburned skeletons where anatomical identification is very successful do not reflect these differences. In other words, the referential that is being used does not seem to fit into the specificities of cremains.

In order to investigate if weight references from unburned skeletons are adequate or not to compare against cremains, an investigation was carried out under a PhD project at a modern crematorium where the complete skeletons of 129 Portuguese individuals were weighed after sieving and the proportion of each skeletal part was assessed (Gonçalves 2012). This procedure lasted for approximately 2 hours for each cremation so no intensive scrutiny of all bone fragments was attained. The results were quite interesting and are given in Table 4.2. One first remark was that, as expected, the average fraction of undetermined bones was quite large (46.1%). Also, this led to smaller proportions of each skeletal part in comparison to those reference values obtained from the results of Lowrance and Latimer (1957). In fact, even if a very conservative approach was adopted – by creating classification intervals with upper and lower bounds that were 50% apart from their published mean values – it was possible to see that, for the sample analysed by Gonçalves (2012), all skeletal parts but the skull would lie outside those intervals and would thus be classified as having unusual skeletal representation. Then, this apparently means that those reference values are only adequate to skeletal remains for which successful anatomical identification is quite high.

Another interesting outcome was the significant correlation found between the identification rate and the skull [rho (127) = 0.475, $p < 0.001$], the trunk [r (127) = 0.703, $p < 0.001$], the upper limbs [r (127) = 0.794, $p < 0.001$] and the lower limbs [r (127) = 0.817, $p < 0.001$]. This meant that the identification rate could potentially be used to predict the proportion of each skeletal part in any given cremation through linear regression. Such procedure would allow the construction of skeletal representation references that are specific to each individual cremains instead of relying in general and inflexible references. The coefficients for the equations are presented in Table 4.3. The sample used to calculate these coefficients included the 129 modern cremations – of both cadavers and skeletons – with identification rates that varied between 25%

Table 4.2: Results for the proportion of the cranium, the trunk and the limbs in relation to total skeletal weight in burned skeletons and comparison with the reference values from unburned skeletons.

	Gonçalves (2012)		Unburned Skeletons ±50%		
	Mean	*SD*	*Mean*	*Upper Bound*	*Lower Bound*
Cranium	13.89	4.22	20	10	30
Trunk	7.72	3.33	17	8.5	25.5
Upper Limbs	6.41	3.04	18	9	27
Lower Limbs	18.06	7.25	45	22.5	67.5

Table 4.3: *Coefficients of the linear regression analysis for the proportion of anatomically identified bone fragments predicting the proportions of the cranium, the trunk, the upper limbs and the lower limbs.*

Model	Unstandardised Coefficients		Standardised Coefficients	t	Sig.	99.0% Confidence Interval for B	
	B	Std. Error	Beta			Lower Bound	Upper Bound
(Constant)	6.785	1.126		6.026	.000	3.841	9.729
Skull	.154	.023	.499	6.570	.000	.093	.215
(Constant)	-.795	.665		-1.195	.234	-2.534	.944
Trunk	.185	.014	.760	13.349	.000	.149	.221
(Constant)	-2.386	.475		-5.025	.000	-3.628	-1.145
Upper Limbs	.191	.010	.861	19.318	.000	.165	.217
(Constant)	-3.434	1.056		-3.252	.001	-6.195	-.674
Lower Limbs	.466	.022	.881	21.226	.000	.409	.524

and 78%. Both samples were pooled despite their mean overall absolute weight being significantly different. This was possible because only relative values were used. The sex-pooled reference values from Lowrance and Latimer (1957) as well as those of females and males from Silva *et al.* (2009) were also included in this analysis in order to better calibrate the equations to contemplate cases with proportions of anatomically identified bone fragments that are higher than 78%.

The following step was to test these linear regression equations on an independent sample. Therefore, a test-sample of 20 cremated skeletons with normal skeletal representation was assembled and the expected proportion of each skeletal part, as well as the 99% classification intervals, were calculated and compared with their actual proportions. Classification intervals based on the reference values from Lowrance and Latimer (1957) were also tested on the same sample so that a comparison between both approaches could be carried out. Duday *et al.* (2000) used these references on the skull – adopting a classification interval between 10% and 30% – and on the trunk – adopting a classification interval between 10% and 24%. The upper limbs and the lower limbs were not targeted in this examination because their proportions were considered to be uninformative due to the fact that a large amount of the fragments belonging to these skeletal parts are often anatomically unidentified. In contrast, Lenorzer (2006) used the same intervals for the skull and the trunk but opted to pay particular attention only to over-representations of 20% and 50% in upper and lower limbs respectively. In our own testing of these references, we chose to use a more conservative approach and thus adopted classification intervals with bounds that were 50% apart from the mean values of proposed by Lowrance and Latimer (1957).

Table 4.4: Results for the classification of normally represented skeletons by using two different classification intervals based on 1) the unburned skeletons weight references of Lowrance and Latimer (1957) (LL) with interval bounds within 50% of the mean and on 2) the linear regressions (LR) taking into account the identification rate (ID%) that were developed from the skeletal weight of cremated modern individuals. Values are given in percentage and unusual representations are highlighted for each skeletal part.

Sk	Sex	ID%	Skull	LL	LR Mean (99% int.)	Trunk	LL	LR Mean (99% int.)	U. Limbs	LL	LR Mean (99% int.)	L. Limbs	LL	LR Mean (99% int.)
1	F	49.4	17.63	(10; 30)	14.4 (8.4; 20.4)	5.03	(8.5; 25.5)	8.3 (4.8; 11.9)	6.16	(9; 27)	7.0 (4.5; 9.6)	20.58	(22.5; 67.5)	19.6 (14.0; 25.2)
2	F	60.5	13.30	(10; 30)	16.1 (9.5; 22.7)	11.93	(8.5; 25.5)	10.4 (6.5; 14.3)	6.40	(9; 27)	9.2 (6.4; 12.0)	28.88	(22.5; 67.5)	24.8 (18.6; 31.0)
3	M	54.6	15.15	(10; 30)	15.2 (8.9; 21.5)	7.18	(8.5; 25.5)	9.3 (5.6; 13.0)	7.96	(9; 27)	8.0 (5.4; 10.7)	24.27	(22.5; 67.5)	22.0 (16.1; 27.9)
4	F	73.1	24.84	(10; 30)	18.0 (10.6; 25.5)	13.85	(8.5; 25.5)	12.7 (8.4; 17.1)	11.97	(9; 27)	11.6 (8.4; 14.7)	22.48	(22.5; 67.5)	30.6 (23.7; 37.7)
5	M	65.2	17.71	(10; 30)	16.8 (9.9; 23.8)	8.00	(8.5; 25.5)	11.3 (7.2; 15.4)	10.19	(9; 27)	10.1 (7.1; 13.0)	29.33	(22.5; 67.5)	27.0 (20.5; 33.5)
6	M	51.3	22.73	(10; 30)	14.7 (8.6; 20.8)	9.87	(8.5; 25.5)	8.7 (5.1; 12.3)	5.69	(9; 27)	7.4 (4.8; 10.0)	13.02	(22.5; 67.5)	20.5 (14.8; 26.2)
7	M	63.6	16.29	(10; 30)	16.6 (9.8; 23.4)	10.90	(8.5; 25.5)	11.0 (6.9; 15.0)	11.90	(9; 27)	9.8 (6.9; 12.7)	24.49	(22.5; 67.5)	26.2 (19.8; 32.6)
8	M	63.9	15.49	(10; 30)	16.6 (9.8; 23.5)	10.51	(8.5; 25.5)	11.0 (7.0; 15.1)	10.35	(9; 27)	9.8 (6.9; 12.7)	27.51	(22.5; 67.5)	26.3 (19.9; 32.8)
9	M	50.1	13.54	(10; 30)	14.5 (8.5; 20.3)	10.69	(8.5; 25.5)	8.5 (4.9; 12.0)	8.31	(9; 27)	7.2 (4.6; 9.7)	17.51	(22.5; 67.5)	19.9 (14.3; 25.6)
10	M	54.4	18.32	(10; 30)	15.2 (8.9; 21.4)	7.49	(8.5; 25.5)	9.3 (5.6; 13.0)	9.96	(9; 27)	8.0 (5.3; 10.7)	18.59	(22.5; 67.5)	21.9 (16.0; 27.8)

11	M	52.5	19.55	(10; 30)	14.9 (8.7; 21.0)	9.88	(8.5; 25.5)	8.9 (5.3; 12.5)	9.07	(9; 27)	7.6 (5.0; 10.2)	13.98	(22.5; 67.5)	21.0 (15.3; 26.8)
12	F	50.9	13.66	(10; 30)	14.6 (8.6; 20.7)	12.33	(8.5; 25.5)	8.6 (5.1; 12.2)	7.55	(9; 27)	7.3 (4.8; 9.9)	17.36	(22.5; 67.5)	20.3 (14.6; 26.0)
13	F	50.2	16.46	(10; 30)	14.5 (8.5; 20.5)	8.72	(8.5; 25.5)	8.5 (4.9; 12.0)	7.28	(9; 27)	7.2 (4.7; 9.7)	17.7	(22.5; 67.5)	19.9 (14.3; 25.6)
14	F	50.3	13.63	(10; 30)	14.5 (8.5; 20.6)	9.34	(8.5; 25.5)	8.5 (5.0; 12.1)	7.61	(9; 27)	7.2 (4.7; 9.8)	19.77	(22.5; 67.5)	20.0 (14.4; 25.7)
15	M	53.4	12.90	(10; 30)	15.0 (8.8; 21.2)	8.23	(8.5; 25.5)	9.1 (5.4; 12.7)	11.02	(9; 27)	7.8 (5.2; 10.4)	21.23	(22.5; 67.5)	21.4 (15.6; 27.3)
16	F	53.2	17.94	(10; 30)	15.0 (8.8; 21.2)	11.99	(8.5; 25.5)	9.1 (5.4; 12.7)	4.25	(9; 27)	7.8 (5.1; 10.4)	19.01	(22.5; 67.5)	21.4 (15.6; 27.2)
17	F	69.9	21.04	(10; 30)	17.5 (10.3; 24.8)	12.02	(8.5; 25.5)	12.1 (7.9; 16.4)	8.40	(9; 27)	11.0 (7.9; 14.0)	28.42	(22.5; 67.5)	29.1 (22.4; 35.9)
18	M	53.4	12.50	(10; 30)	15.0 (8.8; 21.2)	8.34	(8.5; 25.5)	9.1 (5.4; 12.7)	12.01	(9; 27)	7.8 (5.2; 10.4)	20.51	(22.5; 67.5)	21.4 (15.6; 27.3)
19	F	54.0	11.97	(10; 30)	15.1 (8.9; 21.3)	10.60	(8.5; 25.5)	9.2 (5.5; 12.9)	8.02	(9; 27)	7.9 (5.3; 10.6)	23.39	(22.5; 67.5)	21.7 (15.9; 27.6)
20	F	59.7	16.10	(10; 30)	16.0 (9.4; 22.6)	12.52	(8.5; 25.5)	10.3 (6.4; 14.1)	6.75	(9; 27)	9.0 (6.2; 11.8)	24.36	(22.5; 67.5)	24.4 (18.2; 30.6)
Correct Classification				100%	95%		65%	95%		40%	85%		50%	85%

Table 4.5: Data from the examination of the cremations from Tera.

Urn	ID%	Weight (g)	Condition	MNI	Age	Sex	Inventory*	Fauna
[29 - 2001]	42.3	133.9	Cadaver	1	Adult	?	Unidentified: mandible, hyoid, sternum, ulna, hip bone, femur, patella and foot	-
[31 - 2001]	36.9	310.3	Cadaver	1	> 15 years	?	Unidentified: hyoid, sternum, scapula and hip bone	Possible burned fauna
[78]	48.5	359.9	Cadaver	1	Adult	?	Unidentified: hyoid, sternum, scapula, clavicle, radius, ulna, hip bone, patella and tibia	-
[82]	43.7	782.5	Cadaver	1	Adult	F?	Unidentified: hyoid, sternum and patella	-
[111]	0.0	1.5	?	1	?	?	Unidentified: all	-
[120]	60.1	301.2	Cadaver?	1	Adult	F?	Unidentified: all but the skull, mandible, ribs, vertebrae, clavicle and hip bone	-
[128]	36.6	965.2	Cadaver?	1	Adult	M?	Unidentified: hyoid, sternum, clavicle, ulna and hip bone	Possible burned fauna
[193]	48.0	1260.4	Cadaver	2	1 Adult/1?	?	Unidentified: hyoid, sternum and scapula	Burned fauna: ovies/capra
[216]	39.6	2338.9	Cadaver	2	1 Adult/1?	1= M?/2 =?	Unidentified: hyoid, sternum and clavicle	Burned fauna: species unident.
[217]	48.0	2555.4	Cadaver	2	1 Adult/1?	1= F/2 =?	Unidentified: hyoid and sternum	Burned fauna: species unident.
[278]	41.6	1242.9	Cadaver	1	Adult	F?	Unidentified: hyoid and sternum	Possible burned fauna
[300]	57.5	1566.4	Cadaver	1	> 16 years	M?	Unidentified: hyoid, sternum, clavicle and patella	Burned fauna: species unident.

Results are given in Table 4.4 and demonstrated that the approach based on Lowrance and Latimer (1957) values is quite reliable for the assessment of the proportion of the skull. However, successful classification was much worse for the remaining skeletal parts and varied between 40% and 65%. On the other hand, the linear regression equations allowed for quite successful classification of each skeletal part proportion that varied between 85% and 95%. Therefore, this approach generally provided better results than the one based on the references from unburned skeletons even though this one relied on classification intervals with ranges that could be twice or three times as large and, therefore, much more conservative. In fact, the prediction of the mean proportion was on average just a few percentage points apart from the observed proportion in this test sample of 20 skeletons – 2.5% for the skull, 1.6% for the trunk, 1.5% for the upper limbs and 2.6% for the lower limbs. All of this means that the sensitivity of the linear regression equations to detect normal representation of the skeletal parts was much better than the approach based on the references from Lowrance and Latimer (1957). Even in the cases that were mistakenly classified, it is possible to see that the observed proportions were within just two percentage points of the respective classification interval. Nonetheless, the test demonstrated that this approach was not fool-proof and must therefore be used conservatively.

Discussion

The analysis of the cremation urns from Tera is still ongoing but we have some preliminary results that illustrate the potential of cremation weight for bioarchaeology. Some details of these cremations – which were all largely composed of calcined skeletal elements – are given in Table 4.5. In summary, the identification rate for the cremains of these urns varied from 0.0% to 60.1% while the weight ranged between 1.5 g and 2555.4 g. The analysis did not take age into consideration because, although all individuals were either adults or of adult size, a more precise estimation was not possible to obtain. As for sex, only one individual from a minimum of 11[5] was quite confidently determined as a female. Therefore, sex-specific weight references were only used in this case.

For nine urns – [29 - 2001], [31 - 2001],[6] [78], [82], [111], [120], [128], [278] and [300] – a minimum number of one individual was estimated through the inventory and this result was supported by the weight of each cremation since none was larger than the recorded maximum cremation weight of 3805 g or even the second largest of 3287 g (accounting only for sieved weights in both cases). References from cadavers were used because findings suggest that these cremations occurred on cadavers – thumbnail fractures and bone warping (Figs 4.6 and 4.7) were present and are more usual under these circumstances, although may sometimes occur during the cremation of dry skeletal remains (Gonçalves *et al.* 2011; Gonçalves 2012) as well as small bones with labile joints – the absence of which is common in secondary cremations (Roksandic

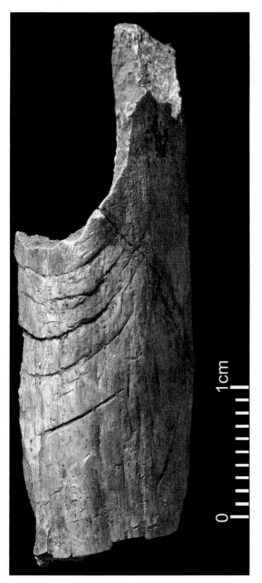

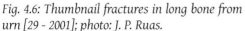

Fig. 4.6: Thumbnail fractures in long bone from urn [29 - 2001]; photo: J. P. Ruas.

Fig. 4.7: Bone warping in tibia from urn [31 - 2001]; photo: J. P. Ruas.

2002; Duday 2006) – and some had clothing-related artefacts (*fibulae*) suggestive of complete bodies. None of these is absolute evidence of the burning of a cadaver but the three together are quite indicative of that.

Duplicated bones were found in urns [193], [216] and [217] demonstrating the presence of at least two different individuals. However, these duplicates referred only to a few bones in the first two cases – right frontal in urn [193]; atlas and right hip

Fig. 4.8: Two repeated petrous bones from urn [217] evidencing two distinct individuals.

bone in urn [216]. In contrast, urn [217] included repeated right petrous pyramid, mandible, left ulna, right hip bone, patella and right calcaneus thus more indicative of a true double burial (Fig. 4.8).

It is probable that the repeated bones in urn [193] and [216] were mere intrusions from previous cremations that resulted from deficient cleansing of the *ustrinum* although the identification rate was less than 50% for both cases, which complicated any conclusion. The weight of the cremations was of little help for the estimation of MNI in urns [193] and [216]. It could refer both to one or more individuals. As for urn [217], one of the individuals was most probably a female[7] and this means that the cremation weight of 2555 g was higher than the recorded maximum sieved weight for modern female cremations of 2420 g. Therefore, the cremation weight gave some support to the estimation of at least two individuals.

In regards to skeletal completeness, five cremations were clearly incompletely present in the container since several bone categories were not found and their weight was clearly lower than the minimum recorded reference of 876 g – [29 - 2001], [31 - 2001], [78], [111] and [120]. These inferences were the only ones that could be made reliably. The skeleton of all other probable single cremations – [82], [128], [278] and [300] – was possibly completely present in the urns but this is impossible to say for certain especially because some bone categories were not identified for all of them. This scenario shows nonetheless that some variation ruled the retrieval of cremains from the extinguished pyre and subsequent deposition in the grave. In some cases, only part of the skeleton was recovered while most of it was retrieved in the others. The assessment of the burials containing at least two individuals was much more complicated because the variables to take into consideration – age, sex and pre-cremation conditions of the remains – had to be multiplied by at least two and some of those variables were almost always unknown to us. This rendered the analysis impractical.

The use of skeletal weight for sex determination was the most complicated one. As mentioned previously, its successful application depends on being sure that each cremation was from a single and almost complete skeleton and this was not the case for the Tera cremations. Under these circumstances, this approach would only be useful to corroborate or contradict any sex estimation based on the observation of bone diagnostic features, but the only such case in Tera was from the double burial composed of urn [217] which included at least one female and this was somewhat corroborated by the presence of a circumstantial evidence – a heart-shaped bracelet. In urn [300], weaponry was found composed of blades which could suggest the presence of a male. However, the only preserved skeletal sex diagnostic feature was a mastoid with some masculine configuration so no reliable determination could be made in this case. Because only one female was confirmed – and this was from a double burial – we refrained from using the cremains weight approach to give support to sex determination in our collection.

The results for the assessment of skeletal representation in the cremations from Tera are presented in Table 4.6. Urn [111] was not analysed due to its small amount of bones. Although it was not possible to test the linear regressions approach (LR) in archaeological cremations because results were evidently not verifiable, it was nonetheless possible to see how different would the results be if compared with the approach based on the reference values from Lowrance and Latimer (1957) hence forth referred to as LL. Therefore, the results from this latter approach are also presented in Table 4.6.

By using the LL approach, all cremations were classified as unusual since one or more skeletal part presented comparatively clear under- or over-representation. This was especially the case for the trunk and the lower limbs where systematic under-representation was found. The result of using the LR approach on the same skeletal parts was quite distinct. In the case of the lower limbs, only two cases were considered to be unusual. In the case of the trunk, only less than half the cases were classified as unusual and some of these had only a very light under-representation up to 1.3% beyond the lower bound of the 99% interval – urns [31 - 2001] and [82].

The analysis of the other skeletal parts was also somewhat distinct between both approaches. In the case of the upper limbs, both the LL approach and the LR approach detected six unusual cases but only coincided in two – urns [120] and [128]. In the case

Table 4.6: Results for the classification of the skeletal representation of the Tera burials according to the approaches based on 1) the unburned skeletons weight references of Lowrance and Latimer (LL) with interval bounds within 50% of the mean and on 2) the linear regressions (LR) taking into account the identification rate (ID%) that were developed from the skeletal weight of cremated modern individuals. Values are given in percentage and unusual representations are highlighted for each skeletal part. Overall skeletal representations (O) classified as clearly unusual are marked as "U" while those classified as normal are marked as "N". A conservative approach was adopted so slightly unusual skeletal representations (with values that were less than ±3 percentage points outside the classification intervals) were also classified as normal.

Urn	ID%	Skull	LL	LR Mean (99% int.)	Trunk	LL	LR Mean (99% int.)	U. Limbs	LL	LR Mean (99% int.)	L.Limbs	LL	LR Mean (99% int.)	O-LL	O-LR
[29 – 2001]	42.3	16.3	(10; 30)	13.3 (7.8; 18.8)	6.6	(8.5; 25.5)	7.0 (3.8;10.3)	9.9	(9; 27)	5.7 (3.4; 8.0)	9.5	(22.5; 67.5)	16.3 (11.1; 21.5)	U	N
[31 – 2001]	36.9	8.5	(10; 30)	12.5 (7.3; 17.7)	0.9	(8.5; 25.5)	6.0 (3.0; 9.1)	13.7	(9; 27)	4.7 (2.5; 6.9)	13.7	(22.5; 67.5)	13.8 (8.9; 18.7)	U	U
[78]	48.5	14.9	(10; 30)	14.3 (8.4; 20.2)	2.0	(8.5; 25.5)	8.2 (4.7; 11.7)	12.6	(9; 27)	6.9 (4.4; 9.4)	19.0	(22.5; 67.5)	19.2 (13.6; 24.7)	U	N
[82]	43.7	20.9	(10; 30)	13.5 (7.9; 19.1)	2.7	(8.5; 25.5)	7.3 (4.0; 10.6)	8.1	(9; 27)	6.0 (3.6; 8.3)	12.0	(22.5; 67.5)	16.9 (11.7; 22.2)	U	N
[120]	60.1	49.9	(10; 30)	16.0 (9.4; 22.7)	3.4	(8.5; 25.5)	10.3 (6.4; 14.2)	2.2	(9; 27)	9.1 (6.3; 11.9)	4.5	(22.5; 67.5)	24.6 (18.4; 30.8)	U	U
[128]	36.6	14.5	(10; 30)	12.4 (7.3; 17.6)	3.9	(8.5; 25.5)	6.0 (2.9; 9.0)	7.8	(9; 27)	4.6 (2.4; 6.8)	10.4	(22.5; 67.5)	13.6 (8.8; 18.5)	U	N
[193]	48	19.0	(10; 30)	14.2 (8.3; 20.1)	8.1	(8.5; 25.5)	8.1 (4.6; 11.6)	5.0	(9; 27)	6.8 (4.3; 9.3)	15.9	(22.5; 67.5)	18.9 (13.4; 24.5)	U	N
[216]	39.6	17.1	(10; 30)	12.9 (7.5; 18.2)	4.3	(8.5; 25.5)	6.5 (3.4; 9.7)	4.4	(9; 27)	5.2 (2.9; 7.4)	13.9	(22.5; 67.5)	15.0 (10.0; 20.1)	U	N
[217]	48	15.7	(10; 30)	14.2 (8.3; 20.1)	6.9	(8.5; 25.5)	8.1 (4.6; 11.6)	10.0	(9; 27)	6.8 (4.3; 9.3)	15.4	(22.5; 67.5)	18.9 (13.4; 24.5)	U	N
[278]	41.6	12.9	(10; 30)	13.2 (7.7; 18.7)	8.0	(8.5; 25.5)	6.9 (3.7; 10.1)	7.1	(9; 27)	5.6 (3.2; 7.9)	13.5	(22.5; 67.5)	16.0 (10.8; 21.1)	U	N
[300]	57.5	26.0	(10; 30)	15.6 (9.2; 22.1)	1.7	(8.5; 25.5)	9.8 (6.0; 13.7)	10.6	(9; 27)	8.6 (5.9; 11.3)	19.2	(22.5; 67.5)	23.4 (17.3; 29.5)	U	U
Total	45.7	18.3	(10; 30)	13.8 (8.1; 19.6)	5.0	(8.5; 25.5)	7.7 (4.3; 11.0)	7.8	(9; 27)	6.3 (3.9; 8.8)	14.7	(22.5; 67.5)	17.9 (12.5; 23.3)	U	N

of the skull, the LL approach detected a single cremation with unusual representation – urn [120] clearly presented over-representation of this skeletal part which represented almost 50% of total cremation weight. In contrast, the LR approach identified two additional burials beside this one – urn [82] and urn [300] – although the former was not clearly unusual. Only the latter could be considered to have an unusual skeletal representation (almost 4% outside the LR 99% classification interval). In contrast, the large interval range of the LL approach would not let this to be detected.

The LL approach that we used here was quite conservative given the range of the classification intervals. Even so, no cremations were found to have an overall normal skeletal representation and this probably reflected the tendency to over-detect unusual cases, as was demonstrated in the test sample from a modern crematorium. That is because this approach tends to over-estimate the expected proportion of all skeletal parts but the skull. Most probably this is the outcome of using weight references from unburned skeletons without taking into account the effect that the fraction of undetermined bones and of the differential identification rate of each skeletal part has on the observed proportions. As a result, the references from Lowrance and Latimer (1957) seem fitting only to detect unusual representation of the skull and to detect any over-representation of the trunk, upper limbs and the lower limbs.

If we conservatively interpret the results from the LR approach, we conclude that only three cremations with clear unusual skeletal representation were detected. In fact, urn [120] was half composed of skull leading to the under-representation of the other skeletal parts. Also, urn [31 - 2001] had a clear over-representation of the upper limbs that constituted about three times what was expected for a cremation, with an identification rate of 36.9%. Therefore, these skeletal parts were intensively recovered from the extinguished pyre. The case of urn [300] is a bit different. Here, some neglect of the trunk was present because the observed proportion was almost six times smaller than the expected value. This did not led to the clear over-representation of the remaining skeletal parts although some was indeed detected for the skull. In urns [31 - 2001], [78] and [82], the trunk was also somewhat neglected although not clearly. In the other cremations, only slightly unusual skeletal representation was found and they were therefore classified as normal. This was supported by other data – after adding the weight of all cremations and calculating the proportion of each skeletal part in relation to it, it was possible to see that no general unusual representation was present in the burials from Tera that have been examined so far (Table 4.5). This result radically contrasted with the interpretation based on the LL approach.

Taking into consideration the results obtained on the testing of the independent sample at the crematorium – in which the LL approach performed worse than the LR approach – the latter apparently allowed for a more perceptive detection of burials with both normal and unusual skeletal representations. In particular, it seemed to be better than the LL approach at identifying the under-represented trunk and limbs. However, its use has to be conservative since the 99% intervals are not fool-proof.

Conclusions

Skeletal weight analysis certainly has the potential for some bioarchaeological inferences and this claim was supported by our examination of the cremation burials of the Iron Age necropolis of Tera. Only a small part of these burials has been examined so our conclusions are still preliminary. No clear age discriminating practice was present at Tera. Although the burials reported here only comprised adults or individuals of adult appearance, a perinate has also been previously mentioned for burial 2 by a former research team (Rocha 2003). In addition, the recent laboratorial excavation of urn [290], a single burial, also contained an infant. As for the sexual composition of the necropolis, although this parameter was not successfully attained for most of the remains, there are some indications that both sexes were indeed present – a female from burial [217] and probable males in burials [128], [216] and [300].

The funerary practice was somewhat uniform. The cremation took place at an undisclosed location hitherto and went on until most of the skeleton was calcined and faunal remains sometimes accompanied the body. Actually, this may have happened for all cremations since fauna was clearly absent only in burials containing incomplete skeletons. Therefore, its absence may have just been the result of incomplete recovery from the pyre. The nature of these faunal findings is yet undetermined. Only one was identified as being a sheep or a goat so this suggests a food offering or sacrifice of some sort. Besides this, not every burial contained artefacts.

All burials were secondary and included the deposition of remains in urns of wheel made pottery of medium size. As we have seen, the retrieval of remains from the pyre for subsequent allocation into those urns was somewhat varied. In some cases, only a fraction of the skeleton was deposited in the urn while in other cases, almost all skeletal elements were allocated to them. The reasons for this are unknown and it is not possible to determine if it was the result of random behaviour or of deliberate practice. As for any preferential inclusion of specific skeletal parts into the urns, the major but still meaningless trends referred to the under-representation of the trunk and the over-representation of the upper limbs. None had a clear pattern revealing of a specific and rather homogeneous funerary practice though. After the allocation of the cremains to the urns, grave goods – mainly brooches, iron knifes and ceramics – were in some cases carefully placed on top of them. The urns were then covered up with plates and deposited into the pits. Sometimes, ashes and cremains were placed around the urns along with small vessels, probably *unguentaria*, oil and perfume bottles possibly used to prepare the body prior to the cremation or to attenuate the powerful odour resulting from it.

The analysis of cremation weight was useful to look for incompatibilities between weight and MNI based on the skeletal inventory – none was found. Our initial suppositions regarding sex determination were confirmed by the examination of the cremains from Tera. No inferences could be carried out since we had no certainties about the assumptions that are required in order to proceed with this method – the burial must reportedly be single and the skeleton must be rather complete.

The linear regression equations revealed to be more reliable at assessing skeletal representation than the method based on weight references from unburned skeletons. This was so because the latter do not account for the effect of anatomically undetermined fragments on skeletal proportions and thus tend to inflate the expected representation of each skeletal part. Also, the differential identification rate of each skeletal part is obviously not taken into consideration in skeletal weight references from unburned skeletons.

The greatest advantage of the linear regression relies on its ability to be case-specific. Instead of using general references for every cremation – such as the one based on the results of Lowrance and Latimer (1957), the equations allow for the building of references that are specific to each cremation. Nonetheless, this method has its own problems to overcome. Firstly, it is based on the identification rate and this depends on the ability of each observer to anatomically identify each skeletal fragment. It can present some inter-observer variation which was not calculated for this research – since only one of the co-authors did the research at the modern crematorium – so its impact on the results is not known.

Another problem of the method was that it was not fool-proof. Some mistaken classifications of normally represented modern cremains occurred, although in these cases, the observed proportions were not too far from the 99% interval bounds. Therefore, these need to be used conservatively and this means that some subjectivity is still part of the process. Such problem is probably more serious for archaeological cremations because, as was seen previously, their weight may not be completely comparable with modern skeletal weight references. In addition, the effect of differential post-depositional preservation on the representation of burned skeletons is not known.

Low identification rates render the assessment of skeletal representation much more difficult. Usually, the composition of the undetermined fraction includes an important portion of bone fragments from the limbs. Therefore, instead of making a distinction between upper and lower limbs, the solution may lie on the agglomeration of these two skeletal parts into a single category designated as "limbs". This way, only three skeletal parts would be assessed and the undetermined fraction would be much smaller because the skull and the trunk tend to be easily identified. As a result, the assessment of skeletal representation would not be too dependent of the undetermined fraction and thus much more reliable.

As a final note, although unusual skeletal representation can be detected by using skeletal weight, such occurrence is not equal to say that this was the result of deliberate practice. Unusual skeletal representation can also result of random and unintended behaviour. Only clear trends may in fact reveal and confirm a premeditated practice regarding the preferential selection of specific skeletal parts, so the examination of multiple burials before making an assessment of this sort is recommendable. Assuming that the LR approach is reliable, no such trend was indeed found for Tera suggesting that the burials with unusual skeletal representation were the result of random or episodic behaviour thus not reflecting a specific funerary practice shared by all or most of the members of this population.

Acknowledgements

The authors would like to thank the municipality of Porto for allowing us to do research at the local crematorium, especially to Cidália Duarte, José Luis, Amarante, Marques and Joaquim Neves. We also would like to convey our appreciation to Leonor Rocha for giving us research access to urns [29 – 2001] and [31 – 2001] recovered from Tera and to Catarina Alves and Leigh Oldershaw for their expertise on the excavation campaigns. In addition, our gratitude goes to the municipalities of Mora and Redondo and to the Direcção Geral do Património Cultural (DGPC, IP) for the accommodation of the field team and laboratorial logistics; to José Paulo Ruas who took some of the pictures presented in this paper; to Eugénia Cunha who read a previous draft of it; and to Sandra Jesus and the Hospital Escolar Veterinário (Faculdade de Medicina Veterinária – Universidade Técnica de Lisboa) for CT-scans of cremation urns. Finally, this investigation would not have been possible without the contribution of many students who attended the Redondo Osteological Programs and helped to excavate some of the urns. David Gonçalves (SFRH/BPD/84268/2012) and Vanessa Campanacho (SFRH/BD/77962/2011) are funded by the Fundação para a Ciência e Tecnologia .

Notes

1   As far as we know, no references for the burned skeleton of sub-adults based on large samples and different age groups have been published to date.

2   The values obtained by McKinley (1993) were not included here due to the small sample size. Also, the values from Herrmann (1976) were not accounted because the sample was not sexually dimorphic. As for the results of Malinowski and Porawski (1969), the weights were not obtained on a sample of complete skeletons. They merely weighed the bones that were preserved after each cremation, calculated the mean weight for each skeletal element (e.g.: clavicle; humerus; etc) and then added these to obtain the theoretical mean weight of an entire skeleton. Therefore, each skeletal element had different samples and the sum did not reflect the actual mean weight of the skeletons.

3   The skeletal part of the skull is composed of the cranium, the mandible and the hyoid; the trunk is composed of the vertebral column, the rib cage and the sternum; the upper limbs are composed of the scapulae, clavicles, humeri, radii, ulnae and bones from the hands; and the lower limbs are composed of the hip bones, femora, patellae, tibiae, fibulae and bones from the feet.

4   Males: skull = 21.0%; trunk = 16.7%; upper limbs = 15.1%; lower limbs = 47.2%. Females: skull = 21.6%; trunk = 21.1%; upper limbs = 12.8%; lower limbs = 44.5%.

5   Although remains from 13 individuals have been found, some of those from the double burials may refer to individuals also present in the other burials. Therefore, the MNI is indeed 11 for the time being.

6   Urns [29 – 2001] and [31 – 2001] were exhumed from Tera under a previous project coordinated by Leonor Rocha (2003).

7   Sex determination was based on the morphology of the greater sciatic notch and the mastoid process (Ferembach *et al.* 1980), on the metrics of the femur, the medial cuneiform and the intermediate cuneiform (Gonçalves 2012; Gonçalves *et al.* 2013b), on the metrics of the mandibular canine (Cardoso 2008) and indirectly on the presence of a heart-shaped bracelet.

References

André A., Leahy, R. and Rottier, S. 2013. Cremated human remains deposited in two phases: evidence from the necropolis of the Tuileries site (Lyon, France: 2nd century AD). *International Journal of Osteoarchaeology*, DOI http://onlinelibrary.wiley.com/doi/10.1002/oa.2317/abstract.

Argente Oliver, J. L., Díaz, A. and Bescós, A. 2000. *Tiermes V, Carratiermes, Necrópolis celtibérica*. Valladolid: Junta de Castilla Y Léon, Memorias 9.

Bass, W. M. and Jantz, R. L. 2004. Cremation weights in East Tennessee. *Journal of Forensic Sciences* 49(5), 901–4.

Beckett, S., Rogers, K. D. and Clement, J. G. 2011. Inter-species variation in bone mineral behavior upon heating. *Journal of Forensic Sciences* 56(3), 571–9.

Blaizot, F, and Georjon, C. 2005. Les pratiques funéraires au Bronze Final – Hallstatt Ancien en Alsace: l'apport de Sainte-Croix-en-Plaine «zone artisanale». In: Mordant C. and Depierre G. (eds), *Les pratiques funéraires à l'Âge du Bronze en France*, 213–41. Paris: Comité des Travaux Historiques et Scientifiques.

Brown, K. A., O'Donoghue, K. and Brown, T. A. 1995. DNA in cremated bones from an early Bronze Age cemetery cairn. *International Journal of Anthropology* 5, 181–7.

Buikstra, J. and Ubelaker, D. 1994. *Standards For Data Collection From Human Skeletal Remains: Proceedings of a Seminar at the Field Museum of Natural History*. Arkansas: Arkansas Archaeological Survey Report 44.

Cardoso, H. 2008. Sample-specific (universal) metric approaches for determining the sex of immature human skeletal remains using permanent tooth dimensions. *Journal of Archaeological Science* 35, 158–68.

Cattaneo, C., Gelsthorpe, K., Sokol, R. J. and Phillips, P. 1994. Immunological detection of albumin in ancient human cremations using ELISA and monoclonal antibodies. *Journal of Archaeological Science* 21, 565–71.

Cattaneo, C., Porta, D., Gibelli, D. and Gamba, C. 2009. Histological determination of the human origin of bone fragments. *Journal of Forensic Sciences* 54(3), 531–3.

Chirachariyavej, T., Amnueypol, C., Sanggarnjanavanich, S. and Tiensuwan, M. 2006. The relationship between bone and ash weight to age, body weight and body length of Thai adults after cremation. *Journal of the Medical Association of Thailand* 89(11), 1940–5.

Cuijpers, A. 2006. Histological identification of bone fragments in archaeology: telling humans apart from horses and cattle. *International Journal of Osteoarchaeology* 16(6), 465–80.

Dias, M. M. A. and Coelho, I. 1983. Objectos Arqueológicos de um Túmulo de Incineração da Necrópole Proto-Histórica da Herdade da Favela Nova (Ourique). *O Arqueólogo Português Série IV* 1, 197–206.

Duday, H. 2006. L'archaéothanatalogie ou l'archaeologie de la mort. In: Gowland, R. and Knüsel, C. (eds), Social Archaeology of Funerary Remains, 30–56. Oxford: Oxbow Books.

Duday, H., Depierre, G. and Janin, T. 2000. Validation des paramètres de quantification, protocoles et stratégies dans l'étude anthropologique des sépultures secondaires à incinération. L'exemple des nécropoles protohistoriques du midi de la France. In: Dedet, B., Gruat, P., Marchand, G., Py, M. and Schwaller, M. (eds), *Archéologie de La Mort, Archéologie de la Tombe au Premier Âge du -Fer*, 7–29. Lattes: UMR.

Enzo, S., Bazzoni, M., Mazzarello, V., Piga, G., Bandiera, P. and Melis, P. 2007. A study by thermal treatment and X-ray powder diffraction on burnt fragmented bones from tombs II, IV and IX belonging to the hypogeic necropolis of 'Sa Figu' near Ittiri, Sassari (Sardinia, Italy). *Journal of Archaeological Science* 34, 1731–7.

Ferembach, D., Schwidetzky, I. and Stloukal, M. 1980. Recomendations for age and sex diagnoses of skeletons. *Journal of Human Evolution* 9, 517–49.

Gonçalves, D. 2012. Cremains: the value of quantitative analysis for the bioanthropological research of burned human skeletal remains. PhD thesis, Coimbra: University of Coimbra.

Gonçalves, D., Thompson, T. J. U. and Cunha, E. 2011. Implications of heat-induced changes in bone on the interpretation of funerary behaviour and practice. *Journal of Archaeological Science* 3 8,1308–13.

Gonçalves, D., Cunha, E. and Thompson, T. 2013a. Weight references for burned human skeletal remains from Portuguese samples. *Journal of Forensic Sciences.* DOI: 10.1111/1556-4029.12167.

Gonçalves, D., Thompson, T. J. U. and Cunha, E. 2013b. Osteometric sex determination of burned human skeletal remains. *Journal of Forensic and Legal Medicine* 20, 906–11.

Greenwood, C., Rogers, K., Beckett, S. and Clement, J. 2013. Initial observations of dynamically heated bone. *Crystal Research and Technology.* DOI: 10.1002/crat.201300254.

Grupe, G. and Hummel, S. 1991. Trace element studies on experimentally cremated bone. I. Alteration of the chemical composition at high temperatures. *Journal of Archaeological Science* 18, 177–86.

Harbeck, M., Schleuder, R., Schneider, J., Wiechmann, I., Schmahl, W. W. and Grupe, G. 2011. Research potential and limitations of trace analyses of cremated remains. *Forensic Science International* 204, 191–200.

Harden, D. 1981. *Catalogue of Greek and Roman Glass in the British Museum.* London: British Museum.

Herrmann, B. 1976. Neuere Ergebnisse zur Beurteilung menschlicher Brandknochen. *Zeitschrift für Rechtsmedizin* 77, 191–200.

Hiller, J. C., Thompson, T. J. U., Evison, M. P., Chamberlain, A. T. and Wess, T. J. 2003. Bone mineral change during experimental heating: an X-ray scattering investigation. *Biomaterials* 24, 5091–7.

Jiménez Ávila, J. 1999. Los objetos de vidrio procedentes del yacimiento de Pajares: estudio preliminar. In: Celestino, S. (ed.), *El yacimiento Protohistórico de Pajares, Villanueva de la Vera, Cáceres,* 139–53. Memorias de Arqueología Extremeña 3.

Jiménez Ávila, J. 2002. *La toréutica orientalizante en la Península Ibérica.* Madrid: Real Academia de la História. Bibliotheca Archaeologica Hispana 16.

Jiménez Ávila, J. 2003. Las sandalias de Apolo: sobre el origen griego de los cinturones 'célticos'. *Archivo Español de Arqueología* 76, 31–46.

Langley, M., Mataloto, R., Boaventura, R. and Gonçalves, D. 2007. A ocupação da Idade do Ferro de Torre de Palma: "escavando nos fundos" do Museu Nacional de Arqueologia. *O Arqueólogo Português* 25, 229–90.

Lenorzer, S. 2006. *Pratiques funéraires du Bronze final IIIb au premier âge du Fer en Languedoc occidental et Midi-Pyrénées: Approche archéo-anthropologique des nécropoles à incinération.* Bordeaux: Université de Bordeaux.

Lorrio, A. J. 1997. *Los Celtíberos.* Alicante/Madrid: Universidad Alicante/Complutense. Complutum Extra 7.

Lorrio, A. J. 2008. Cerámica Gris. In: Almagro-Gorbea, M. (ed.) *La necrópolis de Medellín. II - Estudios de los hallazgos,* 673–723. Madrid: Biblioteca Archaeologica Hispana 26(2).

Lowrance, E.W. and Latimer, H. B. 1957. Weight and linear measurements of 105 human skeletons from Asia. *American Journal of Anatomy* 101(3), 445–59.

Malinowski, A. and Porawski, R. 1969. Identifikationsmöglichkeiten menschlicher Brandknochen mit besonder Berücksichtigung ihres Gewichts. *Zacchia* 5, 1–19.

Mataloto, R. 2013. Os senhores da terra: necrópoles e comunidades rurais do território alto alentejano do sécs. VI–V aC. *Arqueologia & História,* 77–100.

May, S. E. 2011. The effects of body mass on cremation weight. *Journal of Forensic Sciences* 56(1), 3–9.

Mayne Correia, P. (ed.). 1997. *Fire Modification of Bone: a Review of the Literature.* New York: CRC Press.

Mays, S. 1998. *The Archaeology of Human Bones.* New York: Routledge.

McKinley, J. 1993. Bone fragment size and weights of bone from British cremations and the implications for the interpretation of archaeological cremations. *International Journal of Osteoarchaeology* 3(4), 283–7.

McKinley, J. I. 1994. Bone fragment size in British cremation burials and its implications for pyre technology and ritual. *Journal of Archaeological Science* 21, 339–42.

McKinley, J. 1995. East London Romano-British cemeteries; publication report on the cremation burials and cremation related contexts. http://archaeologydataservice.ac.uk/archiveDS/archiveDownload?t=arch-921-2/dissemination/pdf/documents/human_bone_reports/JMcKinley_cremation_archive_rep.pdf

Munro, L. E., Longstaffe, F. J. and White, C. D. 2007. Burning and boiling of modern deer bone: effects on crystallinity and oxygen isotope composition of bioapatite phosphate. *Palaeogeography, Palaeoclimatology, Palaeoecology* 249(1–2), 90–102.

Piga, G., Solinas, G., Thompson, T., Brunetti, A., Malgosa, A. and Enzo, S. 2013. Is X-ray diffraction able to distinguish between animal and human bones? *Journal of Archaeological Science* 40(1),778–85.

Person, A., Bocherens, H., Mariotti, A. and Renard, M. 1996. Diagenetic evolution and experimental heating of bone phosphate. *Palaeogeography, Palaeoclimatology, Palaeoecology* 126, 135–49.

Richier, A. 2005. Sépultures primaires à incineration: nouvelles données et nouvelles problématiques. In: Mordant, C. and Depierre, G. (eds), *Les Pratiques Funéraires à l'Âge du Bronze en France*, 199–210. Paris: Comité des Travaux Historiques et Scientifiques.

Rocha, L. 2003. O monumento megalítico da I Idade do Ferro do Monte da Tera (Pavia, Mora): Sectores 1 e 2. *Revista Portuguesa de Arqueologia* 6(1), 121–9.

Rocha, L. 2012. Anta do Monte das Figueiras. In: Calado, M., Rocha, L. and Alvim, P. *O Tempo das Pedras-Carta Arqueológica de Mora*, 119–20. Mora: Câmara Municipal de Mora.

Roksandic, M. 2002. Position of skeletal remains as key to understand mortuary behavior. In: Haglund, W. D. and Sorg, M. H. (eds), *Advances in Forensic Taphonomy*, 95–113. Boca Raton FL: CRC Press.

Ruiz Delgado, M. M. 1989. *Fíbulas Protohistóricas en el Sur de la Península Ibérica*. Sevilla: Servicio de Publicaciones de la Universidad de Sevilla.

Shipman, P., Foster, G. and Schoeninger, M. 1984. Burnt bones and teeth: an experimental study of colour, morphology, crystal structure and shrinkage. *Journal of Archaeological Science* 11(4), 307–25.

Sweet, D. J. and Sweet, C. H. 1995. DNA analysis to dental pulp to link incinerated remains to homicide victim in crime scene. *Journal of Forensic Sciences* 40(2), 310–14.

Thompson, T. J. U. 2004. Recent advances in the study of burned bone and their implications for forensic anthropology. *Forensic Science International* 146S, 203–5.

Thompson, T. J. U. 2005. Heat-induced dimensional changes in bone and their consequences for forensic anthropology. *Journal of Forensic Sciences* 50(5), 185–93.

Trotter, M. and Peterson, R. R. 1962. The relationship of ash weight and organic weight of human skeletons. *Journal of Bone and Joint Surgery* 44(4), 669–81.

Ubelaker, D. 1974. *Reconstruction of Demographic Profiles from Ossuary Skeletal Samples: A Case from the Tidewater Potomac*. Washington DC: Smithsonian Contributions to Anthropology 18.

van Deest, T. L., Murad, T. A. and Bartelink, E. J. 2011. A re-examination of cremains weight: sex and age variation in a Northern Californian sample. *Journal of Forensic Sciences* 56(2), 344–9.

Walker, P. L., Miller, K. W. P. and Richman, R. 2008. Time, temperature and oxygen availability: an experimental study of the effects of environmental conditions on the color and organic content of cremated bone. In: Schmidt, C. W. and Symes, S. A. (eds), *The Analysis of Burned Human Remains*, 129–37. London: Academic Press.

Warren, M. W. and Maples, W. R. 1997. The anthropometry of contemporary commercial cremation. *Journal of Forensic Sciences* 42(3), 417–23.

Williams, D., Lewis, M., Franzen, T., Lissett, V., Adams, C., Whittaker, D., Tysoe, C. and Butler, R. 2004. Sex determination by PCR analysis of DNA extracted from incinerated, deciduous teeth. *Science and Justice* 44(2), 89–94.

Wurmb-Schwark, Nv., Simeoni, E., Ringleb,. A. and Oehmichen, M. 2004. Genetic investigation of modern burned corpses. *International Congress Series* 1261, 50–2.

Ye, J., Ji, A., Parra, E., Zheng, X., Jiang, C., Zhao, X., Hu, L. and Tu, Z. 2004. A simple and efficient method for extracting DNA from old and burned bone. *Journal of Forensic Sciences* 49(4), 754–9.

Chapter 5

Funerary rituals and ideologies in the Phoenician-Punic necropolis of Monte Sirai (Carbonia, Sardinia, Italy)

Giampaolo Piga, Michele Guirguis and Ethel Allue

Introduction

The site of *Monte Sirai* is located in the south-western part of Sardinia near the city of Carbonia (Fig. 5.1a and b). It is thought to have been established by the Phoenicians of *Sulky* (today known as *S. Antioco*) or by the early settlers living in the anonymous downtown of Portoscuso around 740 BC (Botto 1994), and soon after assumed importance for its strategic position near the coastline and leading to the Campidano plane of the island. Around the year 540 BC, Carthago decided to occupy the island using force, but a coalition of Phoenician cities in Sardinia, certainly involving Sulcis and *Monte Sirai*, firmly resisted to this expansion. Undeterred, Carthago organised a second military expedition a few years later that finally defeated the Phoenician alliance. The population of *Monte Sirai* was massacred and the city almost completely destroyed. It is estimated that after this event only a dozen families were inhabiting the village.

This was surmised from presence of 13 Punic-type tombs in hypogeal chambers of the necropolis of that period, which probably represented family tombs. In fact, the rite of body cremation was mainly used in the Phoenician era. Conversely, during the Punic period, after the Carthaginian conquest, inhumation was the prevailing funerary rite, with the bodies often placed within the hypogeal chamber tombs (Bartoloni 2000).

This situation remained approximately the same until 360 BC, when Carthago decided to strengthen various Sardinian sites, including *Monte Sirai*. After 238 BC, and during the neo-Punic period, the fortress of *Monte Sirai* was completely demolished and a new city plan, which utilised four large building arrays, was established. By 110 BC the site was abandoned and only sporadically inhabited thereafter (Bartoloni 2000). This abrupt end, with the absence of the hallmarks of imperial Roman life, allows for the thorough and privileged investigation of Phoenician and Punic customs, which are preserved in an excellent manner – unlike in other major Sardinian settlements

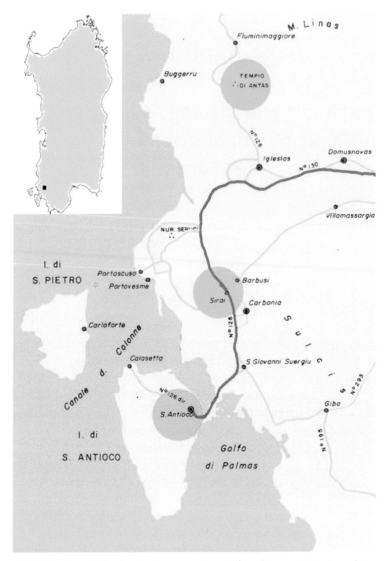

Fig. 5.1: (inset) the location of Monte Sirai necropolis and (map) a magnification of its nearby context in the island of Sardinia (reproduced by kind permission of Prof Bartoloni).

(e.g., Sulky, Tharros, Cagliari, Nora) which were more routinely occupied during the Roman and Medieval periods.

Excavations of the site were conducted between 1963 and 1966 and then again from 1980 and between 2005 and 2010 (Bartoloni 2000; Guirguis 2005; 2010; 2012). In the period 2005–2010, 96 burials were identified, attributed to an extended chronological period between the end of the seventh and the second half of the fourth centuries BC. In the documentation gathered during the latest excavations it was noted that the oldest contexts do not go further back than the seventh century BC. During the early development of the necropolis (i.e., from the end of the seventh to the second half of the fourth centuries BC) there is some variety in funeral rites adopted among which primary incineration is predominant.

The funerary context

The rite of inhumation started to appear early in the sixth century BC in competition with incineration and cremation, later becoming the prevailing funerary rite (Guirguis 2011). It was observed that, during the Archaic period, some graves contained burnt skeletal remains in rectangular pits that did not display any sign of a combustion event. We can consider those burials as secondary, meaning that the ultimate location of osteological materials do not coincide with the place of their combustion.

Currently, the necropolis (Fig. 5.2) consists of three areas spaced at some distance from each other and allows detection of a diachronic use of a large burial area. This

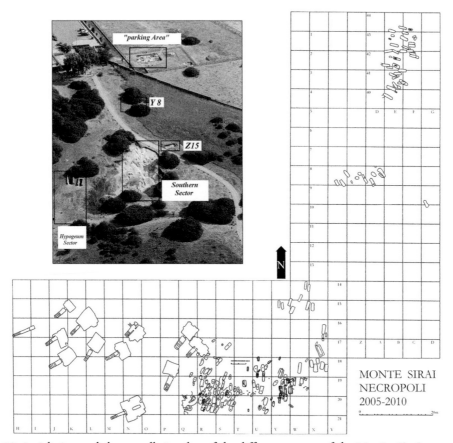

Fig. 5.2: Aerial view and the overall site plan of the different sectors of the Monte Sirai necropolis (elaboration by Rosana Pla Orquín).

occupies a broad valley that opens just east of chamber tombs of Punic age (Hypogeum sector) with two other distinct areas to the north-east. The southern sector has returned the oldest evidence of late sixth century BC, while the Y8 square to its east and the northernmost area, the so-called "parking area", gradually achieve the horizons of late archaic and early Punic age.

Within the *Monte Sirai* necropolis, tombs 250 and 252 are typical Phoenician primary cremation burials in graves, whose ritual performance was described in detail by Bartoloni (2000). In *Monte Sirai*, necropolis graves were only used for the cremation of bodies. First, an ellipsoid cavity was dug in the ground surface and below the turf, about 2 m in length and *c.* 40 cm in depth. During the excavation, the gravediggers retained the larger blocks of turf to be used later. From analysis of ancient funerary kits it is likely that the bodies were cleaned and anointed with special ritual vessels. This is suggested by the presence of pitchers with so-called "hem fungus" and pitchers referred to as "bilobed" or "biconical". Presumably the latter contained an ointment, while the first were used to sprinkle its content because of the strongly expanded rim. After the anointing, the body was equipped with jewels, amulets and other objects. In addition to personal items the bodies of women were accompanied by a set of pots. This was composed of two rituals pitchers, and by one or more plates or cups. Generally five vessels, including the ritual vessels, accompanied women, while three were placed with men and only one with children. The body was then wrapped in a shroud and laid on some boards that had served as a deathbed. In the meantime, branches of oleaginous shrubs were collected and placed along the length of the grave. Firewood was stacked above the branches and the body laid on the woodpile, which was then set alight.

The combustion was of relatively short duration, but continued until the bones were calcined and to the point when the wood was charred completely and collapsed into the grave. The remaining flames and hot coals were probably extinguished with water. This proposal is further strengthened by the discovery of elements in tomb 250 with equipment in close contact with a large trunk of charred wood – residue from the funeral pyre, which overlooks the shallow grave where they went once the osteological remains and artifacts were deposited, after the fire extinction. The funerary kit appeared homogeneously blackened with the ceramic parts in contact with the charred wood. However, one cannot speak of a real burning surface of the vessels. In fact it appears that the pitcher, plates and rituals were placed directly above the burning remains when the original funeral pyre and the result of burning had already fallen into the grave, and the temperature had dropped suddenly as a result of quenching the fire with water. This is suggested by the excellent state of preservation of charred wood, recovered in large fragments (Guirguis 2010) (Fig. 5.3).

The major bones, such as the skull and the pelvis, pots, especially dishes or cups, or some large fragments of amphorae wall sherds fell into the grave, while the two jugs used for ritual anointing of the body were placed at the bottom. After deposition, the bones and charred wood were completely covered and sealed with turf previously

Fig. 5.3: A large trunk of charred wood found in the tomb 250, residue of the funeral pyre, which overlooks the shallow pit where the bones and funerary kit were deposited, after turning off the fire intentionally (photo courtesy of Dr Michele Guirguis).

set aside and placed together with clays. Thus, the grave was covered with a mound formed by stones and earth. Finally, a stone was used to indicate the tomb.

The disposition of the bones, along with the mixture of charcoal and soil, suggests that the cremation was carried out *in situ*. This is indicated also by the smallest bones recovered during excavation, such as wormian bones and phalanges, whose inventory is not usual when the remains of a cremation are collected for deposition in an urn or in a grave dedicated only to contain the remains from the ustrinum.

The cremated remains

The primary cremation graves were located mainly in the southern sector of the necropolis (Fig. 5.4). The chronology of these tombs extends from the late seventh century BC until the second half of the sixth century BC (Guirguis 2011).

A series of graves belonging to the Phoenician period were investigated after the campaign excavation of 2007. Specifically one tomb (252) is described because of its uniqueness. In tomb 252, burnt fragments and remains of an individual, probably male, could be reconstructed into a skeleton. The comparison of the excavation images and rebuilding of bone material has determined the position in which the individual was placed for incineration, demonstrating that the body was cremated in a prone position (Piga *et al.* 2012; Guirguis *et al.* 2011b). It represents the first case of prone cremation reported in the literature.

On the other hand, nearby tomb 250 contained the remains of a large trunk of fossil carbonised wood, clearly the residue of a funeral pyre. By using metallographic microscope observations the type of wood that was used for the primary rite of cremation in the Necropolis was identified. The discovery of almost all parts of the skeletons allowed a detailed analysis which is not always possible in such contexts,

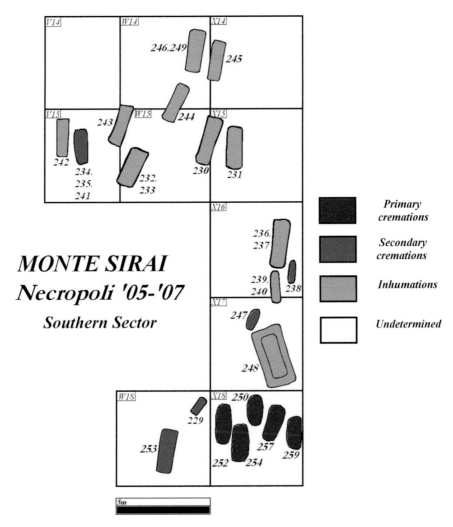

Fig. 5.4: Plan of the southern sector with an indication of the burial rituals identified.

i.e to analyse the homogeneity of the temperature and intensity of fire in various parts representative of the whole body.

The recent study points out the existence of a rite between incineration and inhumation, termed 'semi-combustion'. It was found in the burials of the late Archaic to early Punic age (from the late sixth and throughout the fifth centuries BC), located in the most peripheral necropolis sector. With the terms 'semi-combustion' or 'semi-cremation', essentially equivalent, we refer to incomplete forms of incineration. This particular rite appears to be peculiar to only this site (Piga *et al.* 2010).

In order to ascertain objectively whether all the bodies were subjected to burning and to what extent, the bones recovered from tombs were investigated both by XRD and FT-IR techniques which have been demonstrated to be able to discriminate the degree of fire treatment to which the bones were possibly subjected. The main aim of this study is to analyse all the biological elements of the funerary rituals studied in *Monte Sirai* necropolis, to determine the kind of combustible material used, the temperature of the pyre, the state and position of the body and an estimate of the temperature reached for cremation.

Methods of analysis

Both X-ray powder diffraction (XRD) and Fourier Transform Infrared (FT-IR) techniques can be used to assess the nature of the crystal structure of burned bone and this in turn can be related to the temperature or intensity of burning. The XRD approach correlates crystal size with temperature (Piga *et al.* 2008; 2009), while the FT-IR method links changes in crystallinity (namely the so-called splitting factor, SF) with the same. Both approaches have been used in many experimental studies (e.g. Rogers and Daniels 2002; Piga *et al.* 2010a; Rogers *et al.* 2010; Thompson *et al.* 2009; 2011; 2013) and are now being increasingly applied to real-world archaeological sites and contexts (e.g. Enzo *et al.* 2007; Piga *et al.* 2008; 2010a; 2010b; Squires *et al.* 2011). Further, their application is becoming increasingly accepted and sophisticated, and allows for better interpretation of ancient funerary practices (Piga 2012).

XRD analysis

A sample of 0.5 g of each bone fragment was ball-milled in an agate jar for one-minute using a SPEX mixer-mill model 8000. Our sample holder for XRD analysis is a circular cavity 25 mm in diameter and 0.3 mm in depth. It contains about 420 mg of powder bone. The XRD patterns were recorded overnight using Bruker D8 and Siemens D-500 diffractometers in the Bragg/Brentano geometry with CuKα radiation (λ = 1.54178 Å). The X-ray generator worked at a power of 40 kV and 30 mA and the resolution of the instruments (divergent and antiscatter slits of 0.5°) was determined using α-SiO$_2$ and α-Al$_2$O$_3$ standards free from the effect of reduced crystallite size and lattice defects (Enzo *et al.* 1988).

The goniometer was equipped with a graphite monochromator in the diffracted beam and the patterns were collected with 0.05° of step size which turned out to be adequate for the range of crystallite sizes in the apatite phases here investigated. The powder patterns were collected in the angular range 9–140° in 2θ, with counting time of 40 s per point. Digitised diagrams were analysed according to the Rietveld method (Rietveld 1967), using the programme MAUD (*Materials Analysis Using Diffraction*; Lutterotti and Bortolotti 2003).

FT-IR analysis

FT-IR spectra were collected with a Bruker Vertex 70V interferometer in terms of absorbance vs wavenumber v in the range 400–4500 cm⁻¹, with a resolution of 4 cm⁻¹. Samples of about 3 mg bone were hand-ground and mixed with KBr in the weight ratio 1:100 respectively, to make pellets suitable for beam irradiation. Every spectrum was obtained by averaging 250 interferograms. It should be considered that bands of the infrared spectrum of recent and fossil bones are relevant to obtain molecular information concerning the phosphate/carbonate group ratio. Additional bands may also be evaluable due to minerals other than those related to the apatite-like structure.

Crystallinity Index and other ratios

The Crystallinity Index adopted here is the same as has been used in the majority of archaeological applications. The absorption bands at 605 and 565 cm⁻¹ were used following baseline correction, and the heights of these absorptions peaks were summed and then divided by the height of the minimum between them (Weiner and Bar-Yosef 1990). The carbonate/phosphate ratio (CP) was also calculated. Here the absorption peak at 1415 cm⁻¹ was divided by the peak at 1035 cm⁻¹ as used in Shemesh (1990), Wright and Schwarcz (1996), Koon *et al.* (2003), Olsen *et al.* (2008), Thompson *et al.* (2009; 2011) and Piga *et al.* (2010a). Note that some publications use a slightly different definition for this ratio (Pucéat *et al.* 2004). Since these peaks correlate to the amount of carbonate and phosphate, this ratio allows one to comment upon changes to the carbonate content bone following burning (Thompson *et al.* 2009).

Combination of both CI and CP has been used to successfully show differences in cremation and funerary practices (Squires *et al.* 2011).

Charcoal analysis

Analysis of a sample of the carbonised wood from *Monte Sirai* necropolis has been undertaken using a metallographic microscope (BX41 Olympus) with reflected light and bright and dark fields with ×5, ×20, ×50 magnifications. For the identification the three anatomical sections of a piece fragmented were observed by hand. Each section allowed us to observe the cell structure which characterises the taxa. Cell structure characteristics are described on the basis of a reference collection (in this case the Schweingruber (1990) wood anatomy atlas).

Discussion

In the tomb 252, cremated fragments and remains of an individual, probably male, appeared acceptably relatable to the skeleton. The markers to determine age are limited to the epiphyses and the state of the cranial sutures. Concerning the first, the humeral, femoral and tibial epiphyses show no trace of the epiphyseal line. On the other hand, the coronal obliteration shows an onset of intracranial suture subtracting exocraneal at fully open and so are the rest of sutures.

Overall, both markers suggest that this is a fairly young adult, but we cannot go further. (The epiphysis fusion is observed in the range 14–18 years old for women and in 16–19 years old for men; Krenzer 2006). With regard to biological sex, the orbital rim, the maxilla and mandible, and the epiphyses of the bones of the forearms all show a gracile nature. The pelvis shows a narrow sciatic notch, typical of male individuals, although bone shrinkage and fragmentation of the cortex may have caused some changes. The diameter of the left femoral head (42.20 mm) is intermediate, although the bicondilar width (73.35 mm) falls within the range of an individual male (Krenzer 2006). Again, shrinkage can have an impact here, but generally this is to mask males as females (Thompson 2002; Gonçalves *et al.* 2013).

No major morphological changes are observed related to arthritic problems or anomalies due to special pathologies. However the presence of *cribra orbitalia* (Subirà *et al.* 1999) in the right orbital roof and Schmorl nodules in at least two vertebral bodies is worth of note; the former being an affliction of childhood.

In the centre of the grave, next to an offering dish (Fig. 5.5), we can clearly see the left proximal femoral epiphysis, as well as remains relevant to the diaphysis and distal epiphysis of the femur and proximal tibia epiphysis in a situation corresponding.

Two diaphyseal bone fragments of the upper extremities are observed in the northern part of the grave, particularly the proximal epiphysis and diaphysis of the left ulna (Fig. 5.6).

Overall, it is possible to reconstruct the original situation of the body, oriented north–south (head to toe). Bone fragments corresponding to the left half of the body (ulna, coxal, femur and tibia) were found in the western half of the tomb retaining some joints (coxal, femur, tibia and femur, left), and the bones of the right half of the body (the proximal epiphysis of right humerus, the proximal fragment of the right olecranon base of radium, the proximal region of right femur with surgical neck and neck anatomy) in the opposite side, which is an anomaly when one considers the usual cremation of the body in supine position. In fact it seems impossible that all the bones from one part of the body move to the opposite side after sinking through the pyre or afterwards when the remains are in the bottom of the grave. This strongly suggests a deliberate deposition of the body in a prone position (Guirguis *et al.* 2011b; Piga *et al.* 2012). As further evidence we observe that the front of the distal left femur shows blackening from contact with charcoal, a situation which, in the case of the supine position of the body, should have been found in the reverse side (Fig. 5.6, detail C).

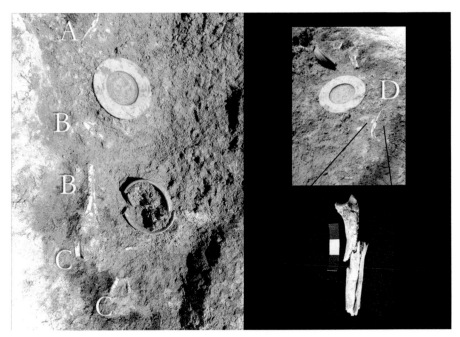

Fig. 5.5: Tomb 252 which shows the arrangement of various bones compatible with: ulna (AD), femur (B) and tibia (C).

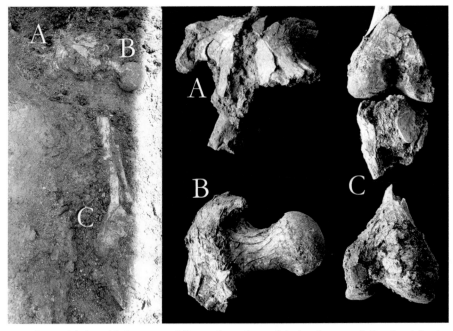

Fig. 5.6: Left coxal (A) and left proximal femoral epiphysis (B), diaphysis and distal epiphysis of the left femur and proximal epiphysis of the left tibia (C), in situ and in the laboratory.

The prone position in the burials is generally rare although some graves have been found with this position. Caroline Arcini (2009), in her first global study of prone burials, suggests that it was a practice used in all societies to indicate disrespect or humiliation of the dead. According to Simmer (1982), the prone position may be related to fear or reverence for the dead. Brothwell (1982) suggests another explanation for this and other special positions that may be associated with hasty burials or deaths in battles, in which the phenomenon of *rigor mortis* prevents any manipulation of the body. Other authors think that the reasons may be in a ritual, ceremonial, or perhaps reflects a position related to deliberate irreverence, neglect or absence of the person responsible for burial (McWhirr *et al.* 1982). Some burials indicate that the practice is probably linked to different social status and religious beliefs (Murphy 2008); indeed the correspondence of individuals buried in prone position with marked signs of violence or infectious diseases such as leprosy or tuberculosis has been highlighted (McWhirr *et al.* 1982; Philpott, 1992; Boylston *et al.* 2000; Prosper and Cerdà 2002; Murphy 2008). In Spain, France, Germany and Italy there are very few cases, mostly of Roman period. In the region of Veneto (Italy) especially the practice of burying the dead in the prone position appears to be a tradition of long duration; in fact Veneto is the territory in which the oldest cases in Italy have been found (Zamboni and Zanoni 2010). The case of Monte Sirai turns out to be the oldest in Europe as well as in the entire world, according to all the examined cases by Arcini (2009), and is the first case of cremation in which the body has been found in a prone position (Piga *et al.* 2012; Guirguis *et al.* 2011b).

The reasons that justify this particular position, perhaps linked to social factors, are difficult to understand because of their specificity. No other apparent case of anomalous deposition was observed in the *Monte Sirai* necropolis and there are no other known cases in Sardinia at the moment.

It was observed in the *Monte Sirai* necropolis that several graves with the skeletons were covered with rocks. This was interpreted as a ritual gesture intended to contain the spirits of the dead within the tomb (called *Rephaim*) so they could not disturb the living (Bartoloni 2000), in keeping with the interpretation of Simmer (1982). Therefore, a possible explanation might be related to the wrapping of the body in a shroud, as described in the rite of primary incineration by Bartoloni (2000), and a subsequent wrong? deposition in the pyre. Another plausible hypothesis may be the deliberate prone deposition of the body during the incineration ritual, perhaps to emphasise some diversity of the individual within the community. It is interesting to note, in all of this discussion, that tomb 252 is not removed from other supine burials at this site, and has therefore not been made peripheral in terms of the actual burial.

XRD/FT-IR analysis

The exceptional state of preservation of almost the entire skeleton belonging to tomb 252 (Fig. 5.7) provides the possibility of assessing the distribution of temperature on representative parts of the whole body, and to determine the possible existence of a central focus.

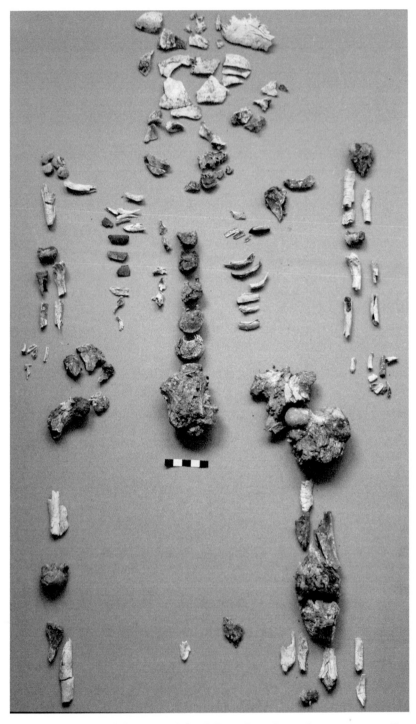

Fig. 5.7: Reconstruction in the laboratory of the skeleton from the tomb 252, exceptionally preserved.

Table 5.1: *Average crystallite size of hydroxyapatite, Splitting Factor, C/P values and estimating the temperatures calculated with both spectrometric techniques according to Piga et al. (2008; 2009; 2010a; in prep.). Both techniques give concordant results.*

Part of the body analysed	Average crystallite size/ (Å) (± 10%)	Est. temp./XRD (Piga *et al.* 2008; 2009)/ °C	SF–(KBr) FT–IR (± 0.05)	SF C/P (±0.05)	Est. temp./IR–KBr (Piga *et al.* in prep.)/°C
Cranium	1520	900<T<1000	7.32	0.05	≅ 988
Cranium	1900	1000	6.33	0.07	≅ 992
Mandible	2297	1000	6.18	0.06	≅ 985
Mandible	1400	900	6.06	0.07	≅ 977
Mandible (blue)	230	700	4.32	0.11	≅ 717
Rib	2306	1000	6.93	0.06	≅ 1001
Rib	1350	900	6.31	0.07	≅ 992
Rib (blue)	224	700	4.30	0.13	≅ 717
Vertebra	2200	1000	6.66	0.06	≅ 1001
Vertebra	1940	1000	7.16	0.05	≅ 995
Vertebra	1900	1000	6.52	0.03	≅ 998
Vertebra	2248	1000	7.26	0.04	≅ 992
Vertebra	2303	1000	7.21	0.09	≅ 995
Vertebra	1950	1000	7.17	0.07	≅ 995
Vertebra	1870	1000	8.08	0.05	≅ 944
Right ulna	2079	1000	7.08	0.07	≅ 999
Left ulna	1724	1000	6.67	0.10	≅ 1001
Right femur	2316	1000	6.86	0.10	≅ 1002
Right femur	1600	900<T<1000	6.37	0.08	≅ 994
Left femur	1480	900<T<1000	5.58	0.10	< 940
Left tibia	1364	900	6.08	0.09	≅ 980
Left tibia	1140	825	5.46	0.09	≅ 922
Right tibia	1655	900<T<1000	6.68	0.08	≅ 1001

Figure 5.8 shows the experimental XRD patterns of two specimens that shows the greatest difference in terms of crystallinity found in the course of the present investigation.

The data are depicted in the y-axis according to the experimental intensity times the variable $q = 4(\pi/\lambda)\sin\theta$ (logarithmic scale) in order to emphasise the presence of weak peaks, that are very important in diffraction in order to reveal the fine details of the whole structure inspected. The full curves are their relevant fit according to the Rietveld method. The featureless curves represent the background line determined by the numerical procedure. As usual, at the bottom of each pattern we show the band of residuals which supplies a complementary insight of how "good" is the fit with respect to the experimental data, so-called goodness-of-fit. Moreover, the two specimens turned out to be made by a single bioapatite phase and the sequence of bars represents the location of each peak expected on the basis of the monoclinic apatite structure (Elliot *et al.* 1973).

The different degree of crystallinity in the two patterns is related to the different peak sharpening clearly evaluable from the direct comparison of the data. In turn, the degree of sharpening has been used to estimate the temperature to which the bioapatite of bones were treated during the cremation process.

Table 5.1 shows in detail the results obtained through the techniques of XRD/FT–IR, according to the methodology established by Piga *et al.* (2008; 2009; 2010a; in prep.) for both techniques and their application on burnt remains (Piga *et al.* 2010b; Squires *et al.* 2011). Both the X-Ray crystallinity and the SF value of the v_4 phospate band converge to similar

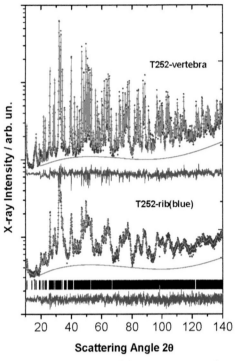

Fig. 5.8: *A comparison of the XRD patterns from blue mandible and vertebra showing the different degree of peak broadening enabling to estimate a different temperature reached by the bones after the cremation process. See text for details about the curves.*

values of temperature, which is further supported by those deducible from C/P of v_3 CO_3^{2-} and v_3 PO_4^{3-} bands, used in the study of cremated bones. In particular, the C/P values are in the range between 0.04 and 0.10, suggesting an intense and/or complete cremation carried out to the body (Squires *et al.* 2011). However, in just two cases (blue rib and blue mandible) we observe a C/P values of 0.13 and 0.11 respectively, which indicates less intense cremation, in agreement with the lower crystallinity values measured by SF FT-IR and XRD, respectively.

As it can be seen from the FT-IR (Fig. 5.9), the carbonate bands in the range 1400–1500 cm⁻¹ can be referred either to the main band of the phosphate group v_3 in the range 1000–1100 cm⁻¹ or to the phosphate v_4 band in the range 500–700 cm⁻¹. An additional carbonate band occurs at *c.* 870 cm⁻¹. In any case, the figure points out a sensible difference between the two cases examined such as the blue rib (bottom curve) and the vertebra (top curve) in terms of carbonate group content. It can be surmised that, in the former case, the bone was subjected to a mild thermal treatment

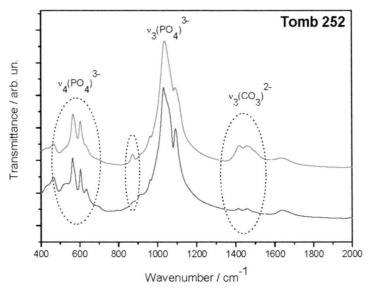

Fig. 5.9: The FT-IR patterns of two cremates specimens: blue rib (upper curve) and the vertebra (bottom curve). The spectra are reported in the wave-number v range from 400 to 2000 cm⁻¹. It is possible to recognize three main groups of band in the range 500–700 cm⁻¹, 1000–1200 cm⁻¹ and 1400–1600 cm⁻¹, which are generally assigned to the energy mode v4 of phosphate groups, v3 of phosphate groups and to the v3 of carbonate groups respectively. The figure points out a sensible difference between the two cases in terms of carbonate group content. Note also the presence of a shoulder at 633 cm⁻¹ in the vertebra 4 spectra, that indicates a higher cremation temperature on this specimen.

(temperature estimated of 700°C) while in the latter all the indices extracted suggest a stronger thermal treatment (equivalent to 1000°C or above).

Data obtained with the two techniques are almost concordant, except in a few cases (mandible, rib and left tibia) where the temperatures obtained with the analysis of FT-IR are a little higher. These differences do not exceed 100°C and are not worth of further interpretation since they may be thought to coincide within their experimental uncertainty.

The values of the splitting factor SF determined by the FT-IR technique in the bone remains are systematically much higher than the values of the laboratory calibration (Piga *et al.* 2008; 2009; 2010a; Thompson *et al.* 2009; 2011). This may be due to at least three reasons:

1. a "real" cremation differs from a cremation in the laboratory for various factors: the presence of organs and soft tissues (which can act as additional fuel), the physical characteristics of the cadaver, such as its weight (Bohnert 1998; Shannon 2011), etc. So a real fire can be much more intense and longer-lasting that a heat treatment in a muffle, and that bones have effectively undergone a heat treatment to temperatures over 1000°C.

2. the bones have been subjected to further processes of "aging" as a result of the subsequent burial, that are superimposed on the thermal process and consequently in the values of the crystallinity index.

3. differences can also result from the use of different equipment and sample preparation (Piga *et al.* 2010a; Thompson 2011).

    Therefore, we conclude that the skeletal remains of tomb 252 have been treated with fire in a temperature range of 825–1000°C, across the whole of the body, while some specific parts (see the evaluation for the blue mandible and rib in Table 5.1) may have been subjected to sensibly? lower temperature values (e.g. 700°C) because of uncompleted combustion processes related to the oxygen available and/or to dynamics of the fire influenced by contact of the body with the wood branches.

Charcoal analysis

The taxonomic identification shows that the carbonised wood of tomb 250 is an evergreen *Quercus* ssp. This taxonomic category includes *Quercus ilex* (holm oak), *Quecus coccifera* (kermes oak) and *Quercus suber* (cork oak) that, due to cell structure similarities, cannot be distinguished. This wood has a transversal section characterised by a pore distribution in flames, tangential section showing uniseriate and multiseriated rays (Fig. 5.10).

Quercus suber usually presents larger pores than *Quercus ilex* and *Q. coccifera* (Heinz *et al.* 1988) and the analysed sample show large pores and clear thylloses, which appear more often in *Quercus suber* (Fig. 5.11).

All the physical characters shown by the fragment permit us to determine it as *Quercus ilex/suber* type. *Quercus ilex* and *Quercus suber* have an important economic interest and are nowadays present in Sardinia (Vogiatzakis and Careddu 2003). The lack

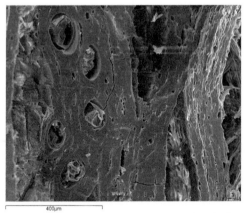 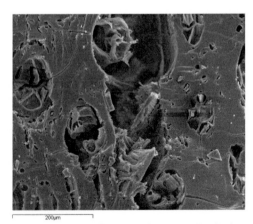

Fig. 5.10: Transversal section of Quercus ilex/suber *from Monte Sirai showing pores and multiseriated rays with vitrified pattern of the cell structure (×120).*

Fig. 5.11: Transversal section of Quercus ilex/suber *from Monte Sirai showing pores with thyloses and vitrified pattern of the cell structure (×200).*

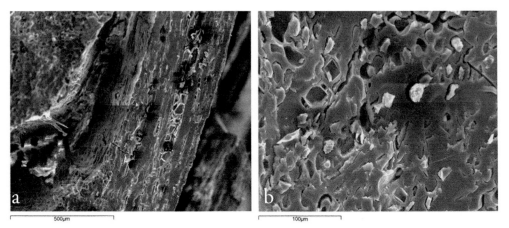

Fig. 5.12: (a) tangential section of Quercus ilex/suber *from Monte Sirai showing multiseriated rays with vitrified pattern of the cell structure (×100); (b) tangential section of* Quercus ilex/suber *from Monte Sirai showing a vitrified pattern of the cell structure (×400).*

of a specific morphology of the object does not permit further interpretation on its precise use or origin. Additionally the cell structure shows alterations which modify its appearance. The main alteration is vitrification, which is not homogeneous in the entire surface (Fig. 5.12a andb).

This alteration causes a glassy appearance of the charcoal noticeable by the fusion of the cells. The cause of the alteration has been traditionally related to high temperatures and combustion in closed environments (Théry-Parisot 2001), although recent studies show that there is no clear relation between temperature and vitrification, but is probably due to several processes affecting wood before and/ or after combustion (McParland *et al.* 2010).

Rite of semi-combustion

The most recent excavation of the site has brought to light 30 tombs contextually attributed to a period from the early sixth to the early 5th centuries BC, which coincides with the beginning of the Carthago influence in Sardinia. In this type of interred burials the skeletal remains, sometimes of two superimposed bodies, were discovered in a primary position and with very good anatomical connection (Fig. 5.13). In some bodies a dark brown colour was observed on the bones that may be attributed to a burning process (Fig. 5.14).

In order to ascertain objectively whether all the bodies were subjected to burning and to what extent, the bones recovered from tombs were investigated both by the X-ray powder diffraction (XRD) and Fourier Transform Infrared (FT-IR) techniques.

In Figure 5.15 we show some experimental diffraction patterns (data points) and the relevant Rietveld fit (full lines) of representative specimens that are of peculiar significance for the *Monte Sirai* necropolis situation brought to light in the excavations.

Fig. 5.13: These two tombs supply an example of human bone remains in primary position and good anatomic connection (photos courtesy of Dr Michele Guirguis).

Fig. 5.14: A detail of a femur with a dark brown colour suggesting that the bone was subjected to a firing process.

As expected, the XRD points to the presence of HA as the main mineralogical phase, which is accompanied by varying quantities of Calcite ($CaCO_3$) up to a maximum level of 31 wt%.

Sometimes, weak quantities of quartz and clay minerals were also observed at the limit of the technique detection. At the moment we attribute calcite to an exogenous origin with respect to the osseous material, since the presence of carbonates units CO_3^{2-} that may substitute for phosphates groups PO_4^{3-} in the apatite structure and that can be likely separated during the deposition times of the bones, may amount to no more than 7–8 wt% (Wopenka and Pasteris 2005). The varying amount of calcite found in some *Monte Sirai* bones may be related to the tufa ground that was filling the excavated sepulchres capped on top by flat stones.

It is likely that soil penetrated into the burial chamber through the interstices at the top due to weathering effects. The fact that small amphora and other ceramics with narrow necks were discovered empty inside, further supports this hypothesis.

In Figure 5.16 we report the IR bands of phosphate groups for the specimens there indicated, ordered according to increasing values of SF. Note that, for the bone of Tomb 8–2, the band at 634 cm^{-1}, normally assigned to the OH$^-$ group, appears to emerge more clearly than in the other samples.

Because of the sigmoidal behaviour of experimental data located at *c.* 750°C, both techniques are not reliable for assessing cremations carried out at temperature lower than 500°C. In any case, the FT-IR and XRD data confirm unambiguously that all the

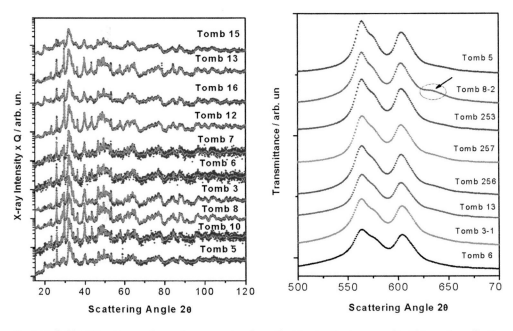

Fig. 5.15: (left) XRD patterns of some bones coming from the Monte Sirai *necropolis. This entire collection of XRD patterns points out to the important approximations assumed in devising the microstructure properties of Hydroxylapatite (HA) just from one or few selected peak profiles. With the Rietveld method the goodness of the fit between calculated and experimental pattern is measured in terms of numerical agreement factors so this approach appears the most complete for evaluating simultaneously experimental data quality (i.e. signal-to-noise-ratio) and/or credibility of model assumptions.*

Fig. 5.16: (right) The IR bands of phosphate groups for some of the bone remains from tombs here indicated. The spectra are ordered on increasing SF factor. Note that for tomb 8-2 the shoulder at 634 cm^{-1} appears more defined with respect to other specimens.

bodies brought to light in the recent *Monte Sirai* excavations (except for tombs 9, 15, 281 and 293) were burnt. The specimens from tombs 271, 279, 281 and 293 show an average domain size and SF-IR in close agreement with values determined in inhumed bones (Piga *et al.* 2008; 2010a).

This observation permits us to exclude an important role of diagenetic effects in the sharpening of XRD lines that was advanced in the case of ancient bodies buried in acid grounds (Sillen and Le Gros 1991). Actually rhe limestone (calcite)-based ground of our burials is supposed to maintain a chemically alkaline character to the local environment (pH≈8.2) that should preserve the microstructure of bones rather than deteriorating it in terms of apparent growth of crystallites with consequent false attribution to a temperature effect.

Overall, all bodies seem to have been burned to the temperatures range 400–850°C. In the case of tomb 263 we determined a fire temperature of 300°C but this value has a relatively high variance associated because, as stated above, below 500°C both XRD line broadening and FT-IR spectroscopy may not be very precise. The estimated temperature values retrieved from the SF of FT-IR bands are reported in column 6 of Table 5.2 and appear to be in overall agreement with the XRD determinations. Within the uncertainty level of experimental error, it is possible that various discrepancies (e.g: Tomb 265) may derive from small systematic errors in our calibration procedure.

In any case, the precise modalities according to which the bodies were burned are not totally clear because neither traces of combustion nor charcoal or wood were recognised at the bottom and walls of burials as well as in the funerary ceramic miscellanea. Because of this absence it is admissible that the bodies were first burned and only later buried in the tomb. An alternative possibility is that the bodies were first burned in the "ustrinum" place (discovered close to the grave area during the recent excavations) and later transferred and deposed into the burials together with the funerary items. However, preservation of the anatomic connection during transportation appears difficult to justify entirely, unless the combustion process occurred with limited time of exposure at the maximum fire intensity.

Nevertheless, it is still possible that an intense fire carried out in the "ustrinum" for a short time did not completely destroy the bodies, allowing their subsequent transportation to the tomb.

Other literature on Phoenician and Punic customs (Benichou Safar 1982; Rodero Riaza 2001) does not report observations similar to the case of *Monte Sirai* discussed here. In any case, it is possible that the typical rite documented here was simply aiming at eliminating the fleshy parts of the bodies. If this is the case, we could identify the rite as a hygienic/cleaning process, primarily be adopted for deaths due to contagious diseases and/or infection pathologies. However, even the simple hygienic motivation cannot be entirely convincing. The care given to the bodies, the valuable items found in the tombs and the persistent adoption of this practice across the period suggest that the "semi-combustion" process had also a symbolic motivation, probably related to faiths well-established in the community of the necropolis.

Table 5.2: XRD average crystallite size, their estimated temperature, FT–IR SF and its estimated temperature for the bones belonging to Monte Sirai *necropolis.*

Sample code	Part of the body examined	Average crystallize size/(Å) (± 10%)	Est. temp./°C with XRD technique	Splitting Factor (SF) calculated (± 0.05)	Est. temp./°C with FT–IR technique
Tomb 230	Femur	223	≅ 600	3.51	504
Tomb 242	Femur	203	≅ 400	3.25	426
Tomb 248	Femur	224	≅ 600	3.53	≅ 510
Tomb 253	Femur	264	< 750	4.45	750
Tomb 245	Femur	241	650	3.83	≅ 600
Tomb 256	Tibia	288	≅ 700	4.26	≅ 703
Tomb 257	Femur	240	650	4.20	694
Tomb 255	Diaphysis	205	400	3.27	≅ 430
Tomb 267	Femur	233	≅ 650	4.23	700
Tomb 271	Foot phalanx	169	Not burned	2.99	Not burned
Tomb 262	Humerus	252	650	3.67	< 575
Tomb 236	Humerus	245	650	4.21	≅ 695
Tomb 263	Humerus	187	≅ 300	3.25	≅ 426
Tomb 265	Fibula	260	650<T<750	5.00	854
Tomb 266	Sacrum	250	650	3.61	≅ 530
Tomb 277	Cranium (parietal)	220	600<T< 700	3.59	≅ 530
Tomb 278	Fibula	222	600<T< 700	3.71	< 575
Tomb 279	Femur	172	Not burned	2.99	Not burned
Tomb 268	Rib	251	≅ 650	4.20	694
Tomb 269	Femur	248	≅ 650	4.45	750
Tomb 274	Fibula	258	≅ 650	3.96	≅ 640
Tomb 273	Femur	220	600<T< 700	3.59	529
Tomb 275	Femur	202	500	3.97	≅ 640
Tomb 280	Femur	218	≅ 650	3.55	613
Tomb 281	Cranium (parietal)	169	Not burned	2.98	Not burned
Tomb 282	Cranium (parietal)	215	≅ 650	3.53	≅ 523
Tomb 283	Cranium (temporal)	218	≅ 650	3.54	≅ 510
Tomb 284	Cranium (temporal)	229	700	3.84	600
Tomb 285	Cranium (parietal)	237	≅ 650	3.59	≅ 529
Tomb 287	Humerus	209	≅ 500	3.32	449
Tomb 292	Humerus	175	Not burned	2.97	Not burned
Tomb 293	Humerus	212	≅ 650	3.50	505
Tomb 296	Cranium (parietal)	205	500	3.24	426

We may hypothesise that in the sixth–fifth centuries BC, at the start of Punic domination, part of the population of *Monte Sirai*, which had strong ties with the original Phoenician community from the near-east Mediterranean, maintained a strong affiliation for the funerary practice of cremation. This seems demonstrated by the whole temporal evolution in the necropolis of the fifth century that evidenced the coexistence of a row of tombs with hypogeal rooms and of another row with ground burials.

Conclusions

In the Phenician-Punic necropolis of *Monte Sirai* there is rich and detailed archaeological evidence of different and peculiar funeral rites. The recent excavations (still ongoing) have brought to light 30 tombs, contextually attributed to a period from early sixth to the early fifth centuries BC, showing the skeletons in a primary position and fine anatomic articulation.

A comparative analysis using X-ray diffraction and Fourier Transform-Infrared spectroscopy established that all the bodies examined, except four cases, were burned before burial in a temperature range of 400–850°C. This investigation has permitted us to ascertain with very fine detail the conversion from incineration rite to inhumation, pointing out the practice of an intermediate process of "semi-combustion". This funerary rite, perhaps limited to the period of early fifth century BC, appears to be peculiar to just this site.

Another extremely interesting case concerns the case of tomb 252 that contained the cremated remains of an individual, probably male. Comparison of the excavation records alongside reconstruction of the bone material itself makes it clear that the individual was cremated in a prone position. This is the first case of prone cremation reported in the literature. The exceptional state of preservation of almost the entire skeleton allows us to determine the distribution of temperature on representative parts of the whole body; moreover the discovery of a very well preserved fragment of burnt wood, in the nearby tomb 250, allowed us to analyse the type of wood used for the cremation of the bodies. All the physical characteristics showed by the fragment permits us to determine it as *Quercus ilex/suber* type.

Acknowledgements

The authors thank: Prof. Piero Bartoloni (Università di Sassari, Italy) for having made available the bones analysed in this study and for the detailed archaeological context, Prof Stefano Enzo (Università di Sassari, Italy), Prof Assumpció Malgosa (Universitat Autonoma de Barcelona, Spain) and Dr Tim Thompson (School of Science & Engineering, Teesside University, UK) for their scientific support.

References

Arcini, C. 2009. Buried faced down: prone burials. *Current Archaeology* 20, 30–5.

Bartoloni, P. 2000. *La necropoli di Monte Sirai.* Roma: Collezione di Studi Fenici 41.

Benichou Safar, H. 1982. Les tombes puniques de Carthage. Topographie, structures, inscriptions et rites funéraires. In: *Etudes d'Antiquités Africaines.* Paris: CNRS, 237–48.

Bohnert, M., Rost, T. and Pollak, S. 1998. The degree of destruction of human bodies in relation to the duration of the fire. *Forensic Science International* 95, 11–21.

Botto, M. 1994. Monte Sirai 1. Analisi del materiale anforico relativo alle campagne di scavo 1990 e 1991. *Rivista di Studi Fenici* 22, 83–116.

Boylston, A., Knüsel, C. J. and Roberts, C. A. 2000. Investigation of a Romano-British rural ritual in Bedford, England. *Journal of Archaeological Science* 27, 241–54.

Brothwell, D. R. 1981. *Digging up Bones. The Excavation, Treatment, and Study of Human Skeletal Remains.* Ithaca, N.Y. and London: Cornell University Press.

Elliott, J. C., Mackie, P. E. and Young, R. A. 1973. Monoclinic hydroxyapatite. *Science* 180, 1055–7.

Enzo, S., Fagherazzi, G., Benedetti, A. and Polizzi, S. 1988. A profile-fitting procedure for analysis of broadened X-ray diffraction peaks. I Methodology. *Journal of Applied Crystallography* 21, 536–42.

Enzo, S., Bazzoni, M., Mazzarello, V., Piga, G., Bandiera, P. and Melis, P. 2007. A study by thermal treatment and X-ray powder diffraction on burnt fragmented bones from Tombs II, IV and IX belonging to the hypogeic necropolis of "Sa Figu" near Ittiri-SS (Sardinia-Italy). *Journal of Archaeological Science* 34, 1731–7.

Gonçalves, D., Thompson, T. J. U. and Cunha, E. 2013. Osteometric sex determination of burned human skeletal remains. *Journal of Forensic and Legal Medicine* 20, 906–11.

Guirguis, M. 2005. Storia degli studi e degli scavi a Sulky e a Monte Sirai. *Rivista di Studi Fenici* XXXIII, 13–30.

Guirguis, M. 2010. *Necropoli fenicia e punica di Monte Sirai. Indagini archeologiche 2005-2007.* Cagliari: Studi di Storia Antica e di Archeologia 7.

Guirguis, M. 2011. Gli spazi della morte a Monte Sirai (Carbonia–Sardegna). Rituali e ideologie funerarie nella necropoli fenicia e punica (scavi 2005–2010). *Fasti On Line Documents & Research*, 230.

Guirguis, M. 2012. Monte Sirai 2005–2010. Bilanci e prospettive. *Vicino & Medio Oriente* 16, 51–82.

Guirguis, M., Malgosa, A. and Piga, G. 2011. Un caso de posición prona en el la Tumba 252 de incineración primaria de la Necropolis de Monte Sirai (Cerdeña, Italia). *Sardinia, Corsica et Baleares Antiquae–International Journal of Archaeology* IX, 73–86.

Heinz, C., Badal, E., Figueiral, I., Grau, E., Ros Mora, M. T. and Thiébault, S. 1988. Identification des charbons de bois préhistoriques méditerranéens, chronologie et répartition. *PACT* 22(III), 161–72.

Knight, B. 1996. Burns and scalds. In: B. Knight, *Forensic Pathology* (2nd edn). London: Edward Arnold, 305–17.

Koon, H. E. C., Nicholson, R. A. and Collins, M. J. 2003. A practical approach to the identification of low temperature heated bone using TEM. *Journal of Archaeological Science* 30, 1393–9.

Krenzer, U. 2006. *Compendio de métodos antropológico forenses para la reconstrucción del perfil osteo-biológico. Tomo II: Métodos para la determinación del sexo.* Guatemala: CAFCA.

Lutterotti, L. and Bortolotti, M. 2003. Object oriented programming and fast computation techniques in Maud, a program for powder diffraction analysis written in java. *IUCr: Compcomm Newsletter* 1, 43–50.

McParland, L. C., Collinson, M. E., Scott, A. C., Campbell, G and Veal, R. 2010. Is vitrification in charcoal a result of high temperature burning of wood? *Journal of Archaeological Science* 37 (10), 2679–87.

McWhirr, A., Viner, L. and Wells, C. 1982. *Romano-British Cementeries at Cirencester. Cirencester Excavations II.* Cirencester: Cirencester Excavation Committee.

Murphy, E. M. (ed.) 2008. *Deviant Burial in the Archaeological Record.* Oxford: Oxbow Books.

Olsen, J., Heinemeier, J., Bennike, P., Krause, C., Hornstrup, K. M. and Thrane, H. 2008. Characterisation and blind testing of radiocarbon dating of cremated bone. *Journal of Archaeological Science* 35, 791–800.

Philpott, R. 1992. Burial practices in Roman Britain. *A Survey of Grave Treatment and Furnishing AD 43-410*. Oxford: British Archaeological Report 219.

Piga G. 2012. The use of spectroscopy and diffraction techniques in the study of bones and implications in Anthropology, Paleontology and Forensic sciences. PhD Thesis. Biblioteca de Comunicación y Hemeroteca general, Universitat Autónoma de Barcelona. www.educacion.es/teseo/mostrarRef.do?ref=996840

Piga, G., Malgosa, A., Thompson, T. J. U. and Enzo, S. 2008. A new calibration of the XRD technique for the study of archaeological burnt remains. *Journal of Archaeological Science* 35, 2171–8.

Piga, G., Thompson, T. J. U., Malgosa, A. and Enzo, S. 2009. The potential of X-Ray Diffraction (XRD) in the analysis of burned remains from forensic contexts. *Journal of Forensic Sciences* 54(3), 534–9.

Piga, G., Guirguis, M., Bartoloni, P., Malgosa, A. and Enzo, S. 2010a. A funerary rite study in the Phoenician-Punic necropolis of Mount Sirai (Carbonia-Sardinia-Italy), *International Journal of Osteoarchaeology* 20, 144–57.

Piga, G., Hernández-Gasch, J. H., Malgosa, A., Ganadu, M. L. and Enzo, S. 2010b. Cremation practices coexisting at the "S'Illot des Porros" Necropolis during the Second Iron Age in the Balearic Islands (Spain). *Homo* 61, 440–52.

Piga, G., Malgosa, A., Thompson, T. J. U., Guirguis, M. and Enzo, S. 2012. A unique case of prone position in the primary cremation Tomb 252 of Monte Sirai necropolis (Carbonia, Sardinia, Italy). *International Journal of Osteoarchaeology* (DOI: 10.1002/oa.2270).

Piga, G,, Thompson, T. J. U., Solinas, M. G., Brunetti, A., Malgosa, A. and Enzo, S. in prep. Advantages and limitations of the Fourier Transform Infrared Spectroscopy (FT-IR) in the study of burned bones. *Journal of Forensic Sciences*.

Polo Cerda, M. and Garcia Prosper, E. 2002. Ritual, violencia y enfermedad. Los enterramientos en decúbito prono de la necrópolis fundacional de Valentia. *Saguntum* 34, 137–48.

Pucéat, E., Reynard, B. and Lécuyer, C. 2004. Can crystallinity be used to determine the degree of chemical alteration of biogenic apatites? *Chemical Geology* 205, 83–97.

Rietveld, H. 1967. Line profiles of neutron powder-diffraction peaks for structure refinement. *Acta Crystallographica* 22, 151–2.

Rodero Riaza, A. 2001. El ritual funerario en las necrópolis coloniales andaluzas. In: García Huerta, R. and Morales Hervás, F. J. (eds), *Arqueología funeraria: las necrópolis de incineración*. Cuidad Real, 79–90.

Rogers, K. D. and Daniels, P. 2002. An X-ray diffraction study of the effects of heat treatment on bone mineral microstructure. *Biomaterials* 23, 2577–85.

Rogers, K. D., Beckett, S., Kuhn, S., Chamberlain, A. and Clement, J. 2010. Contrasting the crystallinity indicators of heated and diagenetically altered bone mineral. *Palaeogeography, Palaeoclimateology, Palaeoecology* 296, 125–9.

Schweingruber, F. H. 1990. *Anatomie europäischer Hölzer ein Atlas zur Bestimmung europäischer Baum-, Strauch- und Zwergstrauchhölzer/Anatomy of European woods an atlas for the identification of European trees shrubs and dwarf shrubs*. Stuttgart: Verlag Paul Haupt.

Shemesh, A. 1990. Crystallinity and diagenesis of sedimentary apatites. *Geochimica and Cosmochimica Acta* 54, 2433–8.

Sillen, A. and Le Gros, R. 1991. Solubility profiles of synthetic apatites and of modern and fossil bones. *Journal of Archaeological Science* 18, 385–97.

Simmer, A. 1982. Le prelevement des cranes dans l'est de la France a l'epoque merovingienne, *Archeologie Medievale* 12, 35–49.

Squires, K. E., Thompson, T. J. U., Islam, M and Chamberlain, A. 2011. The application of histomorphometry and Fourier Transform Infrared Spectroscopy to the analysis of early Anglo-Saxon burned bone. *Journal of Archaeological Science* 38, 2399–409.

Subirà, M. E., Alesan, A. and Malgosa, A. 1992. Cribra orbitalia y déficit nutricional. Estudios de elementos traza. *Munibe* 8, 153–8.

Théry-Parisot, I. 2001. *Économie des combustibles au Paléolithique*. Paris: Dossier de Documentation Archéologique 20 CNRS.

Thompson, T. J. U. 2002. The assessment of sex in cremated individuals: some cautionary notes. *Canadian Society of Forensic Science Journal* 35, 49–56.

Thompson, T. J. U., Gauthier, M. and Islam, M. 2009. The application of a new method of Fourier Transform Infrared Spectroscopy to the analysis of burned bone. *Journal of Archaeological Science* 36, 910–14.

Thompson, T. J. U., Islam, M., Piduru, K. and Marcel, A. 2011. An investigation into the internal and external variables acting on crystallinity index using Fourier Transform Infrared Spectroscopy on unaltered and burned bone. *Palaeogeography, Palaeoclimateology, Palaeoecology* 299, 168–74.

Thompson, T. J. U., Islam, M. and Bonniere, M. 2013. A new statistical approach for determining the crystallinity of heat-altered bone mineral from FTIR spectra. *Journal of Archaeological Science* 40, 416–22.

Vogiatzakis, I. N. and Careddu, M. B. 2003. Mapping the distribution and extent of *Quercus suber* habitats in Sardinia: a literature review and a proposed methodology. *Geographical Paper* 171, 1–30.

Weiner, S. and Bar-Yosef, O. 1990. States of preservation of bones from prehistoric sites in the Near East: a survey. *Journal of Archaeological Science* 17, 187–96.

Wopenka, B. and Pasteris, J. D. 2005. A mineralogical perspective on the apatite in bone. *Materials Science and Engineering* C25, 131–43.

Wright, L. E. and Schwarcz, H. P. 1996. Infrared and isotopic evidence for diagenesis of bone apatite at Dos Pilas, Guatemala: palaeodietary implications. *Journal of Archaeological Science* 23, 933–44.

Zamboni, L. and Zanoni, V. 2010. Giaciture non convenzionali in Italia nord-occidentale durante l'età del Ferro. *Quaderni di archeologia dell'Emilia Romagna* 28, 147–60.

Chapter 6

The funerary practice of cremation at *Augusta Emerita* (Mérida, Spain) during High Empire: contributions from the anthropological analysis of burned human bone

Filipa Cortesão Silva

Introduction

Augusta Emerita (actually Mérida, Spain) was a Roman colony founded by the Emperor Augustus in 25 BC (Saquete 2004) to allow veteran soldiers from legions *V Alaudae* and *X Gemina* to settle following their successful military service on the campaigns carried out against Cantabrians and Astures (Arce 2004; Feijoo and Alba 2008). According to archaeological and ancient sources this city was an entirely new build – although signs of settlements dated from Final Neolithic, Copper Age and Final Bronze Age have been found (Jiménez 2011; Mateos 2001). Moreover, in 19 BC, *Augusta Emerita* (Fig. 6.1) became the capital of *Lusitania* (Arce 2004, 9), one of the three Roman provinces of *Hispania* (currently Iberian Peninsula) during the High Empire.

The strategic location of *Augusta Emerita* and its role as an administration and economic centre (Saquete 2011) allowed the construction of buildings like the theatre, amphitheatre (Mateos and Pizzo 2011) and the circus (Gijón and Montalvo 2011) whose magnificence led to the nickname "Rome in Spain" or "Little Rome" by chroniclers and travellers (Mora 2004, 15). Mérida had been declared UNESCO World Heritage Site in 1993 (Mora 2004) and its numerous preserved roman buildings and infrastructures are frequently visited by tourists.

Over the last 100 years intense archaeological activity (Álvarez and Mateos 2010a) and research, including the organisation of scientific events, expositions and publications (e.g. Alba and Álvarez 2012; Álvarez and Mateos 2010b; 2011; Álvarez 2011; Mateos 2011; Palma 2010; Vélazquez 2011) were carried out by institutions such as the *Consorcio de la Ciudad Monumental, Histórico-Artística Y Arqueológica de Mérida*, the *Museo Nacional de Arte Romano* and the *Instituto de Arqueología de Mérida*.

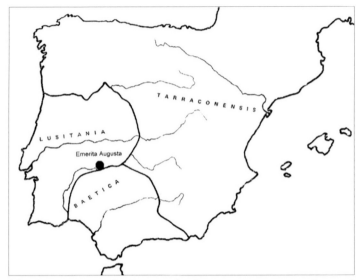

Fig. 6.1: *Map of the Iberian Peninsula showing the three Roman provinces during the High Empire and the location of* Augusta Emerita *in Lusitania (after Sánchez, 2004, 102).*

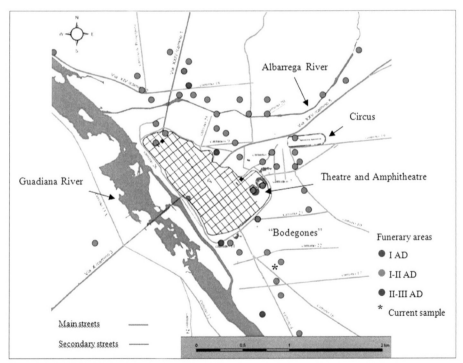

Fig. 6.2: *The distribution of* Augusta Emerita *funerary areas, from the first to the third centuries AD, including the sample of the present study (star). Map elaborated by Juana Márquez Pérez with some modifications.*

The funerary areas had been identified in the outskirts of the Roman city (Fig. 6.2), near the main roads (Bendala 2004; Gijón 2006/2007; Márquez 2008; 2012a; Nogales and Márquez 2002; Murciano 2010). Most of the burials dated between first to second centuries AD are cremations although some inhumations were also found (Bejarano 2004; Nogalez and Márquez 2002). From the third century AD onwards the opposite scenario occurs with the predominance of inhumations (Ayerbe 2001; Ayerbe and Márquez 1998; Márquez 1998; 2006; 2012a; Nogalez and Márquez 2002; Sánchez 2001).

The present paper aims to discuss the cremation burials with preserved human remains, dated to the first–second centuries AD (Márquez 2005a; 2005b; 2005c; 2012b), located in the southern area of Mérida, on a place nowadays called "Los Bodegones" (Márquez 2007).

The funerary context

Based on the detailed information from archaeological reports, burial photos and so on (Márquez 2005a; 2005b; 2005c; 2012b) it was possible to develop a picture of the main characteristics of the 60 cremation burials (Fig. 6.2), corresponding to archaeological intervention numbers 5036–5039 (totaling 2816.21 m²). From those interventions 18 inhumations had also been studied. One of the burials included both rites, namely, an urned cremation and an inhumation (Silva *et al.* 2008; 2014).

The majority of the graves were set in rectangular pits (n=51; 85%) that could be single (n=31) or double (n=20), three had a small rounded pit (5%) and for six burials (10%) it was impossible to identified any pit. Seven rectangular pit burials (13.7%) also presented a brick box (Fig. 6.3). The cremated bones were found unurned in 52 (86.7%) burials (which in 46 cases had a pit and/or brick box) and urned (Fig. 6.4) in eight (13.3%) (seven in ceramic urns and one in a *dolium*). Most of the bone deposits concern primary cremation burials (n=33; 55%), even though 20 (33.3%) were secondary and for seven (11.7%) it was impossible to determine their nature.

Fig. 6.3: Example of a brick box cremation burial (5037/A3): A) At the beginning of excavation process. B) The ongoing of the excavation shows a double pit. Juana Márquez Pérez photos.

Methods of analysis

The anthropological analysis followed standard procedures (Buikstra and Ubelaker 1994; Duday *et al.* 2000; McKinley 2004a).

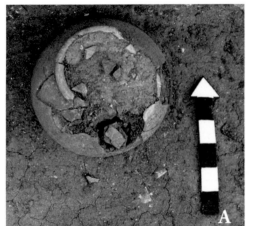

Fig. 6.4: Urned cremation burials: A) Ceramic urn (5036/A21) and B) On a dolium (5037/A14). Juana Márquez Pérez photos.

After cleaning, remains were separated between human and non-human (Depierre 1995). The human bones were then weighed (scale Blauscal AH Series, 0.01 g accuracy) and measured (caliper Mitutoyo 500-181-1). To analyse the degree of fragmentation (McKinley 2004a) the bones were sieved (mesh: 10 mm, 5 mm and 2 mm). Bone identification (Duday *et al.* 2000; McKinley 2004a), colour and deformation (Buikstra and Ubelaker 1994), and thermal fractures (Herrmann and Bennett 1999) were evaluated.

The minimum number of individuals (McKinley 2000a; 2004a; Duday *et al.* 2000), sex (Buikstra and Ubelaker 1994; Ferembach *et al.* 1980; Van Vark *et al.* 1996; Wahl 1996) and age-at-death (Brooks and Suchey 1990; Buikstra and Ubelaker 1994; Lovejoy *et al.* 1985; Ferembach *et al.* 1980) were determined. The statistical analysis was made through the Statistical Package for Social Sciences (SPSS, version 19).

Results and discussion

From the 60 cremation burials, seven (11.7%) were double, so there was a minimum number of 67 individuals. The age-at-death estimation revealed 11 (16.4%) non-adults, 44 (65.7%) adults and for 12 individuals (17.9%) the age was undetermined. Among the non-adults, five (45.5%) were infants I (1–6 years), one (9.1%) infants II (7–12 years), one (9.1%) infant I or II and four (36.4%) juveniles (13–19 years).

The proportion between non-adults and adults found on this sample was compared to other studies of roman cremation burials (Table 6.1). It is below the 30.1% recorded at the Tiel-Passewaaij site, Netherlands (Van den Bos and Maat 2002), or the 30.4% found by Wahl (2008) which encompassed several imperial Roman sites in Germany. If the juveniles are excluded from the non-adult group this proportion decreases to 12.7% which is close to the values found by Barrand (2012) at "84–86 André Malreux"

Table 6.1: Percentages of non-adults in cremation burials from several Roman sites.

Individuals			Roman site (s) location	Author (s)
Total	*Non-adults*			
N	n	(%)		
91	10	11[a]	Eastern Cemetery, London, UK	McKinley (2000b)
142	43	29[a]	Cemetery at Brougham, Cumbria, UK	McKinley (2004b)
181	32	17.7[b]	St Lambert necropolis, Fréjus, Var, France	Berato *et al.* (1990)
124	21	16.9[a]	"La Fache des Près Aulnoys", Bavay, France	Barrand (2012)
264	31	11.7[a]	"84-86 André Malreux", Metz, France	
186	56	30.1[b]	Tiel Passewaaij, Netherlands	Van den Bos and Maat (2002)
673	n. d.	30.4[b]	Several Roman imperial sites, Germany	Wahl (2008)
72	8	11.1[a]	Porta Nocera necropolis, Pompeii, Italy	Duday (2013a)
55	11	20[b]	Southern funerary area, Mérida, Spain	Present study
	7	12.7[a]		

Total: Sum of adults and non-adults; a. Excluding juveniles; b. Including juveniles; n. d. no data.

site, Metz France, or the 11% achieved by McKinley (2000b) at the Eastern Roman cemetery London, UK, as well as Duday (2013a) at Porta Nocera necropolis, Pompeii, Italy.

The different approaches to considering juveniles as non-adults (e.g. Berato *et al.* 1990; Van den Bos and Maat 2002; Wahl, 2008) or adults (e.g. Barrand 2012; Duday 2013a) are related to authors' choice between a biologic immaturity *versus* a social maturity of past populations as pointed out by Ancel (2010), Duday *et al.* (2000) and Barrand (2012). Furthermore, authors such as McKinley (2000b; 2004b) also use a distinct group called subadult/adult for individuals older than 13 years. Thus, the discussion of this issue should be taken with caution because it depends on the inclusion of juveniles in a specific age group. Moreover, the reality could also be masked by the individuals whose age could not be determined.

The absence of individuals under 1 year of age in cremation burials is frequently reported on Roman sites (e.g. Smits 2006; Béguin and Le Goff 2001 in Durand 2008; McKinley 2000b; Van den Bos and Maat 2002). Ancient authors, namely Pliny or Juvenal (cf. Carroll 2011; Dansen 2011; Hope 2007) mentioned that children who have not teethed are not cremated. Despite that, cremated babies of less than 6 months had been reported, for instance at Évora, Portugal (Fernandes *et al.* 2012), Valladas, Drôme, France (Bel *et al.* 2002), Évreux, France (Pluton *et al.* 2008), Chalon-sur-Saône, France (Depierre 1995), Pompéi, Italy (Duday 2013a), von Stettfeld I, Germany (Wahl 1988), and King Harry Lane, St Albans, England (Stirland 1989 in McKinley 2008). Furthermore, infants aged less than 1 year could be inhumed in other places, outside the formal cemetery, such as within houses or outside houses along walls (e.g. Alapont and

Bouneau 2010; Blaizot *et al.* 2003; Dansen 2011; Durand 2005; Gowland 2001; Philpott 1991; Tranoy 2000). At *Augusta Emerita* the anthropological study of the inhumations indicates the presence of four individuals younger than 1 year old on this funerary area (Silva in prep.).

The fact that the majority of the cremated non-adults from this sample died under 6 years was predictable since infant mortality (0–5 years) in the Roman period was near 50% (Rawson 2003, 341). Besides, 63.3% of the non-adults died at less than 10 years, although this is lower than the values found by Van den Bos and Maat (2002) and Depierre (1995), of 71.4% and 77.8%, respectively. During Roman times at least half of the children who survived the first year died before reaching the age of 10 (Garnsey 1998, 256; Parkin 1992, 92). A similar point of view was also presented by Laes (2011, 26) who claims that 30–35% of the newborns did not survive past the first month and that less than 50% attain 15 years.

It must be keep in mind that comparisons with other studies can be difficult or impossible since some authors did not clarify the anthropological methods and the age group adopted as well as the terminology used (e.g. infants, babies, immatures, subadults, children). In addition to these methodological problems, babies and/ or infants could have been buried in specific zones of a funerary area (Durand 2008; Pearce 2001) and/or in an unexcavated area of a necropolis. These issues are compounded in the cremation context.

Regarding the 44 adults, two (4.5%) were young adults (< 30 years), nine (20.5%) middle adults (30–49 years) and two (4.5%) old adults (50+ years), although for the remaining 31 (70.5%) it was impossible to be precise with an age-at-death range. In other Roman burial sites (Wahl 2008; McKinley 2000b; 2004b; Van den Bos and Maat 2002), the majority of the adults died between 30 and 45 years old (Table 6.2). Studies based on epigraphic sources from *Hispania* by authors such as García Merino (1975 in Gozalbes 2007) or García y Bellido (1954; Gozalbes 2007) also suggest an average age-at-death close to the late 30s, although there was a high mortality in women and men between 20 and 30 years (Gozalves 2007).

The sex diagnosis of the 44 adults revealed that ten (22.7%) were male, nine (20.5%) female and 25 (56.8%) undetermined. A predominance of males *versus* females was

Table 6.2: *Age-at-death estimations of cremated adults from Roman burial sites.*

Age-at-death (years)	Roman site (s) location	Author (s)
26–45 (majority)	Eastern Cemetery, London, UK	McKinley (2000b)
30–45 (majority)	Cemetery at Brougham, Cumbria, UK	McKinley (2004b)
20–40 (majority)	Cemeteries of Valkenburg, Museum Kamstraat, Moers-Asberg and Gregeld-Gellep, Netherlands	Smits (2006)
35–40 (majority)	Tiel-Passewaaij, Netherlands	van den Bos and Maat (2002)
34.7 (average)	Several Roman imperial sites from Germany	Wahl (2008)
30–39 (majority)	Southern funerary area, Mérida, Spain	Present study

also reported on funerary sites such as Espinal, Navarra, Spain (Unzu and Peréx 2010), Porta Nocera, Pompeii, Italy (Duday 2013a) or at Krefeld-Gellep, Netherlands (Smits 2006) although the opposite scenario also had been documented (Table 6.3). Nevertheless, the fairly similar distribution between sexes in this *Augusta Emerita* sample had parallels in other sites (Unzu and Peréx 2010; Van den Bos and Maat 2002; Wahl 2008).

The fragmentation, shrinkage and deformation associated with the cremation process, combined with the absence of skeletal elements due to post-cremation funerary practice on archaeological cremated bone deposits (Silva 2007) limit considerably the sex diagnosis and could lead to misclassifications (Holck 2005). Moreover, the reliability of conventional sex osteometric methods is affected by shrinkage (Gonçalves 2011; Thompson 2004; 2005). Morphological sex criteria should also be used with caution since there is a considerable anatomical variation between individuals (Holck 1997/2008). Nonetheless, the nature of grave goods occurring with the cremation burials sample from *Augusta Emerita* seem to support most of the anthropological data achieved concerning females individuals.

Sex diagnosis was possible in 43.2% (19/44) of the adult individuals which is close to the 51% and the 53% found respectively by McKinley (2000b; 2004b), but lower than the 75% presented by Van den Bos and Maat (2002). Smits (2006) diagnosed the sex in 52–89% of individuals. According to Holck (2005, 116) "it is common for more than 50% of the cremated bone to remain undetermined" in relation to sex determination.

Table 6.3: *Male and female percentages of sexed adults from Roman cremation burial sites.*

Sex estimatation (%)		Roman site (s) location	Author (s)
Male	Female		
30.9	69.1	Verona Porta Palio and Spianà, Italy	Drusini *et al.* (1997)
57	43	Porta Nocera necropolis, Pompeii, Italy	Duday (2013a)
60.6	39.4	Necropolis d'Avenches "En Chaplix", Suisse	Porro *et al.* (1999)
30.4	69.6	Eastern Cemetery, London, UK	McKinley (2000b)
37.8	62.2	Cemetery at Brougham, Cumbria, UK	McKinley (2004b)
40.7	59.3	Valkenburg-Marktveld, Netherlands	Smits (2006)
54.5	45.5	Krefeld-Gellep, Netherlands	
48.4	51.6	Tiel-Passewaaij, Netherlands	Van den Bos and Maat (2002)
52	48	Several imperial roman sites from Germany	Wahl (2008)
38.1	61.9	Santa Criz necropolis, Eslava, Spain	Armendáriz *et al.* (2001)
53.8	46.2	Espinal second cemetery, Navarra, Spain	Unzu and Peréx (2010)
52.6	47.4	Southern funerary area, Mérida, Spain	Present study

Single versus double burials

Seven double burials were recorded (Table 6.4), which corresponds to 11.7% of the total. This result is quite similar to the values found by Barrand (2012) at Bavay necropolis at France but higher than those presented by Duday (2013a), Barrand (2012), Van den Bos and Maat (2002) and McKinley (2000b; 2004b), all less than 5%. Wahl (2008, 151) reviewing data from German sites stated: "Real double burials are relatively rare on graveyards from the Imperial Period. Their percentage mostly lies below 5%".

Three double burials had one non-adult and an adult (42.9%), two non-adults (28.6% n=2) and two adults individuals (28.6%; n=2). Among those burials were identified two situations of infants buried with unsexed adults and that of a juvenile with a male. Furthermore, two burials concerning a female with an adult of undetermined sex were also found.

In terms of double burials, the combination most reported is of an adult and a child (e.g. Bel *et al.* 2002; Billard 1987; Blaizot *et al.* 2009; McKinley 2000b; Van den Bos and Maat 2002; Wahl 2008). However, graves containing two adults were also recognised on Roman burial sites, namely, at Porta Nocera, Italy (Duday 2013a), the Eastern Cemetery of London, UK (McKinley 2000b), at Brougham, UK (McKinley 2004b), at Tiel-Passewaaij, Netherlands (Van den Bos and Maat 2002), at von Stettfeld I, Germany (Walh 1988) and at "Solar de la Morería" Sagunto, Spain (Polo *et al.* 2005). Cremation burials containing two non-adults are the less frequent, although documented for instance at von Stettfeld I roman burial site, Germany by Wahl (1988).

Identifying a double burial requires a sufficient representation of anatomical parts of the skeletons from each person (Duday 2013b). At *Augusta Emerita* three of these deposits concerned primary cremation burials. The remaining four cases were secondary cremation burials but none of them seemed to fit the notion of commingling of human remains due to a contamination occurring at the moment of

Table 6.4: Biological profile of the individuals in double cremation burials.

Double burials	N	%	Biological profile of individuals
2 Non-adults	2	28.6	1 Infant II + 1 Juvenile
			2 Infants I
1 Non-adult + 1 adult	3	42.9	1 Infant I + 1 Adult (undetermined sex)
			1 Infant I/II + 1 Adult (undetermined sex)
			1 Juvenile + 1 Adult (male)
2 Adults	2	28.6	1 Adult (undetermined sex) + 1 Adult (female)
			1 Adult (undetermined sex) + 1 Adult (female)
Total	7	100	7 Non-adults (5 infants and 2 juveniles)
			7 Adults (4 undetermined sex, 1 male and 2 females)

bone collecting from the cremation area, as was suggested by Duday (2013a) at Porta Nocera necropolis and Gonçalves *et al.* (2010) at Encosta de Sant'Ana Roman funerary site, Lisbon Portugal.

Biologic profile of the individuals according to burial type

The distribution of the non-adults and adults as well as the male and females of the sample according to burial type is presented on Figure 6.5. The analysis of the data allows draw up some interesting aspects about funerary practices at *Augusta Emerita* during High Empire.

The non-adults are more common than adults in the double burials (63.6% of non-adults were found with another individual while this happens with only 15.9% of the adults). The number of non-adults and adults found on single and on double burials differ significantly (Fisher test, $p=0.003$). Furthermore the remains of children are preferably put on urns (54.5%), particularly those in the infants I category, which contrasts to the 90.9% of unurned burials presented by the adults. There are differences statistically significant between number of non-adult and adults present on unurned *versus* urned burials (Fischer test, $p=0.002$).

The number of non-adults and adults found on primary as opposed to secondary burials is not significantly different (Fisher test, $p=0.19$). However, if the individuals from double burials containing a non-adult with an adult were excluded, the difference become statistically significant (Fisher test, $p=0.038$). Those data suggest a trend to put non-adults into secondary burials while adults were mainly associated to primary burials. There are no differences statistically significant between males and females

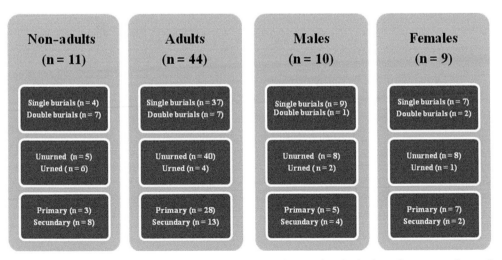

Fig. 6.5: Distribution of non-adults and adults, as well as males and females by burial type, namely, single versus double, unurned versus urned and primary versus secondary burial. The cases concerning unknown burial type and individuals with unknown age and/or sex are not included.

put on urned *versus* unurned burials (Fisher test, *p*=1) or on primary *versus* secondary burials (Fisher test, *p*=0.620). If only individuals from single burials are considered the absence of significant statistically differences maintain (Fisher test, *p*=0.608). There is a special funerary treatment concerning young children which differs from the adults. On other roman funerary sites with predominance of primary cremation burials such as at La Favorite, Lyon France (Tranoy 1995 in Bel *et al.* 2002), or at Pupput, Tunisia (Ben Abed and Griesheimer 2008) it will be interesting to find out if this trend was also observed.

Among males and females there are no differences concerning the place where the cremation and the burial of their remains occurs. Nevertheless one hypothesis to explore in future studies is if the most elaborate burials, namely with brick box, are allocated to males and/or to individuals of high social status. Of the sample here, two of those seven burials had one male each, although for the remaining five burials it was impossible to sex the individuals.

It is necessary to point out that the burials under analysis in this chapter represent a portion of the total amount of burials excavated by Juana Márquez Pérez, namely approximately 101 cremation burials (and/or cremation bone deposits) and 23 inhumations. Furthermore, other archaeological interventions made on nearby soils (Palma 2002; Estévez 2002; Silva 2002; Méndez 2006) also revealed similar burials (Márquez 2005b; e.g. Silva in prep.). So all these interventions indicate a much broader Roman funerary area with burials (mainly cremations) dated between the first and the first half of the second centuries AD (Márquez 2005a; 2005b; 2005c). After a period of abandonment it was again the place of burials from 4th century onwards (Márquez 2005a; 2005b; 2005c). So the anthropological results attained must be seen with caution.

Weight

The average weight of the 60 bone deposits was 754.56 g with a variation between 1.69 g and 4261.6 g. For the 53 single burials (Table 6.5) the average weight was 598.37 g, ranging between 1.69 g and 2565.53 g, while on the seven double burials it was 1937.12 g, ranging from 456.97 g to 4261.6 g. In this sample the average weight of the human cremated bone per burial is higher than those found by Drusini *et al.* (1997) at Verona Porta Palio and Spianà, Italy, which are lower than 200 g (n=994), or the 300–400 g recorded by Wahl (2008) on several Roman imperial sites from Germany (n=850) and by Van den Bos and Maat (2002) at Tie Passewaaij, Netherlands (n=189).

On the whole, the higher average weights found at *Augusta Emerita* could be due to factors such as the burial type (55% are primary), the undisturbed nature of most bone deposits (62%), a favourable environment for bone preservation, a detailed excavation, and/ or a regional variation on the cremation ritual.

Among the single burials, the average weight of the 31 undisturbed deposits was 810.94 g, ranging from 87.29 g to 2565.53 g, while the 22 disturbed burials had 298.85 g, ranging from 1.69 g to 1469.20 g. The smaller quantities of bone recovered

Table 6.5: Weight averages of cremated bone from single burials by burial type and condition, as well as by age and sex of the individual.

Burial (single)				Weight (g)		
Variables			N	Average	Variation	
					Minimum	Maximum
Type	Urned		6	1024.37	34.55	2565.53
	Unurned		47	543.99	1.69	2314.78
	Primary		30	577.88	14.77	1581.00
	Secondary		16	698.87	1.69	2565.53
	Primary unurned		30	577.88	14.77	1581.00
	Secondary	Unurned	10	503.57	1.69	1409.46
		Urned	6	1024.37	34.55	2565.63
		All	16	698.87	1.69	2565.53
Condition	Undisturbed		31	810.94	87.29	2565.63
	Disturbed		22	298.85	1.69	1496.20
Age	Non-adult		4	583.70	164.80	1581.00
	Adult		37	761.46	34.55	2565.53
	Undetermined		12	100.41	1.69	371.93
Sex	Male		9	1303.59	589.93	2565.53
	Female		7	1169.06	360.02	2144.70
	Undetermined			393.25	34.55	1463.65
All burials			53	598.37	1.69	2565.53

from the disturbed burials are reported in other studies (McKinley 2000b; 2004b; Silva and Santos 2009/2010) and probably result from taphonomic factors.

The average weight of the six single urned and the 47 single unurned burials is 1024.37 g and 543.99 g, respectively. Without the disturbed burials those values increase to 1324.80 g on the urned (n=4) and 734.81 g on the unurned (n=27) burials. This difference may be explained by several hypotheses: a more favourable environment to bone preservation on the urned burials (McKinley 1993), the specific characteristics of the cremated individuals, or the more likely situation that not all the bones from unurned burials were recovered during excavation (Blaizot and Tranoy 2004).

The four non-adults from single burials had an average weight of 583.70 g, ranging between 164.80 g and 1581 g. According to age group the values of the two infants I and the two juveniles were respectively 294.49 g and 872.9 g. These average weights are quite higher than those found by Wahl (1988) at von Stettfeld I, namely 126.8 g (n=14) and 412.5 g (n=2). Furthermore, is also superior to the average weight of 106 g achieved on 39 "subadults" from several Roman imperial sites at Germany (Wahl 2008, 152) or the 148.15 g concerning four infants I–II on a Roman burial site located at

30–32 Rue de Bourgogne, Lyon, France (Schmitt *et al.* 2010). At Porta Nocera necropolis, on the contrary, the average weight of five children aged 3–10/13 years old was 311.46 g (Duday 2013a), which is equivalent to infants average weight of the present study.

One possible explanation to the higher values found at *Augusta Emerita* could be the undisturbed condition of all non-adult burials and the fact that two of them (pertaining to two juveniles) are primary deposits. Even so, they are below the average weight presented by Trotter and Hixon (1974) on a crematory study, namely 300.6 g on 29 children aged 6 months–3 years, and 1225.0 g to 37 children aged 3–13 years. For the moment the results achieved should be with caution due to the small number of individuals studied.

The 37 adults from single burials had an average weight of 761.46 g, ranging between 34.55 g and 2565.53 g. The average weights of adults by burial type were: 650.0 g for the primary unurned (n=23), 645.60 g to the secondary unurned (n=7) and 1389.31 g to the urned secondary burials (n=4). Those values are above the 326.8 g calculated for 31 primary deposits from Lyon, France (Blaizot *et al.* 2009), the 424.3 g achieved on 33 secondary cremation burials from Valladas necropolis, at Saint-Paul-Trois-Châteaux, France (Bel *et al.* 2002) or the average weights recorded at the French Roman funerary sites of Champ de l'Image (Saint-Marcel), Lazenay (Bourges) and Vieux Domaine (Vierzon), all lower than 250 g on a sample of 119 individuals (Durand 2005). Nevertheless, they are below the average weights found on primary deposits from several French Roman sites, namely 1163.7 g on 19 pyres from Languedoc (Blaizot *et al.* 2009), 1066.84 g regarding seven at Lyon region (Bel 1996) or the weights achieved by Bura (2001) on two deposits (1387 g for burial 5 from Thérouanne and 1298.5 g for burial 1 at Bruay-La-Buissière). It is also considerably lower than the average weight of 1259.8 g found on 47 secondary cremation burials at Porta Nocera necropolis, Pompeii, Italy (Duday 2013a).

The average adult weight of this sample is lower than the values obtained from commercial crematoria (Warren and Maples 1997; McKinley 1993; Gonçalves 2012), specifically 2430 g (n=91), 1625.9 g (n=15; excluding the 2 mm fraction) and 1674.1 g (n=88; excluding the 2 mm fraction). This average weight represents 31.3%, 46.8% and 45.5% of the expected bone, according to Warren and Maples (1997), McKinley (1993) and Gonçalves (2012). This is to be expected though, and highlights one of the key issues when using such crematoria-based studies for comparisons with remains from the archaeological context.

When these data are analysed by sex (Table 6.6), the nine males show an average weight of 1303.59 g while the females had 1169.06 g. Both sexes show higher average weights than those presented by McKinley (2004b), Van den Bos and Maat (2002) or Wahl (1988; 2008). The superior average weight of males *versus* females was also noticed at several Roman sites (McKinley 2004b; Smits 2006; Wahl 1988; 2008) and commercial crematoria (Gonçalves 2012; McKinley 1993; Warren and Maples 1997; Van Deest *et al.* 2011).

Table 6.6: *Male and female weight averages from single burials according to the type of burial.*

Burial type	Male weight (g)				Female weight (g)			
	N	Average	Variation		N	Average	Variation	
			Minimum	Maximum			Minimum	Maximum
Unurned	7	1193.48	598.93	2314.78	6	1006.45	360.02	1496.20
Urned	2	1688.99	812.45	2565.53	1	2144.70	–	–
Primary	4	1018.22	694.77	1229.14	5	925.85	360.02	1496.20
Secondary	4	1336.17	589.93	2565.53	2	1777.08	409.46	2144.70
Primary unurned	4	1018.22	694.77	1229.14	5	925.85	360.02	1496.20
Secondary unurned	2	938.35	589.93	1376.77	1	1409.46	–	–
Secondary urned	2	1688.99	812.45	2565.53	1	2144.70	–	–
All burials	9	1303.59	589.93	2565.53	7	1169.06	360.02	2144.70

Bone fragmentation

Of the 60 burials, 91.0% of bone pieces had a size greater or equal to 10 mm, while 8% and 1% fit on 5 mm and 2 mm sieves, respectively. The range in proportions in each category are 100–57.2% at 10 mm, 38.5–0% at 5 mm, and 11.4–0% at the 2 mm size. Regarding the average size of the largest fragment per burial it was 63.02 mm, ranging from 14 mm (on a disturbed unurned secondary burial) to 131.23 mm (on an undisturbed unurned double primary burial). Most of those fragments (88.3%; n=53) are long bones shafts from limbs namely from the femur (n=14), tibia (n=13), ulna (n=2) and radius (n=3). Table 6.7 displays the values for bone fragmentation on single burials.

Burial type and condition display the most differences, especially with regard the percentages of bone pieces recovered from the 10 mm and 5 mm sieves and on the average maximum fragment size. The undisturbed burials have a higher average maximum fragment size than the disturbed ones.

Regarding bone fragment size on the 37 adults (Table 6.8), 91.8% of the pieces stay on the 10 mm sieve, 7.7% on the 5 mm, and 0.9% on the 2 mm. McKinley (2004b) found averages of 72–76% to the 10 mm fraction. The average of the maximum bone size on adult burials was 67.97 mm, ranging between 22.22 mm and 106.79 mm, which is higher than the averages of 48–58 mm recorded by McKinley (2004b), not including the 76 mm achieved on undisturbed urned lidded burials, but lower than the 128 mm detected on a crematory study (McKinley 1993).

Bone fragmentation among males and females is analogous. Even so, males show a superior average of bone pieces in the 10 mm sieve while the females present higher values concerning the average size of the biggest fragment, which for the last item, is opposite to Wahl's (1988) findings.

Table 6.7: Average bone fragmentation on single burials by burial type, condition, age and sex of individuals.

Variables			N	Fragmentation (%)			Average > frag (mm)	Variation > frag (mm)
				10 mm	5 mm	2 mm		
Burial Type	Unurned		47	92.0	7.2	0.7	60.57	14.00–104.46
	Urned		6	92.2	7.3	0.5	61.95	22.22–106.79
	Primary		30	91.8	7.3	0.9	65.48	32.09–104.46
	Secondary		16	93.8	5.7	0.4	60.32	14.00–106.79
	Primary unurned		30	91.8	7.3	0.9	65.48	32.09–104.46
	Secondary	unurned	10	94.8	4.8	0.4	59.34	14.00–85.07
		urned	6	92.2	7.3	0.5	61.95	22.22–106.79
		all	16	93.8	5.7	0.4	61.95	14.00–106.79
Condition	Undisturbed		31	92.2	7.0	0.8	70.26	42.85–106.79
	Disturbed		22	91.8	7.6	0.6	47.29	14.00–104.46
Age	Non-adult		4	90.1	8.1	1.9	58.78	42.85–88.77
	Adult		37	91.8	7.5	0.7	67.97	22.22–106.79
Sex	Male		9	94.5	5.2	0.3	78.67	60.84–89.66
	Female		7	91.6	8.3	0.1	84.0	63.90–106.79
All burials			53	92.1	7.2	0.7	60.72	14.00–104.46

Table 6.8: Average bone fragmentation on adults from single burials by type and condition of the burial.

Adults			N	Average fragmentation (%)			Average > frag (mm)	Variation > frag (mm)
				10 mm	5 mm	2 mm		
Burial Type	Unurned		33	91.9	7.6	0.9	68.06	32.09–104.46
	Urned		4	91.0	8.5	0.5	67.23	22.22–106.79
	Primary		23	91.5	7.6	0.9	68.24	32.09–104.46
	Secondary		11	92.2	7.3	0.6	68.06	22.22–106.79
	Primary unurned		23	91.5	7.6	0.9	68.24	32.09–104.46
	Secondary	unurned	7	92.9	6.6	0.6	68.53	50.81–85.07
		urned	4	91.0	8.5	0.5	67.27	22.22–106.79
		all	11	92.2	7.3	0.6	68.06	22.22–106.79
Condition	Undisturbed		23	92.2	7.4	0.8	74.29	50.81–106.79
	Disturbed		14	91.2	8.1	0.8	57.60	22.22–104.46
All burials			37	91.8	7.7	0.9	67.97	22.22–106.79

The discrepancies between bone fragmentation values could be due to differences with the cremation ritual such as: burning process, namely the degree of bone combustion (McKinley 1994; Stiner *et al.* 1995); the pyre structure, intervention of an *ustor* (a professional pyre-burner) during cremation process; the burial type or bone manipulation (McKinley 1994). The observation of current cremations of approximately 170 individuals, in India and Nepal, indicate that the bone manipulation that occurs during the combustion process followed, sometimes, by an extinction of the fire with water, are the major responsible for the bone fragmentation (Grévin 2009).

Anatomical regions of the skeletal elements

The percentages of weight distribution by anatomical regions (namely, skull, axial skeleton, upper limbs, lower limbs and unidentified fragments) among the 37 adults (Fig. 6.6) and the two infants I from single burials were also analysed. For the non-adults the values achieved were: 55.8% skull, 2.2% axial, 4.3% upper limbs, 7.7% lower limbs and 29.9% unidentified. Due to the lack of studies about those individuals it only can be said that skull percentage overlaps what Lenorzer (2006, 185) calls the "normal values", namely 30–50% for an infant I and that the axial skeleton is under-represented, a phenomenon also observed by Duday (2013a). Moreover, since both cases correspond to secondary urned burials this data could be seen as a consequence of partial collection from the funerary pyre perhaps privileging skull bone pieces.

Of the 60 burials studied, the undetermined bones represent on average 35.6% of the bone deposit which fits McKinley's (2000a) values. This author estimates that

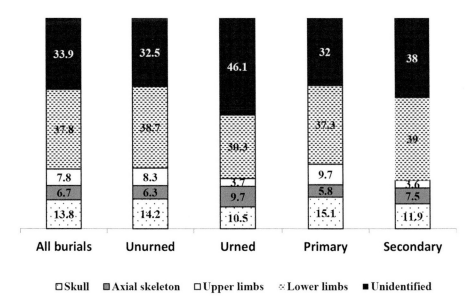

Fig. 6.6: Percentages of weight distribution by anatomical region for the 37 adults from single burials by burial type.

only 30–50% of the bone from a cremation burial may be identifiable to a specific skeletal element. For the 37 adult single burials, bone identification was on average possible in 66.1% of the pieces, which is similar to the data presented by McKinley (2004b).

As depicted on Figure 6.6, the values for the skull (10.5–15.1%) are below the theoretical value expected to this anatomical region (20.40%) by Lowrance and Latimer (1957) – although Duday *et al.* (2000) considered this normal as it is included within the range of 10–30%. There are 14 (37.8%) burials (seven primary, five secondary, two undetermined) values inside normal range, 17 (45.9%) bellow and six (16.2%) above (five primary, one secondary). The maximum found was 41.5% for a primary burial. The analysis of skull percentage according to the type of burials is quite similar despite the higher values on primary *versus* secondary burials.

With the axial skeleton the values (3.6–9.7%) are below the theoretical value of 17% (Lowrance and Latimer 1957) and the normal range of Duday *et al.* (2000) of 10–24%. Only eight (21.6%) burials (four primary, three secondary and one undetermined) present values inside the normal range, while 27 (18 primary, seven secondary, two undetermined) are below, only two (one primary, one secondary) are above. The under-representation of axial skeleton is found in numerous cremation burials (Duday 2013a), such as at the necropolis of the Tuileries site, Lyon, France (André *et al.* 2013). One exception to this "rule" was found at Porta Nocera necropolis where most of the burials fit the normal range (Duday 2013a).

The upper and lower limbs are below the expected values, namely, 17.6% and 45.0% (Lowrance and Latimer 1957). The percentages concerning the limbs are usually small since bone pieces from these regions can be placed within the undetermined category (Duday *et al.* 2000). Possibly this explains the high percentage of undetermined bone fragments and the low values for the limbs found at urned adult burials.

Despite these results, it is important to refer that some bone pieces are easier to identify than others (Holck 1997/2008) and that bone preservation, which depends on intrinsic and extrinsic factors, has possibly influenced the values achieved.

Colour

The main colours of the bones within the burials were: pale yellow in 28 (46.7%), white in 22 (36.7%), gray/blue in nine (15%) and one (1.7%) black. Moreover, oxidation variations on bone pieces were found on 39 burials (65%). This is common in Romano-British cremation burials (McKinley 2000b; 2008) being also reported at Tiel-Passewaaij Roman site, Netherlands (Van den Bos and Maat (2002).

The pale colour of almost half of the bone deposits from *Augusta Emerita* contrasts to the findings on others Roman burial sites, for instance in England (Márquez-Grant 2008; McKinley 2000b; 2004b), Netherlands (Van den Bos and Maat 2002), Greece (Ubelaker and Rife 2007), France (Berato *et al.* 1990) or Portugal (Fernandes *et al.* 2012; Silva and Santos 2009/2010) where the vast majority of bone deposits were white. This suggests that there may be differences in burning practices.

According to burial type, most of bone deposits from the 52 unurned burials were pale yellow (23; 44.2%), followed by 19 (36.5%) white, nine (17.3%) gray/blue and one (1.9%) black. In the eight urned burials, pale yellow was also predominant (62.5%) with the remaining three (37.5%) being white. The majority of bone deposits from primary burials were white (n=15; 45.5%), then pale yellow (n=13; 39.4%), gray/blue (n=3; 12.1%) and black (n=1; 3%) while the secondary burials were mainly pale yellow (n=12; 60%), gray/blue (n=2; 10%) and white (n=6; 30%). Apparently, unurned burials had a higher degree of bone combustion than urned burials, as McKinley (2008) also point out, although this could be only a coincidence since pale yellow was found on unurned burials.

Among non-adults in single burials the major colour of the bone deposits concerning two unurned burials was yellow (100%) while the two urned were white. For the 37 adults the main colour was pale yellow (20 or 54.1%, on five males, six females and nine individuals of undetermined sex). On other nine (24.3%) were white, namely three males, one female and five individuals of undetermined sex. Finally, the gray/blue colour was found in seven burials (18.9%): one male and six individuals of undetermined sex while black was observed on bones pertaining to one individual of undetermined sex.

The frequencies of the main colour by anatomical region indicate some differences on its distribution (Fig. 6.7). The skull has higher values of white whereas on the axial skeleton this colour was not observed, with yellow being predominant. The upper and lower limbs had similar values of white and gray despite the distinct frequencies between them, when these colours were seen separately. Nevertheless near 50% of bone pieces from a given anatomical region were pale yellow.

According to Symes *et al.* (2008, 37) thermally altered bone is subject to visual changes that "result in a scale that gradually evolves from a translucent yellowish (unaltered bone), to an opaque white (heat line and border), to a blackened appearance

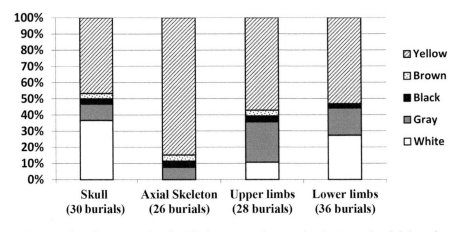

Fig. 6.7: *Colour frequencies by identified anatomical region for the 37 single adult burials.*

(char), and eventually to a totally ash-colour, calcined condition". Pale yellow possibly corresponds to the grade 0 defined by Holck (1997/2008) which refers to bones minimally affected by heat and with no external signs of having been exposed to fire. The pale yellow bones, although not oxidised, most likely experimented dehydration that is accompanied by fracture patterns and weight loss at temperatures ranging between 100°C to 600°C (Thompson 2004). So, this colour reveals incomplete combustions (Holck 1997/2008). Moreover, the colour change is expressed when the bone is subject to decomposition (Shipman *et al.* 1984; Mayne 1997; Thompson 2004). The white colour indicates a calcinated bone which lost its organic material and moisture (Mayne 1997).

Bone oxidation depends of factors such as oxygen, temperature (McKinley 2008; Walker *et al.* 2008), duration of exposure to fire (Symes *et al.* 2008; Walker *et al.* 2008), and may be the result of factors such as the body position on the pyre, body mass, quantity of fuel used to build the pyre, and/or an insufficient temperature applied to elements on the peripheries of the pyre (McKinley 2008). The differences between bone oxidation among anatomical regions could be due to the "pugilistic posture" of the body (Symes *et al.* 2008) and "variability in the thickness of soft tissues within different parts of the body" (McKinley 2008, 165). The main colour distribution per anatomical region found in this sample is in agreement with the studies of McKinley (2008), with the axial skeletal exhibiting a smaller grade of combustion. Moreover, the variation in bone oxidation can have been influenced by human action during the cremation in response to the aims of the funerary ritual. As McKinley (2000b; 2006) points out, it is likely that the concept of a "complete" cremation (e.g. Noy 2000) varies not only temporally but geographically, and in some Romano-British cremations full oxidation seems not to be the goal – as seems to be the case here.

Besides all the conditions that occurred during cremation and burial, the evaluation of the bone colour from archaeological contexts is influenced by the perception of the researcher, even when using a scale for comparison. Furthermore, it depends on taphonomic agents (Nicholson 1993; Duday 2013b; Duday *et al.* 2000; Holck 2005) and brightness during the observation.

Deformation
Deformation was visible in bones (Fig. 6.8) from 27 (45%) of the 60 burials. The frequency of deformation by anatomical region indicates that the upper (64%) and lower limb (53.8%) shafts were the more affected, followed by bone pieces of the skull (42%), and axial skeleton (12%). On single burials deformation was observed on bone pieces from 21 (39.6%), namely on two of the four non-adults (50%) and 17 of the 37 adults (45.9%). There are no differences that are statistically significant (Fisher test, p=0.639) between frequencies of burials with bone deformation and the age-at-death of the individual (non-adult *versus* adult).

The deformation is caused by the effect of temperature on the bone structure. Long bone shafts are more prone to deformation (Depierre 1995) as they essentially constituted by compact tissue. Deformation indicates also a fresh cremation (e.g.

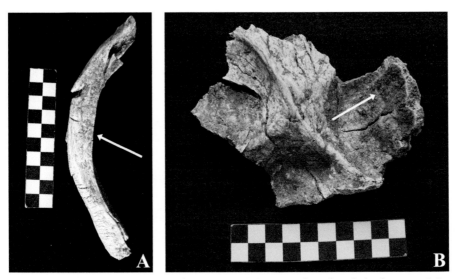

Fig. 6.8: *Examples of bone deformation. A) Radius shaft fragment (5038/A12/56). B) Occipital fragment (5036/A8/139).*

Ubelaker 1989 in Ubelaker and Rife 2007; Silva 2007). The cases of an "extreme morphological disfigurement", associated with bone calcination, are interpreted by Ubelaker and Rife (2007, 50) as the "melting" effect "in which temperatures reaching 1600° transform bone salts".

Thermal fractures
These fractures were observed on bone pieces from 50 (83.3%) of the 60 burials studied. Furthermore, distinct types of fractures were noticed on bones from the same burial and/or even on the same bone fragment. The most frequent fracture types were lamination and curved and/or concentric transverse fractures, both present on 33 (66%) burials. Next were transversal fractures on 30 (60%), and patina on 27 (54%) while the longitudinal fractures on nine (18%) and step on three (6%) were less common.

The location of the distinct thermal fractures by anatomical regions show that the pieces of skull were the more affected by lamination while fragment of shafts of upper and lower limbs exhibit most of the curved transverse, transversal, longitudinal and step fractures (Fig. 6.9). Patina was mainly found on skull pieces and on the extremities of long bones. The incidence of curved transverse fractures and deformation indicates a flesh on bone cremation (Herrmann and Bennett 1999; Thurman and Willmore 1980/1981; Ubelaker and Rife 2007). The location of distinct patterns of thermal fractures is due to the characteristics of the bone, such as the proportion of spongy and compact tissue (Herrmann and Bennett 1999; Symes *et al.* 2008). Despite the studies on thermal fractures (Symes *et al.* 2008), there is a lack of standardisation regarding designations employed and most authors do not present results about it, thus their discussion was impossible.

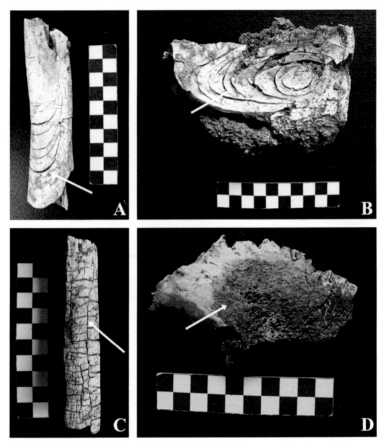

Fig. 6.9: Examples of thermal fractures on the Augusta Emerita sample. A) Curved transverse on the humerus shaft (5038/A29/163; B) Concentric transverse on a hip bone fragment (5036/A32/321; C) Step fracture on a long bone shaft (5038/A28/182; D) Lamination on a skull fragment (5038/A28/182).

Conclusions

According to archaeological sources, during the High Empire, most of the dead at *Augusta Emerita* were cremated (e.g. Márquez 2006; 2008). Nevertheless, until this present study, there was no anthropological data regarding those individuals or the funerary practice of cremation at this important capital of the *Lusitania* province. Based on the analysis of cremated bone from a minimum of 67 individuals found in 60 burials, dated to the first–second centuries AD, some interesting and novel interpretations can be made.

Usually, cremation occurred shortly after death, as evidenced by the presence of curved transverse and/or concentric fractures, sometimes associated with strong deformation. In most cases the combustion took place on funerary pyres placed in rectangular pits dug into the ground, although there are also situations where cremation was performed on an *ustrinum*.

While cremations at this time could be made under the supervision of professional undertakers (Bodel 2000), at *Augusta Emerita*, for the most part, the burnings do not give rise to calcined bones. Moreover, the low bone oxidation, depicted on the majority of burials analysed, suggests that this was not a matter of concern for the participants, and that the creation of ashes was not vital (e.g. Noy 2000). Nevertheless, other reasons such as adverse weather conditions or an inadequate supply of combustible material to produce a complete combustion could also be significant. Neither the age nor the sex of the deceased seemed to influence distinct funerary gestures concerning the degree of combustion of the individuals.

Following cremation, the human bones generally remained *in situ*, being buried with a range of grave goods such as ceramic, glass, metal and bone objects and/or personal ornaments in a primary cremation burial, also called *bustum* on ancient sources (e.g. Bel *et al.* 2008; 2009; Blaizot and Tranoy 2004; McKinley 2000c; Weekes 2008). Less often, the remains were collected from the funerary pyre and buried unurned. At least 32 individuals (29 adults and three non-adults) had been subjected to the former type of cremation burial while 19 (11 adults and eight non-adults) to the latter. Note the tendency for adults to undergo primary cremation burials while the non-adults were integrated into secondary cremation burials.

Most of the 60 cremation burials were individual in nature, although seven burials had remains of two human individuals (chiefly one non-adult with one adult although some had two non-adults or two adults). Seven of the 11 non-adults were found in double cremation burials, with five infants and two juveniles, which seems to indicate a predisposition to bury non-adults with others individuals.

The cremated bones of 44 adults were found unurned within 40 burials and urned within four. Among the 11 non-adults, six were urned while five were unurned. This data suggests that there could be a trend to bury the cremated bones of the adults unurned, while the non-adults, mainly the infants I, were put in cinerary urns. The city of *Augusta Emerita* was an important place within this period of Roman history, and this study demonstrates that the practice of cremation undertaken here seems to have some differences with other Roman cities. In the future we hope that the continuation of these studies in Mérida will help us all to understand the characteristics of the Roman cremation ritual in *Lusitania* and the roman funerary world abroad in more depth. Meanwhile, it is advisable to develop methodology specific to cremated bone found on ancient burials and to use standard methods which enable the discussion of results within similar studies. This will maximise the anthropological and archaeological data achieved.

Acknowledgments

Thanks to Tim Thompson, Teesside University (UK), to Ana Luísa Santos, University of Coimbra (Portugal), to Juana Márquez Pérez, Consorcio de Mérida (Spain), to Pedro Mateos, Instituto de Arqueología de Mérida (Spain), to Consorcio de Mérida (Spain) and to FCT (Portugal) (Grant SFRH/BD/31943/2006).

References

Alapont Martin, Ll. and Bouneau, C. 2010. Les sépultures de sujets périnatals du Vicus de Falacrinae (Cittareale, Italie). Evidences anthropologiques du rituel des suggrundaria. *Bulletins et Mémoires de la Société d'Anthropologie de Paris* 22(3–4), 117–44.

Alba Calzado, M. and Álvarez Martínez, J. M. (eds). 2012. *El Consorcio y la Arqueología emeritense: de la excavación al museo. Catálogo de la Exposición*. Mérida: Consorcio de la Ciudad Monumental Histórico-Artística y Arqueológica de Mérida, Ministerio de Educación, Cultura y Deporte.

Álvarez Martínez, J. M. 2011. Obras públicas e infraestructuras en la Colonia Augusta Emerita. Puentes y acueductos. In: Álvarez Martínez, J. M. and Mateos Cruz, P. (eds), *Actas Congreso Internacional 1910-2010: El Yacimiento Emeritense*. Mérida: CSIC, 145–71.

Álvarez Martínez, J. M. and Mateos Cruz, P. 2010a. 100 años de Arqueología en Mérida. In: Álvarez Martínez, J. M. and Mateos Cruz, P. (eds) *Mérida. 2000 años de Historia, 100 años de Arqueología. Cien años de excavaciones arqueológicas en Mérida 1910-2010*. Mérida: Consorcio de la Ciudad Monumental, Histórico-Artística y Arqueológica de Mérida, 27–43.

Álvarez Martínez, J. M. and Mateos Cruz, P. (eds). 2010b. *Mérida 200 años de Historia, 100 años de Arqueología. Cien años de excavaciones Arqueológicas en Mérida 1919-2010*. Mérida: Consorcio de la Ciudad Monumental, Histórico-Artística y Arqueológica de Mérida.

Álvarez Martínez, J. M. and Mateos Cruz, P. (eds). 2011. *Actas Congreso Internacional 1910-2010: El Yacimiento Emeritense*. Mérida: CSIC.

Ancel, M.-J. 2010. *La crémation en milieu rural en Gaule Belgique romaine: les exemples de la Lorraine et du Nord-Pas-de-Calais*. Thèse de Doctorat. Université Lumière Lyon 2, [Online], Available: http://theses.univ-lyon2.fr/documents/lyon2/2010/ancel_mj/download, [7 April 2011].

André, A., Leahy, R. and Rottier, S. 2013. Cremated human remains deposited in two phases: evidence from the necropolis of the Tuileries site (Lyon, France: 2nd century AD). *International Journal of Osteoarchaeology* [Electronic], Available: Wiley Online Library/DOI: 10.1002/oa.2317 [2 July 2013].

Arce, J. 2004. Introducción histórica. In: Dupré Raventós, X. (ed.), *Mérida: Colonia Augusta Emerita*. Roma: L'Erma di Bretschneider, 7–13.

Armendáriz, R. M., Mateo, M. R. and Sáez de Albéniz, M. P. 2001. Santa Criz, ciudad romana. Resultados de los estudios metalográficos y paleopatológicos. *Isturitz* 11, 259–63.

Ayerbe Vélez, R. 2001. Excavación de un área funeraria del s. III en los alrededores de la Vía de la Plata. Intervención arqueológica realizada en Avda. Vía de la Plata s/n. Mérida Excavaciones Arqueológicas 1999. *Memoria* 5, 21–47.

Ayerbe Vélez, R. and Márquez Pérez, J. 1998. Intervención arqueológica en el solar de la calle Cabo Verde. Espacio funerario del sitio del Disco, Mérida Excavaciones Arqueológicas 1996. *Memoria* 2, 135–66.

Barrand, H. 2012. *Les pratiques funéraires liées à la crémation dans les ensembles funéraires des capitales de cités du haut-empire en Gaule Belgique: Metz-Dividorum, Bavay-Bagacium, Thérouanne-Tervanna*. Thèse de doctorat en Langues, Histoire et civilisations des mondes anciens. Lyon, Université Lumière Lyon 2. [Online], Available: http://theses.univ-lyon2.fr/documents/lyon2/2012/barrand_h#p=0&a=top, [15 June 2013].

Bejarano Osorio, A. M. 2004. *El mausoleo del Dintel de los ríos: los contextos funerarios tardíos en Augusta Emerita*. Cuadernos Emeritenses 27, Mérida: Museo Nacional de Arte Romano.

Bel, V. 1996 Étude spatial de sept incinérations primaires Gallo-romaines de la région Lyonnaise. *Bulletins et Mémoires de la Société d'Anthropologie de Paris* 8(3–4), 207–22.

Bel, V., Bui Thi, M., Feugere, M., Girard, M., Heinz, C. and Olive, C. 2002 *Pratiques funéraires du Haut-Empire dans le Midi de la Gaule. La nécropole gallo-romaine du Valladas à Saint-Paul-Trois-Châteaux (Drôme)*. Lattes, ADAL Monographies d'Archéologie Méditerranéenne 11, Lattes: Association pour le Développement de l'Archéologie en Languedoc-Rousillon.

Bel, V., Blaizot, F. and Duday, H. 2008. Bûchers en fosse et tombes bûcher. Problématiques et méthodes de fouille. In: Scheid, J. (ed.), *Pour une archéologie du rite: nouvelles perspectives de l'archéologie funéraire*. Rome: École Française de Rome 407, 233–47.

Bel, V., Blaizot, F., Bonnet, C., Gagnol, M.-E., Georges, P., Gisclow, J.-L., Lisfranc, R., Richier, A. and Wittmann, A. 2009. L'étape de la crémation: les bûchers funéraires. In: Blaizot, F. (ed.), *Pratiques et espaces funéraires de la Gaule durant l'Antiquité*. *Gallia* 66(1). Paris: CNRS Éditions, 89–150.

Ben Abed, A. and Griesheimer, M. 2008. Pupput (Hammamet), une nécropole d'époque romaine. *Les Dossiers d'Archéologie* 330, 82–91.

Bendala Galán, M. 2004. Arquitectura funeraria. In: Dupré Raventós, X. (ed.), *Mérida: Colonia Augusta Emerita*. Roma: L'Erma di Bretschneider, 85–100.

Berato, J., Dutour, O. and Williams, J. 1990. Incinérations et inhumations du Haut-Empire Saint-Lambert, Fréjus-Var. *Paleobios* 6(2–3), 43–61.

Billard, M. 1987. Etude anthropologique des sépultures par incinération de la nécropole de la rue des Cordiers a Macon (Sâone et Loire). *Paleobios* 3(2–3), 37–60.

Blaizot, F., Alix, G. and Ferber, E. 2003. Le traitement funéraire des enfants décédés avant un an dans l'Antiquité: études de cas. *Bulletins et Mémoires de la Société d'Anthropologie de Paris* 15(1–2), 49–77.

Blaizot, F. and Tranoy, L. 2004. La notion de sépulture au Haut-Empire. Identification et interprétation des structures funéraires liées aux cremations. In: Baray, L. (ed.), *Archéologie des pratiques funéraires. Approches critiques. Actes de la table ronde des 7 et 9 juin 2001 (Glux-en-Glenne - F. 58)*. Glux-en-Gienne, Bibracte: Centre Archéologique Européen, 171–87.

Blaizot, F., Bel, V., Bonnet, C., Georges, P. and Richier, A. 2009. Les pratiques post crématoires dans les bûchers. In: Blaizot, F. (ed.) *Pratiques et espaces funéraires de la Gaule durant l'Antiquité*. *Gallia* 66(1), Paris: CNRS Éditions, 151–74.

Bodel, J. 2000. Dealing with the dead. Undertakers, executioners and potter's fields in ancient Rome. In: Hope, V. and Marshall, E. (eds), *Death and Disease in the Ancient City*. London: Routledge, 128–51.

Brooks, S. and Suchey, J. 1990. Skeletal age determination based on the os pubis: a comparison of the Acsádi-Neméskeri and Suchey Brooks methods. *Human Evolution* 5(3), 227–38.

Buikstra, J. and Ubelaker, D. 1994. *Standards for Data Collection from Human Skeletal Remains: Proceedings of a Seminar at the Field Museum of Natural History*. Fayetteville AS: Arkansas Archaeological Survey Research Series 44.

Bura, P. 2001. Autopsie d'une tombe-bûcher: les exemples de Thérouanne et de Bruay-La-Buissière. In: Geoffroy, J.-F. and Barbe, H. (eds), *Les nécropoles à incinérations en Gaule Belgique, synthèses régionales et méthodologie. Actes du XIXème Colloque international du Centre de Recherches Archéologiques de l'Université Charlesde- Gaulle - Lille 3, 13-14 Décembre 1996. Revue du Nord* Hors série 8. Lille: Université Charles-de-Gaulle, 167–76.

Carroll, M. 2011. Death and society: social and economic aspects of death in the Roman world. In: Andreu, J., Espinosa, D. and Pastor, S. (eds), *Mors omnibus instat: aspectos arqueológicos, epigráficos y rituales de la muerte en el Occidente Romano, Colección Estudios*. Madrid: Ediciones Liceus, 23–50.

Dansen, V. 2011. Childbirth and infancy in Greek and Roman Antiquity. In: Rawson, B. (ed.), *A Companion to Families in Greek and Roman Worlds*, Oxford: Blackwell, 291–314.

Depierre, G. 1995. *Les pratiques funéraires gallo-romaines, liées à l'incinération: apports spécifiques de l'osteologie, de l'archeologie et de l'ethnologie*. Diplôme d'Études Approfondies. Bordeaux: Université de Bordeaux [unpublished work].

Drusini, A. G., Ranzato, C., Onisto, N., Rippa, A. and Bonati, M. 1997. Anthropological study of cremated bones from northern Italy (9th century B.C.–3rd century A.D.). In: Smits, E., Iregren, E. and Drusini, A. G. (eds), *Cremation Studies in Archaeology. Proceedings of the Symposium Cremation Studies in Archaeology (Amsterdam, 26-27 October 1995)*. Saonara: Logos Edizioni, 51–72.

Duday, H. 2013a. Des défunts, des bûchers et des tombes: les enseignements de l'Anthropologie, le renouveau des méthodes. In: Van Andringa, W., Duday, H. and Lepetz, S. (eds), *Mourir à Pompei - Fouille d'un quartier funéraire de la nécropole romaine de Porta Nocera (2003-2007)*. Collection de l'École Française de Rome 468, Rome: Ecole Française de Rome 1, 861–907.

Duday, H. 2013b. L'étude anthropologique des sépultures à crémation. In: Van Andringa, W. Duday, H. and Lepetz, S. (eds), *Mourir à Pompei - Fouille d'un quartier funéraire de la nécropole romaine de*

Porta Nocera (2003-2007). Collection de l'École Française de Rome 468, Rome: Ecole Française de Rome 1, 5–16.

Duday, H., Depierre, G. and Janin, T. 2000. Validation des paramètres de quantification, protocoles et stratégies dans l'étude anthropologique des sépultures secondaires à incinération. L'exemple des nécropoles protohistoriques du Midi de la France'. In: Dedet, B., Gruat, P., Marchand, G., Michel, P. Y. and Schwaller, M. (eds), *Archéologie de la mort, archéologie de la tombe au premier Âge du Fer. Actes du XXI Colloque International de l'Association Française pour l'Étude de l'Âge du Fer. Conques-Montrozier, 8-11 mai 1997*. Monographies d'Archéologie Méditerranéenne 5, 7–30.

Durand, R. 2005. *La mort chez les Bituriges Cubes: approches archéologiques et données anthropologiques d'une cité de Gaule romaine*. Thèse de doctorat. Université de Paris I – Panthéon Sorbonne. [Online], Available: http://tel.archives-ouvertes.fr/tel-00337828, [7 April 2011].

Durand, R. 2008. Données paléodémographiques et classes d'âges d'immatures: recrutement et gestion d'enfants dans les espaces funéraires gallo-romains. In: Gusi, F. Muriel, S. and Olària, C. (eds), *Nasciturus, infans, puerulus vobis mater terra. La muerte en la infancia*. Castelló: Servei d'Investigacions Arqueològiques I Prehistòriques, Diputación de Castelló, 41–56.

Estévez Morales, J. A. 2002. Nuevos hallazgos de naturaleza funeraria en un espacio situado extramuros de la ciudad en época romana. Restos aparecidos en un solar de la calle Tomás Romero de Castilla. Mérida Excavaciones Arqueológicas 2000. *Memoria* 6, 93–102.

Feijoo Martínez, S. and Alba Calzado, M. 2008. Consideraciones sobre la fundación de Avgvsta Emerita. In: Colegio de Ingenieros Técnicos de Obras Públicas (ed.) *IV Congreso de las Obras Públicas en la Ciudad Romana*. Lugo/Guitiriz: Cyan, Proyectos y Producciones Editoriales, S.A., 97–124.

Ferembach, D., Schwidetzky, I. and Stloukal, M. 1980. Recommendations for age and sex diagnoses of skeletons. *Journal of Human Evolution* 9, 517–49.

Fernandes, T. M., Paredes, J., Rebocho, L., Lopes, M. L. and Janeirinho, V. 2012. Área funerária romana em Évora: dos restos ósseos aos rituais funerários. *Antropologia Portuguesa* 29, 183–201.

Garnsey, P. 1998. Child rearing in ancient Italy. In: Scheidel, W. (ed.), *Cities, Peasants and Food in Classical Antiquity: Essays in Social and Economic History*. Cambridge: Cambridge University Press, 253–71.

Gijón Gabriel, E. 2006/2007. Una via sepulchralis en la necrópolis oriental de Augusta Emerita. *Anas* 19–20, 107–38.

Gijón Gabriel, E. and Montalvo Frías, A. N. 2011. El circo romano de Mérida. In: Álvarez Martínez, J. M. and Mateos Cruz, P. (eds), *Actas Congreso Internacional 1910-2010: El Yacimiento Emeritense*. Mérida: CSIC, 195–227.

Gonçalves, D. 2011. The reliability of osteometric techniques for the sex determination of burned human skeletal remains. *Homo - Journal of Comparative Human Biology* 62(5), 351–8.

Gonçalves, D. 2012. *Cremains: The value of quantitative analysis for the bioanthropological research of burned human skeletal remains*. PhD thesis, University of Coimbra, [Unpublished work].

Gonçalves, D., Duarte, C., Costa, C., Muralha, J., Campanacho, V., Costa, A. M. and Angelucci, D. E. 2010. The Roman cremation burials of Encosta de Sant'Ana (Lisbon). *Revista Portuguesa de Arqueologia* 13, 125–44.

Gowland, R. 2001. Playing death: implications of mortuary evidence for the social construction of childhood in Roman Britain. In: Davies, G, Gardner, A. and Lockyear, K. (eds), *TRAC 2000: Proceedings of the Tenth Annual Theorethical Roman Archaeology Conference*. Oxford: Oxbow Books, 152–67.

Gozalves Cravioto, E. 2007. La Demografía de la Hispania romana tres décadas después. *Hispania Antiqua* 31, 181–208.

Grévin, G. 2009. Les crémations sur bûchers: de nos jours et dans l'Antiquité. In: Goudineau, C. (ed.) *Rites funéraires à Lvgdvnvm*. Paris: Éditions Errance, 229–35.

Herrmann, N. and Bennett, J. 1999. The differentiation of traumatic and heat-related fractures in burned bone. *Journal of Forensic Sciences* 44(3), 461–9.

Holck, P. 1997/2008. *Cremated Bones: A Medical-Anthropological Study of an Archaeological Material on Cremation Burials*. Oslo: Anatomical Institute, University of Oslo.

Holck, P. 2005. Cremated bones. In: Byard, R., Payne-Jones, J., Corey, T. and Henderson, C. (eds), *Encyclopedia of Forensic and Legal Medicine.* Oxford: Elsevier, 113–19.

Hope, V. M. 2007. *Death in Ancient Rome: a sourcebook.* London: Routledge.

Jiménez Ávila, J. 2011. Mérida Pre y Protohistórica. In: Álvarez Martínez, J. M. and Mateos Cruz, P. (eds), *Actas Congreso Internacional 1910-2010: El Yacimiento Emeritense.* Mérida: CSIC, 35–58.

Laes, C. 2011. *Children in the Roman Empire: outsiders within.* Cambridge: Cambridge University Press.

Lenorzer, S. 2006 *Pratiques funéraires du Bronze final IIIB au Premier Age du Fer en Languedoc occidental et Midi-Pyrénées: Approche archéo-anthropologique des nécropoles à incinération.* Thèse de doctorat en Anthropologie biologique. Bordeaux, Université Bordeaux I, [Online], Available: http://tel. archives-ouvertes.fr/tel-00151432, [9 April 2012].

Lovejoy, C., Meindl, R., Pryzbeck, T. and Mensforth, R. 1985. Chronological metamorphosis of the auricular surface of the ilium: a new method for the adult skeletal age at death. *American Journal of Physical Anthropology* 68, 15–28.

Lowrance, E. W. and Latimer, H. B. 1957. Weights and linear measurements of 105 skeletons from Asia. *American Journal of Anatomy* 103(3), 445–59.

Márquez-Grant, N. 2008. The burnt human bone. In: Simmonds, A., Márquez-Grant, N. and Loe, L. (eds), *Life and Death in a Roman City. Excavation of a Roman Cemetery with a Mass Grave at 120-122 London Road, Gloucester,* Oxford Archaeology Monograph 6, Oxford: Oxford Archaeology, 72–9.

Márquez Pérez, J. 1998. Nuevos datos sobre la dispersión de las áreas funerarias de Emerita Augusta. Mérida Excavaciones Arqueológicas 1996. *Memoria* 2, 291–301.

Márquez Pérez, J. 2005a. *Informe gráfico de los resultados de la intervención arqueológica en un solar sito en la c/ Tomás Romero de Castilla s/n (12040/20-10S). Intervención arqueológica nº 5037,* Mérida, Consorcio de la Ciudad Monumental de Mérida [unpublished work].

Márquez Pérez, J. 2005b. *Informe gráfico de los resultados de la intervención arqueológica en un solar sito en la c/ González Serrano s/n (12040/21-10S). Intervención arqueológica nº 5038,* Mérida, Consorcio de la Ciudad Monumental de Mérida [unpublished work].

Márquez Pérez, J. 2005c. *Informe gráfico de los resultados de la intervención arqueológica en un solar sito en la c/ Tomás Romero de Castilla s/n (12040/20-10S). Intervención arqueológica nº 5039,* Mérida, Consorcio de la Ciudad Monumental de Mérida [unpublished work].

Márquez Pérez, J. 2006. *Los Columbarios: arquitectura y paisaje funerario en Augusta Emerita.* Serie Ataecina 2. Mérida: Asamblea de Extremadura.

Márquez Pérez, J. 2007. Recuperación de varios edificios funerarios en el área conocida como "La Cueva del Latero" o "Los Bodegones" de Mérida. Presentación de los resultados obtenidos en dos intervenciones arqueológicas realizadas en el solar de "Los Columbarios" de Mérida', Mérida Excavaciones Arqueológicas 2004. *Memoria* 10, 333–54.

Márquez Pérez, J. 2008. Las áreas funerarias de *Augusta Emerita* entre los siglos I y III d. C. In: Mangas, J. and Ángel Novillo, M. (eds), *El territorio de las ciudades romanas.* Madrid: Ediciones Sísifo, S. L., 443–76.

Márquez Pérez, J. 2012a. Las áreas funerarias altoimperiales de *Augusta Emerita.* In: Alba Calzado, M. and Álvarez Martínez, J. M. (eds), *El Consorcio y la Arqueología emeritense: de la excavación al museo. Catálogo de la Exposición.* Mérida: Consorcio de la Ciudad Monumental Histórico-Artística y Arqueológica de Mérida, Ministerio de Educación, Cultura y Deporte, 87–9.

Márquez Pérez, J. 2012b. *Informe gráfico de los resultados de la intervención arqueológica en un solar sito en la c/ Bartolomé José Gallardo n 5 (12040/21-10S). Intervención arqueológica nº 5036,* Mérida, Consorcio de la Ciudad Monumental de Mérida [unpublished work].

Mateos Cruz, P. 2001. *Augusta Emerita.* La investigación arqueológica en una ciudad de época romana. *Archivo Español de Arqueología* 74, 183–208.

Mateos Cruz, P. 2011. Topografía y Urbanismo en *Augusta Emerita.* In: Álvarez Martínez, J. M. and Mateos Cruz, P. (eds), *Actas Congreso Internacional 1910-2010: El Yacimiento Emeritense.* Mérida: CSIC, 127–44.

Mateos Cruz, P. and Pizzo, A. 2011. Los edificios de ocio y representación. El teatro y el anfiteatro de Augusta Emerita. In: Álvarez Martínez, J. M. and Mateos Cruz, P. (eds), *Actas Congreso Internacional 1910-2010: El Yacimiento Emeritense.* Mérida: CSIC, 173–93.

Mayne Correia, P. 1997. Fire modification of bone: a review of the literature. In: Haglund, W. and Sorg, M. (eds), *Forensic Taphonomy: the post-mortem fate of human remains.* New York: CRC Press, 275–93.

McKinley, J. 1993. Bone fragment size and weights of bone from modern British cremations and its implications for the archaeological cremations. *International Journal of Osteoarchaeology* 3(4), 283–7.

McKinley, J. 1994. Bone fragment size in British cremation burials and its implications for pyre technology and ritual. *Journal of Archaeological Science* 21(3), 339–42.

McKinley, J. 2000a. The analysis of cremated bone. In: Cox, M. and Mays, S. (eds), *Human Osteology in Archaeology and Forensic Science.* London: Greenwich Medical Media, 403–21.

McKinley, J. 2000b. Cremation burials. In: Barber, B. and Bowsher, D. (eds) *The Eastern Cemetery of Roman London: Excavations 1983-1990.* London: Museum of London Archaeological Services Monograph, 264–77.

McKinley, J. 2000c. Phoenix rising: aspects of cremation in Roman Britain. In: Pearce, J., Millet, M. and Struck, M. (eds), *Burial, Society and Context in the Roman World.* Oxford: Oxbow Books, 38–44.

McKinley, J. 2004a. Compiling a skeletal inventory: cremated human bone. In: Brickley, M. and McKinley, J. (eds), *Guidelines to the Standards for Recording Human Remains.* Reading: British Association for Biological Anthropology and Osteoarchaeology and Institute of Field Archaeologists, 9–13.

McKinley, J. 2004b. The human remains and aspects of pyre technology and cremation rituals. In: Cool, H. E. M. (ed.), *The Roman Cemetery at Brougham, Cumbria: Excavations 1966-67*, Britannia Monograph 21. London: Society for the Promotion of Roman Studies, 283–310.

McKinley, J. 2006. Cremation ... the cheap option? In: Gowland, R. and Knüsel, C. (eds), *Social Archaeology of Funerary Remains.* Oxford: Oxbow Books, 81–8.

McKinley, J. 2008. In the heat of the pyre: efficiency of oxidation in Romano-British cremations – did it really matter?' In: Schmidt, C. W. and Symes, S. A. (eds), *The Analysis of Burned Human Remains.* London: Elsevier, 163–83.

Méndez Grande, G. 2006. Desarrollo de un espacio agropecuario y funerario en la zona sur de la ciudad. Intervención arqueológica realizada entre las c/ Tomás Romero de Castilla y Antonio Hernández Gil (Mérida). Mérida Excavaciones Arqueológicas 2003. *Memoria* 9, 313–56.

Mora, G. 2004. Historia de la investigación. In: Dupré Raventós, X. (ed.), *Mérida: Colonia Augusta Emérita.* Roma: L'Erma di Bretschneider, 15–26.

Murciano Calles, J. M. 2010. *Historiografía de los aspectos funerarios de Augusta Emerita (siglo I-IV).* Cuadernos Emeritenses 36. Mérida: Museo Nacional de Arte Romano.

Nicholson, R. A. 1993. A morphological investigation of burnt animal bone and an evaluation of its utility in Archaeology. *Journal of Archaeological Science* 20(4), 411–28.

Nogales Basarrate, T. and Márquez Pérez, J. 2002. Espacios y tipos funerarios en *Augusta Emerita*. In: Vaquerizo, D. (ed.), *Espacios y usos funerarios en el Occidente Romano. Actas del Congreso Internacional celebrado en la Facultad de Filosofía y Letras de la Universidad de Córdoba (5-9 de Junio, 2001).* Córdoba: Universidad de Córdoba 1, 113–44.

Noy, D. 2000. Half-burnt on a emergency pyre: roman cremations which went wrong. *Greece and Rome* 2nd Ser. 47(2), 186–96.

Palma García, F. 2002. Ocupación industrial y funeraria de un espacio suburbano en la Colonia *Augusta Emerita*. Intervención arqueológica realizada en un solar de la calle Tomás Romero de Castilla s/n. Mérida Excavaciones Arqueológicas 2000. *Memoria* 6, 79–92.

Palma García, F. 2010. Las competencias autonómicas: una nueva etapa en la arqueología emeritense (1984-2010). In: Álvarez Martínez, J. M. and Mateos Cruz, P. (eds), *Mérida. 2000 años de Historia, 100 años de Arqueología. Cien años de excavaciones arqueológicas en Mérida 1910-2010.* Mérida: Consorcio de la Ciudad Monumental, Histórico-Artística y Arqueológica de Mérida, 175–92.

Parkin, T. G. 1992. *Demography and Roman Society*. Baltimore: Johns Hopkins University Press.

Pearce, J. 2001. Infants, cemeteries and communities in the roman provinces. In: Davies, G., Gardner, A. and Lockyear, K. (eds), *TRAC 2000: Proceedings of the Tenth Annual Theorethical Roman Archaeology Conference*. Oxford: Oxbow Books, 125–42.

Philpott, R. 1991. *Burial Practices in Roman Britain. A Survey of Grave Treatment and Furnishing A.D. 43-410*. Oxford: British Archaeological Report 219.

Pluton, S., Adrian, Y.-M., Kliesch, F. and Cottard, A. 2008. La nécropole gallo-romaine du "Clos au Duc" à Évreux (Eure): des sépultures du Ier siècle apr. J.-C. *Revue archéologique de l'Ouest* [Electronic] 28, 209–60, Available: URL: http:// rao.revues.org/666, [7 June 2013].

Polo Cerdá, M., García-Prósper, E. and Sanchis Serra, A. 2005. Estudio bioarqueológico de las cremaciones del monumento funerario romano del "Solar de la Morería" de Sagunto. *ARSE* 39, 229–68.

Porro, M. A., Simon, C. and Kramar, C. 1999. Etude anthropologique. In: Castela, D. (ed.), *La nécropole gallo-romaine d'Avenches "En Chaplix". Fouilles 1987-1992, Volume 1. Étude des sépultures.* Cahiers d'Archeologie Romande 77. Lausanne: Aventicum IX, 105–13.

Rawson, B. 2003. *Children and Childhood in Roman Italy*. Oxford: Oxford University Press.

Sánchez Barrero, P. D. 2004. El territorio. In: Dupré Raventós, X. (ed.) *Mérida: Colonia Augusta Emerita.* Roma: L'Erma di Bretschneider, 101–11.

Sánchez Sánchez, G. 2001. Ejemplo de continuidad en un espacio funerario de Mérida. Intervención arqueológica en un solar s/n de la c/ Travesía Marquesa de Pinares. Mérida Excavaciones Arqueológicas 1999. *Memoria* 5, 49–82.

Saquete Chamizo, J. C. 2004. Territorios y gentes en el contexto histórico de la fundación de la colonia Augusta Emerita. In: Nogales Basarrate, T. (ed.) *Augusta Emerita: territorios, espacios, imágenes y gentes en Lusitania Romana.* Monografías Emeritenses 8. Mérida: Secretaria General Técnica, 373–97.

Saquete Chamizo, J. C. 2011. Aspectos políticos, estratégicos y económicos en la fundación de Augusta Emerita. In: Álvarez Martínez, J. M. and Mateos Cruz, P. (eds), *Actas Congreso Internacional 1910-2010: El Yacimiento Emeritense.* Mérida: CSIC, 111–24.

Schmitt, A., Monin, M., Bertrand, E., Bouvard, E. and Carrara, S. 2010. Un ensemble funéraire du Haut-Empire le long de la voie de l'Océan (Lyon 9e). *Revue Archéologique de l'Est* [Electronic] 59, 287–51, Available: URL: http:// rao.revues.org/666, [12 July 2013].

Shipman, P., Foster, G. and Schoeninger, M. 1984. Burnt bones and teeth: an experimental study of color, morphology, crystal structure and shrinkage. *Journal of Archaeological Science* 11(4), 307–25.

Silva Cordero, A. F. 2002. Intervención arqueológica realizada en un solar en la c/ Tomás Romero de Castilla, esquina con c/ San Pedro de Alcántara. Mérida Excavaciones Arqueológicas 2000. *Memoria* 6, 103–9.

Silva, F. C. 2007. Abordagem ao ritual da cremação através da análise dos restos ósseos. *Al-Madan* 15, 40–8.

Silva, F. C. forthcoming. Mundo funerário sob o prisma da cremação: análise antropológica de amostras altoimperiais da Lusitania. Tese de Doutoramento em Antropologia Biológica, Universidade de Coimbra.

Silva, F. C., Márquez Pérez, J., Rosa, J. and Santos, A. L. 2008. Cranial trauma on a child from a double Roman burial at *Augusta Emerita*, Spain. Paleopathology Association: scientific program & abstracts. 17th European Meeting of the Paleopathology Association. 25–27 August 2008, Copenhagen, Denmark. Supplement to the *Paleopathology Newsletter* 62.

Silva, F. C. and Santos, A. L. 2009/2010. Análise antropológica: restos ósseos cremados da necrópole romana de Monteiras (Bustelo-Penafiel). *Cadernos do Museu* 12/13, 223–45.

Silva, F. C., Márquez Pérez, J., Rosa, J. and Santos, A. L. 2014. Health care and survival of a child with cranial trauma at *Augusta Emerita* (Mérida, Spain). In: Michaelides, D. (ed.), *Medicine and Healing in the Ancient Mediterranean.* Oxford: Oxbow Books, 218–22.

Smits, E. 2006. Leven en Sterven Langs de Limes. Het fysisch-antropologisch onderzoek van vier gragveldpopulaties uit de noordelijke grenszone van Germania inferior in de Vroeg-en Midden-Romeinse tijd. PhD Thesis, Universiteit van Amsterdam, [Online], Available: http://dare.uva.nl/document/89773, [10 February 2010].

Stiner, M. C., Kuhn, S. L., Weiner, S. and Bar-Yosef, O. 1995. Differential burning, recrystallization, and fragmentation of archaeological bone. *Journal of Archaeological Science* 22(2), 223–37.

Symes, S. A., Rainwater, C. W., Chapman, E. N., Gipson, D. R. and Piper, A. L. 2008. Patterned thermal destruction of human remains in a forensic setting. In: Schmidt, C. W. and Symes, S. A. (eds), *The Analysis of Burned Human Remains.* London: Elsevier, 15–54.

Thompson, T. J. U. 2004. Recent advances in the study of burned bone and their implications for forensic anthropology. *Forensic Science International.* 146 supplement 1, S203–S205.

Thompson, T. J. U. 2005. Heat-induced dimensional changes in bone and their consequences for Forensic Anthropology. *Journal of Forensic Sciences* 50(5), 185–93.

Thurman, M. and Willmore, L. 1980–1981. A replicative cremation experiment. *North American Archeologist* 2(4), 275–83.

Tranoy, L. 2000. La mort en Gaule romaine. In: Crubézy, E., Masset, C., Lorans, E., Perrin, F. and Tranoy, L. (eds), *Archéologie funéraire.* Paris: Éditions Errance, 105–54.

Trotter, M. and Hixon, B. B. 1974. Sequencial changes in weight, density, and percentage ash weight of human skeleton from an early fetal period through old Age. *Anatomical Record* 179(1), 1–18.

Ubelaker, D. H. and Rife, J. L. 2007. The practice of cremation in the Roman-era cemetery at Kenchreai, Greece: the perspective from archeology and forensic science. *Bioarchaeology of the Near East* 1, 35–57.

Unzu Urmeneta, M. and Peréx Agorreta, M. J. 2010. Segunda necrópolis de incineración de época romana en Espinal (Navarra). *Trabajos de Arqueología Navarra (TAN)* 22, 93–114.

Van Den Bos, R. P. M. and Maat, G. J. R. 2002. Cremated remains from a Roman burial site in Tiel-Passewaaij (Gelderland). *Barge's Anthropologica* 9. Leiden: Barge's Anthropologica.

Van Deest, T. L., Murad, T. A. and Bartelink, E. J. 2011. A re-examination of cremains weight: sex and age variation in a northern California sample. *Journal of Forensic Sciences* 56(2), 344–9.

Van Vark, G.-N., Amesz-voorhoeve, W. and Cuijpers, A. 1996. Sex-diagnosis of human cremated skeletal material by means of mathematical-statistical and data-analytical methods. *Homo* 47(1–3), 305–38.

Velázquez Jiménez, A. 2011. *Repertorio de bibliografía arqueológica emeritense III. Emerita 2010.* Mérida: Consorcio de la Ciudad Monumental, Histórico-Artística y Arqueológica de Mérida.

Wahl, J. 1988. Menschenknochen. In: Wahl, J. and Kokabi, M. (eds), *Das römische Gräberfeld von Stettfeld I. Osteologische Untersuchung der Knochenreste aus dem Gräberfeld.* Stuttgart, Kommissionsverlag: Konrad Verlag, 46–223.

Wahl, J. 1996. Erfahrungen zur metrischen Geschlechtsdiagnose bei Leichenbranden. *Homo* 47(1–3), 339–59.

Wahl, J. 2008. Investigations on pre-roman and roman cremation remains from southwestern Germany: results, potentialities and limits. In: Schmidt, C. W. and Symes, S. A. (eds), *The Analysis of Burned Human Remains.* London: Elsevier, 145–61.

Walker, P. L., Miller, K. W. P. and Richman, R. 2008. Time, temperature, and oxygen availability: an experimental study of the effects of the environmental conditions on the color and organic content of cremated bone. In: Schmidt, C. W. and Symes, S. A. (eds). *The Analysis of Burned Human Remains.* London: Elsevier, 129–35.

Warren, M. and Maples, W. 1997. The anthropometry of contemporary commercial cremation. *Journal of Forensic Sciences* 42(3), 417–23.

Weekes, J. 2008. Classification and analysis of archaeological contexts for the reconstruction of early Roman-British cremation funerals. *Britannia* 39, 145–60.

Chapter 7

The integration of microscopic techniques in cremation studies

A new approach to understanding social identity among cremation practicing groups from early Anglo-Saxon England

Kirsty E. Squires

Introduction

Cremation has long been a favoured mortuary practice among many societies in the prehistoric and historic past. Communities inhabiting eastern England during the early Anglo-Saxon period (fifth–sixth centuries AD) are no exception. Archaeological excavations in this region have uncovered multiple large cemeteries where cremation was the prevalent funerary rite (Fig. 7.1). Cremation burials have also been recorded from inhumation dominant sites. An examination of the funerary remains show that the cremation rite was complex and involved a number of stages. This paper will focus on two large cemeteries in North Lincolnshire, namely Elsham and Cleatham, alongside other contemporary sites.

The funerary context

A great deal of our understanding of early Anglo-Saxon society derives from examinations of burials from this period. Inhumation practising groups attracted more attention in the past due to the rich grave provisions buried with the dead. Inhumations therefore provide the majority of evidence concerning social identity owing to the wealth of information that can be obtained from the skeletal remains and their associated artefacts. The most well-known feature of early Anglo-Saxon inhumation burials is the binary grave assemblages of men and women. Weapons are strongly associated with males while females are frequently found with elaborate jewellery (Lucy 2000, 87). In addition, the different combinations of grave goods recovered from inhumation burials have been used to further our understanding of

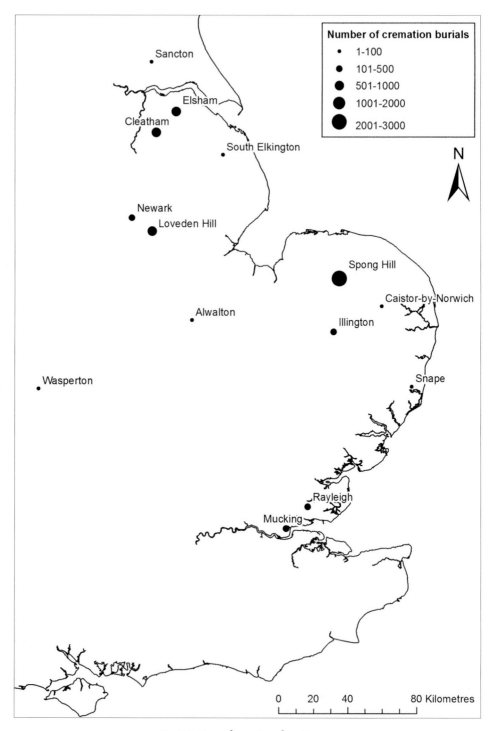

Fig. 7.1: Map of cemetery locations.

stages of the lifecycle (Härke 1997; Crawford 1999; Stoodley 1999; 2000; 2011; Gowland 2006; Martin 2013), hierarchical status (Carver 1989) and wealth of the dead (Arnold 1980). Other factors that have also been considered in the analysis of inhumation dominant cemeteries include the position of the deceased in the grave (Lucy 2000; Reynolds 2009) and spatial distribution of social groups in community cemeteries (Pader 1982; Hirst 1985; Penn and Brugmann 2007; Sayer 2009; 2010; Sayer and Wienhold 2013). The latter two lines of investigation aim to show whether certain individuals or, indeed, specific social groups, were treated unlike the rest of the burial population owing to their position within the community.

Cemeteries where cremation was the preferred funerary rite are larger than those where inhumation was favoured. The quantity of material recovered from these sites has led scholars to explore the social identity of these groups using methods that are more commonly employed in early Anglo-Saxon inhumation studies (Ravn 1999; 2003; Williams 2005; 2007; Devlin 2007; Squires 2011; 2013). However, the grave assemblages of inhuming and cremating populations are very different. Animal offerings and cinerary urns are particularly common in the cremation rite while weapons are extremely rare. Relationships between social identity of the dead, particularly gender, and their associated grave assemblages are less clear-cut in cremation burials (Richards 1987; McKinley 1994; Squires 2011; 2013). Yet, a small number of positive associations have been identified. Infants and children, for instance, were less likely to have been provided with animal offerings than adolescents and adults and were often interred in shorter vessels (Richards 1987; Harman 1989; McKinley 1993; 1994; Hirst and Clark 2009; Squires 2011; 2013). The spatial distribution of both cremation and inhumation burials rarely show any distinct grave groupings (based on age, sex and type and number of grave goods) leading to the recurrent theory that individuals were buried in household groups (Harman 1989; Malim and Hines 1998; Ravn 1999; 2003; Penn and Brugmann 2007; Carver 2009; Hirst and Clark 2009; Squires 2011; 2013). Furthermore, the destructive nature of cremation also makes an examination of social identity by traditional means challenging. The cremation process causes the fragmentation of burned bone and loss of diagnostic skeletal elements required for in-depth osteological analyses. In many cases it is not possible to establish all of the biological attributes of every member of a cemetery population. This factor alone limits the information that can be extracted about social identity. Similarly, the differential survival of artefacts that were placed on the funerary pyre, and even those that made it into the ground, can leave gaps in the available evidence. Therefore, given the limited amount of evidence available from grave provisions and cemetery organisation alone, it is clear that we must supplement traditional methods used to understand social identity in inhumations with new approaches that can be applied more effectively to cremation practicing groups.

The cremated remains

The early Anglo-Saxon cemeteries of Elsham (NGR: TA 046 125) and Cleatham (NGR: SE 932 008) are located in north Lincolnshire (Fig. 7.1). At Elsham, 566 cremation and six inhumation burials dating to the early Anglo-Saxon period and two Bronze Age inhumations were identified and analysed by the author (Berisford and Knowles n.d., 8; Squires 2011, 133–4, 144–5; 2012, 316, 318). Each burial containing human cremated bone was found within, or was associated with, a ceramic cinerary urn with the exception of 23 deposits that were discovered in an unurned state (Squires 2011, 158–9). Although three burials were missing at the time of analysis, 552 of the 566 burials examined contained cremated human bone, while the remaining 14 deposits were largely, if not entirely, composed of animal remains (Squires 2012, 319). The minimum number of individuals (MNI) afforded the cremation rite totalled 564 persons. In addition, seven individuals were recorded from the Anglo-Saxon inhumations and two individuals were identified from the Bronze Age burials (*ibid.*, 319). At Cleatham, 977 cremation and 62 inhumation early Anglo-Saxon burials were discovered (Jakob 1999; Leahy 2007, 29; Squires 2011, 3). The cremated bones were subjected to osteological analyses by the author (Squires 2011). Only 11 of the cremation burials from Cleatham were not interred within, or associated with, a ceramic funerary vessel (Squires 2011, 223). Two burned bone deposits (1101 and 1102) were missing at the time of analysis. However, of the 977 burials examined, a total of 969 interments contained human bone while the remaining eight deposits were primarily composed of animal bone with minimal, if any, burned human bone (Squires 2012, 323). The MNI belonging to the cremation and inhumation practising groups at this site totalled 1009 and 60 persons, respectively (Leahy 2007, 60; Squires 2012, 323). The multiple burials from Elsham and Cleatham account for the larger number of individuals than burials. The archaeological evidence from both Elsham and Cleatham largely conforms to those recorded from contemporary cremation practising groups. An examination of the contents of these burials has showed that funerary provisions, such as grave and pyre goods and faunal offerings, played a key role in the mortuary rituals at these cemeteries (Squires in prep.).

The aim of this paper is to illustrate the utility of combining macro- and microscopic analyses of cremated bone with social interpretation in order to gain a more comprehensive understanding of social identity, particularly hierarchical status. Thompson (2004, 204) has noted that primary level changes, at the microscopic level, are closely linked to secondary level alterations which are manifested at the macroscopic level. Thus, in order to assess differential burning patterns between burials, thin-sections of bone and samples of unburned and burned remains (taken for Fourier Transform Infrared (FT-IR) spectroscopy) obtained from the Elsham skeletal assemblage will be examined alongside the macroscopic appearance of cremated bone from Elsham and contemporary cemeteries. An exploration of burning patterns between, and within, burials can shed light upon the differential funerary treatment of individuals, which was perhaps an expression of their social identity. On a social level, an examination of the cremated remains will provide information about the variability of pyre conditions, which can be viewed in terms of investment. The thin-section and FT-IR spectroscopy case study observations and results employed in this chapter derive from an earlier paper (Squires *et al.* 2011) and the author's doctoral research (Squires 2011). However, unlike the former works, this paper will explore how the application of microscopic techniques, such as histomorphometry, and macroscopic examinations of cremated bone can provide valuable information about social identity.

Methods of analysis

Macroscopic characteristics of the Elsham and Cleatham cremated bone were assessed during the initial stages of osteological analysis. Further details of the complete methodology employed in the analysis of these bone assemblages can be found in Squires (2011; 2012). The skeletal remains from each burial were weighed then sieved through 2 mm, 5 mm and 10 mm sieves, before weighing these compartments individually. The maximum fragment size from each of these sieves was measured using digital callipers. Weight and fragment size were recorded as these measurements can provide useful information about the cremation process itself, for example tending the pyre, and subsequent stages of the funerary rite, such as the amount of bone collected from the pyre site and deposited in urns. Munsell soil colour charts (2000) were employed to record the colour and discoloration of bone. Such an examination of colour is the traditional method used to establish pyre conditions (i.e. temperature and oxidising conditions), taphonomic characteristics of the burial environment and the presence of staining that derived from pyre and grave goods (Franchet 1933; Shipman *et al.* 1984; McCutcheon 1992; McKinley 1994; Taylor *et al.* 1995, 116; Shahack-Gross *et al.* 1997; Devlin and Herrmann 2008; Walker *et al.* 2008). Next, the degree of shrinkage, fracturing and warping of burned bone from each burial was assessed to establish cremation intensity and pyre conditions. The present author devised a scale whereby the shrinkage, fissuring and warping of each burned bone deposit could be efficiently noted since no standardised recording procedure was available at the time of analysis (Squires 2011). This scale ranged from no modification ('none') through to a small amount of modification ('moderate') to significant amounts of modification ('severe') (*ibid.*, 114). A written record was also produced alongside this method as a means of justifying the scores ascribed to each heat-induced modification. Past research has shown that the shrinkage of burned bone is extremely variable and many factors affect the size of skeletal remains that have endured heat modification (Herrmann 1977, 102; Wahl 1982, 10–11; Shipman *et al.* 1984, 322; McKinley 1994, 77; Bush *et al.* 2007, 158). Therefore, metric analyses were not employed to establish the shrinkage of bone from Elsham and Cleatham.

   In addition to the more conventional means of assessing cremated bone, thin-section analysis and FT-IR spectroscopy were also implemented, although samples were only selected from the Elsham assemblage. The detailed results from these analyses will not be addressed here but, instead, an overview of the methods and findings will be discussed. A comprehensive assessment of the methods used in these analyses can be found in Squires *et al.* (2011). Thin-section analysis, or histomorphometry, facilitates the examination of structural changes that occur to bone as a result of the burning process. Together with macroscopic examination, histomorphometry is extremely useful as it not only provides a better understanding of pyre temperatures during the early Anglo-Saxon period but it also supplies evidence for the differential burning of body parts, potentially indicative of the position of the deceased on the pyre. In total, 16 samples from the Elsham assemblage were selected at random, each from a single burial. The only condition of this sampling method was that the remains were taken from adult long bones, as these are the most suited to thin-sectioning. The colour of bone from each sample was documented using Munsell soil colour charts (2000). Due to the fragile nature of burned bone, sections were cut at 60, 75 or 100 microns (Squires *et al.* 2011, 2404). Each thin-section was mounted between two glass slides and examined under a microscope (×25 at all times). Micrographs were taken of each sample to allow a more detailed analysis of bone microstructure.

The microstructure of the archaeological samples was compared with experimental specimens, where temperature of burning was known (Bhayro 2003). Based on these observations, the author devised three standardised categories that could be used to classify varying degrees of heat-induced changes to bone microstructure (Squires *et al.* 2011, 2401). The first category of burned bone is classified as "less intensely cremated". Bones that fell into this grouping were exposed to temperatures between 300°C and 600°C and less than 50% of bone microstructure had been destroyed. Characteristics of "less intensely cremated" bone include the presence and preservation of many Haversian systems, a small number of Volkmann's Canals, organic material and canaliculi. However, some hydroxyapatite (inorganic) crystals show signs of fusion. Macroscopic observations of "less intensely cremated" bone should be very dark grey in colour throughout the section of bone.

Burned bone that falls into the second category, referred to as "intensely cremated" bone, provides evidence for the destruction of over 50% of bone microstructure. These skeletal remains were subjected to temperatures of 600–900°C. Less than 50% of the organic content of bone is preserved at this stage. The outline of Haversian systems are defined and are brown in colour when examined under plane polarised light. Canaliculi are still preserved at this stage, though very few, if any, Volkmann's Canals survive. "Intensely cremated" bone also displays the fusion of many hydroxyapatite crystals, which results in a disorganised arrangement of bone microstructure. Skeletal remains that fall into this category should be light grey to white in colour throughout the cross-section of bone when examined macroscopically.

"Completely cremated" is the final category devised for the purpose of classifying burned bone. Specimens that were allocated to this category were heated to temperatures in excess of 900°C and show the complete absence of Haversian systems,

Volkmann's Canals, organic material and canaliculi. All hydroxyapatite crystals have completely fused at this stage. Hence, 100% of the bone microstructure has been destroyed. Macroscopically, "completely cremated" bone should be white in colour throughout the sample's section. Surviving artefact and pyre debris was also recorded as further evidence of temperature. The presence of glass globules from the Elsham and Cleatham burials indicate that funerary pyres reached temperatures of 800–900°C while the identification of molten copper-alloy suggests temperatures over 1000°C (Holck 1986, 42; Mays 2009, 439). An examination of early Anglo-Saxon cremation slag from Illington, Norfolk, and Elsham by Henderson *et al.* (1987, 93) showed that this by-product was formed through the fusion of silica (cadaver, plant and wood ash), calcium (human body and wood ash) and alkali (plants) at temperatures in excess of 900°C.

FT-IR spectroscopy can be used to identify varying degrees of burning intensity in archaeological bone and discrete temperature variation between samples (Thompson *et al.* 2009; Squires *et al.* 2011). In total, eight samples from the Elsham bone assemblage were selected at random for this analysis, all of which derived from single adult burials. Two of these specimens were taken from individuals that had been afforded the inhumation rite as a control. These samples were different to those employed in thin-section analysis. Samples were taken from the anterior distal third of femoral diaphyses. Again, the colour of each bone sample was recorded using Munsell soil colour charts (2000).

The FT-IR-ATR technique was used in this study. This method measures changes that take place within a reflected infrared ray as soon as it makes contact with the bone sample (Thompson *et al.* 2009, 911). The application of FT-IR spectroscopy permits an assessment of the carbonyl to carbonate ratio, the carbonate to phosphate ratio and the Crystallinity Index of burned bone. The latter two measurements are examined in Squires *et al.* (2011). Crystallinity Index measures the crystal structure and order of bone, which is closely associated with the mean length of these crystals (Trueman *et al.* 2008, 161). When these crystals are heated they become more ordered and larger, which corresponds with the increased Crystallinity Index value (Stiner *et al.* 2001, 650). Similar to the effects of heating on the organic content of bone, exposure to increasing temperatures causes a decrease in the carbonate to phosphate value of cremated remains (Thompson *et al.* 2009, 911). Each sample was processed three times using a Nicolet 5700 FT-IR Spectrometer and the resultant spectra were recorded using OMNIC software (Squires *et al.* 2011, 2405).

Discussion

Position of the deceased on the pyre

The majority of cremated bones from Elsham and Cleatham were white in colour, which indicates the overall high efficiency of cremation and oxidising conditions that were achieved on the pyre. Yet the colour of bone frequently varied within each burial from both Elsham and Cleatham. Despite the high frequency of bones that

Fig. 7.2: Vertebra fragment (Elsham).   _Fig. 7.3: Femur fragment (Cleatham)._

experienced successful oxidation, skeletal remains exposed to reducing conditions were also recorded among these assemblages. Vertebrae, pelves, proximal femora and certain bones of the crania, particularly the petrous portion of the temporal bone, were frequently subject to incomplete cremation (Figs 7.2 and 7.3). These bones often showed minimal amounts of shrinkage and ranged in colour from brown to black. The anatomical location of these bones and the position of the deceased on the pyre possibly explain their exposure to reducing conditions. This is particularly noticeable on the dorsal surface of the bones in question, as they would have been in direct contact with the pyre structure and would therefore have been subjected to a lesser oxygen flow. These observations suggest an extended supine position on top of the pyre. If the body was prone, the ventral surface of bones would show evidence of reducing conditions, which is not the case from the sites in question. Similar burning patterns have been identified from other early Anglo-Saxon cemeteries, including Illington (Wells 1960, 33–4), Sancton, East Riding of Yorkshire (McKinley 1993, 296), Spong Hill, Norfolk (McKinley 1994, 83) and Snape, Suffolk (Steele and Mays 2001, 227).

Iron and copper-alloy staining, as well as adhering globules of metal and glass, were recorded from numerous fragments of cremated bone from the Elsham and Cleatham assemblages. Metal staining was most frequently identified on cranial bones, ribs and the upper limb, particularly on the bones of the hand (Figs 7.4 and 7.5). These observations agree with the patterns of artefact staining on burned bone from Sancton (McKinley 1993, 298) and Spong Hill (McKinley 1994, 83), providing evidence for the type of artefacts that accompanied the deceased on the pyre (_ibid._, 83). For example, copper-alloy staining and adhering globules of the same material were identified on a number of metacarpals and hand phalanges from the Elsham and Cleatham skeletal assemblages (Fig. 7.4). This implies that some individuals were wearing finger rings at the time of cremation.

The location of staining on skeletal elements offers further evidence for the supine position of the deceased on the pyre. If the body was prone or on its side, dress accessories that were usually situated on the upper torso or waist would have

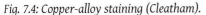

Fig. 7.4: Copper-alloy staining (Cleatham).   Fig. 7.5: Iron staining (Cleatham).

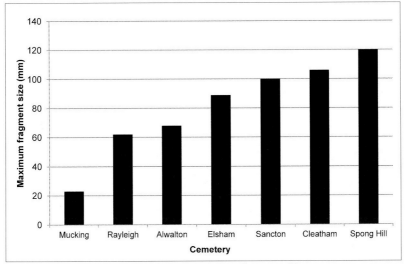

Fig. 7.6: Maximum fragment size of cremated bone.

fallen away from the body at an early stage of the cremation. This would prevent staining and the adherence of artefact debris to bone. The fact that artefact debris and staining was identified where objects would have been positioned by mourners suggests that physical disturbances to the pyre, perhaps to encourage oxidising conditions, are unlikely. This is of particular importance as the maximum fragment size of cremated bones from Anglo-Saxon England, compared to modern cremations, is extremely small (Fig. 7.6). McKinley (1994, 84) notes that the maximum fragment size of burned bone retrieved from modern crematoria before raking lies at around 250 mm. These observations highlight that the cremated bone from Anglo-Saxon England underwent extensive fragmentation, though the cause of which cannot be attributed to intensive tending of the pyre. Instead, other factors such as unintentional fragmentation of the body on the pyre (e.g. when the pyre collapses), collection of burned bone from the pyre site, deposition of the skeletal remains in funerary vessels and the excavation and osteological analysis of these assemblages are all likely to have contributed to further fragmentation of these remains (see Squires 2012 for a more in-depth discussion on this topic).

Once the cadaver had been placed on top of the pyre, the mourners appear to have paid special attention to the positioning of the deceased and their accompanying artefacts to ensure the body underwent a successful cremation. The body undergoes numerous transformations on the pyre. One of these stages is the loosening of ligaments. On an open pyre this would have caused the appendages, particularly the hands and feet, to fall away from the body and towards the edge of the pyre, or away from the pyre completely (McKinley 1989, 72; 2008, 176), resulting in the curtailed combustion of these remains. McKinley (1994, 83–4) has proposed that the deceased was placed in a supine position with their arms folded across their torso. This arrangement would have kept their arms and hands away from the edge of the pyre, ensuring that they did not fall away from the body. Cultural practices may have also influenced the position of the dead on the funerary pyre. Haphazard bodily positioning could result in incomplete cremation. Communities that practiced cremation may have held the belief that cremation was a means of releasing the spirit from the physical body (Oestigaard 2004, 25). Therefore, the decision to place the dead specifically in a supine position at the very top of the pyre may have been seen to facilitate the safe passage of the soul into the afterlife (Meaney 2003, 238; Richards *et al.* 2004, 96).

Pyre conditions

The application of FT-IR spectroscopy to eight samples selected from the Elsham assemblage demonstrated that this method can identify discrete differences between archaeological bone burned at low, medium and high intensities as well as distinguishing burned from unburned bone (Squires *et al.* 2011, 2406). These analyses identified the difference between the two unburned samples, three less intensely cremated, one intensely cremated and two completely cremated specimens (*ibid.*). It was clear that increased burning intensity correlated with a rise in the CI and a drop in the C/P ratio (*ibid.*). These results correspond with those obtained in studies that have employed this method in the analysis of modern samples heated at known temperatures and set intervals (Thompson *et al.* 2009; 2011; 2013). Given that the samples used in the present study are all derived from the same bone, but from different individuals, demonstrates the variability of cremation during the early Anglo-Saxon period.

An examination of bone microstructure using histomorphometry showed that eight of the Elsham samples were heated to temperatures up to, and in excess, of 900°C. These specimens were therefore identified as "completely cremated". The exposure of skeletal elements to high intensity cremation conditions was exhibited through the destruction of organic material, the incineration of bone microstructure and the fusion of hydroxyapatite crystals. Identifiable changes to the inorganic fraction of bone included increased diameter size of Haversian canals, disappearance of osteocyte lacunae and decreased osteon diameter size. Only two samples exhibited the complete loss of microstructure, which occurs at over 900°C (Figs 7.7 and 7.8). The remaining six samples displayed a very small number of osteons, suggesting that these bones were exposed to temperatures of around 900°C (Figs 7.9 and 7.10).

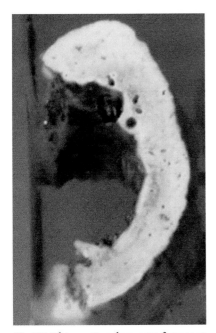

Fig. 7.7. Thin-section: humerus fragment
(EL75BK).

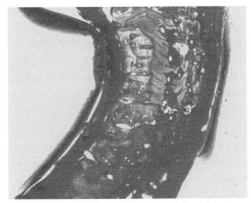

Fig. 7.8. Humerus fragment (EL75BK) under plane
polarised light.

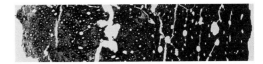

Fig. 7.10. Tibia fragment (EL75BQ) under plane
polarised light.

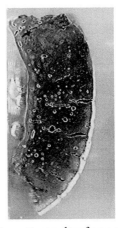

Fig. 7.11. Thin-section: radius fragment (EL75CR).

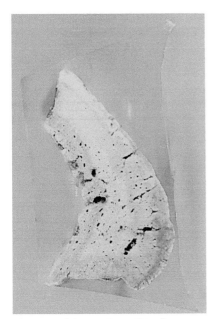

Fig. 7.9. Thin-section: tibia fragment
(EL75BQ).

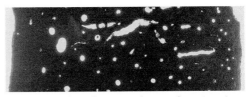

Fig. 7.12. Radius fragment (EL75CR) under plane
polarised light.

The remaining eight samples displayed signs of burning at lower temperatures and were recorded as 'intensely cremated'. These thin-sections revealed the presence of surviving osteons in at least one area of the micrograph, suggesting that these bones were exposed to temperatures below 900°C. An assessment of both archaeological and modern material (the latter prepared by Bhayro, 2003) highlighted that the Elsham samples were exposed to temperatures between 600°C and 900°C (Figs 7.11 and 7.12). These observations imply that the outer cortical bone attained higher temperatures than the mid- and inner-cortical sections, which could in part be attributable to differential duration of the burning process. Cremation that took place over an extended period facilitated complete incineration as heat permeates through the bone at a relatively constant rate. In contrast, curtailed cremation causes differential burning patterns on the inner and outer cortical bone. The inner cortical bone would have endured lower temperatures as well as reducing conditions and hence, it would not have experienced complete incineration. The recovery of large fragments of trabecular bone from a number of cremation burials from Elsham and Cleatham supports this theory. This type of bone contains an elevated amount of organic components compared to cortical bone and, as a result, trabecular bone takes longer to oxidise. Therefore, curtailed cremation may explain why numerous burials contain large fragments of trabecular bone that display signs of incomplete oxidisation.

Three intensely cremated bone samples, namely EL75GA (FN 101); EL75PMb (FN 273b) and EL76NN (FN 549), are of particular interest since burning intensity varied throughout each of these specimens (Figs 7.13–7.18). McKinley (2008, 176) refers to this type of burning as the "sandwich effect". Natural disturbance to the pyre, or bones that fell away from the body, could explain these unusual patterns of burning. For example, bone normally shielded from intense burning conditions would have been directly exposed to high temperatures and an oxidising environment.

Overall, it appears early Anglo-Saxon cremations reached relatively high temperatures and achieved oxidising conditions, though their duration varied. The presence of glass and copper-alloy globules as well as fuel ash slag from a number of the Elsham and Cleatham burials indicate temperatures of at least 800°C to over 1000°C (Holck 1986, 42; Henderson, *et al.* 1987, 93; Mays 2009, 439). Furthermore, the macroscopic external appearance of cremated bone from Elsham and Cleatham exhibited minimal amounts of fracturing and warping, which highlights the oxidation of skeletal remains at a steady rate and at relatively high temperatures. This agrees with the presence of radiating fractures identified on a number of the Elsham thin-section samples. Some degree of variation is to be expected from open air cremations. However, differential rates of complete cremation between individuals demand an interpretation taking both practical and cultural factors into consideration.

Early Anglo-Saxon inhumation and cremation practicing communities expressed their identity differently through their respective mortuary rites (Squires 2013). The visual display of a large funerary pyre may have paralleled contemporary richly furnished inhumation burials. Weapon burials were likely to have been visually

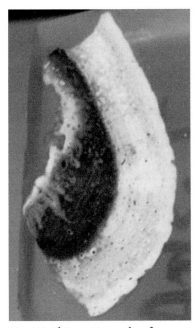

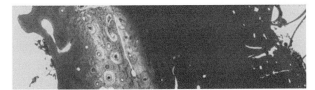

Fig. 7.14: Radius fragment (EL75GA) under plane polarised light.

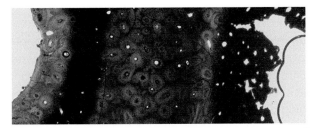

Fig. 7.16. Humerus fragment (EL75PMb) under plane polarised light.

Fig. 7.13: Thin-section: radius fragment (EL75GA).

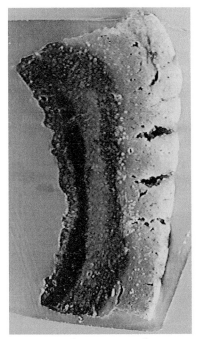

Fig. 7.17. Thin-section: femur fragment (EL76NN).

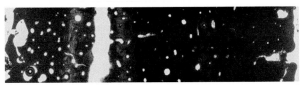

Fig. 7.15: Thin-section: humerus fragment (EL75PMb).

Fig. 7.18: Femur fragment (EL76NN) under plane polarised light.

impressive, especially on the rare occasions when a horse was also included (Fern 2010, 131). Similarly, the construction of a large pyre and the provision of whole and/ or multiple animal offerings placed on its top, either at the sides or by the feet of the deceased (McKinley 1994, 98), would have created an impressive spectacle that would have undoubtedly become part of a collective social memory (Williams 2004, 273). This type of funeral would certainly have been an overwhelming sensory experience. Furthermore, part of the importance of such a large ceremony may have been to evoke and create personal memories of the deceased even for those that were not immediate kin (*ibid.*). A more impressive mortuary display may have been reserved for an individual whose death was deemed a great loss to the community. The additional expenditure of resources, such as fuel, food and labour, would have been essential for this type of funeral. A larger fire would have been necessary, especially if the dead was accompanied by multiple or large faunal offerings. The construction of a bigger pyre would have required the community to invest more time in the collection of fuel and erection of the pyre. In addition, the maintenance of such a large pyre would have required particular attention, for example removing wood ash from under-pyre pits to encourage oxidising conditions (McKinley 1994, 80). Whole horses were cremated and buried at Elsham and Cleatham (Squires 2011). If these creatures were placed on the same pyre as humans, the cremation process would have taken longer due to their size. It is worth mentioning that the cremated faunal remains were primarily blue and grey in colour, suggestive of incomplete cremation, perhaps explained by a peripheral position on the pyre. The placement of faunal offerings on the edge of the pyre would have facilitated the identification of the more thoroughly burned human remains. Alternatively, horses may have been afforded a separate funerary pyre but were cremated for the same duration as the human. This scenario would also account for the less intense burning patterns identified on burned faunal remains from Elsham and Cleatham. It is difficult to differentiate whether faunal offerings, particularly large animals such as horses, were placed on the peripheries of the funerary pyre or were afforded a separate pyre. A detailed examination of these bones and a subsequent investigation into pyre conditions is necessary if we are to reach any conclusions about the cremation of animal offerings in Anglo-Saxon England.

It is clear that all individuals, regardless of hierarchical status, received an adequate cremation. However, it may be possible to make the case that an individual of lower social standing received a smaller cremation pyre, demanding less in terms of both labour and resources. The duration of their funerals may also have been shorter and, as a result, the bones endured less intense cremation than those that were cremated on a more substantial structure. This could account for bones that were classified as "less intensely" and "intensely" cremated from the Elsham cemetery. Despite varying degrees of heat-induced changes to bones from early Anglo-Saxon England, there are no known examples of failed cremations. Nevertheless, this is not to say that unsuccessful cremations did not occur during the period in question. It is possible that cremations did fail, resulting in incomplete combustion of the cadaver, and were carried out again to ensure that the body was reduced to bones with no adhering soft tissues. Given the evidence at hand, it is clear that these communities not only had a good understanding of the cremation process but possessed social values, such as respect for the dead, and perhaps ideological beliefs that assured the success of cremations. This contrasts with the preceding Roman period. Literary accounts from the Continent during the Roman period reference "half-burnt bodies" (Noy 2000). The practicalities of this funerary technology can be accountable for incomplete cremations (*ibid.* 193; McKinley 2008, 178). Yet, on some occasions, the incomplete cremation of a body may have been an intentional mark of dishonour (*ibid.* 191–3).

The presence of artefact debris adhering to burnt bone at Elsham and Cleatham, alongside the lack of pyre debris in the urns, suggests that cremation lasted until the pyre died out (Squires 2011, 293). If the pyre was left to run its course, a number of factors would affect the duration of cremation, such as adverse weather conditions (Squires in prep.). Curtailed cremation, by our definition, was not necessarily significant or even recognised in the past. If a cremation was cut short, mourners may have taken this cue to collect and inter the cremated remains, providing the bones appeared to be burnt. During the Anglo-Saxon period, the colour change in bone, which developed from pale yellow through brown, black, bluish grey, light grey and finally to white, may have signified a complete cremation (Shipman *et al.* 1984, 312–13; McKinley 2008, 180; Squires 2011, 291), and could account for the high proportion of white bones from Elsham and Cleatham. However, the white external appearance of bone may only indicate that the outer cortical exterior had been affected by high temperatures under oxidising conditions. On one hand, an individual afforded a large pyre and cremated under favourable weather conditions would have produced "completely cremated" bones that were entirely white in colour. On the other hand, the cremation of an individual on a smaller pyre under the same weather conditions would have lasted for a shorter duration, but would have produced bones that were similarly white. This colour would have only extended to the outer cortical surface, while the trabecular bone and inner cortical bone would have experienced incomplete cremation, remaining darker in colour.

The collection and burial of cremated bone

The Elsham and Cleatham cremated bone assemblages produced average burial weights of 523 g and 525 g, respectively (Fig. 7.19). These measurements closely correspond with the mean weight of burned bone from contemporary cemeteries, including Sancton (566 g) and Spong Hill (514 g) (McKinley 1993, 296; 1994). Cremated bone deposits from Mucking (147 g) and Rayleigh (326 g), both in Essex, produced significantly smaller average burial weights (Mays 2009, 436; Powers 2008, 48), while the cemetery at Alwalton, Cambridgeshire, yielded a much greater mean burial weight (680 g) (Gibson 2007, 345–8). Based on observations from modern day cremation, McKinley (1994, 75) has identified that a complete adult skeleton produces in the region of 1600–3600 g of burned bone, with an average weight of 2500–3000 g. The

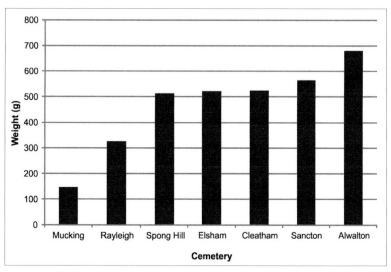

Fig. 7.19: Average weight of cremation burials.

weights of burned bone from Anglo-Saxon cremation burials have highlighted that it was extremely rare to collect and bury the majority, let alone the entirety, of skeletal remains deriving from a whole body. These results hold significant implications in terms of the processing strategies of cremated bone on a site and regional level (see Squires 2012 for a more in-depth discussion of this topic) as well as social factors that may have affected this stage of the funerary rite.

Based on ethnographic evidence and experimental cremations, McKinley (1997, 68) has estimated that the collection process would take at least 3 hours if one individual gathered all of the burned bone from a pyre site by hand. An assessment of 114 cremation burials (or 20% of the burned bone assemblage) from Elsham has illustrated that there was no partiality towards the collection and subsequent burial of bones from one particular skeletal area (Squires 2011, 140). This observation corresponds to the findings from Sancton (McKinley 1993, 298) and Spong Hill (McKinley 1994, 85). It appears that, the primary objective during the collection process was to gather a representative amount of bone from each part of the skeleton. Yet the amount of labour invested in the collection of burned bone is likely to have varied between cremations, depending perhaps on the social standing of the deceased (McKinley 2006, 85). This is illustrated by the variable amounts of bone recovered from early Anglo-Saxon cremation burials (Table 7.1). Analyses have shown that biological sex did not influence the amount of cremated material collected and interred at the Elsham and Cleatham cemeteries (Squires 2011, 150, 213). Analogous findings were recorded from the Spong Hill (McKinley 1994, 85) and Mucking (Hirst and Clark 2009, 630) assemblages. However, age seems to have been an influential factor as infants and children were represented by a smaller amount of cremated bone than adolescents and adults. This can be explained by the fact that they produce a smaller quantity

Table 7.1: Minimum and maximum weight of cremated bone deposits from early Anglo-Saxon England.

Cemetery	Minimum weight (g)	Average weight (g)	Maximum weight (g)	Source
Mucking	0.2	147.4	1164.5	Hirst and Clark 2009, Data Table 9; Mays 2009, 436
Rayleigh	0.4	325.9	1241.6	Powers 2008, 48
Spong Hill	0.1	514.0	3105.1	McKinley 1994, Table 2
Elsham	0.8	523.0	3722.0	Squires 2011, Appendix 1
Cleatham	0.6	525.0	3972.8	Squires 2011, Appendix 2
Sancton	6.0	566.0	3733.0	McKinley 1993, 296–297
Alwalton	5.0	680.0	1659.0	Gibson 2007, Appendix 3

of skeletal remains than older individuals. Furthermore, the fragment size of adult cremated bone would have been larger and easier to identify than the burned remains of an infant or child and this probably accounts for the weight discrepancy between age groups. Yet cultural factors, such as hierarchical status, may have also influenced the amount of cremated material collected and buried after the cremation rite. For example, the skeletal remains of an individual cremated with a horse would have demanded more time. Additionally, if this type of funeral was reserved for individuals of higher status, such as the head of a household, a greater number of mourners may have been involved at this stage of the funerary rite. As a result, a greater quantity of material would have been retrieved

One important question remains unanswered: why is the quantity of cremated remains obtained from early Anglo-Saxon cremation burials frequently less than the expected weight of bone from a complete cadaver? Post-depositional disturbance may account for the low weight of many of these burials, but it is also possible that some burials in cremation cemeteries represent token deposits (McKinley 1998, 19). Perhaps, following a cremation, the remains were distributed among mourners which were retained and buried at a later date, sometimes along with the remains of others (Williams 2004, 282). On the other hand, these bones may have been used in subsequent ceremonies. As an ethnographic parallel, some East Asian Buddhist communities practice a rite that involves family members of the deceased using chopsticks to pick out specific bone fragments which are subsequently placed in special cinerary vessels for later use in commemorative ceremonies (Davies 2005, 58). Alternatively, very small deposits of cremated bone may represent skeletal remains that were collected during the clearance of a pyre site. The burial of a minute quantity of bone may not have warranted reopening a grave, but its interment was still felt to be necessary.

Conclusions

The macro- and microscopic characteristics of burned bone can provide invaluable information about the pyre conditions of early Anglo-Saxon cremations. But what can these observations tell us about the social identity of cremation practicing groups? Rather than basing our understanding on grave assemblages alone, it is equally likely that the time and resources expended on the cremation process were just as significant to these communities. Through the combined use of macro- and microscopic analyses further details relating to the early Anglo-Saxon cremation rite have emerged. The discrete differences in cremation intensity identified through the application of histomorphometry and FT-IR spectroscopy would have gone undetected if only a macroscopic assessment of the Elsham assemblage was undertaken. However, the intention here is not to undermine analyses based only on the macroscopic appearance of bone. Important information pertaining to the differential collection strategies of burned bone, position of the dead on the pyre and more general observations pertaining to pyre conditions can be gathered through such studies. The heat modification of bone highlights differential investment in cremation processes, which is perhaps related to social identity. A person whose death was deemed a great loss to the household or wider community may have been granted a more elaborate funeral, requiring a greater amount of resources and labour. This could explain why the bone from some burials was "completely cremated". Future research into this area will undoubtedly provide a better understanding of the amount of resources and labour invested into the cremation of different members of early Anglo-Saxon society. The application of microscopic methods to a larger sample of individuals from various biological groups (i.e. age and sex) would potentially highlight differences between the cremations of different sectors of society. An examination of burial location and associated grave provisions in conjunction with burning patterns may result in the emergence of spatial burial clusters and artefact groupings that have yet to be recognised. An advantage of the methodological approach used in this chapter is that it can be employed in all osteological studies that deal with cremation practicing societies regardless of time frame and geographical location. The application of this method in future studies will enhance our understanding of how the cremation process and funerary rites differed within and between communities over time and space.

Acknowledgements

The author would like to thank Dawn Hadley, Andrew Chamberlain, Tim Thompson, Meez Islam, Toby Martin, Lisa Bhayro, Derek Pitman, Gareth Perry, Rose Nicholson, Freda Berisford and Chris Knowles for their help in the preparation of this paper. Many thanks to the anonymous referees for their useful comments and constructive feedback. Special thanks to the AHRC for funding the author's PhD research. All photographs were taken by the present author with kind permission from North Lincolnshire Museum.

References

Arnold, C. J. 1980. Wealth and social structure: a matter of life and death. In: Rahtz, P., Dickinson, T. and Watts, L. (eds), *Anglo-Saxon Cemeteries 1979: The Fourth Anglo-Saxon Symposium at Oxford.* Oxford: British Archaeological Report 82, 81–142.

Berisford, F. and Knowles, C. n.d. Elsham Cremation Cemetery. Unpublished draft report.

Bhayro, L. 2003. Histological quantitative and morphological analysis of burned and unburned bone. Unpublished MSc dissertation. Sheffield University.

Bush, M. A., Miller, R. G., Prutsman-Pfeiffer, J. and Bush, P. J. 2007. Identification through X-Ray fluorescence analysis of dental restorative resin materials: a comprehensive study of noncremated, cremated, and processed-cremated individuals. *Journal of Forensic Sciences* 52(1), 157–65.

Carver, M. 1989. Kingship and material culture in early Anglo-Saxon East Anglia. In: Bassett, S. (ed.), *The Origins of Anglo-Saxon Kingdoms.* Leicester: Leicester University Press, 141–58.

Carver, M. 2009. Arguments for the sequence. In: Carver, M., Hills, C. and Scheschkewitz, J., *Wasperton: A Roman, British and Anglo-Saxon Community in Central England.* Anglo-Saxon Studies 11. Woodbridge: Boydell Press, 95–125.

Crawford, S. 1999. *Childhood in Anglo-Saxon England*, Stroud: Sutton.

Davies, D. J. 2005. Remains. In: Davies, D. J. and Mates, L. H. (eds), *Encyclopedia of Cremation.* London: Ashgate, 57–60.

Devlin, J. B. and Herrmann, N. P. 2008. Bone color as an interpretive tool of the depositional history of archaeological cremains. In: Schmidt, C. W. and Symes, S. A. (eds), *The Analysis of Burned Human Remains.* London: Academic Press, 109–128.

Devlin, Z. 2007. *Remembering the Dead in Anglo-Saxon England: Memory Theory in Archaeology and History.* Oxford: British Archaeological Report 446.

Fern, C. 2010. Horses in mind. In: Carver, M., Sanmark, A. and Semple, S. (eds), *Signals of Belief in Early England: Anglo-Saxon Paganism Revisited.* Oxford: Oxbow Books, 128–157.

Franchet, L. 1933. La coloration des os dans le sol: le bouillage des cadavres au moyen age. L'incinération et ses phénominènes. *Revue Scientifique,* 483–95.

Gibson, C. 2007. Minerva: an early Anglo-Saxon mixed-rite cemetery in Alwalton, Cambridgeshire. In: Semple, S. and Williams, H. (eds), *Early Medieval Mortuary Practices.* Anglo-Saxon Studies in Archaeology and History 14. Oxford: Oxford University School of Archaeology, 238–350.

Gowland, R. 2006. Ageing the past: examining age identity from funerary evidence. In: Gowland, R. and Knüsel, C. (eds), *Social Archaeology of Funerary Remains.* Oxford: Oxbow Books, 134–54.

Härke, H. 1997. Early Anglo-Saxon social structure. In: Hines, J. (ed.), *The Anglo-Saxons from the migration period to the eighth century: an ethnographic perspective.* Woodbridge: Boydell Press, 125–70.

Harman, M. 1989. Discussion of the finds: cremations. In: Kinsley, A. G., *The Anglo-Saxon Cemetery at Millgate, Newark-on-Trent, Nottinghamshire.* Nottingham Archaeological Monograph 2. Nottingham: University of Nottingham, 23–5.

Henderson, J., Janaway, R. C. and Richards, J. R. 1987. Cremation slag: a substance found in funerary urns. In: Boddington, A., Garland, A. N. and Janaway, R. C. (eds), *Death, Decay and Reconstruction: Approaches to archaeology and forensic science.* Manchester: Manchester University Press, 81–100.

Herrmann, B. 1977. On histological investigations of cremated human remains. *Journal of Human Evolution* 6, 101–3.

Hirst, S. M. 1985. *An Anglo-Saxon Inhumation Cemetery at Sewerby, East Yorkshire.* York University Archaeological Publications 4. York: University of York.

Hirst, S. and Clark, D. 2009. *Excavations at Mucking: Volume 3, The Anglo-Saxon Cemeteries.* London: Museum of London Archaeology.

Holck, P. 1986. Cremated bones: A medical-anthropological study of archaeological material on cremation burials. *Anthropologiske skrifter* 1. Oslo: Anatomisk institutt, Universitetet i Oslo.

Jakob, B. 1999. The Inhumations from the Mixed Rite Anglo-Saxon Cemetery 'Kirton in Lindsey', Cleatham, North Lincolnshire. Unpublished MSc dissertation. University of Sheffield.

Leahy, K. 2007. "*Interrupting the Pots*": *The excavation of Cleatham Anglo-Saxon Cemetery, North Lincolnshire*. York: Council for British Archaeology Research Report 155.

Lucy, S. 2000. *The Anglo-Saxon Way of Death*. Stroud: Sutton.

Malim, T. and Hines, J. 1998. *The Anglo-Saxon Cemetery at Edix Hill (Barrington A), Cambridgeshire. Excavations 1981-1991 and a summary catalogue of material from 19th century interventions*. York: Council for British Archaeology Research Report 112.

Martin, T. F. 2013. Women, knowledge and power: the iconography of early Anglo-Saxon cruciform brooches. In: Hamerow, H. (ed.), *Anglo-Saxon Studies in Archaeology and History* 18. Oxford: Oxford University School of Archaeology, 1–18.

Mays, S. 2009. The human remains. In: Hirst, S. and Clark, D. (eds), *Excavations at Mucking: Volume 3, The Anglo-Saxon Cemeteries*. London: Museum of London Archaeology, 436–40.

McCutcheon, P. T. 1992. Burned archaeological bone. In: Stein, J. K. (ed.), *Deciphering a Shell Midden*. London: Academic Press, 347–70.

McKinley, J. I. 1989. Cremations: expectations, methodologies and realities. In: Roberts, C. A., Lee, F. and Bintliff, J. (eds), *Burial Archaeology: Current Research, Methods and Developments*. Oxford: British Archaeological Report S211, 65–76.

McKinley, J. I. 1993. Cremated bone. In: Timby, J., Sancton I Anglo-Saxon Cemetery excavations carried out between 1976 and 1980, 287–316. *Archaeological Journal* 150, 243–365.

McKinley, J. I. 1994. *The Anglo-Saxon Cemetery at Spong Hill, North Elmham Part VIII: The Cremations*, East Dereham: East Anglian Archaeology 69.

McKinley, J. I. 1997. The cremated bone from burial and cremation-related contexts. In: Fitzpatrick A. P., *Archaeological Excavations on the Route of the A27 Westhampnett Bypass, West Sussex, 1992. Volume 2: the Late Iron Age, Romano-British, and Anglo-Saxon cemeteries*. Salisbury: Wessex Archaeology Report 12, 55–73.

McKinley, J. I. 1998. Archaeological manifestations of cremation. *Archaeologist* 33, 18–20.

McKinley, J. I. 2006. Cremation ... the cheap option? In: Gowland, R. and Knüsel, C. (eds), *Social Archaeology of Funerary Remains*. Oxford: Oxbow Books, 81–8.

McKinley, J. I. 2007. Cremation Burial 1296. In: C. Gibson. Minerva: an early Anglo-Saxon mixed-rite cemetery in Alwalton, Cambridgeshire, 276-279. In: S. Semple and H. Williams (eds) *Early Medieval Mortuary Practices. Anglo-Saxon Studies in Archaeology and History* 14. Oxford: Oxford University School of Archaeology, 238–350.

McKinley, J. I. 2008. In the heat of the pyre: efficiency of oxidation in Romano-British cremations – did it really matter? In: Schmidt, C. W. and Symes, S. A. (eds), *The Analysis of Burned Human Remains*. London: Academic Press, 163–83.

Meaney, A. L. 2003. Anglo-Saxon Pagan and Early Christian attitudes to the dead. In: Carver, M., *The Cross Goes North: Processes of Conversion in Northern Europe, AD 300-1300*, Woodbridge: Boydell Press, 229–41.

Noy, D. 2000. "Half-Burnt on an emergency pyre": Roman cremations which went wrong. *Greece and Rome* 47(2): 186–96.

Oestigaard, T. 2004. Death and ambivalent materiality – human flesh as culture and cosmology. In: Oestigaard, T. Anfinset, N. and Saetersdal, T. (eds), *Combining the Past and the Present: Archaeological Perspectives on Society* Oxford: British Archaeological Report S1210, 23–30.

Pader, E-J. 1982. *Symbolism, Social Relations and the Interpretation of Mortuary Remains*. Oxford: British Archaeological Report 130.

Penn, K. and Brugmann, B. 2007. *Aspects of Anglo-Saxon Inhumation Burial: Morning Thorpe, Spong Hill, Bergh Apton and Westgarth Gardens*. East Dereham: East Anglian Archaeology Report 119.

Powers, N. 2008. Cremated human remains. In: Ennis, T., *An Early Saxon Cemetery at Rayleigh, Essex: Excavations at the Former Park School*. Chelmsford: East Anglian Archaeology 127, 46–50.

Ravn, M. 1999. Theoretical and methodological approaches to Migration Period burials. In: Rundkvist, M. (ed.), *Grave Matters: Eight Studies of First Millennium AD Burials in Crimea, England and Southern Scandinavia* Oxford: British Archaeological Report S781, 41–56.

Ravn, M. 2003. *Death Ritual and Germanic Social Structure (c. AD 200-600)*. Oxford: British Archaeological Report S1164.

Reynolds. A. 2009. *Anglo-Saxon Deviant Burial Customs*. Oxford: Oxford University Press.

Richards, J. D. 1987. *The Significance of Form and Decoration of Anglo-Saxon Cremation Urns*. Oxford: British Archaeological Report 166.

Richards, J. D., Beswick, P., Bond, J., Jecock, M., McKinley, J., Rowland, S. and Worley, F. 2004. Excavations at the Viking barrow cemetery at the Heath Wood, Ingleby, Derbyshire. *Antiquaries Journal* 84, 23–116.

Sayer, D. 2009. Laws, funerals and cemetery organisation: the seventh-century Kentish family. In: Sayer, D. and Williams, H. (eds), *Mortuary Practices and Social Identities in the Middle Ages*. Liverpool: Liverpool University Press, 141–69.

Sayer, D. 2010. Death and the family: developing generational chronologies. *Journal of Social Archaeology* 10(1), 59–91.

Sayer, D. and Wienhold, M. 2013. A GIS-investigation of four early Anglo-Saxon cemeteries: Ripley's K-function analysis of spatial groupings amongst graves. *Social Science Computer Review* 31(1), 71–89.

Shahack-Gross, R., Bar-Yosef, O. and Weiner, S. 1997. Black-coloured bones in Hayonim Cave, Israel: differentiating between burning and oxide staining. *Journal of Archaeological Science* 24, 439–46.

Shipman, P., Foster, G. and Schoeninger, M. 1984. Burnt bones and teeth: an experimental study of color, morphology, crystal structure and shrinkage. *Journal of Archaeological Science* 11, 307–25.

Squires, K. E. 2011. An Osteological Analysis and Social Investigation of the Cremation Rite at the Cemeteries of Elsham and Cleatham, North Lincolnshire. Ph D dissertation, University of Sheffield.

Squires, K. E. 2012. Populating the pots: The demography of the early Anglo-Saxon cemeteries at Elsham and Cleatham, North Lincolnshire. *Archaeological Journal* 169, 312–42.

Squires, K. E. 2013. Piecing together identity: A social investigation of early Anglo-Saxon cremation practices. *Archaeological Journal* 170, 154–200.

Squires, K. E. in prep. Come rain or shine? The social implications of seasonality and weather on the cremation rite in early Anglo-Saxon England. In: Cerezo-Román, J. I., Wessman, A. and Williams, H. (eds), *Cremation in European Archaeology*. Cambridge: Cambridge University Press.

Squires, K. E., Thompson, T. J. U., Islam, M. and Chamberlain, A. 2011. The application of histomorphometry and Fourier Transform Infrared Spectroscopy to the analysis of early Anglo-Saxon burned bone. *Journal of Archaeological Science* 38(9), 2399–409.

Steele, J. and Mays, S. 2001. The cremated bone. In: Filmer-Sankey, W. and Pestell, T. (eds), *Snape Anglo-Saxon Cemetery: Excavations and Surveys 1824-1992*. Ipswich: East Anglian Archaeology 95, 227–228.

Stiner, M. C., Kuhn, S. L., Surovell, T. A., Goldberg, P., Meignen, L., Weiner, S. and Bar-Yosef, O. 2001. Bone preservation in Hayonim Cave (Israel): a macroscopic and mineralogical study. *Journal of Archaeological Science* 28, 643–59.

Stoodley, N. 1999. *The Spindle and the Spear: a Critical Enquiry into the Construction and Meaning of Gender in the Early Anglo-Saxon Burial Rite*. Oxford: British Archaeological Report 288.

Stoodley, N. 2000. From the cradle to the grave: age organization and the early Anglo-Saxon burial rite. *World Archaeology* 31(3), 456–72.

Stoodley, N. 2011. Childhood to old age. In: Hamerow, H., Hinton, D. A. and Crawford, S. (eds), *The Oxford Handbook of Anglo-Saxon Archaeology*. Oxford: Oxford University Press, 641–66.

Taylor, R. E., Hare, P. E. and White, T. D. 1995. Geochemical Criteria for thermal alteration of bone. *Journal of Archaeological Science* 22, 115–19.

Thompson, T. J. U. 2004. Recent advances in the study of burned bone and their implications for forensic anthropology. *Forensic Science International* 146, S203–S205.

Thompson, T. J. U., Gauthier, M. and Islam, M. 2009. The application of a new method of Fourier Transform Infrared Spectroscopy to the analysis of burned bone. *Journal of Archaeological Science* 36, 910–14.

Thompson, T. J. U., Islam, M., Piduru, K. and Marcel, A. 2011. An investigation into the internal and external variables acting on crystallinity index using Fourier Transform Infrared Spectroscopy on unaltered and burned bone. *Palaeogeography, Palaeoclimatology, Palaeoecology* 299, 168–74.

Thompson, T. J. U., Islam, M. and Bonniere, M. 2013. A new statistical approach for determining the crystallinity of heat-altered bone mineral from FTIR spectra. *Journal of Archaeological Science* 40, 416–22.

Trueman, C. N., Privat, K. and Field, J. 2008. Why do crystallinity values fail to predict the extent of diagenetic alteration of bone mineral? *Palaeogeography, Palaeoclimatology, Palaeoecology* 266, 160–7.

Wahl, J. 1982. Leichenbranduntersuchungen: Ein Überblick über die Bearbeitungs – und Aussagemöglichkeiten von Brandgräbern. *Praehistorische Zeitschrift* 57(1), 1–125.

Walker, P. L., Miller, K. W. P. and Richman, R. 2008. Time, temperature, and oxygen availability: an experimental study of the effects of environmental conditions on the color and organic content of cremated bone. In: Schmidt, C. W. and Symes, S. A. (eds), *The Analysis of Burned Human Remains.* London: Academic Press, 129–35.

Wells, C. 1960. A study of cremation. *Antiquity* 34, 29–37.

Williams, H. 2004. Death warmed up: the agency of bodies and bones in early Anglo-Saxon cremation rites. *Journal of Material Culture* 9(3), 263–91.

Williams, H. 2005. Keeping the dead at arm's length: memory, weaponry and early medieval mortuary technologies. *Journal of Social Archaeology* 5(2), 253–75.

Williams, H. 2007. Transforming body and soul: toilet implements in early Anglo-Saxon graves. In: Semple, S. and Williams, H. (eds), *Early Medieval Mortuary Practices. Anglo-Saxon Studies in Archaeology and History 14.* Oxford: Oxford University School of Archaeology, 66–91.

Chapter 8

Analysing cremated human remains from the southern Brazilian highlands
Interpreting archaeological evidence of funerary practice at mound and enclosure complexes in the Pelotas River Valley

Priscilla Ferreira Ulguim

Significant evidence exists for funerary practices associated with earthwork mound and enclosure complexes situated at elevated locations within carefully constructed landscapes in the southern Brazilian highlands and surrounding regions. Increasing archaeological research at sites associated with prehistoric Jê populations provides a variety of evidence from at least 220 BC, and possibly from as early as 2860 BC, intensifying until the contact period (De Masi 2006; 2009; Copé *et al.* 2002; Araújo 2007; Corteletti 2012; Iriarte *et al.* 2008; 2013). The cremated human remains from these complexes indicate an intrinsic link to cremation practice, evidencing discernible regional patterns (Herberts and Müller 2007; Copé 2007; Iriarte *et al.* 2008; De Masi 2009; De Souza and Copé 2010). This chapter analyses cremated human remains excavated at three mound and enclosure complexes, RS-PE-21, RS-PE-29, SC-AG-108, along the Pelotas River in the southern Brazilian highlands, all dating to between AD 1405 and 1655 (OxCal v4.2.3 Bronk Ramsey 2009; SHCal13 southern hemisphere atmospheric curve Hogg *et al.* 2013) (Figs 8.1 snd 8.2). The analysis of cremated remains has the potential to reveal fundamental evidence about cremation practice in prehistory, and new approaches and analysis in this area are developing rapidly (Shipman *et al.* 1984; McKinley 1997; Devlin and Herrmann 2008; Walker *et al.* 2008; Gonçalves *et al.* 2011; Thompson *et al.* 2009; 2011; Squires *et al.* 2011). Such analysis is especially effective in conjunction with detailed contextual information as part of an interdisciplinary approach, integrating data from experimental and forensic research with a range of archaeological and ethnohistorical information. This allows greater understanding of the processes central to the disposal of the deceased in specific contexts, as well as improved interpretation of funerary practices with implications for broader research questions. This study aims to integrate interdisciplinary research with the analysis of the cremated remains, investigating the nature of the cremation practice through the

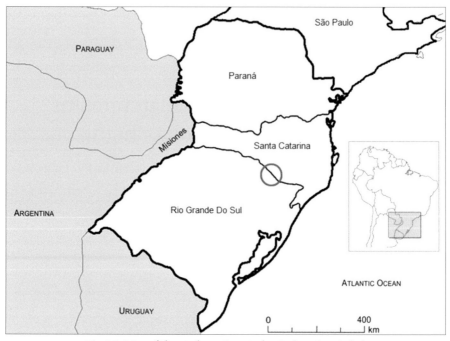

Fig. 8.1: Map of the study region, study site location circled.

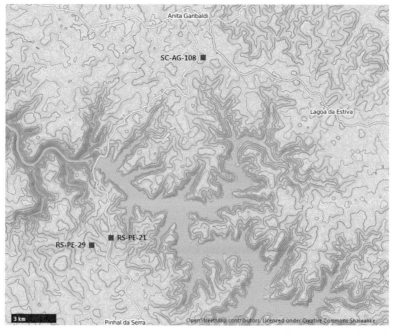

Fig. 8.2: Sites RS-PE-21 RS-PE-29 and SC-AG-108 on either side of the Pelotas River, the boundary between the states of Santa Catarina and Rio Grande do Sul (OpenStreetMap Contributors).

analysis of secondary-level changes within the bone and the nature of the individuals through bioarchaeological analysis, relating this to information from the funerary contexts and the broader 'sacred' landscape (Iriarte *et al.* 2013), linking archaeological, ethnohistorical and experimentally derived evidence.

Introduction

The synthesis of archaeological, ethnographic and linguistic data suggest that these sites form a continuum linking prehistoric inhabitants of the region with ethnographically recorded regional groups of Macro-Jê linguistic stock; the Kaingang and Xokleng (Wiesemann 1978; Noelli 1999; Prous 1992; Da Silva 2001). Through this methodological framework their ancestors are seen as proponents of this carefully constructed landscape. Implications for the interpretation of the cremated material are explored in the course of the chapter.

Southern Jê archaeology corresponds to a range of sites, landscapes and material culture across the highlands of southern Brazil; Rio Grande do Sul, Santa Catarina, Paraná, São Paulo, north-eastern Argentina; in Misiones and Paraguay (Beber 2004; Iriarte *et al.* 2008) (Fig. 8.1). Various traditions were defined to describe these groupings: Eldoradense (Menghin 1957), Casa de Pedra, Itararé (Chmyz 1968) and Taquara, later consolidated as Taquara/Itararé (Prous 1992; Araújo 2007). Links have been proposed between these and the material culture and sites of contemporary Kaingang and Xokleng groups since early research (Menghin 1957; Miller 1971; 1978; Chmyz 1967; Brochado 1984; Schmitz and Becker 1991). However, recent interdisciplinary revisions explicitly associate this archaeological evidence with proposed migrations of Jê speaking groups southwards from central Brazil (Noelli 1999; 2005), the southern branch of the Jê language family, including Kaingang and Xokleng, having possibly diverged from the others around *c.* 1000 BC (Urban 1992).

Archaeological evidence for this expansion exists from *c.* 220 BC, comprising mound and enclosure complexes, pithouses, terraces and thin-walled, dark clay-coloured ceramics with impressed designs (Ribeiro 1980; Reis 1980; 2002; Schmitz and Becker 1997, 252; Schmitz *et al.* 2002; Iriarte *et al.* 2008; Schmitz 1988; Araújo 2001; 2007). Palaeoenvironmental evidence reveals that increased human activity in this region coincides with the southward expansion of *Araucaria angustifolia* (Araucaria tree or Paraná pine), replacing *campos* vegetation *c.* AD 600 in Paraná, *c.* AD 950 in Rio Grande do Sul and *c.* AD 1100 in Santa Catarina (Bitencourt and Krauspenhar 2006, 110; Bronk Ramsey 2009; Hogg *et al.* 2013). This is associated with elevated regional frequencies of charcoal particulates, possibly of anthropogenic origin (Iriarte and Behling 2007, 116–20). Archaeological evidence exists for hunting, riverine fishing, plant and seeds exploitation, including *pinhão* of the Araucaria tree whose charred remains are found at domestic sites (Copé and Saldanha 2002), as well as horticulture, with palaeobotanical evidence for the presence of *Zea mays* L. *Cucurbita sp. Manihot sp. Phaseolus sp.* and *Dioscorea sp.* (De Masi 2007; Gessert *et al.* 2011; Corteletti 2012).

The mound and enclosure complexes are of significance due to their link with funerary practice and cremation. Here the term enclosure is used to translate the Portuguese *estrutura anelar* or *anel* (ring structure or ring), those containing mounds are noted as a mound and enclosure, and when grouped, as complexes (following Iriarte *et al.* 2008; 2013). Commonly found in elevated locations with a wide viewshed, or area of land with a broad vista (Saldanha 2005; Iriarte *et al.* 2013), these comprise circular, elliptical or keyhole-shaped earthworks 3–6 m wide and 20–180 m in diameter, generally in low relief *c.* 0.5 m high, though there are much larger examples, frequently enclosing single or multiple mounds (Caldarelli 2002; De Masi 2005; 2009; Iriarte *et al.* 2008). First described in Misiones, Argentina by Menghin (1957), he theorised a possible funerary function due to their monumental form and apparent paucity of domestic refuse. As systematic research developed these type-sites were noted across the Brazilian highlands (Chmyz *et al.* 1968; Chmyz and Sauner 1971; Rohr 1971; Miller 1971; Ribeiro and Ribeiro 1985). However, function was debated due to the lack of excavation evidence and understanding of variability in form, patterning within the landscape, and relation to other sites such as pithouses. Although Chmyz and Sauner (1971) noted the presence of cremated remains beneath the mound of an enclosure at PR-UB-4 as providing evidence for a funerary function, emphasis was placed on the interpretation as fortified villages with palisaded embankments for defence (Rohr 1971; Ribeiro and Ribeiro 1985).

The advent of a series of focused research programmes has shed more light on their function and context, including in the Canoas and Pelotas River valleys (Caldarelli 2002; Copé *et al.* 2002; Copé 2007; 2008a; 2008b; Müller 2008; 2011; Iriarte *et al.* 2008; Scientia Sul 2006; De Masi 2005; 2006; 2009). Cremated human remains were recovered in Pinhal da Serra, Rio Grande do Sul at two sites analysed in this study: RS-PE-21 and RS-PE-29, in a programme which identified several mound and enclosure complexes (Copé *et al.* 2002; Copé 2008). Further research in Santa Catarina provided evidence for a range of similar sites including cremated human remains: one, SC-AG-108, is also analysed here (Caldarelli 2002; Müller 2008; 2011; Scientia Sul 2006; De Masi 2005; 2006; 2009). Calibrated radiocarbon dates for these sites indicate use between AD 1405 and 1655 (Figs 8.2–8.4).

Themes emerge at the various sites presenting cremated remains. Their location on intervisible hilltops and ridges in proximity to pithouses was probably not arbitrary as GIS-based research reveals placement at nodal points, often aligned with each other, suggesting careful positioning within a formally defined landscape. Location may have both a symbolic meaning in terms of social and public space, as well as possibly demarking territories (Saldanha 2005; Iriarte *et al.* 2013). Often, though not always, the enclosures occur in complexes: regularly paired. Though variation exists (De Souza and Copé 2010; Iriarte *et al.* 2008; 2013) many of the paired enclosures are composed of low banks encircling a single central mound, these are regularly found on an east–west axis, with NW–SE or SW–NE alignment, with the larger mound to the west. This is true of the three sites which form the basis for this chapter (Fig. 8.3).

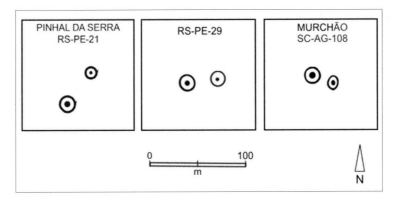

Fig. 8.3: The mound and enclosure complex study sites RS-PE-21, RS-PE-29 and SC-AG-108, this reveals alignment of the mounds and the patterns in the size of the earthworks (after Iriarte et al. 2008, fig. 2 and Ulguim 2011, fig. 8).

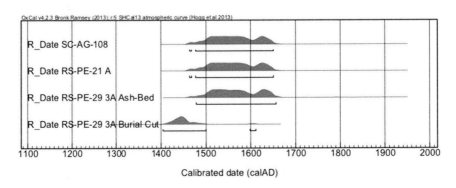

Fig. 8.4: Calibrated radiocarbon dates for archaeological material from the sites (Oxcal 4.2.3, Bronk Ramsey 2009, SHCal13, Hogg et al. 2013).

At RS-PE-21 a twin mound and enclosure complex was identified, Enclosure A is larger and more westerly, with an earthwork bank of 20 m diameter, while B is 15 m in diameter. Only A was excavated, revealing 54.6 g of cremated human remains mixed with charcoal throughout an ash-bed dating to between AD 1465 and 1650 (350±40 uncal. BP, Copé 2007; all cited radiocarbon dates were calibrated using OxCal 4.2.3, SHCal13: Bronk Ramsey 2009; Hogg *et al.* 2013) (Figs 8.4 and 8.5), and pot sherds apparently deposited as pyre goods, similar to specific forms found at other sites. Below the ash-bed was a block of burnt clay forming a pyre base, extending to the limit of the mound. Outside the enclosure pot sherds, stone flakes, small balls of burnt clay and burnt clay rollers were recovered, possibly indicating ritual activities (Copé *et al.* 2002; Saldanha 2005).

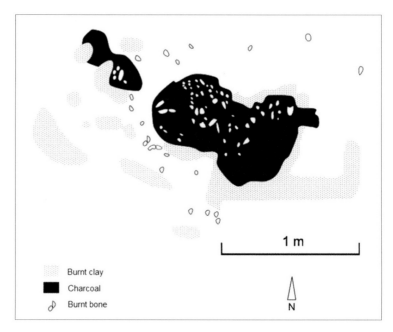

Fig. 8.5: Plan of the excavated context containing cremated remains at RS-PE-21 (after De Souza 2012, fig. 4.7).

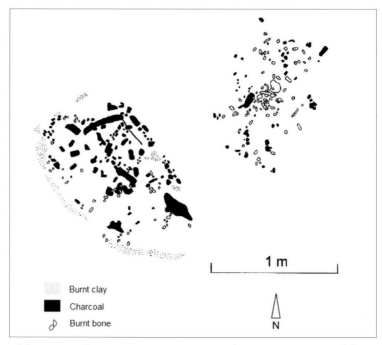

Fig. 8.6: Plan of the excavated contexts containing cremated remains at RS-PE-29 (after De Souza 2012, fig. 4.36).

At RS-PE-29, the complex included another pair of enclosures, 3A and 3B, with single mounds. A, the westerly enclosure has a greater diameter of 20 m, while B has 15 m. Both were excavated, only A provided evidence of cremated remains, but recorded in two separate contexts. The first, an ash-bed feature below the mound with charcoal logs in rectilinear form underlain by a pyre-base, was indicative of a structure measuring approximately 0.9 × 1.8 m, to the extent to of the burnt clay. Within the debris 26.5 g of cremated material in relatively friable condition was recovered. Material from this feature dates to AD 1479–1655 (340±40 uncal. BP, De Souza and Copé 2010) (Figs 8.4 and 8.6). Fragments of associated ceramics were found, though in insufficient quantity to reconstruct the vessel.

The second context at Enclosure A is dated earlier, to AD 1405–1610 (490±40 uncal. BP, De Souza and Copé 2010) (Fig. 8.4). This grey oval feature, identified as a burial cut, exceeded 30 cm deep and 0.70 m in diameter at the widest point and contained 209.5 g of calcined bones with charcoal and burnt orange clay (Fig. 8.6). The form, lack of ash-bed and concentration of the remains support an interpretation as a cremated deposit.

At the complex of SC-AG-108 another pair of enclosures were excavated; Enclosure 1 and 2, material from this complex was dated to AD 1465–1650 (350±40 uncal. BP, Herberts and Müller 2007) (Fig. 8.4). The larger, westerly Enclosure 1, measures 19 m in diameter, while Enclosure 2 is 15 m. Within Enclosure 1 mound an ash bed containing 298 g of cremated human material was encountered and blocklifted for laboratory excavation (Fig. 8.7). Root action dispersed the material; fragments of vertebrae, proximal and medial pedal phalanges, mandible, humerus and the neck of a left first rib were not anatomically aligned, but long bones appeared to the southwest. Duplicated elements indicate multiple individuals are present. Pot sherds were recovered around the enclosure and as ash-bed pyre goods, while an intentional stone cluster was noted east of the ash-bed.

Beneath the Enclosure 2 mound 79 g of bone was concentrated in a cut 15 cm deep, 0.50 m in diameter (Fig. 8.8). The bones appeared to be mingled, without anatomical alignment, but significantly included a maxilla with intact left and right first and second maxillary molars and the right half of a mandible with post-mortem dentition loss. The cut, concentration, mingling and lack of ash-bed indicate a cremated deposit. A single undecorated pot sherd was recorded in the context, while a cluster of unflaked and unburnt stone was recovered below the burial.

In summary, the sites consist of paired circular enclosures of similar dimensions, consistently larger in the west. The central mounds reveal cremated remains in ash-beds or cut features all associated with specific pot sherds.

The funerary context

The careful use of ethnographic and ethnohistorical documentation is critical in interpreting the archaeological evidence for funerary practices, allowing a deeper understanding of the themes of continuity and change in southern Jê archaeology and the testing of hypotheses in relation to the practices of Kaingang and Xokleng groups. Thousands of ethnohistorical accounts note characteristics of both societies from the sixteenth century onwards (Noelli *et al.* 1998; n.d.; Noelli 1999; 2005), providing a wealth of detail, comparable to archaeological evidence, for technology, sites and activity in the region (Lavina 1994). Although caution is required due to the pitfalls of direct analogy, processes of cultural change, and intense pressures exerted during the colonisation period, there remains significant evidence of cultural continuity that can support a considered approach (Noelli 2005, 177).

Many sources provide information regarding Kaingang funerary rites and the use of mounds and enclosures for burials of chiefs (Métraux 1946; Mabilde 1988; Baldus [1937] 1979; Manizer 2006). Mabilde (1988) notes that after death, the principal chief of the group would be laid with his head to the east and feet to the west, while the family of the dead and chiefs of subordinate groups would gather, after the men covered the body with ether they would then feast around fires. On the following day the principal chief organised the subordinate tribes to return and create a circular mound over the burial (Fig. 8.9). This would be cleared of vegetation and beaten underfoot. Inhumation of the chief in which a pit below a mound is noted in other sources, some of which mention these were sometimes reused for later burials (Borba 1908 cited in Dias 2004; Mabilde 1983; Horta Barbosa 1947; Cimitille cited in Veiga 1992, 165; Manizer 2006).

The strongest evidence for cremation is attributed to Xokleng groups. Multiple sources portray aspects of a rite where deceased are cremated with personal belongings on a pyre, attended by a group of individuals, who leave the fire to burn out, returning later to collect the cremated remains and deposit these in a pit, over which a mound is then raised (Tavares 1910; Vasconcellos 1912, 19 cited in Lavina 1994; Kempf 1947; Henry 1964; D'Angelis 2003). Henry (1964, 185–6) provides a detailed account from a Xokleng named Vamblé:

> "They place him on a blanket. Arrows...beside him. Feathers are placed on him. His arrows are broken. The bowstring is cut and the arrows tied with it; also the wrapping for future arrows. His head is laid to the west and his feet to the east because the kuplēng dwell in the west. He will see the road and go that way. If they were to put him on the other way he would err. The wood is waist-high. They place him on it and pile wood on top of him until it is as high as a man. They sink posts on the side and all around so that the wood with not fall down... they set fire to the pile with flaming bamboo. When they set first they sing... When the fire is out they throw the ashes off the bones and gather them together in bark... they make a big basket for them and...carry the basket with the bones and go to another place to bury them."

Kempf (1947) notes that the individuals are bound with vines in a squatting position and also notes the placement of with a bow, broken, and other personal belongings on the pyre. Vasconcellos (1912, 19 cited in Lavina) adds detail regarding mound construction, noting deposition of cremated remains of chiefs in carefully excavated pits, with the form of a "pot", upon which they raised a mound with a diameter of of half a metre at the widest point, forming a "truncated cone", approximately half a metre high, depending on the status of the deceased.

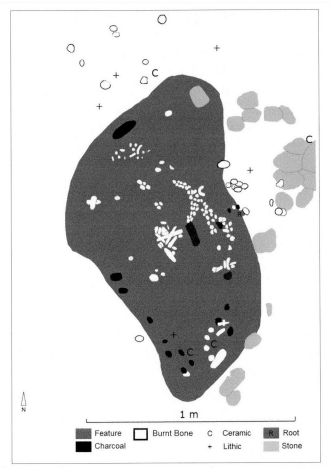

Fig. 8.7: Plan of the excavated contexts containing cremated remains at SC-AG-108 Enclosure 1 (after Müller 2008, fig. 54).

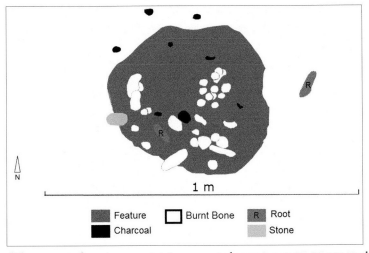

Fig. 8.8: Plan of the excavated contexts containing cremated remains at SC-AG-108 Enclosure 2 (after Müller 2008, fig. 55).

Other rites described ethnographically include Xokleng funerary feasting: *kikikoi* (Veiga 2006), and initiation rites involving the use of lip-plugs or *tembetá* (De Masi 2006). In the archaeological record enclosure size and form are distinguished between those with low banks 15–20 m in diameter and a central mound, and those with large circular embankments 65–70 m in diameter lacking central mounds (Rohr 1971). Evidence from recent research now suggests that larger forms without mounds may have been spaces for social ceremonies, such as initiation rites, where *tembetá* have been recovered (De Masi 2005; 2006; Corteletti 2012), while funerary feasting is also evidenced by earth ovens and remains at larger complexes (Iriarte *et al.* 2008) though it is not proposed that this is directly connected to the *kikikoi* ritual. Mound and enclosure complexes regularly present human cremated remains, providing evidence for funerary practice centred around cremation (Copé *et al.* 2002; Saldanha 2005; Copé 2007; 2008a; 2008b; Muller 2008; De Masi 2005; 2006; 2009). These are examples of a regional pattern of funerary practice. From the descriptions provided, there are recurring themes across the southern Jê in the position of the body, the addition of grave goods and, or pyre goods as accompaniments for the deceased, including bows and arrows, ceramic vessels and other personal possessions. Ethnographic accounts link such practices with social differentiation, mentioning 'chiefs', and note the attendance of groups at a ceremonial site and the construction of earthworks. Understanding whether this is applicable for the archaeological record requires detailed analysis. Such data provides a unique opportunity to make in-depth archaeological comparisons.

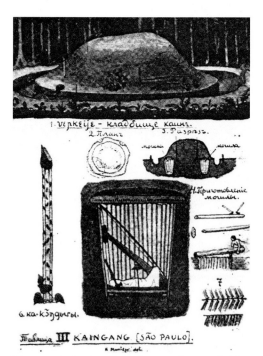

Fig. 8.9: *Kaingang burial mound recorded by Manizer in São Paulo state (Manizer 2006, 47).*

Methods of analysis

A range of analytical techniques was used to link variation in heat-induced changes in bone to specific archaeological contexts and regional studies, allowing interpretation of funerary practice. The analytical techniques are part of a broader methodology developed in forensic and archaeological research into burnt bone (Krogman 1943a; 1943b; Baby 1954; Binford 1963; Herrmann 1977; Bradtmiller and Buikstra 1984; Shipman *et al.* 1984; McCutcheon 1992; Nicholson 1993; Mayne Correia 1997). Recent advanced analysis has refined our understanding of the dynamics of cremation, focusing on microscopic structural and chemical change, termed "primary-level" change (Piga *et al.* 2008; 2009; 2013; Gonçalves *et al.* 2011; Squires *et al.* 2011; Thompson 2005; Thompson *et al.* 2009; 2013). These studies have been crucial in developing an improved understanding of primary and secondary level heat-induced changes in bone, and fundamental to interpreting cremation within a broader archaeological context. A summary of these changes are given and discussed in Chapter 1 of this volume.

This chapter attempts to use this understanding to develop a refined interpretation of the remains. All fragments were categorised and analysed macroscopically (see Table 8.12 for categories). Identifiable features, where found, were investigated microscopically. All fragments were weighed and measured on greatest dimension using circular diameter scales, identifiable fragments were sorted by side, segment, and skeletal region. Heat-induced changes were recorded, including fracture types, warping, fragmentation and RGB colour analysis. Data for age and sex was recorded, though affected by heat exposure (Thompson 2004). The presence of pathological lesions and taphonomic signatures were noted. It is highlighted that recovery and conservation method can affect the study of these changes. In this case the application of Paraloid B-72 and anhydrous acetone to prevent fragmentation in excavation and storage (Müller 2008; Gambim Júnior 2010) were considered with regards to modification of bone weight and colour (Rossi *et al.* 2004).

This study makes use of seven fracture categories standardised by Symes *et al.* (2008, 42–3): Longitudinal, Curved Transverse, Step, Transverse, Burn Line, Patina and Splintering and Delamination (Table 8.1). Fracture types and warping are used as indicators of bone state when burned, with important implications for the interpretation of specific cremation practices, as the presence of warping and curved transverse fractures was linked to burned fleshed bone, their absence with longitudinal fractures and splintering to dry bone (Krogman 1943a; 1943b; Baby 1954; Binford 1963). Recent experimental research reveals that warping and curved transverse fractures can occur when burning dry, unfleshed bone, and may be more indicative of bone properties, such as the preservation of collagen-apatite links, rather than soft tissue presence (Gonçalves *et al.* 2011). Thus, these heat-induced changes should be used with caution when inferring pre-burn state and interpreting funerary practice.

Heat-induced colour change is an important indicator for understanding burn intensity (Shipman *et al.* 1984; Walker *et al.* 2008). As temperature increases, bone carbonises, changing from brown, to black, calcination then causing it to turn grey and white (Table 8.2). Researchers have attempted to increase the accuracy of the link between burn temperature and colour change (Mayne Correia 1997).

Interpretation of bone colour must account for the dependency on exposure duration, environmental conditions, and deposition context, fuel, the presence of soft tissue and the protection it afforded the bone. This also includes factors such as haemoglobin, soil type, oxygen availability, burn duration and temperature achieved, as well as the chemical reaction of organic and inorganic materials (Walker *et al.* 2008). Colour can vary within an assemblage or just a single bone, therefore a nuanced approach is required to understand fire dynamics (Symes *et al.* 2008, 35; Mayne Correia 1997, 276–7).

Colour recording method is an important consideration. Though well standardised with Munsell Soil colour charts (Shipman *et al.* 1984) further research has developed new digital standards using CIELAB and RGB, reducing subjectivity and recording issues. The use of RGB allows calculation of average composite digital colours from a single surface, accounting for burn variability and environmental conditions (Devlin and Herrmann 2008; Walker *et al.* 2008). In this study a computer program provided RGB colours from several points on bone surfaces using digital images of a sample

Table 8.1: Fracture classifications in burnt bone after Symes et al. *2008.*

Fracture	Description
Longitudinal	Regular and predictable, Induced as the bone is heated to the point of structural failure. This occurs along the weakest point of the bone, parallel to the osteon canals therefore travelling longitudinally along the bone. They may also travel helically along the long axis of the bone.
Curved Transverse	Sometimes known as thumbnail fractures, these appear as twisting fractures along the long axis of bones or as concentric rings in regions with fossae or concentrated tissues. This can also result in 'coning', a feature where fractured diaphysis appears arched at the margin of the fracture. Cited as caused by the shrinkage of soft tissues and periosteum during heating which pulls and cracks bone during thermal alteration. In support of this Symes *et al.* (2008) conducted studies on modern burned bone and presented evidence to suggest that these fractures are the result of bundles of muscles shrinking during heating. However, evidence shows that they can occur on dried bone, perhaps due to collagen-apatite links (Gonçalves *et al.* 2011).
Step	Commonly related to longitudinal fractures, as they extend transversely from longitudinal fracture margins through the compact bone of the diaphysis until the margin of another longitudinal fracture.
Transverse	Distinguished by the fact that they transect haversion canals. Common due to the regular transverse direction of burning bone.
Burn Line	Fractures which follow the burn line between burned and unburned bone
Patina	A "fine mesh of uniformly patterned cracks" (Symes *et al.* 2008, 43), which may be due to uniform shrinkage of flat cortical bone. This often appears on flat areas of the postcranial bones, but is also apparent on epiphyseal bones, possibly as the result of broad areas heated uniformly, or the burning of thin soft tissue
Splintering and Delamination	The separation of bone layers, occurring as the separation of cortical bone from cancellous bone. On cranial bones this is apparent as the separation of the inner and outer tables. On epiphyses the cancellous bone is also exposed

Table 8.2: Temperature °C and Bone Colour Observed (after Gonçalves 2007).

Colour	Shipman et al. 1984	Etxeberria 1994	Mays 1998	Walker et al. 2008	Wahl 2008	McCutcheon 1992	Bonucci and Graziani 1975
No Change	<285	-	185	-	<200	-	
Red/ Orange	285–645	-	185	-	-	-	200–300
Brown	285–525	-	285	>100	300	<240	200–300
Black	525–645	>300	285	300	400	<340	300–350
Grey	>645	-	440/525	600	550	<600	550–600
White	>645	700	645-1200	>800	>650	<650	650~

of elements selected to cover variation in colour and provide information about burn patterning and temperature change. Multiple surface points were selected for measurement on each fragment accounting for intra-surface variation. Effectiveness depends on light control conditions, which were controlled with the use of colour scale is recommended for calibration. The analysis of a sample provides a partial view of the burn temperature for the total assemblage, but allows a detailed analysis of key changes which permit further interpretation.

Experiments have provided average cremated bone weights of male and female individuals, cataloguing discrepancies resulting from sex-related differences in stature (Tables 8.3 and 8.4) (Trotter and Peterson 1955; Warren and Maples 1997; Adams and Byrd 2008). Caution is required when using experimental data to estimate pre-cremation body weight as this assumes the complete preservation and recovery of all cremated remains (Warren and Maples 1997). Archaeological material can be subject to manipulation pre- or post-cremation, and taphonomy, sampling strategy and recovery method can all bias results. A variety of cremation procedures were used in the past, also influencing preservation. For example bone may be removed from the ash-bed for deposition, leaving samples of bone at the pyre-site, and a proportion in the final deposit. Inconsistencies in experimental bone weight research have also been exposed (Birkby 1991; Bass and Jantz 2004; Adams and Byrd 2008). Used as a guideline weights exceeding experimental values may be indicative of a greater than one individual, whilst lower weights could be indicative of an infant or juvenile cremation. However, this method is also subject to regional or temporal variation in stature, body weight values, diet and interpopulation variation.

Challenges exist in age and sex determination of cremated remains due to heat-induced changes (Mayne Correia 1997; Thompson 2005; Gonçalves 2011). Shrinkage can complicate estimation of sex, mass and stature from cremated remains (Stewart 1979). Experimental studies demonstrate variation in heat-induced shrinkage up to

Table 8.3: Post-Cremation Weight of remains from experimental studies.

Adult Cremated Remains Weight	Females	Males	Mean
Weight (g)	>1887	<2750	2430
Bass and Jantz (2004)		1865–5379 (mean 2350)	

Table 8.4: Weight of cremated remains as a proportion of pre-cremated body weight.

Type	Adult	Children	Infants
Cremated remains weight as proportion of precremation body weight (Ubelaker 2009, 4)	3.50%	2.50%	1%

25% of bone length (Van Vark 1970; Ubelaker 1978; 1989; Maples and Browning 1994), others stating 2% of the original length up to 800°C, while temperatures exceeding this could increase shrinkage to 10–15% (Byers 2002). This depends on bone type (Grupe and Herrmann 1983; Hummel and Schutkowski 1986; Buikstra and Swegle 1989). Nonetheless metric data is recommended for sex determination (Warren and Maples 1997; Byers 2002; Gonçalves *et al.* 2013), as well as the morphology of cranial, mandibular and pelvic elements, including size and shape of the mastoid process, occipital protuberance, sharpness of the supraorbital rim and emphasis of the brow edges, mandible morphology, and the sciatic notch and preauricular sulcus (Mayne Correia and Beattie 2002; Brickley and McKinley 2004; Buikstra and Ubelaker 1994; Mays 2002; White and Folkens 2005; Wahl 2008; Buikstra and Uberlaker 1994; Meindl and Lovejoy 1985).

Standard age determination methods can apply to cremated material (Wahl 2008) including degrees of epiphyseal fusion (Krogman and İşcan 1986; McKern and Stewart 1957; Redfield 1970; Suchey *et al.* 1984; Ubelaker 1989) and cranial suture closure (Todd and Lyon 1924; 1925a–c; Krogman and İşcan 1986; Buikstra and Ubelaker 1994; Baker 1984; Meindl and Lovejoy 1985) though sutures tend to fragment (Lisowski 1968; Buikstra and Goldstein 1973). Tooth eruption (Van Beek 1983; Anderson *et al.* 1976) and dental wear (Lovejoy *et al.* 1985) can be used, although teeth are degraded from *c.* 300°C or destroyed above *c.* 700°C (Shipman *et al.* 1984; Schmidt and Symes 2008). Rib end analysis (İşcan *et al.* 1984; 1985), and auricular and pubic symphysis scoring (Lovejoy *et al.* 1985) are other methods. The most accurate age at death estimations will always be provided by the application of a range of methods.

Pathological lesion identification in burned remains can be framed in relation to their differential preservation. Preservation is linked to burn temperature and duration, age, weight and body mass, as well as the resilience of specific elements. Thinner, delicate bones are less likely to survive, whilst dense bones, such as vertebrae survive better, meaning that pathologies in these areas may be more frequently noted. However, indices created from comparable and contemporaneous archaeological contexts to review differential loss of distinguishable pathological lesions in cremated and unburned material have confirmed similar levels of preservation for several conditions (Reinhard and Fink 1994). Though cremated material may not always preserve evidence of dental disease well, other aspects were noted at similar levels in both bone types. Poorer survival rates were noted for *Cribra orbitalia* in cremations, possibly due to thin bone incineration, but porotic hyperostosis of the parietal and occipital was better preserved (Reinhard and Fink 1994).

Finally, funerary practice and human activity has an impact on all methods of analysis, in affecting preservation through variation of temperature, exposure and duration. Post-cremation treatment including the gleaning of remains from the ash-bed for deposition or the addition of other cremated remains to the deposit, or the cremation of multiple individuals must be also be considered.

Results

Overall, the sample was heavily fragmented; the least fragmented was the burial cut from SC-AG-108 Enclosure 2, where a number of cranial bones were in a more complete state (Table 8.5, Fig. 8.10). Fragment size was relatively regular, high frequencies of smaller fragment sizes being indicative of the fragmented nature. Larger numbers of fragments over 20 mm and 30mm were recovered at RS-PE-29 3A Burial Cut, and the Ash-bed of SC-AG-108 Enclosure 1, which included relatively greater frequencies of cranial elements, though not as different in proportion to the other samples, they maintain the highest percentages of bones over 30mm (Table 8.6). High fracture rates were recorded at the Ash-bed of RS-PE-29, due to high frequencies of delaminated cranial bone. Patina, longitudinal, step and transverse fractures are present across the assemblage, but in greater numbers across RS-PE-29 and RS-PE-21. There is no particular distinction between the burial cut contexts and the ash-bed contexts (Fig. 8.11). Warping was noted in the sample across four of the five contexts, with higher rates in Burial cut of Enclosure 3A at RS-PE-29. None was recorded at the burial cut of SC-AG-108 Enclosure 2 (Table 8.7).

Table 8.8 presents a summary of colour across the sample; relevant photos are displayed in Fig. 10.12 1–7, these were compared against experimental results (Walker *et al.* 2008, pl. 20). Colour patterning was discernible across many of the samples, the colours on each item varied though contamination by soil colouration did impact the analysis.

Evidence from weight and skeletal part abundance for minimum number of individuals, skeletal distribution and identification of age and sex are presented below. No elements were observed with sufficient integrity for metrical data. At RS-PE-21 A Ash-bed undetermined and long bone fragments had the highest weight of the 298 fragments (Tables 8.9 and 8.10). No diagnostic elements were identified to evidence more than a single individual or particular age and sex determination. Spatial differentiation of the proximal and distal skeleton was apparent in fibula and long bone fragments in square 100/99, and cranial fragments in 100/100 possibly indicating body position within the pyre-structure.

At RS-PE-29 3A Ash-bed presented 26.5 g of 181 mainly unidentifiable fragments (Table 8.9). The weight is not indicative of greater than a single individual. A fragment of left supraorbital margin was scored at 2 for sex-related morphology (Buikstra and Ubelaker 1994) possibly indicating a female, but more evidence is required for a reliable determination. The paucity of material may be indicative of removal of remains for deposition elsewhere, though taphonomic processes may be partly responsible.

At RS-PE-29 3A burial cut 209.5 g was recorded of various elements, mainly cranial fragments (Table 8.9). The bone weight and lack of duplicated elements does not indicate multiple individuals (Tables 8.9 and 8.10). Due to fragmentation the petrous temporal could not provide reliable sex evidence. However, an unfused distal tibial epiphysis indicates the presence of an individual younger than 20 years of age (fusion 14–19 years if female, 16–20 if male; Buikstra and Ubelaker 1994; Scheuer and Black 2004). The majority of the cranial sutures identified were at least incompletely closed, though there were insufficient suture sites for composite scoring (Meindl and Lovejoy 1985). Therefore, evidence exists for the presence of a younger individual of indeterminate sex.

SC-AG-108 Enclosure 1 presents the greatest distribution of identifiable fragments including large numbers of cranial fragments (Tables 8.9 and 8.10). A left maxillary

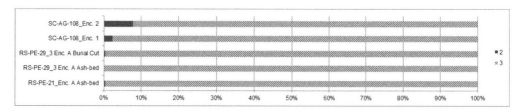

Fig. 8.10: Comparison of fragmentation as a percentage of total fragments for each sample.

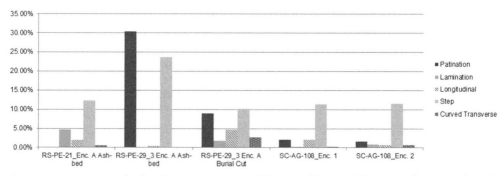

Fig. 8.11: Fracture type, displayed as a percentage of the assemblage total fragment frequency from the respective context.

Table 8.5: *Percentage completeness recorded as a proportion of the total number of fragments analysed.*

Degree Completeness	Category 2 (25–75%)	Category 3 (<25%)
RS-PE-21_Enc. A Ash-bed	0.30%	99.70%
RS-PE-29_3 Enc. A Ash-bed	0%	100%
RS-PE-29_3 Enc. A Burial Cut	0.40%	99.60%
SC-AG-108_Enc. 1	2.40%	97.60%
SC-AG-108_Enc. 2	7.90%	92.10%

Table 8.6: *Fragment size as a percentage of all fragments analysed for each assemblage, colour-coded to show highest percentage (dark red) to lowest (dark green).*

Fragment Size (mm)	10	15	20	30	40	50	60
RS-PE-21_Enc. A Ash-bed	72.80%	16.40%	6.00%	3.70%	1.00%		
RS-PE-29_3 Enc. A Ash-bed	63.00%	27.60%	8.30%	1.10%			
RS-PE-29_3 Enc. A Burial Cut	59.80%	21.20%	11.40%	6.10%	1.50%		
SC-AG-108_Enc. 1	60.40%	25.50%	8.20%	4.60%	0.60%	0.40%	0.20%
SC-AG-108_Enc. 2	71.00%	16.20%	6.20%	3.70%	2.10%	0.80%	

Table 8.7: *Warping frequency within the assemblage.*

Context	Warping Frequency	Total Fragments	% Warped
RS-PE-21 Enclosure A – Ash-bed	2	298	0.70%
RS-PE-29 3 Enclosure A – Ash-bed	2	181	1.10%
RS-PE-29 3 Enclosure A – Burial Cut	25	458	5.50%
SC-AG-108 Enclosure 1 – Ash-bed	3	1020	0.30%
SC-AG-108 Enclosure 2 – Burial Cut	0	241	0%

Table 8.8: *Summary of results of RGB analysis and comparison.*

Context	Temperatures Noted	Comment
RS-PE-21 Ash-bed	Up to 800–900°C in air	
RS-PE-29 Enclosure 3A Ash-bed	Maximum of 900–1000°C in air	Variation in temperature
RS-PE-29 Enclosure 3A Burial Cut	Exceeding 800°C	
SC-AG-108 Enclosure 1 Ash-bed	Maximum of 900–1000°C in air	
SC-AG-108 Enclosure 2 Burial Cut	Exceeding 800°C in places	

Table 8.9: Element Fragment Weight (g).

Site Context	1	2	3	4	5	7	8	9	10	11	14	15	16	19	20	21
RS-PE-21_Enc. A Ash-bed (g)	28.6	11.9	1.7					3.2				0.3				2.2
RS-PE-29_3 Enc. A Ash-bed (g)	20.5	1.8										0.1				4.1
RS-PE-29_3 Enc. A Burial Cut (g)	118	30.2	0.5	5.2			4	17.1	1							33.6
SC-AG-108_Enc. 1 Ash-bed (g)	93.9	24.2	10.3	0.3		14.3	0.4	17.1	31.4	0.3	1.3	4.6	0.4	6.8	2.5	50
SC-AG-108_Enc. 2 Burial Cut (g)	20.5	2			0.7	12.4	9	1.2			1.1	0.7		21.8		0.6

Table 8.10: Element Fragment Frequency.

Site Context	Area	1	2	3	4	5	7	8	9	10	11	14	15	16	19	20	21
RS-PE-21 A Ash-Bed	100/100	133	7	3					2				1				4
RS-PE-21 A Ash-Bed	100/99	83	40														
RS-PE-21 A Ash-Bed	99/99	15	4														
RS-PE-21 A Ash-Bed	Grand Total	231	51	3					2				1				4
RS-PE-29 3 A Ash Bed	91/98	39	4														26
RS-PE-29 3 A Ash Bed	92/97	12	1														
RS-PE-29 3 A Ash Bed	92/98	95	1										1				
RS-PE-29 3 A Ash Bed	93/92	2															
RS-PE-29 3 A Ash Bed	Grand Total	148	6										1				26
RS-PE-29 3 A Burial Cut	92/99	247	67	1	6			4	4	1							64
RS-PE-29 3 A Burial Cut	93/99	46	16														1
RS-PE-29 3 A Burial Cut	Grand Total	293	83	1	6			4	4	1							65
SC-AG-108_Enc. 1 Ash Bed	Grand Total	718	222	27	4		98	8	36	20	22	14	255	32	171	140	3717
SC-AG-108_Enc. 2 Burial Cut	Grand Total	184	22			10	56	32	18			28	60		133		105

22	24	25	26	27	28	29	30	31	32	33	34	37	38	39	52	54	57	58	Grand Total
1.8	4.9																		**54.6**
																			26.5
				0.3															**209.5**
3.7	15	0.4	0.2	0.7	4		2	6.5	1.9	0.6	3.7	0.1	0.3	0.4	0.2		0.1		**298**
				7.2		0.3	0.9									0.1	0.2	0.2	**79**

22	24	25	26	27	28	29	30	31	32	33	34	37	38	39	52	54	57	58	Grand Total
2																			152
	4																		127
																			19
2	4																		298
																			69
																			13
																			97
																			2
																			181
				1															395
																			63
				1															458
110	96	50	26	162	56		60	217	224	66	272	37	76	78	52		57		7123
				81		87	30									54	114	116	1130

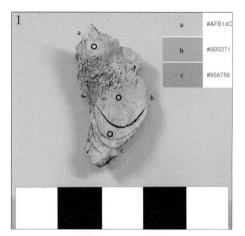

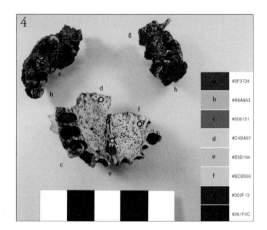

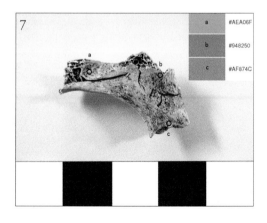

Fig. 8.12: 1: Diaphysis fragment exhibiting clear thumbnail fractures and warping, RS-PE-21. RGB colour analysis results displayed. 2: Diaphysis exhibiting thumbnail fracturing, RS-PE-29. RGB analysis results displayed. 3: Lambdoid suture porosity posterior, SC-AG-108 Enclosure 1. RGB analysis results displayed. 4: Inferior maxilla with porosity on the hard palate, and the presence of canine root, and those of both left and right first and second molars, SC-AG-108 Enclosure 1. RGB analysis results displayed. 5: Diaphysis of a left humerus, SC-AG-108 Enclosure 1. RGB analysis results displayed. 6: Lateral right mandibular ramus, SC-AG-108 Enclosure 1. RGB analysis results displayed. 7: First rib head right inferior, SC-AG-108 Enclosure 2. RGB analysis results displayed.

first incisor and indeterminately sided crown of the first maxillary molar were also noted. Two odontoid processes and two mental protuberance fragments provide evidence for a minimum of two individuals. One mental protuberance provided a possible inference of male sex, scoring 3–4 (Buikstra and Ubelaker 1994; Brickley and McKinley 2004), however the potential for heat-induced changes and interpopulation variation mean this is not the most secure diagnostic sexually dimorphic feature. Scores from the supraorbital margin also indicate a male, but may not be a reliable indicator due to effects of burning and the presence of porosity, influencing bone structure and size.

At the burial cut of SC-AG-108 Enclosure 2 just 79 g of bone was recovered (Tables 8.9 and 8.10), including part of a mandible and maxilla. The maxilla was linked to an unsided maxillary canine and both the left and right maxillary first and second molars, while the alveolar process of the third molars was open. The eruption of the permanent maxillary third molars indicates an older individual over 21 years of age, based on eruption sequences from Ubelaker (1989). The remains of at least one individual were deposited here.

Pathological lesions were noted across the samples, mainly as porosity, including porotic hyperostosis and periodontal disease (Table 8.12). At RS-PE-21 A Ash-bed porosity was distributed across cranial fragments, on the fragment of left supraorbital margin this may represent *cribra orbitalia*. At RS-PE-29 ash-bed porotic hyperostosis was recorded in cranial fragments, including the posterior cranial suture. There similar evidence at RS-PE-29 burial cut where porotic hyperostosis was noted in 20 indeterminate cranial fragments.

At the ash-bed of SC-AG-108 Enclosure 1, multiple cranial fragments exhibited porosity interpreted as porotic hyperostosis. Other fragments including that of a left first rib and long bone also revealed porosity. Porosity on a mandible body and mental protuberance provide evidence for periodontal disease, as does a possible abscess draining from the alveolar process of the left mandibular canine. Another concentration of porosity was recorded in the maxilla around the left alveolar process of the upper left canine.

SC-AG-108 Enclosure 2 presented several fragments with significant porosity from the mandible, maxilla and palate, which in the mandible and maxilla is interpreted as evidence for peridontosis. Porosity was also noted in a vertebra, three fragments of metacarpal diaphysis and undetermined fragments.

Discussion

Site patterns

Repeated patterns at the sites allow us to draw conclusions. The earliest dated archaeological evidence from the three sites is from the burial cut at RS-PE-29, between AD 1405 and 1610, most likely during the fifteenth century; the ash-bed structures all fall in the same range between AD 1465 and 1655, most likely during

Table 8.11: List of Element Numbers.

Element Number	Element	Element Number	Element
1	Undetermined	36	Manual Phalanx Intermediate Row
2	Long Bone Fragment	37	Manual Phalanx Distal Row
3	Temporal	38	Pedal Phalanx Proximal Row
4	Radius	39	Pedal Phalanx Intermediate Row
5	Sphenoid	40	Pedal Phalanx Distal Row
6	Zygomatic	41	Second Rib
7	Mandible	42	Metatarsal 1
8	Maxilla	43	Metatarsal 2
9	Humerus	44	Metatarsal 3
10	Tibia	45	Metatarsal 4
11	Metatarsal	46	Metatarsal 5
12	Cuneiform	47	Metacarpal 1
13	Phalanx	48	Metacarpal 2
14	Scapula	49	Metacarpal 3
15	Vertebra Undetermined	50	Metacarpal 4
16	Femur	51	Metacarpal 5
17	Sternum	52	Maxillary Incisor 1
18	Os innominatum	53	Maxillary Incisor 2
19	Rib	54	Maxillary Canine
20	Ulna	55	Maxillary Premolar 3
21	Cranial Fragment	56	Maxillary Premolar 4
22	Frontal	57	Maxillary Molar 1
23	Ethmoid	58	Maxillary Molar 2
24	Fibula	59	Maxillary Molar 3
25	Tooth Undetermined	60	Mandibular Incisor 1
26	Nasal	61	Mandibular Incisor 2
27	Palatal	62	Mandibular Canine
28	Parietal	63	Mandibular Premolar 3
29	Metacarpal	64	Mandibular Premolar 4
30	First Rib	65	Mandibular Molar 1
31	Occipital	66	Mandibular Molar 2
32	Cervical Vertebra	67	Mandibular Molar 3
33	Thoracic Vertebra	68	Carpal
34	Lumbar Vertebra	69	Tarsal
35	Manual Phalanx Proximal Row	70	Sacrum

Table 8.12: The presence of pathological lesions across the samples.

Site	Cribra Orbitalia	Porotic Hyperostosis	Other Lesions
RS-PE-21 Enc. A Ash-bed	1 Frontal fragment	1 Temporal fragment 3 Unidentified	Porosity: four unidentified fragments
RS-PE-29 Enc. 3A Ash-bed	Not noted	25 cranial fragments, one with posterior cranial suture	Not noted
RS-PE-29 Enc. 3A Burial Cut	Not noted	20 cranial fragments	Not noted
SC-AG-108 Enc. 1 Ash-bed	Not noted	68 cranial fragments	Periodontosis: 3 fragments of mandible mandible body and the mental protuberance
			Mandibular abscess: alveolar process left manidbular canine
			Porosity concentration in the maxilla around the left alveolar process of the left canine
			Porosity: 1 long bone fragment
			Porosity: 1 first rib fragment
			Porosity: Unidentified fragments
			Periodontosis
			Porosity: 2 mandible fragments
			Porosity: 6 fragments of maxilla and palatal bones
SC-AG-108 Enc. 2 Burial Cut	Not noted	Yes	Porosity: Vertebral fragment
			Porosity: 3 fragments of metacarpal diaphysis.
			Porosity: 4 undetermined fragments.

the sixteenth century. This aligns with the most active phase of related regional occupation. Radiocarbon dates from complexes increase in frequency from *c.* AD 1000, and peak between the thirteenth and sixteenth centuries (Iriarte *et al.* 2008). Site forms are consistent, comprising a pair of enclosures 20–30 m apart with earthen enclosures and central mounds. The enclosures measure 15–20 m in diameter and the mounds 5–7 m. The mounds are all approximately 0.5 m in height, constructed on the natural land surface. The complexes are either oriented on a NE–SW axis (RS-PE-21; RS-PE-29) or NW–SE axis (SC-AG-108). In each case the westerly enclosure is larger and in a more elevated location, a feature common to other sites (Iriarte *et al.* 2013). Regular landscape situation at elevated nodal points and monumental construction in repeated forms, containing pyre-debris and/or cremated remains points to a developed funerary tradition of regional significance involving multiple communities (Saldanha 2005; Iriarte *et al.* 2013).

Ethnography of the southern Jê allows contextualisation of this information. There is evidence for a dualistic worldview among the Kaingang, split between east and west (Veiga 2000), apparent in ceremonies relating to death. This is reflected in division between two moieties, the *Kamé* and *Kairu* (Veiga 2006). In the Kaingang creation myth they are ancestral fathers killed by a flood, which devastated everything save a single mountain peak named *Krinjijimbe*. Their souls took residence within the mountain, passing through different sides on the path to rebirth: *Kamé* to the west and *Kairu* to the east (Veiga 2000). Following their rebirth they reconstructed human society with their hands from ashes and cinders, recreating night and important animals; as such the world of the living was created by dead spirits (Veiga 2000). The east and west cardinal associations are of importance and link to other aspects, for example *Kamé* is associated with both the western cardinal point, and strength and intelligence. These provide an interpretative framework for the disparity in size between the larger westerly and smaller easterly enclosures. Though a direct link is not implied, such paired complexes could represent continuity of this idea within regional groups, and have significance in differentiated enclosures related with a similar dualistic cosmology and the identities of the individuals they were reserved for or used by. Descriptions of mound construction among historical groups also bear semblance in the low earthwork banks, mounds with associated plazas (Vasconcellos 1912 cited in Lavina 1994; Kempf 1947). Although regional configurations of mound and enclosure complexes extend beyond paired enclosures, there remain parallels within the ethnographic record. Archaeological examples include evidence for earth ovens and periodic feasting events (Iriarte *et al.* 2008; 2013; De Masi 2009). In local Jê groups different communities gather to commemorate the dead in *kikikoi* with feasting and the ritual preparation of a fermented maize-based beverage (Manizer 2006; Veiga 2006). In this respect, there is further evidence for ceramics across the sites, and additionally, repeated pyre goods in consistent vessel forms reconstructed as small cups and bowls (Fig. 8.13) possibly indicating a link between feasting or consumption and the dead.

Repeated monumental funerary constructions set within carefully controlled landscapes may be viewed as evidence of a developed system of control, and perhaps hierarchy and territoriality, reflecting complexity within society. This has parallels in the ethnographic records, where the complexes were developed as part of the burial of the principal chief and his subordinates were later buried within the same mound after death (Mabilde 1983). Reuse of specific sites is suggested by the cremated remains from RS-PE-29 3A burial cut, which pre-dates the ash-bed in the centre of the mound (see Fig. 8.4). Other sites in the locality also present this pattern, such as SC-AG-98, which has a single mound covering an ash-bed, and a cremated deposit (Caldarelli 2002). In this perspective the enclosures may be interpreted as ritually

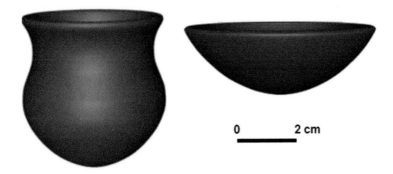

Fig. 8.13: Ceramic vessels reconstructed from SC-AG-98 (Scientia Consultoria Científica).

defined space for events related with the world of the dead, where local communities gathered to commemorate powerful individuals. However, the link between past and present is not direct and while there are general themes there are also discrepancies in historical and ethnographic information. Therefore this evidence acts as a lens to evaluate explanations for patterns and continuity across the region between prehistoric populations and the modern Jê groups (Noelli 1999).

Contexts
Cremated remains were recovered beneath the central mounds of the sites studied, both within ash-bed contexts and as cremated deposits in cut features. This pattern of pyre-structures and cremated deposits is repeated in other local sites (SC-AG-98, Caldarelli 2002; SC-AG-12, De Masi 2009). The following discussion aims to propose explanations for these patterns in conjunction with regional data.

Burning structures and ash-beds
Combustion is often achieved through the construction and destruction of a pyre. Each site presented evidence for ash-beds of pyre-debris and burnt clay forming a pyre-base. The burnt clay of the pyre-base suggests that pyres were constructed on the ground surface, or an area of cleared topsoil. Organisation in the charcoal, including remains of entire logs, provides evidence for rectilinear pyre-structure (Fig. 8.14); at RS-PE-21 measuring approximately 0.9 × 1.8 m. Other complexes present rectilinear forms which may be interpreted as box-pyres similar to this and RS-PE-29 (Fig. 8.15), such as the 1.2 × 1.2 m ash-bed at SC-AG-100 (Müller 2008) (Fig. 8.16). Pyre-base burn patterning is also important, as the greatest burning and oxidation occurs at the pyre edges, leaving red, oxidised sediment in contrast to black material beneath the pyre, shielded from oxidation and intense heat (Marshall 2011, 35) (Fig. 8.17). This phenomenon is clear at RS-PE-21 and 29 where increased oxidation or red colouration is particularly apparent towards the southerly edges of the pyre-base, while internal colouration is grey-black (Figs 8.5, 8.6, 8.15).

Ethnographic parallels allow us further insight into pyre construction. Vamblé's description of Xokleng cremation (Henry 1964) highlights wood being stacked to waist height, the body placed on the pyre with personal effects and covered with wood to the height of a man. The pyre would then be propped with stakes, presumably around the edge of the pyre-structure. Placement of the body within the pyre-structure has implications for the maximum exposure temperature. Exposure temperature has been shown to vary based on environment, burning within a pyre could expose the body to higher temperatures for longer durations.

Several criteria might determine fuel choice: practicality, burn intensity or ritual significance (Marshall 2011, 8). The abundance of Araucaria means it may have been used; anthracological analysis could definitively confirm this. Ethnographic sources describe how Araucaria trees were used in the *kikikoi* rite, which serves to separate the world of the living from the dead (Veiga 2000). During *kikikoi* a tree is felled and the trunk serves as a receptacle for a ritually prepared maize-based drink, the trunk itself represents the deceased and is similarly oriented; head to the west, feet to the east (Veiga 2000). *Pinhão* was also important in diet and this relationship between prehistoric groups and Araucaria may have encouraged them to enable its regional expansion, or the spread of the tree may have enabled their expansion. Experiments show that box-pyres require considerable amounts of fuel for extended burn duration; 956 kg of wood were burnt on one over five hours (Marshall 2011) (Fig. 8.18). A similar quantity of fuel would represent significant effort by those conducting the rites.

The orientation of the mounds may also be reflected in pyre and body orientation. Ethnographies describe specific orientations; in Kaingang burials the deceased lies

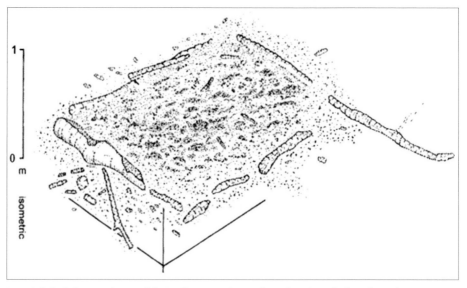

Fig. 8.14: Ash-bed form and pyre-debris after experimental combustion of a box shaped pyre structure (Marshall 2011, fig. 5).

feet to the west and head to the east (Mabilde 1983, 93), while Vamblé's description of Xokleng cremation places the head to the west and feet to the east (Henry 1964), as in the *kikikoi* (Veiga 2000). This presents further evidence for the continuation of an east/west theme in the spatial differentiation of aspects of funerary rites. The orientation of the pyre can affect the burn intensity and duration due to variation in environmental conditions, specifically wind. In this case the ash-beds all provide evidence for a SW–NE orientation. However, this may have been more closely related with the same motivation for the orientation of the sites than burn efficiency concerns. That they are located in elevated positions in the landscape increases the probability that the pyres were exposed to higher or more consistent wind speeds in any case.

The recovery of cremated material direct from the ash-bed is noted for three of the contexts. Though there is variability in the bone weights and remains, it would appear that these are the remains of cremations undertaken *in situ*. The material may have been disturbed in these cases, but definitive proof of whether the low weight from the ash-bed features indicates gleaning or is a result of other cultural or taphonomic processes is not provided. If they were removed for deposition elsewhere, it seems mounds were also raised on the pyre-site itself with some bone left in situ. It may be variation in the practice, where some remains were collected and others left, for example larger bones collected whilst smaller fragments were not.

Cremated deposits

Two samples were analysed from cremated deposits, which most likely represent gleaning of cremated remains from pyre-debris, and subsequent deposition of the disarticulated bone in oval-shaped cuts 45–80 cm in diameter. Low quantities of recovered bone could indicate incomplete collection, and would be causal factor in the low weight of bone recovered in ash-beds, ensuring that neither context contains the complete assemblage. Collection could also account for the fragmented nature of the remains.

The concentration of bone in cremated deposits raises questions as to the use of a container. Accounts of the Xokleng provide evidence for a comparative model, many of those described in this chapter note collection of remains after burning (Kempf 1947), and also deposition of cremated remains below mounds (Vasconcellos 1912 cited in Lavina 1994; Tavares 1910, Boiteux 1911; Paula 1924 in Lavina 1994, 67). Vamblé's account provides clear detail of the creation of baskets for the cremated remains, which were gathered up and taken to another location for burial (Henry 1964, 185–7). This may be linked to cremated deposits at the SC-AG-12 complex which De Masi (2005) suggested might be interpreted as deposition in baskets. It seems likely that a container was used, based on the feature form and the fact that the remains would have required a transport mode; it is therefore feasible to suggest the use of baskets. Redeposition is relatively common in cremation (Reinhard and Fink 1994; Marshall 2011), but whether this was applied to all remains, and the exact rationale for this treatment is unknown.

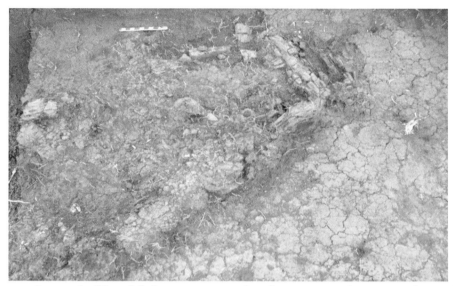

Fig. 8.15: Photograph of the ash-bed at RS-PR-29 revealing the patterns in colouration on the pyre based, indicating form and the more intensely oxidised sides. (NupArq, FURGS 2008).

This question relates to the specific rites and significance of cremation practice for these individuals.

Fracture and warping

Fracture patterns varied across the assemblages, but were most frequently noted at the ash-beds of RS-PE-29 3A and RS-PE-21. The greatest proportions of longitudinal fractures were identified at both sites. Additionally, significant numbers of delaminated cranial fragments were recovered from both contexts at RS-PE-29.

Fig. 8.16: The ash-bed recovered at SC-AG-100, this also contained cremated material (Muller 2008, fig. 14; Scientia Consultoria Científica. Photo: Ana Lucia Herberts).

Warping and curved transverse fracture were noted in many of the assemblages. Though linked with the burning of fleshed bone, this exact interpretation has been called into question as warping and curved transverse fracturing can occur on dry bone (Gonçalves *et al.* 2011). Therefore, these bones may have simply had well preserved collagen-apatite links at the time of burning, though this would not rule out the possibility that they were fresh, if not also fleshed at the time of burning. Ethnographic parallels provide no description of defleshing or burning of dry bones, and no evidence for defleshing was revealed during the analysis of material during this study.

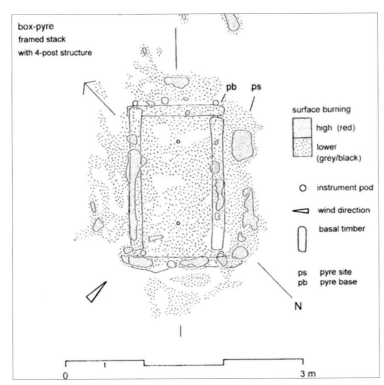

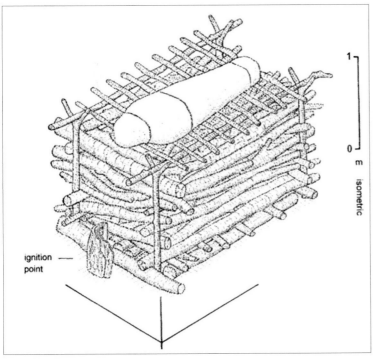

Fig. 8.17: Experimental ash-bed and pyre-base plan from box-shaped pyre combustion with burnt clay areas noted (Marshall 2011, fig. 7).

Fig. 8.18: Experimental reconstruction of a box shaped pyre structure (Marshall 2011, fig. 5).

Colour of the cremated remains

Colour analysis suggested temperatures as high as 800°C and in some cases close to 1000°C. However, the bones seem to have been subject to varied temperatures depending on their position within the pyre, and degree of exposure to the fire itself.

On areas of relatively clean bone there were clear indications of the higher temperature ranges. However, soil contamination, in particular through the application of paraloid, did hinder the application of colour analysis including the use of composite RGB values of bone surfaces.

This data has implications for our understanding of cremation practice. Firstly the construction of the pyre must have been substantial enough to provide burn intensity attaining these temperatures. As discussed, clearly a significant amount of fuel and appropriate environmental conditions were required to combust and expose the bone to such temperatures for long durations (Marshall 2011). This would require time to fully combust to the levels noted in the ash-bed and pyre-debris, lending support to the pyre being left to burn out while the participants in the rite returned to recover the cremated material for deposition as mentioned in ethnographic descriptions (Henry 1964; Kempf 1947).

The individuals

Sample weight and identified elements provide no confirmation of more than one individual in most contexts, except the ash-bed of SC-AG-108 Enclosure 1 where elements represent at least two individuals. There is evidence for cremation of multiple individuals at other sites such as SC-AG-12 (De Masi 2009). The precise circumstances and reasons for the cremation of multiple individuals may vary; this could hold a specific ritual purpose or it could simply be the death of two individuals treated together. The other sites provide evidence for at least single individuals, however, these contexts may evidence a mix of both single or multiple individuals, as low bone weights indicate a depleted sample.

The analysis identified a handful of clues regarding the individuals present. At RS-PE-29 3A burial cut aging evidence from the unfused distal tibial ephiphysis indicates a probable sub-adult of 14–20 years old. RS-PE-29 ash-bed presented a "feminine" type supraorbital margin, which could indicate female sex. Tooth eruption indicates an age of greater than 21 years at SC-AG-108 Enclosure 2. One of the two identified individuals in SC-AG-108 Enclosure 1 had possible male features in the mental protuberance of the mandible and another in the supraorbital margin. Though evidence for age and sex is limited it is possible that a range is represented.

The pathological lesions present may be associated with hygiene, infectious disease and diet. Porosity was noted across the various contexts, mainly affecting cranial elements. Though generally interpreted as porotic hyperostosis, at RS-PE-21 a fragment of the frontal bone presents possible *cribra orbitalia* and there is palatal porosity at SC-AG-108 Enclosure 2. Porosity on mandible fragments was interpreted as periodontal disease at SC-AG-108 Enclosures 1 and 2, while potential abscesses were noted around the alveoli of the upper left canine in SC-AG-108 Enclosure 1. Porotic hyperostosis on the cranial vault may be caused by the expansion of the diploë in response to marrow hypertrophy or pathological processes such as chronic scalp infections and scurvy (Ortner 2003). Traditionally, porotic hyperostosis has been linked to iron-deficiency anaemia however it may be more completely explained by anaemias causing premature red blood cell death and increased erythropoiesis, such as megaloblastic and haemolytic anaemias (Walker *et al.* 2009). *Cribra orbitalia* relates to porosity specifically in the orbits of the frontal bone. Though it presents a more complicated aetiology it can also be caused by megaloblastic and haemolytic anaemia, which can comprise subperiosteal bleeding associated with nutritional deficiencies such as scurvy. In the Americas heavily maize-based diets have been suggested as predisposing individuals to scurvy. For these acquired conditions diet, infections, disease and parasites are important considerations (Holland and O'Brien 1997). Though there is evidence for maize cultivation at related sites (Cortelletti 2012) the populations were not solely dependent on this resource, and the presence of *pinhão* and other foodstuffs in the local diet (Corteletti 2012) provide a source of nutrients and vitamins including iron and phytoferrin, an iron-protein complex which plays an important role in iron metabolism and storage (Panza *et al.* 2002, 280). This could indicate that these pathologies were not caused by the absence of elements in the diet, but may be linked to malabsorbtion. This can occur through the development of diarrheal disease, which contributes to depletion of B-complex vitamins, vitamin C, vitamin E, selenium and iron, together with an average of 20–60% of caloric intake loss (Walker *et al.* 2009). Parasite infection can also cause malabsorbtion, and can be detected archaeologically detected (Reinhard 1990; Ferreira *et al.* 2008) though no study has been undertaken in this region. The periodontosis present at SC-AG-108 may be linked to insufficient dental care as well as overall health status. The potential left mandibular abscess from the assemblage at SC-AG-108 Enclosure 1 would compound this evidence. The fact that each of these pathological lesions are present within the bone indicates that the individuals may have lived with the conditions long enough to induce a bony response, possibly during childhood, revealing resilience to nutrient stress.

Conclusions

Broader questions emerge when the remains are analysed within temporal and regional contexts. What was the significance of these cremation practices to these people? How did the practice change over time? What are the roots of this practice? This study has unravelled details of the cremation, assessing potential hypotheses based on the archaeological, ethnographic and ethnohistorical data available, acknowledging the historical continuity between southern Jê groups and prehistoric populations (Noelli 1999; 1999–2000; 2005; Iriarte *et al.* 2013). Patterns exist in the cremated remains and funerary contexts which, when linked, permit interpretations of rites and ritual. The emergence of a complex funerary tradition based around monumental constructions within a curated landscape, intensifying in fifteenth and sixteenth centuries, points to a population developing intricate social structures and specific hierarchies.

Cremation seems to have been conducted within a ritually defined space, suggesting a gathering of social grouping. Considering the archaeological evidence and accounting for ethnography, it is possible that these individuals were related with the leadership of local groups. Cremation may have been undertaken with a large amount of fuel in box-form, possibly Araucaria, with the body or bodies of the dead and pyre goods within the pyre-structure. The fuel load and extended burn can be inferred from the intensity of the temperatures the bones were exposed to over 800°C in each case. Both single and multiple individuals, of various ages were cremated, and there is possible evidence for both male and female individuals. The recurrence of ceramic forms within the pyres and cremated deposits suggest that these were deposited as pyre goods, possibly personal possessions of the dead, including objects that did not survive cremation or subsequent deposition. Following cremation, in many cases, a portion of the remains were collected from the ash-bed and deposited in small cut features. Ethnographic accounts document similar practices in historic times, where the remains were collected in baskets. The cremated deposits and the location of the pyre structure were covered with low mounds with banks are raised around them; the interior plaza levelled. Evidence from other sites (Iriarte *et al.* 2008; De Masi 2009) reveals reuse of these types of spaces for social ceremonies and ritual feasting, possibly related with the commemoration of the dead. Though it is not possible to make a direct link, there are Jê ethnographic accounts with evidence for the maintenance of ceremonial sites for this type of ritual feasting in the form of *kikikoi*.

The deposition in paired mounds may have been linked to a dualistic worldview and cosmology, exemplified by later Kaingang moieties. However, there may be several explanations for the burial of both the pyre and separate cremated deposit under individual mounds. Perhaps some individuals were left undisturbed within the ash-bed, whilst others were removed and buried elsewhere, or the individuals were generally collected, but mounds raised over both sites. Furthermore, the numbers of individuals present at these sites appear to be a small proportion of the population, given the number of complexes and the intensity of the occupation within the landscape. Unburnt remains interred in rock shelters and caves throughout the region could represent other parts of the population (Brentano and Schmitz 2010; Ulguim 2011, 57–9).

Further studies could address questions regarding the development of cremation practices among Jê groups, using other scientific methods to relate more microstructural changes within the bone to the funerary context. Measures such as Fourier Transform Infrared Spectroscopy (FTIR) could be used to access measures of crystal structure within bone (Crystallinity Index), ratios of carbonate/phosphate and carbonate/carbonate or histology and histomorphometry, revealing more detail of burning intensity, variation in burning and burn efficiency in a quantifiable manner (Thompson *et al.* 2011). Burn duration could be more effectively distinguished by comparison of bone surface and interior, linked to variables such as burn direction (Symes *et al.* 2008), local atmospheric conditions, fuel type, pyre size and physical attributes of the individual (Squires *et al.* 2011). A regional study of RGB values of cremated remains could allow further cross-comparison of burn patterning. Systematic sampling for analysis of absorbed organics within the ceramic assemblages from the sites is also recommended in order to understand the role of the ceramic items often placed with the deceased.

In conclusion, through the combination of evidence from the cremated remains, analysis of the landscapes, sites and archaeological data, historical accounts and ethnographic information, the chapter presented a deeper picture of the cremation and funerary practice at the three sites. This documented the possible construction of the pyre, the duration of the combustion and nature of the individuals involved, proposing explanations for the regional patterns in cremation and the significance of the mound and enclosure complexes and specific archaeological contexts. This evidence has wider implications for our understanding of the development of Jê societies in the region, providing the basis for further investigation into cremated remains from these sites.

References

Adams, J. B. and Byrd, J. E. 2008. *Recovery, Analysis, and Identification of Commingled Human Remains.* Totowa: Humana Press.

Anderson, D. L. Thompson, G. W. and Popovich, F. 1976. Age of attainment of mineralisation stages of the permanent dentition. *Journal of Forensic Sciences* 21, 191–200.

Araújo, A. G. M. 2001. Teoria e Método em Arqueologia Regional: Um Estudo de Caso no Alto Paranapanema, Estado de São Paulo. Unpublished PhD Thesis. São Paulo: Universidade de São Paulo, Faculdade de Filosofia e Ciências Humanas.

Araújo, A. G. M. 2007. Tradição Cerâmica Itararé-Taquara: Características, área de ocorrência e algumas hipóteses sobre a expansão dos grupos Jê no Sudeste do Brasil. *Revista de Arqueologia* 20, 9–38.

Baby, R. S. 1954. *Hopewell Cremation Practices.* Columbus: Ohio Historical Society Papers in Archaeology.

Baker, R. K. 1984. The Relationship of Cranial Suture Closure and Age Analyzed in a Modern Multi-Racial Sample of Males and Females. Unpublished Masters Dissertation. Fullerton: California State University Dept of Anthropology.

Baldus [1937] 1979. *Ensaios De Etnología Brasileira* (2nd edn). São Paulo: Companhia Editora Nacional.

Bass, W. M. and Jantz, R. L. 2004. Cremation weights in East Tennessee. *Journal of Forensic Science* 49(5), 901–4.

Beber, M. V. 2004. O Sistema de Assentamento dos Grupos Ceramistas do Planalto Sul Brasileiro: O caso da Tradição Taquara/Itararé. Unpublished PhD Thesis. São Leopoldo: Universidade do Vale do Rio dos Sinos.

Binford, L. R. 1963. An analysis of cremations from three Michigan Sites. *Wisconsin Archaeologist* 44, 98–110.

Birkby, W. H. 1991 The analysis of cremains. *Proceedings of the 43rd Annual Meeting of the American Academy of Forensic Sciences*, 18–23 February, Anaheim.

Bitencourt, A. L. V. and Kraupenhar, P. M. 2006. possible prehistoric anthropogenic effect on *Araucaria Angustifolia* (Bert.) O. Kunze expansion during the late Holocene. *Revista Brasileira de Paleontologia* 9(1), 109–16.

Boiteux, L. A. 1911. *Notas para a História Catharinense*. Florianópolis: Livraria Moderna.

Bonucci, E. Graziani, G. 1975. Comparative thermogravimetric X-ray diffraction and electron microscope investigations of burnt bones from recent, ancient and prehistoric age. *Atti della accademia Nazionale dei Lincei, Rendiconti, classe di scienze fisiche, matematiche e naturali* 59, 517–532.

Bradtmiller, B. and Buikstra, J. E. 1984. Effects of burning on human bone microstructure: a preliminary study. *Journal of Forensic Sciences* 29, 535–40.

Brentano, C. and Schmitz, P. I. 2010. Remanescentes Ósseos Humanos da gruta do Matemático (RS-A-08). *Pesquisas*. São Leopoldo: Antropologia. Instituto Anchietano de Pesquisas 68, 121–31.

Brickley, M. and McKinley, J. 2004. *Guidance on standards for Recording Human Skeletal Remains*. Reading: Institute For Archaeologists/British Association for Biological Anthropology and Oseoarchaeology Paper 7.

Brochado, J. P. 1984. An Ecological Model of the Spread of Pottery and Agriculture into Eastern South America. Unpublished Doctoral Thesis. University of Illinois at Urbana-Champaign.

Bronk Ramsey, C. 2009. Bayesian analysis of radiocarbon dates. *Radiocarbon* 51(1), 337–60.

Buikstra, J. E. and Goldstein, l. 1973. *The Perrins Ledge Crematory*. Illinois State Museum Reports of Investigation 28/Illinois Valley Archaeological Program Research Papers 8. Springfield: Illinois State Museum

Buikstra, J. E. and Swegle, M. 1989. Bone modification due to burning: experimental evidence. In: Bonnichsen, R. (ed.), *Bone Modification*. Peopling of the Americas Publication. Centre for the Study of the First Americans. Maine: University of Maine, 247–58.

Buikstra, J. E. and Ubelaker, D. H. 1994. Standards for data collection from human skeletal remains. In: Hass, J. (Org.), *Proceedings of Asimilal at the Field Museum of Natural History*. Fayetteville: Arkansas Archaeological Survey Research Series 44.

Byers, S. N. 2002. *Introduction to Forensic Anthropology: A Textbook* (2nd edn). Boston: Allyn and Bacon.

Caldarelli, S. B. (Org.). 2002. *Projeto de levantamento arqueológico na área de inundação e salvamento arqueológico no canteiro de obras da UHE Barra Grande, SC/RS. Relatório Final 1: Salvamento Arqueológico no Canteiro de Obras, Margem Direita e Esquerda do Rio Pelotas: Resultados dos Trabalho de Campo*. São Paulo: Scientia Ambiental.

Chmyz, I. 1967. Dados parciais sobre a arqueologia do Vale do Rio Paranapanema. In: *Publicações Avulsas 6. Programa Nacional de Pesquisas Arqueológicas - Resultados Preliminares do Primeiro Ano 1965-1966*. Belem: Museu Paraense Emílio Goeldi, 59–78.

Chmyz, I. 1968. Subsídios Para o Estudo Arqueológico do Vale do Rio Iguaçu. *Revista do Centro de Ensino e Pesquisas Arqueológicas* 1, 31–52.

Chmyz, I. and Sauner, Z. C. 1971. Nota sobre as pesquisas arqueológicas no vale do rio Piquiri. *Dédalo, Revista do Museu de Arqueologia e Etnologia* 13, 7–36.

Chmyz, I. Perota, C. Mueller, H. I. and Da Rocha, M. L. F. 1968. Nota Sobre a Arqueologia do Vale do Rio Itararé. *Revista do Centro de Ensino e Pesquisas Arqueológicas* 1, 7–23.

Copé, S. M. 2007. El Uso de La Arquitectura Como Artefacto en el Estudio de Paisajes Arqueológicos Del Altiplano Sur Brazilieño, Rio Grande do Sul. *Revista de Arquelogía* 2, 15–34.

Copé, S. M. 2008a. *Escavações arqueológicas em Pinhal da Serra, RS*. 11º Relatório Bimestral. Porto Alegre: NuPArq/UFRGS, IPHAN, BAESA.

Copé, S. M. 2008b. *Escavações Arqueológicas em Pinhal da Serra, RS*. 12º Relatório Bimestral – Fevereiro/ Março. Porto Alegre: NuPArq/UFRGS, IPHAN, BAESA.

Copé, S. M. and Saldanha, J. D. M. 2002. Em busca de um sistema de assentamento para o Planalto Sul-Rio-Grandense: Escavações no sítio RS-AN-03, Bom Jesus, RS. *Pesquisas Antropologia* 58, 107–20.

Copé, S. M. Saldanha, J. D. M. and Cabral, M. P. 2002. Contribuições Para a Pré-História do Planalto: Estudo da variabilidade de sítios arqueológicos de Pinhal da Serra, RS. *Pesquisas, Antropologia* 58, 121–38.

Corteletti, R. 2012. Projeto Arqueológico Alto Canoas – Paraca: Um Estudo da presença Jê no planalto catarinense. Unpublished Doctoral Thesis. Universidade de São Paulo

D'Angelis, W. 2003. O Primeiro século de registro da língua Kaingang (1842–1950): valor e uso da documentação etnográfica. Paper presented at the Third Macro-Jê Meeting. Brasília, LALI-UnB.

Da Silva, S. B. 2001. Etnoarqueologia dos Grafismos Kaingang: Um Modelo para a Compreensão das sociedades Proto-Jê Meridionias. Unpublished Doctoral Thesis. Faculdade de Filosofia, Letras e Ciências Humanas. Universidade de São Paulo.

De Masi, M. A. 2005. *Projeto de Salvamento Arqueológico Usina Hidrelétrica de Campos Novos. Relatorio Final*. Florianópolis: Brazil.

De Masi, M. A. 2006. *Xokleng 2860 a.C. As Terras Altas do Sul do Brasil*. Transcrições do Seminário de Arqueologia e Etnohistória. Tubarão: Editora Unisul.

De Masi, M. A. N. 2007. Análise de isótopos estáveis de 13/12C e 15/14N em resíduos de incrustações carbonizadas de fundo de recipientes cerâmicos das Terras Altas do Sul do Brasil. *Anais do XIV Congresso da Sociedade de Arqueologia Brasileira*. CD-Rom. Florianópolis: Brazil.

De Masi, M. A. 2009. Centros ceremoniais do planalto meridional: uma análise intrasítio. *Revista de Arqueologia SAB* 22, 99–113.

De Souza, J. G. 2012. Paisagem ritual no planalto meridional Brasileiro: Complexos de aterros anelares e montículos funerários Jê do sul em Pinhal da Serra, RS. Unpublished Masters Dissertation. Universidade de São Paulo.

De Souza, J. G. and Copé, S. M. 2010. Novas perspectivas sobre a arquitetura ritual do planalto meridional brasileiro: pesquisas recentes em Pinhal da Serra, RS. *Revista de Arqueologia* 23(2), 98–111.

Devlin, J. B. and Herrmann, N. P. 2008. Bone color as an interpretative tool of the depositional history of archaeological cremations. In: Schmidt, C. W. and Symes, S. A. (eds), *The Analysis of Burned Human Remains*. London: Academic Press, 109–35.

Dias, J. L. Z. 2004. A tradição taquara e sua ligação com o índio kaingang. Unpublished Masters Dissertation. Universidade do Vale do Rio dos Sinos.

Etxeberria, F. 1994. Aspectos macroscópicos del hueso sometido al fuego: revisión de las cremaciones descritas en el País Vasco desde la arqueología. San Sebastián: Munibe, 111–116.

Ferreira, L. F. Reinhard, K. J. and Araújo, A. 2008. *Paleoparasitologia*. Rio de Janeiro: Editora Fiocruz.

Gambim Júnior, A. 2010. Arqueologia dos Ossos Humanos: Práticas Funerárias no Planalto Norte do Rio Grande do Sul. Unpublished Dissertation. Porto Alegre: Pontifícia Universidade Católica do Rio Grande do Sul, Faculdade de Filosofia e Ciências Humanas.

Gessert, S. Iriarte, J. Ríos, R. C. and Behling, H. 2011. Late Holocene vegetation and environmental dynamics of the Araucaria forest region in Misiones Province, NE Argentina. *Review of Palaeobotany and Palynology* 166, 29–37.

Gonçalves, D. 2011. The reliability of osteometric techniques for the sex determination of burned human skeletal remains. *HOMO - Journal of Comparative Human Biology* 62(5), 351–8.

Gonçalves, D. Thompson, T. J. U. and Cunha, E. 2011. Implications of heat-induced changes in bone on the interpretation of funerary behaviour and practice. *Journal of Archaeological Science* 38, 1308–30.

Gonçalves, D. Thompson, T. J. U. and Cunha, E. 2013. Osteometric sex determination of burned human skeletal remains. *Journal of Forensic and Legal Medicine* 20(7), 906–11.

Grupe, G. and Herrmann, B. 1983. Über das schrumpfungsverhalten experimentell verbrannter spongiöser knochen am beispiel des caput femoris. *Zeitschrift für Morphologie und Antrhopologie* 74(2),121–7.

Henry, J. 1964. *Jungle People: A Kaingáng Tribe of the Highlands of Brazil*. New York: Vintage Books.

Herberts, A. L. and Müller, L. M. 2007. Os Sítios Funerários do "Projeto de Arqueologia Compensatória UHE Barra Grande – SC". *Anais do XIII Congresso da Sociedade de Arqueologia Brasileira*. CD-Rom. Florianópolis: Brazil.

Herrmann, B. 1977. On histological investigations of cremated human remains. *Journal of Human Evolution* 6(2), 101–2.

Hogg, A. G., Hua, Q., Blackwell, P. G., Niu, M., Buck, C. E., Guilderson, T. P., Heaton, T. J., Palmer, J. G., Reimer, P. J., Reimer, R. W., Turney, C. S. M., and Zimmerman, S. R. H. 2013. SHCal13 Southern Hemisphere Calibration, 0–50,000 Years cal BP. *Radiocarbon* 55(4), 1165–1176.

Holland, T. D. and O'Brien, M. J. 1997. Parasites, porotic hyperostosis, and the implications of changing perspectives. *American Antiquity* 62(2), 183–93.

Horta Barbosa, L. B. 1947: *A pacificação dos índios Caingangue paulistas. Hábitos, costumes e instituições desses índios.* Publicação n° 88 da Comissão Rondon, Rio de Janeiro: Imprensa Nacional, Conselho Nacional de Proteção aos Índios, 33–72.

Hummel, S. and Schutkowski, H. 1986. Das Verhalten von Knochengewebe unter dem Einfluß höherer Temperaturen. – Bedeutungen für die Leichenbranddiagnose. *Zeitschrift für Morphologie und Anthropologie* 77(1), 1–9.

Iriarte, J. and Behling, H. 2007. The expansion of Araucaria forest in the southern Brazilian highlands during the last 4000 years and its implications for the development of the Taquara/Itararé tradition. *Environmental Archaeology* 12, 115–27.

Iriarte, J., Gillam, J. C. and Marozzi, O. 2008. Monumental burials and memorial feasting: an example from the southern Brazilian highlands. *Antiquity* 82(318), 947–61.

Iriarte, J., Copé, S. M. Fradley, M. Lockhart, J. and Gillam, J. 2013. Sacred landscapes of the southern Brazilian highlands: Understanding southern proto-Jê mound and enclosure complexes. *Journal of Anthropological Archaeology* 32(1), 74–96.

İşcan, M. Y., Loth, S. R. and Wright, R. K. 1984. Age estimation from the ribs by phase analysis: white males. *Journal of Forensic Sciences* 29, 1094–104.

İşcan, M. Y., Loth, S. R. and Wright, R. K. 1985. Age estimation from the rib by phase analysis: white females. *Journal of Forensic Sciences* 30, 853–63.

Kempf, W. G. 1947. Notas sobre um grupo de indígenas de Santa Catarina. *Revista do Arquivo Municipal* CXII, 25–34.

Krogman, W. M. 1943a. Role of the physical anthrolopologist in the identification of human skeletal remains, Part I. *FBI Law Enforcement Bulletin* 12(4), 17–40.

Krogman, W. M. 1943b. Role of the physical anthrolopologist in the identification of human skeletal remains, Part II. *FBI Law Enforcement Bulletin* 12(5): 12–28.

Krogman, W. M. and İşcan, M. Y. 1986. *The Human Skeleton in Forensic Medicine* (2nd edn). Springfield: Charles Thomas.

Lavina, R. 1994. Os Xokleng de Santa Catarina: uma etnohistoria e sugestões para os arqueólogos. Unpublished Masters Dissertation. São Leopoldo: Universidade do Vale do Rio dos Sinos.

Lisowski, F. P. 1968. The investigation of human cremated remains. *Anthropologie und Humangenetik* 4, 76–83.

Lovejoy, C. O., Meindl, R. S. Pryzbeck, T. R. and Mensforth, R. P. 1985. Chronological metamorphosis of the auricular surface of the ilium: a new method for the determination of adult skeletal age at death. *American Journal of Physical Anthropology* 68, 15–28.

Mabilde, P. F. A. B. 1983. *Apontamentos sobre os indígenas selvagens da nação coroados dos matos da Província do Rio Grande do Sul: 1836-1666.* São Paulo: IBRASA/Brasília: INL, Fundação Nacional Pró-Memória.

Mabilde, A. P. T. 1988. O Índio Kaingang do Rio Grande do Sul no Final do Século XIX. *Documentos*. São Leopoldo: Instituto Anchietano de Pesquisas 2, 141–72.

Manizer, H. H. 2006. *Os Kaingang de São Paulo.* Campinas: Curt Nimuendajú.

Maples, W. R. and Browning, M. 1994. *Dead men do tell tales: The strange and fascinating cases of a forensic anthropologist.* New York: Doubleday.

Marshall, A. 2011. *Experimental Archaeology: 1. Early Bronze Age Cremation Pyres 2. Iron Age Grain Storage.* Oxford: British Archaeological Report 530.

Mayne Correia, P. 1997. Fire modifcation of bone: a review of the literature. In: Haglund, W. (ed.), *Taphonomy: The Postmortem Fate of Human Remains.* Boca Raton: CRC Press, 275–93.

Mayne Correia, P. and Beattie, O. 2002. A critical look at methods for recovering, evaluating and interpreting cremated human remains. In: Haglund, W. (ed.), *Advances in Forensic Taphonomy: Methods, Theory, and Archaeological Perspectives.* Boca Raton: CRC Press, 435–50.

Mays, S. 1998. *The archaeology of human bones.* London: Routledge.

McCutcheon, P. T. 1992. Burned archaeological bone. In: Stein, J. (ed.), *Deciphering A Shell Midden.* San Diego: Academic Press, 347–70.

McKern, T. and Stewart, T. 1957. *Skeletal Age Changes in Young American Males, Analyzed from the Standpoint of Identification.* Technical Report EP-45, Natick: Quartermaster Research and Development Command.

McKinley, J. 1997. Bronze Age barrows and funerary rites and rituals of cremation. *Proceedings of the Prehistoric Society* 63, 129–45.

Meindl, R. S. and Lovejoy, C. O. 1985. Ectocranial suture closure: a revised method for the determination of skeletal age at death based on the lateral-anterior sutures. *American Journal of Physical Anthropology* 68, 57–66.

Menghin, O. F. 1957. El Poblamiento prehistórico de Misiones. *Anales de Arqueología y Etnologia* 12, 19–40.

Métraux, A. 1946. The Caingang. In: Steward, J. H. (ed.), *Handbook of South American Indians. Volume 1: The Marginal Tribes.* Washington DC: Smithsonian Institution, 445–77.

Miller, E. T. H. 1971. Pesquisas arqueológicas efetuadas no Planalto Meridional, Rio Grande do Sul. Separata do Programa Nacional de Pesquisas Arqueológicas. *Publicações Avulsas Museu Paraense Emiliano Goeldi* 4 (15).

Miller, E. T. H. 1978. Tecnologia cerâmica dos Kaingang paulista. *Arquivos do Museu Paraense,Nova Série, Etnologia,* Curitiba, 2.

Müller, L. M. 2008. *Sobre Índios e Ossos: Estudo de Três Sítios de Estruturas Anelares Construídos para Enterramento por Populações que Habitavam o Vale do Rio Pelotas no Período Pré-Contato.* Unpublished Masters Dissertation. Porto Alegre: Pontifícia Universidade Católica do Rio Grande do Sul.

Müller, L. M. 2011 (ed). *Estudo e valorização do patrimônio arqueológico do vale do Rio Pelotas, SC: a contribuição da UHE Barra Grande.* Florianópolis: Scientia Consultoria Científica.

Nicholson, R. A. 1993. A morphological investigation of burnt animal bone and an evaluation of its utility in archaeology. *Journal of Archaeological Science* 20, 411–28.

Noelli, F. S. 1999. Repensando os rótulos e a história dos Jê no sul do Brasil a parti de uma interpretação interdisciplinary. *Revista do nuseu de Arqueologia e Etnologia* 3, 285–302.

Noelli, F. S. 1999-2000. A Ocupação Humana na Região do Sul do Brasil: Arqueologia, Debates e Perspectivas 1872–2000. *Revista da Universidade de São Paulo* 44, 218–69.

Noelli, F. S. 2005. Rethinking stereotypes and the history of research on Je populations in south Brazil: an interdisciplinary point of view. In: Funari, P. P. Zarankin, A. and Stovel E. (eds), *Global Archaeological Theory: Contextual Voices and Contemporary Thoughts.* New York: Kluwer, 167–90.

Noelli, F. S. (Org.), Silva, F. Veiga, J. Tommasino, K. Mota, L. T. M. and D'Angelis, W. R. 1998. *Bibliografia Kaingang: referências dobre um povo Jê do sul do Brasil.* Londrina: Editora da Universidade Estadual de Londrina.

Noelli, F. S. (Org.), Silva, F. And Mota, L. T. M. no date. Bibliografia Xokleng: referências dobre um povo Jê do sul do Brasil. Unpublished manuscript.

Ortner, D. J. 2003. *Identification of Pathological Conditions in Human Skeletal Remains* (2nd edn). London: Academic Press.

Panza, V., Lainez, V. Maroder, H. Prego, I. and Maldonado, S. 2002. Storage reserves and celular water in mature seeds of Aruacaria angustifolia. _Botanical Journal of the Linnean Society_ 14, 273–81.

Piga, G., Malgosa, A. Thompson, T. J. U. Enzo, S. 2008. A new calibration of the XRD technique for the study of archaeological burned human remains. _Journal of Archaeological Science_ 35(8), 2171–8.

Piga, G., Thompson, T. J. U. Malgosa, A. Enzo, S. 2009. The potential of X-Ray Diffraction in the analysis of burned remains from forensic contexts. _Journal of Forensic Sciences_ 54(3), 534–9.

Piga, G., Solinas, G. Thompson, T. J. U. Brunetti, A. Malgosa, A. and Enzo, S. 2013. Is X-Ray Diffraction able to distinguish between animal and human bones? _Journal of Archaeological Science_ 40, 778–85.

Prous, A. 1992. _Arqueologia Brasileira._ Brasília: Editora da Universidade de Brasília.

Redfield, A. 1970. A new aid to aging immature skeletons: development of the occipital bone. _American Journal of Physical Anthropology_ 33, 217–20.

Reinhard, K. J. 1990. Archaeoparasitology in North America. _American Journal of Physical Anthropology_ 82, 145–63.

Reinhard, K. J. and Fink T. M. 1994. Cremation in southwestern North America: aspects of taphonomy that affect pathological analysis. _Journal of Archaeological Science_ 21, 597–605.

Reis, M. J. 1980. A Problemática Arqueológica das Estruturas Subterrâneas no Planalto Catarinense. Unpublished Master Dissertation. São Paulo: Universidade de São Paulo, Faculdade de Filosofia e Ciências Humanas.

Reis, J. A. 2002. _Arqueologia dos Buracos de Bugre: Uma pré-história do Planalto meridional._ Caxias do Sul: Editora da Universidade de Caxias do Sul.

Ribeiro, P. A. M. 1980. _Casas subterrâneas no planalto meridional, município de Santa Cruz do Sul._ Revista do CEPA 9.

Ribeiro, P. A. M. and Ribeiro, C. T. 1985. _Levantamentos Arqueológicos no Município de Esmeralda, Rio Grande do Sul, Brasil._ Revista do CEPA 12(14).

Rohr, J. A. 1971. Os Sítios Arqueológicos do Planalto Catarinense, Brasil. _Pesquisas, Antropologia_ 24.

Rossi, D., De Grunchy, S. and Lovell, N. C. 2004. A comparative experiment in the consolidation of cremated bones. _International Journal of Osteoarchaeology_ 14 (2), 104–11.

Saldanha, J. D. M. 2005. Paisagem, Lugares e Cultura Material. Unpublished Masters Dissertation. Porto Alegre, Pontifícia Universidade Católica do Rio Grande do Sul.

Scheuer, L. and Black, S. 2004. _The Juvenile Skeleton._ San Diego: Elsevier.

Schmidt, C. W. and Symes, S. A. (eds). 2008. _The Analysis of Burned Human Remains._ London: Academic Press.

Schmitz, P. I. 1988. _As Tradições Ceramistas do Planalto Sul-brasileiro. Arqueologia do Rio Grande do Sul, Brasil._ Documentos, São Leopoldo 2, 75–130.

Schmitz, P. I. and Becker, I. I. B. 1991. _Os primitivos engenheiros do Planalto e suas estruturas subterrâneas: a Tradição Taquara. Arqueologia do Rio Grande do Sul, Brasil_ (2nd edn). Documentos, São Leopoldo 5, 65–99.

Schmitz, P. I. and Becker, I. I. B. 1997. Os primitivos engenheiros do Planalto e suas estruturas subterrâneas: a Tradição Taquara. In: Kern, A. A. (ed.), _Arqueologia Pré-Histórica do Rio Grande do Sul_ (2nd edn). Porto Alegre: Mercado Aberto, 251–94.

Schmitz, P. I., Rogge, J. H. Rosa, A. Beber, M. V. Mauhs, J. and Arnt, F. V. 2002. O Projeto Vacaria: Casas Subterrâneas no Planalto Rio-Grandense. _Pesquisas, Antropologia._ 58, 11–105.

Scientia Sul 2006. _Projeto de Arqueologia Compensatória - UHE Barra Grande - Santa Catarina. Relatório Parcial 3._ Florianópolis: Scientia Escritório Sul.

Shipman, P., Foster, G. and Schoeninger, M. 1984. Burnt bone and teeth: an experimental study of color, morphology, crystal structure and shrinkage. _Journal of Archaeological Science_ 11, 307–25.

Squires, K. E., Thompson, T. J. U. Islam and M. Chamberlain, A. 2011. The application of histomorphometry and Fourier Transform Infrared Spectroscopy to the analysis of early Anglo-Saxon burned bone. _Journal of Archaeological Science_ 38, 2399–409.

Stewart, T. D. 1979. _Essentials in Forensic Anthropology._ Springfield: Charles Thomas.

Suchey, J. M., Owings, P. A. Wiseley, D. V. and Noguchi, T. T. 1984. Skeletal aging of unidentified persons. In: Rathburn, T. and Buikstra, J. (eds), *Human Identifcation: Case Studies in Forensic Anthropology.* Springfield: Charles Thomas, 278–97.

Symes, S. A., Rainwater, C. W. Chapman, E. N. Gipson, D. R. and Piper, A. L. 2008. Patterned Thermal destruction of human remains in a forensic setting. In: Schmidt, C. and Symes, S. (eds), *The Analysis of Burned Human Remains.* London: Academic Press, 15–54.

Tavares, J. S. 1910. Os botocudos de Santa Catarina. *Brotéria, Série de vulgarização cientifica, Braga* 4, 277–86.

Thompson, T. J. U. 2004. Recent advance in the study of burned bone and their implications for forensic anthropology. *Forensic Science International* 146, 203–5.

Thompson, T. J. U. 2005. Heat-induced dimensional changes in bone and their consequences for forensic anthropology. *Journal of Forensic Sciences* 50(5), 1008–15.

Thompson, T. J. U., Gauthier, M. and Islam, M. 2009. The application of a new method of Fourier Transform Infrared Spectroscopy to the analysis of burned bone. *Journal of Archaeological Science* 36(3), 910–14.

Thompson, T. J. U., Islam, M. Piduru, K. and Marcel, A. 2011. An investigation into the internal and external variables acting on crystallinity index using Fourier Transform Infrared Spectroscopy on unaltered and burned bone. *Palaeogeography, Palaeoclimatology, Palaeoecology* 299, 168–74.

Thompson, T. J. U., Islam, M. and Bonniere, M. 2013. A new statistical approach for determining the crystallinity of heat-altered bone mineral from FTIR spectra. *Journal of Archaeological Science* 40, 416–22.

Todd, T. W. and Lyon, D. W. Jr. 1924. Endocranial suture closure, its progress and age relationship part I: adult males of white stock. *American Journal of Physical Anthropology* 7, 325–84.

Todd, T. W. and Lyon, D. W. Jr. 1925a. Cranial suture closure, its progress and age relationship part II: ectocranial closure in adult males of white stock. *American Journal of Physical Anthropology* 8, 23–45.

Todd, T. W. and Lyon, D. W. Jr. 1925b. Cranial suture closure: its progress and age relationship. part III: endocranial closure in adult males of negro stock. *American Journal of Physical Anthropology* 8, 47–71.

Todd, T. W. and Lyon, D. W. Jr. 1925c. Cranial suture closure: its progress and age relationship. part IV: ectocranial closure in adult males of negro stock. *American Journal of Physical Anthropology* 8, 149–68.

Trotter, M. and Peterson, R. 1955. Ash weight of human skeletons in per cent of their dry, fat-free weight. *Anatomical Record* 123, 341–68.

Ubelaker, D. H. 1978. *Human Skeletal Remains: Excavations, Analysis, Interpretation.* Chicago: Aldine.

Ubelaker, D. H. 1989. The estimation of age at death from immature human bone. In: İşcan, M. (ed.), *Age Markers in the Human Skeleton.* Springfield: Charles Thomas, 55–70.

Ubelaker, D. H. 2009. The forensic evaluation of burned skeletal remains: A synthesis. *Forensic Science International* 183 (1), 1–5.

Ulguim, P. F. 2011. The analysis of cremated archaeological remains from the southern Brazilian highlands: A study of the sites *RS-PE-21, RS-PE-29 and SC-AG-108.* Unpublished Master's Dissertation. University of Exeter.

Urban, G. 1992. A história da cultura brasileira Segundo as línguas nativas. M. Carneiro da Cunha (Org.) *História dos índios no Brasil.* São Paulo: Cia. das Letras/FAPESP/SMC, 87–102.

Van Beek, G. C. 1983. *Dental Morphology: An Illustrated Guide* (2nd edn). Bristol: Wright.

Van Vark, G. N. 1970. Some statistical procedures for the investigation of prehistoric skeletal material. Unpublished Master Thesis. Groningen

Veiga, J. 1992. Revisão Bibliográfica crítica sobre organização social Kaingang. In *Cadernos do Centro de Organização de Memória Sócio Cultural do Oeste de Santa Catarina - CEOM 8.* Chapecó: Universidade do Oeste de Santa Catarina.

Veiga, J. 2000. A retomada da festa do Kikikoi no P.I. Xapecó e a relação desse ritual com os mitos Kaingang. In: Motta, L. T. (ed.), *Uri e Wãxi: Estudos Interdisciplinares dos Kaingang*. Londrina: EUL, 261–92.

Veiga, J. 2006. *Aspectos Fundamentais da Cultura Kaingang*. Campinas: Editora Curt Nimuendajú.

Wahl, J. 2008. Investigations of pre-Roman and Roman cremation remains from southwestern Germany: Results, potentialities and limits. In: Schmidt, C. and Symes, S. (eds), *The Analysis of Burned Human Remains*. London: Academic Press, 145–61.

Walker, P. L., Miller, K. W. P. and Richman, R. 2008. Time, temperature, and oxygen availability: an experimental study of the effects of environmental conditions on the color and organic content of cremated bone. In: Schmidt, C. W. and Symes, S. A. (eds), *The Analysis of Burned Human Remains*. London: Academic Press, 129–35.

Walker, P. L., Bathurst, R. R. Richman, R. Gjerdrum, T. and Andrushko, V. A. 2009. The causes of porotic hyperostosis and cribra orbitalia: a reappraisal of the iron-deficiency-anemia hypothesis. *American Journal of Physical Anthropology* 139, 109–25.

Warren, M. W. and Maples, W. R. 1997. The anthropometry of contemporary commercial cremation. *Journal of Forensic Sciences* 42(3), 417–23.

White, T. D. and Folkens, P. A. 2005. *The Human Bone Manual*. London: Elsevier.

Wiesemann, U. 1978. Os dialetos da língua Kaingáng e Xokléng. *Arquivos de Anatomia e Antropologia* 3, 197–217.

Chapter 9

Case applications of recent research on thermal effects on the skeleton

Douglas H. Ubelaker

Introduction and funerary context

The evaluation of possible thermal effects on the human skeleton represents a major challenge for the skeletal biologist working with ancient remains. Since fragmentation is frequently associated with advanced thermal alterations, the recovered evidence is likely small and incomplete. The discoloration produced by burning further complicates recognition; the heat-altered fragments often appear similar to other materials in the immediate archeological environment. Even with thorough recovery, identification of burned skeletal remains can prove difficult in the laboratory. Once such fragments have been isolated, major questions emerge in analysis. What bones do the fragments represent? How many individuals are represented by the burned remains? What can be said about their sexes except differences between male and female weights and ages at death? Was evidence of trauma preserved and if so, was it ante-mortem or peri-mortem? How can taphonomic factors be excluded when interpreting the evidence of trauma? What temperatures were the remains exposed to and what can be said about the duration of the fire? Were the remains burned in the flesh or as dry bones? Can molecular evidence be recovered from the remains that might assist in the evaluation of the population origin or sex?

Fortunately, considerable research has been conducted to address many of the questions above. Much of this research relates to the practice of forensic anthropology and the myriad of issues that arise in the interpretation of human remains in the legal arena (Carr *et al.* 1986; De Haan and Nurbakhish 2001; Dirkmaat 2002; Fanton *et al.* 2006; Nelson and Winston 2006; Shkrum and Johnston 1992; Sledzik and Rodriguez 2002; Warren and Schultz 2002). Casework in forensic anthropology presents problems and issues that stimulate research ideas and projects. The resulting experimental research is not only applicable to future forensic cases, but also to the analysis of ancient remains. In addition, forensic casework and the associated scenarios provide experienced perspective and useful information. When cases involving the interpretation of thermal alterations are resolved, details of what happened may be forthcoming, clarifying aspects of the effects of burning on the human skeleton.

This chapter attempts to summarise much of the information gleaned from the published literature as it pertains to issues that arise in the study of remains from ancient contexts. Many of these issues are described in the questions outlined above. In essence, they involve determining if remains were exposed to heat and, if so, what can be concluded about the bones/individuals represented and the thermal events to which they were exposed. Although much can be learned from the bones themselves (Gejvall 1969; Kurzawski *et al.* 1987; Lisowski 1968; Masset 1987), the archaeological evidence recovered from careful excavation and documentation of context is paramount. The location of bone fragments *in situ* may reveal a great deal about their position when exposed to fire. Evidence of thermal change in the associated soil and/or other materials may indicate if the human remains were burned *in situ* or transported there from another source. Any evidence of bone articulation may reveal that the bones were burned in the flesh. Thorough excavation and documentation are the keys to success in the analysis of burned remains; a point that cannot be overemphasised (McKinley and Roberts 1993; Mayne-Correia and Beattie 2002).

The published literature relevant to the interpretation of burned remains is substantial and growing. The challenges of interpreting burned remains are well-known and have attracted considerable research attention. While the details inherent in this literature are important with different aspects of analysis, published syntheses are available and particularly useful. These summary works have been published by Fairgrieve (2008), Kurzawski *et al.* (1987), McKinley (2000), Masset (1987), Schmidt and Symes (2008), Thompson (2004) and Ubelaker (2009).

Methods of analysis

Detection of human remains

Exposure to heat can produce extremely variable effects on the human skeleton (Thompson 2005). Even with an intense fire of long duration, alterations to the human body can be minimal (Hurlbut 2000). Some individuals exposed to such thermal events die from smoke inhalation with minimal damage to body morphology. The body can be protected from direct exposure to the fire by clothing or structural features. Such protection may explain why some bodies show little or no heat effects. It also may explain extreme variation in thermal effects in which some body areas exhibit drastic alterations while other areas of the same individual are minimally affected. In cases involving multiple individuals located in close proximity, an extensively affected individual may have provided thermal protection to another displaying minimal effects. In short, forensic casework indicates that absence of thermal change on human remains does not rule out the possibility of a thermal event.

Of course, fire exposure may produce profound alterations to the exposed soft tissue without involving the skeleton. If the soft tissue is affected, protein denaturation and dehydration can lead to contraction of muscles. The extent of such contraction usually varies within the body, frequently producing greater contraction in the flexors than in the less bulky extensors. Such variation can lead to pronounced post-mortem flexion of the body, producing what has been termed the pugilistic pose (Saukko and Knight 2004).

In fires of great intensity and long duration, the soft tissues of the body can be destroyed, leading to exposure and thermal alteration of the hard tissues. As this process proceeds, individual bones will reveal a transition zone between the area with clear heat alteration and that still protected by the soft tissue. Evidence of this zone will be preserved with antiquity once the soft tissue remaining after the fire decomposes. Such a transition zone found on remains from archaeological contexts reveals that they were burned in the flesh and provides information on the body parts with greatest exposure to the heat source.

Prolonged exposure of the skeleton to extreme heat usually leads to severe fragmentation. Such fragmentation not only complicates analysis, but also challenges recovery efforts. The small bone segments can be camouflaged by the surrounding matrix, especially in the aftermath of large structural fires. Burned building materials and associated materials can appear very similar to the burned bone fragments. Forensic casework has demonstrated that some burned human bone fragments can be so morphologically compromised by the burning and other taphonomic factors that they cannot be recognised by external morphology alone. Similarly, some non-skeletal materials from these contexts cannot be distinguished from bone upon external examination. If bone is recognised, it is often difficult to determine from morphology alone if the fragments are of human or non-human origin.

Scanning-electron microscopy/energy dispersive spectroscopy (SEM/EDS) represents a useful tool to distinguish fragments of bone or tooth from other materials. SEM/EDS is frequently employed in forensic science to clarify the structural and elemental composition of evidence. Put simplistically, analysis generates an X-ray spectrum unique to the specimen. This spectrum reveals which elements are present and their approximate proportions. Comparative databases derived from known materials facilitate the identification of the sample being analysed. Such a database has been constructed for bones and teeth representing remains from varied contexts (Ubelaker *et al.* 2002). Spectral analysis of bones and teeth reveal the high proportions of calcium and phosphorus that allow them to be distinguished from other materials commonly found associated with human remains in both forensic and archeological contexts. While this technique is very effective to distinguish bone and tooth from other materials, it does not reveal if the samples are of human or non-human origin. Portable versions of this equipment are now available, making on site analysis possible (Schweitzer *et al.* 2005).

If recovered fragments are known to represent bone or tooth (Chandler 1987), it is important to determine species or at least distinguish human from non-human. Microscopy can be important to recognise non-human bone. Plexiform bone or a banding pattern of histological structures can prove diagnostic for non-human bone. Unfortunately, the human pattern of circumferential lamellar bone, primary osteons, secondary osteons and osteon fragments is shared with some other animals. Human/ non-human differences have been documented for histological structures but lack sufficient magnitude or nature to be diagnostic.

Solid-Phase Double-Antibody Radioimmunoassy (pRIA) offers a method to determine the species of bone and tooth fragments. In this technique, protein is extracted from the specimen and then subjected to a solid-phase double-antibody radioimmunoassay utilising controls of antisera produced in rabbits followed by antibody of rabbit gamma globulin produced in donkeys. The latter analysis is marked with radioactive iodine-125 so that the uptake can be measured and quantified. This technique will not only identify human status but also allow species identification of non-human fragments. The method can be applied to samples weighing 200 mg or less, even those from ancient contexts (Ubelaker *et al.* 2004).

Trauma analysis

Evidence for trauma in skeletons from archeological contexts provides vital information related to life history, likely cause of death, violence and many related social/anthropological factors. Ante-mortem trauma can be recognised if signs of remodelling are preserved. Recognition of peri-mortem trauma can be more complicated since post-mortem alterations can prove difficult to differentiate. Of the various types of trauma, several can be recognised from ancient skeletons, including blunt force, patterned (alterations that reveal class characteristics of the object involved), sharp force, projectile and even thermal.

Thermal exposure complicates trauma interpretation. As noted above, advanced thermal skeletal effects include substantial fragmentation and fracturing. This fracturing is particularly problematic since fractures represent primary evidence for trauma. Obviously, fragmentation complicates trauma analysis making the evidence more difficult to discover and interpret.

Forensic casework and experimental research indicate that significant evidence for trauma can survive post-mortem burning. The extensive analysis of decedents of the Branch Davidian group from Waco, Texas revealed evidence of peri-mortem trauma following the major fire that occurred there in 1993 (Ubelaker *et al.* 1995).

In their examination of preservation of bone peri-mortem trauma following incineration, Herrmann and Bennett (1999) reported that sharp force evidence remained present but required careful analysis of surface morphology and pattern of fractures. In their experimental work, blunt force trauma proved more difficult to differentiate from post-mortem thermal alterations.

In similar experimental research on cranial bone, Pope and Smith (2004) found that evidence for trauma could survive post-mortem burning. De Gruchy and Rogers (2002) further noted that chop- marks could be detected following a thermal event, but fragmentation complicated analysis. Symes *et al.* (2008) also note the problems of differentiating peri-mortem trauma from post-mortem change following burning but conclude that careful analysis of the fracture patterns can facilitate diagnosis.

Careful reconstruction following fragmentation can assist trauma analysis (Grévin *et al.* 1998). Following systematic and careful recovery, there is the potential that fragments can be reassembled to produce larger segments more conducive to trauma interpretation. Although this process can prove time-consuming and challenging, at least some reconstruction is usually possible even with advanced thermal change. The larger segments that result are more likely to produce diagnostic evidence not only for trauma detection, but also for other areas of analysis such as bone identification, determination of animal vs. human status, age at death estimation and other factors.

Temperature exposure

Thermal changes in skeletal remains reflect both the temperature and duration of the fire (Duffy *et al.* 1991). Working with archaeological samples, it may not always be possible to sort out these variables. Nevertheless, extensive experimental research provides information that is very useful in making these assessments (Brooks *et al.* 2006; Shipman *et al.* 1984; Stiner *et al.* 1995). The following presents many of the major studies in chronological order to expose the evolution of methodology and concepts.

Much of the foundations work on cremation studies and temperature assessment in particular can be traced to the classic work by Calvin Wells in 1960. Wells noted that the firing pattern on different bones reveals information on body position relative to the fire source. He referenced gas jet crematoriums at that time reaching temperatures between 820°C and 980°C. He noted in his study of archaeological cremations that the condition of associated glass beads suggested temperatures approximating 900°C.

In 1970 Van Vark reported experimental research involving the burning of fragments of mandible, patella and femur in a controlled electric oven. He found that at 700°C significant shrinkage began and reached a maximum at 800°C. Temperatures above 800°C produced loss of histological structure. Bones became increasingly brittle up to the temperature of 900°C and then no further changes were noted at higher temperatures.

Richards (1977) produced key information on temperature shifts in structure fires. Experimental work suggested that ceiling temperatures increased to 500°C in about 10 minutes. Temperatures then increased to about 700–800°C after about 55 minutes, followed by temperature reduction. In 1987, Wilson and Massey introduced experimental evidence using teeth. They found that the enamel rods structure became altered beginning at 800°C. Structural changes were also noted in dentin beginning at 600°C. The following year, Eckert *et al.* (1988) added detail to the information provided earlier by Wells regarding commercial cremation procedures and cases. They reported that retorts at that time reached temperatures of 1,500–1,600 degrees F.

Several key studies were published in 1989. McKinley added important detail on modern cremation practices, indicating the use of temperatures between 500°C and

1000°C with the procedure usually taking 1–2 hours. Commercial cremation of an adult produces an average of about 3000 g of residue, the approximate weight of the dry skeleton. In regard to archaeological cremations, McKinley noted that cremation in an outside fire would take 7–8 hours and require addition of fuel during the process. She also noted that the centre of the fire would be much hotter than the periphery and suggested that, in ancient times, bodies were likely placed initially on top of the burning fuel to receive oxygen. Also in 1989, Holland reported that low temperature burning (less than 800°C) produced minimal shrinkage to the cranial base. Working with faunal remains, Spennemann and Colley (1989) found that the bone surface texture was not altered up to a temperature of 500°C. Staining of bone resulted from materials in the immediate environment and considerable breakage occurred during recovery. They noted that color generally changed to white as temperature increased, but with considerable variation.

In experimental research, David (1990) reported that bones burned in a controlled brushfire produced fractures and brown/black staining but no calcinations. Bone calcination was achieved in a campfire fueled with eucalyptus reaching a temperature of 840°C after 1 hour and 5 minutes. Bones removed from the campfire after 25 minutes revealed fractures and a color range of brown, black, grey and white/blue. This study suggested that duration of burning is a key factor.

As noted by Grupe and Hummel (1991), caution should be employed in chemical analysis of cremated bone. They found that following exposure to temperatures above 200°C nitrogen and carbon isotope values were altered. Trace element analysis became limited to the modification of crystals and elemental volatilisation.

In 1993, Sillen and Hoering found in a Pretoria study that with temperatures between 200°C and 700°C crystallinity in bone increased; over 700°C apatite was transformed into whitlockite. Supporting earlier work by others, they found that at 300°C bone color changed to blackish-brown. At 500°C the bone colour began to fade and at 700–800°C became white and brittle. They also noted formation of char at temperatures between 300°C and 500°C.

In 1994, Cattaneo *et al.* found that human albumin survives cremation up to a temperature of 300°C. No albumin survived at higher temperatures. Holden *et al.* (1995) found that in heat-treated human bone, the organic component was lost at 400°C. Recrystallisation of the bone mineral occurred beginning at 600°C. At 1600°C the bone mineral melted. In 1997, Mayne-Correia published a key literature review summarising the information discussed above. This synthesis noted that the stress of weight during extreme heat can produce plastic deformation of affected bones. Also in 1997, Warren and Maples reported on residual weights of 100 adults following commercial cremation in Florida. With information on body weight prior to cremation, they were able to examine the relation between original body weight and residual weight after cremation. The mean of the residual weight was 2430 g with a range from 876 g to 3784 g. Residual weight represented 3.5% of body weight in adults, 2.5% in children and only 1% in fetuses.

In 1998, Quatrehomme *et al.* found no correlation of temperature with patterns within bone revealed by scanning electron microscopy. They also reported information from the literature that at 800–1400°C new crystals appear, with crystal fusion occurring above 1000°C. This study revealed that at 1600°C, bone mineral melts and recrystalises upon subsequent cooling. Also in 1998, Murad summarised information on commercial cremations noting that extreme temperatures can sometimes be reached. This publication also summarised previous unpublished research by Sonek noting that, in a study of the commercial cremation of 150 individuals, residual weight was between 892 g and 4056 g with a mean of 2348 g.

In 2002, Christensen experimentally found that type of bone is a factor in heat related fracturing. In her experiments, osteoporotic bone was more likely to fragment than healthy bone. This study has implications for the detection of disease in ancient cremated bone. In 2003, Koon *et al.* studied heat changes in sheep humeri using transmission electron microscopy. They found that low temperature exposure (roasting of bones) produced changes in collagen fibrils. Bass and Jantz (2004) reported experimental data on residual weights following commercial cremation of adults in East Tennessee. They found that adult cremations required 2–3 hours and several hours to subsequently cool, reaching high temperatures of 1600–1800°C. Adult male residual weights ranged from 1865 g to 5379 g with a mean of 3380g. Adult female residual weights ranged from 1050 g to 4000 g with a mean of 2350 g. Walker *et al.* (2005) explored the different factors involved in producing variation in color and organic content of cremated bone. They found that oxygen availability, duration and temperature all influenced the ultimate bone color.

The experimental studies discussed above offer a wealth of scientific information to be utilised in the study of cremated remains from archaeological contexts. These studies indicate the complexity of the issues involved. Variation in research results complicate interpretation and call for a thorough understanding of the issues involved.

Fleshed vs dry bone

In the analysis of burned samples from archaeological contexts, it is important to attempt to differentiate bones burned in the flesh from those burned in the defleshed, dry condition. Research by Baby (1954), Binford (1963) and Thurman and Willmore (1981) collectively indicate that dry bone burning produces longitudinal splitting that generally follows the stress lines of the bone. In addition, bones burned in the dry condition present superficial checking of the external surfaces and minimal evidence of morphological warping. Those bones burned with soft tissue exhibit more warping, more irregular longitudinal splitting and transverse fractures. The transverse fractures frequently present a curvilinear pattern.

More recently, Whyte (2001) reported experimental research utilising non-human animal remains. In support of the previously published research, Whyte found that alterations of burned dry bones displayed less evidence of warping and less variation in fracture patterns.

Ancient DNA

Molecular approaches to the study of ancient remains continue to grow in research importance. Such studies have great potential to examine past population relationships and ancestry issues, as well as disease diagnosis in paleopathology. The recovery of ancient DNA from archeological samples always presents challenges, especially in remains that are poorly preserved. These problems are compounded in the examination of ancient remains that have been burned.

Despite the obvious limitations presented by burning, some research indicates molecular analysis is possible subsequent to the thermal event. Sajantila *et al.* (1991) were successful in DNA typing of all 26 samples from ten individuals with extreme heat alteration in a forensic context. In 1995, Brown *et al.* reported DNA recovery from early Bronze Age cremated human bone excavated at Bedd Branwen, Anglesey, Wales.

Working with dental samples, Tsuchimochi *et al.* (2002) reported successful amplification and typing of dental pulp after the teeth had been heated to 300°C. However, they noted that molecular analysis was not fruitful with teeth exposed to higher temperatures.

Given the quantity and diversity of current DNA research, the prospects remain bright for this area of analysis of burned remains. Projects aimed at working with degraded samples and introducing new technology to increase the purity and yield of DNA (Ye *et al.* 2004) are particularly promising.

Individual representation

One of the major challenges facing the analysis of ancient cremated human remains is to determine the number of individuals present, as well as the sexes (Van Vark 1974; 1975) and ages at death represented. Such information is vital to an understanding of the cremation process itself and its role in the past social matrix. With the extreme fragmentation associated with advanced burning and calcination, analysis requires detailed sorting and inventory with the understanding that valuable information may not be preserved.

Nevertheless, careful sorting by element and extent of maturity can reveal a great deal of information. Even with extreme calcinations, many individual bones can be recognised, or at least sorted into categories such as those of the cranial vault, long bone diaphyses, vertebrae, etc. Evidence of maturity, especially the extent of epiphyseal closure and dental formation will likely be preserved. As noted above, reconstruction can be helpful to better recognise bone morphology and enhance classification. Even bone pathology can survive (Warren *et al.* 1999), although some diseased bone may be more likely to fragment. Sorting by bone type and age at death can reveal the minimal number of individuals present and perhaps some information on the sex ratio and age distribution. Sex estimation may be possible in some cases but usually is compromised by fragmentation. Likewise, some identifying characteristics may survive also depending on the extent of bone morphology reduction.

Recording the weights of the burned samples can be useful as well. This information relates the general amount of bone present in the various categories. Coupled with the analysis of minimal number of individuals and the demographic statistics, weights offer the potential to examine the bone representation in the recovered samples. Such analysis may offer insights into the extent to which remains of individuals were recovered. If the archaeological deposits were secondary, analysis may suggest the extent to which burned remains were recovered and transferred from the primary site of burning. This information leads to a greater understanding of the mortuary process and the social norms it reflects. Forensic-related research summarized above relates the approximate amount of residual material expected following a body cremation (Bass and Jantz 2004; McKinley 1989; Murad 1998; Warren and Maples 1997). This weight information can be compared to the weights of the materials recovered and the minimal number of individuals to estimate the percentage of residual material that was actually recovered archaeologically.

The cremated remains

The methodological research and issues discussed above are relevant in archaeological studies since the practice of cremation was globally widespread among peoples of the past (Childe 1945; Downes 1999; Haüsler 1968; Irion 1968; Oestigaard 2000). Although the details of cremation practice varied considerably, the resulting archaeologically recovered samples present challenges to skeletal biologists/bioarchaeologists working in many continents.

Many excellent studies have been conducted on archaeologically recovered cremated remains (McKinley 1994; McKinley and Roberts 1993; Merbs 1967; Weitzel 2007). An example from ancient Greece offers insight into the role of forensic research on thermal issues in bioarchaeological interpretation. Ubelaker and Rife (2007; 2011) examined human remains recovered from careful excavation of chamber tombs from the Roman-era cemetery of Kenchreai in Greece. Since the tombs had been subject to looting in earlier times, the remains were very fragmented. Analysis involved separation of skeletal remains displaying evidence of burning from those lacking such evidence. Careful inventory documented the presence of recognisable individual bones, as well as the presence of various types of bones and information on disease, sex, age at death and anything else that could be extracted. The weights of the different categories of remains were recorded as well. In analysis, this information was integrated to facilitate an over-all interpretation of the tombs' contents and the mortuary process likely involved.

Table 9.1 presents the weights of burned remains compared to the total weights of samples recovered from three tombs that were completely excavated with total recovery of the tomb contents. These data reveal that between two and 24% of the tombs' skeletal contents were burned. Archaeological evidence suggested that the burned remains likely originated mostly from niches located in the more elevated

Table 9.1: Comparison of the weights of burned remains with the total weights of samples of human remains recovered from three tombs in the cemetery at Kenchreai, Greece (modified from Ubelaker and Rife 2007, 42).

Tomb	Total weight (g)	Total weight burned (g)	% Burned
13	12,245	2949	24
14	34,235	2471	7
22	12,486	221	2
Totals	58,966	5641	10

areas of the tombs. The unburned remains typically originated from loculi located along the sides of the tombs (Ubelaker and Rife 2007).

The considerable variation in bone weight found among the three tombs largely reflected the number of individuals represented. At least 52 individuals were present in the large deposits of Tomb 14 and 19 and 13 individuals within the smaller deposits of Tombs 13 and 22 respectively. Thus at least 84 individuals were represented within the three tombs. The burned samples revealed the calcination, warping and fracture patterns suggestive of extensive burning of fleshed remains. Some bones displayed the plastic deformation suggestive of extreme high temperatures and prolonged duration of the fire. Ages at death of the cremated individuals ranged from young child to adult and all regions of the skeleton were represented (Ubelaker and Rife 2007).

In Tomb 13, 2949 g of cremated bone were recovered. Analysis revealed that a minimum of one adult was represented. According to the forensic research of Warren and Maples (1997) and others this weight could represent one adult. However, archaeological evidence suggested that the cremated remains originated from multiple niches, each representing a separate individual. Collectively, the bioarchaeological evidence indicated that the amount of cremated remains deposited in Tomb 13 was only a fraction of the amount originally available at the primary repository and site of the cremation event (Ubelaker and Rife 2007).

Likewise, Tomb 14 produced 2471 g of cremated bone which is consistent with the expected residual weight following the cremation of one adult. However, analysis of this sample revealed the presence of at least two subadults and one adult, as well as the presence of multiple niches. The weight information combined with the demographic analysis and archaeological evidence indicates that only a portion of the cremated remains were deposited in Tomb 14 (Ubelaker and Rife 2007).

In Tomb 22, less than 5% of the total weight of remains showed evidence of burning, an amount well within the limits of the weight expected from one individual. However, analysis revealed that the burned remains represented at least two subadults and one adult. These data also suggest that only a small portion of the total amount of residual remains following cremation were transferred to the tomb (Ubelaker and Rife 2007).

Analysis combined with archaeological evidence suggested that the original cremation event probably involved an intense fire of prolonged duration with the burning of fleshed bodies. To produce the extreme calcination observed with the remains recovered from the tombs, the original cremation event likely involved the addition of fuel to prolong the fire with limited subsequent recovery of remains. Both adults and subadults were included in the mortuary process involving cremation.

Conclusions

Analysis of cremated remains from archaeological contexts continues to be a challenging process for the bioarchaeologist. However, the methodological approaches to analysis have been greatly enhanced by experimental research largely stimulated by the practice of forensic anthropology. A great deal can be learned, not only about the individuals represented in cremated deposits, but also about the complex social processes reflected in this mortuary practice. The interaction between the two sub-disciplines remains the best way to ensure the accurate and innovative analysis of cremated remains.

References

Baby, R. S. 1954. *Hopewell Cremation Practices*. Columbus: Ohio Historical Society, Papers in Archaeology 1.

Bass, W. M. and Jantz, R. L. 2004. Cremations weights in East Tennessee. *Journal of Forensic Sciences* 49(5), 901–4.

Binford, L. R. 1963. An analysis of cremations from Three Michigan Sites. *Wisconsin Archaeologist* 44, 98–110.

Brooks, T. R., Bodkin, T. E., Potts, G. E. and Smullen, S. A. 2006. Elemental analysis of human cremains using ICP-OES to classify legitimate and contaminated cremains. *Journal of Forensic Sciences* 51(5), 967–73.

Brown, K. A., O'Donoghue, K. and Brown, T. A. 1995. DNA in cremated bones from an Early Bronze Age cemetery cairn. *International Journal of Osteoarchaeology* 5(2), 181–7.

Carr, R. F., Barsley, R. E. and Davenport, W. D. 1986. Postmortem examination of incinerated teeth with the Scanning Electron Microscope. *Journal of Forensic Sciences* 31(1), 307–11.

Cattaneo, C., Gelsthorpe, K., Sokol, R. J. and Phillips, P. 1994. Immunological detection of albumin in ancient human cremations using ELISA and monoclonal antibodies. *Journal of Archaeological Science* 21(4), 565–71.

Chandler, N. P. 1987. Cremated teeth. *Archaeology Today* 8(7), 41–5.

Childe, V. G. 1945. Directional changes in funerary practices during 50,000 years. *Man* 45, 13–19.

Christensen, A. M. 2002. Experiments in the combustibility of the human body. *Journal of Forensic Sciences* 47(3), 466–70.

David, B. 1990. How was this bone burnt? In: Solomon, S., Davidson, I. and Watson, D. (eds), *Problem Solving in Taphonomy: Archaeological and Palaeontological Studies from Europe, Africa and Oceania*, Tempus, Archaeology and Material Culture Studies in Anthropology Vol. 2. Queensland: University of Queensland, 65–79.

de Gruchy, S. and Rogers, T. L. 2002. Identifying chop marks on cremated bone: a preliminary study. *Journal of Forensic Sciences* 47(5), 933–6.

De Haan, J. D. and Nurbakhsh, S. 2001. Sustained combustion of an animal carcass and its implications for the consumption of human bodies in fires. *Journal of Forensic Sciences* 46(5), 1076–81.

Dirkmaat, D. C. 2002 Recovery and interpretation of the fatal fire victim: the role of forensic anthropology. In: Haglund, W. D. and Sorg, M. H. (eds), *Advances in Forensic Taphonomy: Method, Theory, and Archaeological Perspectives.* Boca Raton: CRC Press, 451–72.

Downes, J. 1999. Cremation: a spectacle and a journey. In: Downes, J. and Pollard, T. (eds), *The Loved Body's Corruptions: Archaeological Contributions to the Study of Human Mortality.* Glasgow: Cruithne Press, 19–29.

Duffy, J. B., Waterfield, J. D. and Skinner, M. F. 1991. Isolation of tooth pulp cells for sex chromatin studies in experimental dehydrated and cremated remains. *Forensic Science International* 49(2), 127–41.

Eckert, W. G., James, S. and Katchis, S. 1988. Investigation of cremations and severely burned bodies. *American Journal of Forensic Medicine and Pathology* 9(3), 188–200.

Fairgrieve, S. I. 2008. *Forensic Cremation: Recovery and Analysis.* Boca Raton: CRC Press.

Fanton, L., Jdeed, K., Tilhet-Coartet, S. and Malicier, D. 2006 Criminal burning. *Forensic Science International* 158(2–3), 87–93.

Gejvall, N. 1969. Cremations. In: Brothwell, D. and Higgs, E. (eds), *Science in Archaeology* (2nd edn). London: Thames and Hudson, 468–79.

Grévin, G., Bailet, P., Quatrehomme, G. and Ollier, A. 1998. Anatomical reconstruction of fragments of burned human bones: a necessary means for forensic identification. *Forensic Science International* 96(2–3), 129–34.

Grupe, G. and Hummel, S. 1991. Trace element studies on experimentally cremated bone. I. alteration of the chemical composition at high temperatures. *Journal of Archaeological Science* 18(2), 177–86.

Häusler, A. 1968. Burial customs of the ancient hunters and fishers of northern Eurasia. *Arctic Anthropology* 5(1), 62–7.

Herrmann, N. P. and Bennett, J. L. 1999. The differentiation of traumatic and heat-related fractures in burned bone. *Journal of Forensic Sciences* 44(3), 461–9.

Holden, J. L., Phakey, P. P. and Clement, J. G. 1995. Scanning electron microscope observations of heat-treated human bone. *Forensic Science International* 74(1–2), 29–45.

Holland, T. D. 1989. Use of the cranial base in the identification of fire victims. *Journal of Forensic Sciences* 34(2), 458–60.

Hurlbut, S. A. 2000. The taphonomy of cannibalism: a review of anthropogenic bone modification in the American Southwest. *International Journal of Osteoarchaeology* 10(1), 4–26.

Koon, H. E. C., Nicholson, R. A. and Collins, M. J. 2003. A practical approach to the identification of low temperature heated bone using TEM. *Journal of Archaeological Science* 30(11), 1393–9.

Kurzawski, V., Bouville, C. and Totoyan, C. 1987. Fouille d'un ensemble des sépultures à cremation à Martigues (Bouches-du-Rhône). In: Duday, H. and Masset, C. (eds), *Anthropologie physique et archéologie: méthodes d'étude des sépultures, Actes du colloque de Toulouse, 4, 5 et 6 novembre 1982.* Paris: Presses du CNRS, 67–72.

Lisowski, F. P. 1968. The investigation of human cremations. In: Saller, K. (ed.), *Anthropologie und Humangenetik.* Stuttgart: Gustav Fischer Verlag, 76–83.

McKinley, J. I. 1989. Cremations: expectations, methodologies, and reality. In: Roberts, C. A., Lee, F. and Bintliff, J. (eds), *Burial Archaeology: Current Research, Methods, and Developments.* Oxford: British Archaeological Report 211, 65–76.

McKinley, J. I. 1994. Bone fragment size in British cremation burials and its implications for pyre technology and ritual. *Journal of Archaeological Science* 21(3), 339–42.

McKinley, J. I. 2000. The analysis of cremated bone. In: Cox, M. and Mays, S. (eds), *Human Osteology: In Archaeology and Forensic Science.* London: Greenwich Medical Media, 403–21.

McKinley, J. I. and Roberts, C. 1993. *Excavation and Post-Excavation Treatment of Cremated and Inhumed Human Remains.* Reading: Institute of Field Archaeologists Technical Paper 13.

Masset, C. 1987. Le "Recrutement" d'un ensemble funéraire. In: Duday, H. and Masset, C. (eds), *Anthropologie physique et archéologie: méthodes d'étude des sépultures, Actes du colloque de Toulouse, 4, 5 et 6 novembre 1982.* Paris: Presses du CNRS, 111–34.

Mayne-Correia, P. 1997. Fire modification of bone: a review of the literature. In: Haglund, W. D. and Sorg, M. H. (eds), *Forensic Taphonomy: The Postmortem Fate of Human Remains*. Boca Raton: CRC Press, 275–93.

Mayne-Correia, P. and Beattie, O. 2002. A critical look at methods for recovering, evaluating, and interpreting cremated human remains. In: Haglund, W. D. and Sorg, M. H. (eds), *Advances in Forensic Taphonomy: Method, Theory, and Archaeological Perspectives*. Boca Raton: CRC Press, 435–50.

Merbs, C. F. 1967. Cremated human remains from Point of Pines, Arizona: a new approach. *American Antiquity* 32(4), 498–506.

Murad, T. A. 1998. The growing popularity of cremation versus inhumation: some forensic implications. In: Reichs, K. J. (ed.), *Forensic Osteology: Advances in the Identification of Human Remains* (2nd edn). Springfield: Charles Thomas, 86–105.

Nelson, C. L. and Winston, D. C. 2006. Detection of medical examiner cases from review of cremation requests. *American Journal of Forensic Medicine and Pathology* 27(2), 103–5.

Oestigaard, T. 2000. *The Deceased's Life Cycle Rituals in Nepal: Present Cremation Burials for the Interpretation of the Past*. Oxford: British Archaeological Report S835.

Pope, E. J. and Smith, O. C. 2004 Identification of traumatic injury in burned cranial bone: an experimental approach. *Journal of Forensic Sciences* 49(3), 431–40.

Quatrehomme, G., Bolla, M., Muller, M., Rocca, J. P., Grévin, G., Bailet, P. and Ollier, A. 1998. Experimental Single controlled study of burned bones: contribution of Scanning Electron Microscopy. *Journal of Forensic Sciences* 43(2), 417–22.

Richards, N. F. 1977 Fire investigations– destruction of corpses. *Medicine, Science, and the Law* 17(2), 79–82.

Sajantila, A., Ström, M., Budowle, B., Karhunen, P. J. and Peltonen, L. 1991. The polymerase chain reaction and post-mortem forensic identity testing: application of Amplified D1S80 and HLA-DQα Loci to the identification of fire victims. *Forensic Science International* 51(1), 23–34.

Saukko, P. and Knight, B. 2004. *Knight's Forensic Pathology* (3rd edn). London: Hodder Arnold.

Schmidt, C. W. and Symes, S. A. 2008. *The Analysis of Burned Human Remains*. London: Academic Press.

Schweitzer, J. S., Trombka, J. I., Floyd, S., Selavka, C., Zeosky, G., Gahn, N., McClanahan, T. and Burbine, T. 2005. Portable generator–based XRF instrument for non-destructive analysis at crime scenes. *Nuclear Instruments and Methods in Physics Research Section B: Beam Interactions with Materials and Atoms* 241(1–4), 816–19.

Shkrum, M. J. and Johnston, K. A. 1992 Fire and suicide: a three-year study of self-immolation deaths. *Journal of Forensic Sciences* 37(1), 208–21.

Shipman, P., Foster, G. and Schoeninger, M. 1984. Burnt bones and teeth: an experimental study of color, morphology, crystal structure and shrinkage. *Journal of Archaeological Science* 11(4), 307–25.

Sillen, A. and Hoering, T. 1993. Chemical characterization of burnt bones from Swartkrans. In: Brain, C. K. (ed.), *Swartkrans: A Cave's Chronicle of Early Man*. Transvaal Museum Monograph 8. Pretoria: Transvaal Museum, 243–9.

Sledzik, P. S. and Rodriguez, W. C. 2002. *Damnum Fatale*: the taphonomic fate of human remains in mass disasters. In: Haglund, W. D. and Sorg, M. H. (eds), *Advances in Forensic Taphonomy: Method, Theory and Archaeological Perspectives*. Boca Raton: CRC Press, 321–30.

Spennemann, D. H. R. and Colley, S. M. 1989. Fire in a pit: the effects of burning of faunal remains. *Archaeozoologia* 3(1–2), 51–64.

Stiner, M. C., Kuhn, S. L., Weiner, S. and Bar-Yosef, O. 1995. Differential burning, recrystallization, and fragmentation of archaeological bone. *Journal of Archaeological Science* 22(2), 223–37.

Symes, S. A., Rainwater, C. W., Chapman, E. N., Gipson, D. R. and Piper, A. L. 2008. Patterned thermal destruction of human remains in a forensic setting. In: Schmidt, C. W. and Symes, S. A. (eds), *The Analysis of Burned Human Remains*. London: Academic Press, 15–54.

Thompson, T. J. U. 2004. Recent advances in the study of burned bone and their implications for forensic anthropology. *Forensic Science International* 146S: S203–5.

Thompson, T. J. U. 2005. Heat-induced dimensional changes in bone and their consequences for forensic anthropology. *Journal Forensic Science* 50(5), 1008–15.

Thurman, M. D. and Willmore, L. J. 1981. A replicative cremation experiment. *North American Archaeologist* 2(4), 275–83.

Toulouse, J. H. 1944. Cremation among the Indians of New Mexico. *American Antiquity* 10(1), 65–74.

Tsuchimochi. T., Iwasa, M., Maeno, Y., Koyama, H., Inoue, H., Isobe, I., Matoba, R., Yokoi, M. and Nagao, M. 2002. Chelating resin-based extraction of DNA from dental pulp and sex determination from incinerated teeth with Y-Chromosomal alphoid repeat and short tandem repeats. *American Journal of Forensic Medicine and Pathology* 23(3), 268–71.

Ubelaker, D. H. 2009. The forensic evaluation of burned skeletal remains: a synthesis. *Forensic Science International* 183(1–3), 1–5.

Ubelaker, D. H. and Rife, J. L. 2007. The practice of cremation in the Roman-era cemetery at Kenchreai, Greece: The perspective from archeology and forensic science. *Bioarchaeology of the Near East* 1, 35–57.

Ubelaker, D. H. and Rife, J. L. 2011. Skeletal analysis and mortuary practice in an Early Roman chamber tomb at Kenchreai, Greece. *International Journal of Osteoarchaeology* 21(1), 1–18.

Ubelaker, D. H., Lowenstein, J. M. and Hood, D. G. 2004. Use of solid-phase double-antibody radioimmunoassay to identify species from small skeletal fragments. *Journal of Forensic Sciences* 49(5), 924–9.

Ubelaker, D. H., Ward, D. C., Braz, V. S. and Stewart, J. 2002. The use of SEM/EDS analysis to distinguish dental and osseus tissue from other materials. *Journal of Forensic Sciences* 47(5), 940–3.

Ubelaker, D. H., Owsley, D. W., Houck, M. M., Craig, E., Grant, W., Woltanski, T., Fram, R., Sandness, K. and Peerwani, N. 1995. The role of forensic anthropology in the recovery and analysis of Branch Davidian Compound victims: recovery procedures and characteristics of the victims. *Journal of Forensic Sciences* 40(3), 335–40.

Van Vark, G. N. 1970. *Some Statistical Procedures for the Investigation of Prehistoric Human Skeletal Material.* Groningen: Rijksuniversiteit te Groningen.

Van Vark, G. N. 1974. the investigation of human cremated skeletal material by multivariate statistical methods, I. Methodology. *Ossa* 1, 63–95.

Van Vark, G. N. 1975. The investigation of human cremated skeletal material by multivariate statistical methods, II. Measures. *Ossa* 2(1), 47–68.

Walker, P. L., Miller, K. P. and Richman, R. 2005. Time, temperature, and oxygen availability: an experimental study of the effects of environmental conditions on the color and organic content of cremated bone. *American Journal of Physical Anthropology* Supplement 40, 216–17.

Warren, M. W. and Maples, W. R. 1997. The anthropometry of contemporary commercial cremation. *Journal of Forensic Sciences* 42(3), 417–23.

Warren, M. W. and Schultz, J. J. 2002. Post-cremation taphonomy and artifact preservation. *Journal of Forensic Sciences* 47(3), 656–9.

Warren, M. W., Falsetti, A. B., Hamilton, W. F. and Levine, L. J. 1999. Evidence of arteriosclerosis in cremated remains. *American Journal of Forensic Medicine and Pathology* 20(3), 277–80.

Weitzel, M. A. 2007. Mortuary use of fire: An experimental approach. In: Weber, A., Katzenberg, M. and Goriunova, O. (eds), *KHUZHIR-NUGE XIV, a Middle Holocene Hunter-Gatherer Cemetery on Lake Baikal, Siberia: Osteological Materials.* Edmonton: CCI Press, 253–66.

Wells, C. 1960 A study of cremation. *Antiquity* 34(133), 29–37.

Whyte, T. R. 2001. Distinguishing remains of human cremations from burned animal bones. *Journal of Field Archaeology* 28(3/4), 437–48.

Wilson, D. F. and Massey, W. 1987 Scanning Electron Microscopy of incinerated teeth. *American Journal of Forensic Medicine and Pathology* 8(1), 32–8.

Ye, J., Ji, A., Parra, E. J., Zheng, X., Jiang, C., Zhao, X., Hu, L. and Tu, Z. 2004 A simple and efficient method for extracting DNA from old and burned bone. *Journal of Forensic Sciences* 49(4), 754–9.

Chapter 10

The interpretation and reconstruction of the post-mortem events in a case of scattered burned remains in Chile

Claudia Garrido-Varas and Marisol Intriago-Leiva

Introduction and funerary context

Scattered human remains were discovered by a forest ranger in "La Campana" national park, which is situated in the commune of Limache in the V Region of Chile. Geographically, the national park is part of the Coastal Mountain of central Chile between the coordinates 32°55'–33°01' south latitude and 71°09'–71°01' west longitude and it covers an area of 8000 hectares (Elórtegui and Moreira 2002).

The climate of this region corresponds to Mediterranean-type climate (warm temperate) with yearly average temperatures of 18°C maximum, and 8°C minimum. Rainfall is usually restrained to the winter months (May–August) and between September and April a prolonged dry season sets in. The remains discussed here were discovered on the 21 February 2007, in the mid-summer of the southern hemisphere. During the month of January 2007, 13 days registered maximum temperatures above 25°C (Dirección General de Aeronáutica Civil 2008).

During a routine patrol, a forest ranger detected the smell of decomposition in the area of "Quebrada Larga". According to the police report, he noticed the presence of garments, shoes and what might have been human remains in an extinguished fire pit. Remains in an advanced state of decomposition were also found scattered in the area surrounding the fire pit and in the bushes. The site was surveyed and the remains were recovered by the police force and later remitted to the Special Unit of Forensic Identification of the Forensic Service for analyses.

This Unit is a multidisciplinary team, highly trained in the areas of forensic anthropology, archaeology, odontology, pathology and photography. The number of cases studied each year is over a hundred, including mainly Human Rights investigations, mass disasters and criminal cases that require special expertise such as burnt, dismembered, putrefact and skeletonised individuals (Garrido Varas and Intriago Leiva 2012).

The cremated remains

One of the main challenges faced in this case was the necessity to determine the time, in respect to the moment of death, when these remains had been burned. It was important to understand the context of death in order to determine whether the body was burned peri-mortem or post-mortem. If the burning took place at the time of death, some possible explanations could be:

- A murder: where the perpetrator/s burnt the cadaver to get rid of the body and therefore the evidence.
- A suicide: the victim could have committed suicide close to a fire pit and caught fire after dying.
- An accidental death: the victim could have lost consciousness due to many possible reasons, for example because of the consumption of alcohol, and caught fire from the pit that he or she had earlier lit.

On the other hand, if these remains had been burnt post-mortem, there is not much place for doubt about the intentionality if this action, which can be interpreted as the intention of getting rid of the remains. The chances of the remains being burnt post-mortem accidentally were ruled out since there were no reports of bush fires for the previous ten years since the moment of the discovery of the remains. Also, the presence of a unique fire pit in the area, in which some remains were found, was a clear indication of human activity.

To solve this puzzle the anthropological analysis had the following specific objectives:

a) To analyse the burn patterns of the remains.
b) To establish the minimal number of individuals (MNI).
c) To construct a biological profile, establishing the presence of individualising traits.
d) To identify the presence of pre-, peri- and post-mortem trauma.
e) To establish the cause of death.
f) To estimate the time since death.

Laboratory activities included cleaning, compiling the inventory, anatomical articulation, anthropological and odontological analyses, radiography and photography. All the bones that had not been exposed to the action of heat, with exception of a tibia, were macerated in warm water, soft tissue was removed with the aid of paper towel, and were then left to dry at room temperature. This was done after radiographing and photographing the remains in order to detect any hidden marks on the bone surface. The tibia[1] was left intact for posterior sample selection for genetic analysis, following the protocols of the genetic laboratory in regards to sample selection.

The construction of the biological profile was performed according to the Standards for Data Collection from Human Skeletal Remains (Buikstra and Ubelaker 1994), pathologies were diagnosed using the reference criteria of Ortner (2003) and taphonomy was assessed using the criteria published by Behrensmeyer (1978),

Haglund (1991; 1997), Haglund, Reay *et al.* (1988; 1989) and Thompson (2005). All the remains were examined with the aid of a Leica Stereoscope. Minimal number of individuals was determined through the repetition of anatomical units.

Inventory and description of the remains

An important part of the skeleton was not present and the remains that were recovered showed a completely different preservation since some of them were exposed to fire and the rest were not (Fig. 10.1).

The remains that were not exposed to the action of fire presented a very homogeneous state of preservation, with a considerable amount of soft tissue adhering to the surface, mainly periosteum and ligaments. The bones exhibited a yellowish colour and some areas presented erosion of the cortical region. The bones had a fatty appearance, felt greasy to the touch and had the smell of decomposition. The group of bones exposed to the action of fire presented greater fragmentation, different colouration and an absolute absence of soft tissue or greasy appearance.

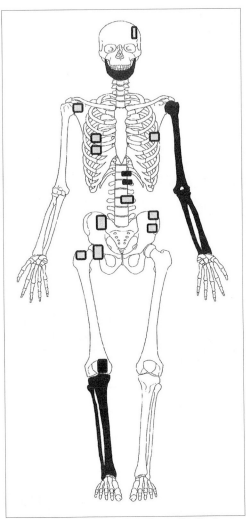

Remains not exposed to fire

MANDIBLE

The mandible was well preserved; it presented remains of soft tissue, mainly ligaments and periostium on the body, coronoid and mental spines. The condyles were incomplete showing splintered borders, exposure of cancellous bone and punctures on the neck of the condyles. The left sigmoid notch presented a fracture, and the right, a puncture of 1 mm diameter (which compromised the internal and external walls of the diploe). Splintered borders were observed on both coronoid processes.

The external surface of the right ramus and the mental area presented scoring; these are produced when teeth slip and drag over the cortex of the bone, the

Fig. 10.1: Skeletal elements recovered – displaying bones not heat altered (in black, note only the diaphysis present), fragments of bone exposed to fire (grey) and bones not recovered (white).

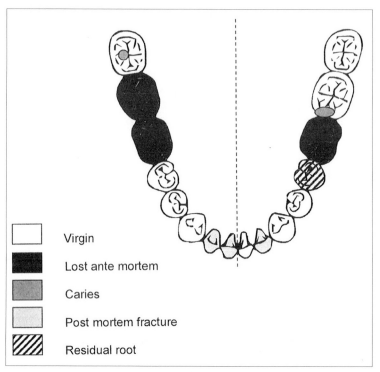

Fig. 10.2: Odontogram.

vertical lines presented various longitudes from 3 mm to 15 mm. The left ramus presented on the external surface three pits of 1 mm diameter (pits are marks left by chewing on the bone on only one surface without perforating the bone). The internal surface of the left mandibular angle also exhibited three pits. There was no evidence of heat damage to the bone or teeth. the surviving dentition is shown in Figure 10.2.

Third right molar: Oclusal caries, attrition of the enamel with loss of the distal cusps anatomy.

Second right molar: Lost ante-mortem, socket partially healed. Radio lucid areas in the socket.

First right molar: Lost ante-mortem, healed socket.

Second right premolar: Virgin, attrition of the enamel with partial loss of the vestibular cusp anatomy.

First right premolar: Virgin, attrition of the enamel with loss of the vestibular cusp anatomy and dentine exposure.

Right canine: Virgin, marked attrition of the distal slope with exposure of dentin.

Right lateral incisor: Post-mortem fracture of the crown, distal angle absent.

Right central incisor: Post-mortem fracture of the crown, incise border absent.

Left central incisor: Virgin, attrition of the enamel with dentine exposition.
Left lateral incisor: Virgin, post-mortem fracture of the crown.
Left canine: Virgin, marked attrition of the distal slope with exposure of dentin.
First left premolar: Virgin, attrition of the enamel with partial loss of the vestibular cusp anatomy.
Second left premolar: Residual root, polished dentine surface, rotated.
First left molar: Lost ante-mortem, healed socket.
Second left molar: Mesial caries, enamel attrition with dentin exposure.
Third left molar: Virgin, enamel attrition with dentin exposure.

The roots of the right incisors and second right premolar presented change of coloration of the exposed root area, which was dark reddish. There was subtle presence of calculus, more abundant on the lingual surfaces, accompanied to minor osseous reabsorption compatible with incipient periodontal disease.

VERTEBRAL FRAGMENTS

Two vertebral fragments were found. They were incomplete posterior arches. One of them corresponded either to the 12th thoracic or 1st lumbar vertebra. The borders were splintered. The base of the spinous process presented a puncture and after the removal of the soft tissue a pit in the inferior right articular facet was observed. Asymmetry of the inferior articular facets was noted, the right being smaller. The other fragment was a posterior arc of a lumbar vertebra, displaying the same asymmetry pattern. The spinous process was absent displaying jagged borders. After removing the adhering soft tissue, pits were revealed in the anterior surface of the posterior arch. All the damage described is compatible with the action of gnawing by canids.

Although it was not possible to directly articulate both fragments, they shared a similar morphology, preservation status and asymmetry pattern of the inferior articular facets. This could be an indication that they belong to the same individual since asymmetries are not always present at this level; Dia and Jia (1996) reported that facet angle asymmetry was present in a 27% on healthy patients and in 49% of patients with lumbar spine disorders.

LEFT HUMERUS

The head of the humerus and the inferior margin of the distal epiphysis were absent, displaying borders with gnawing marks. Scoring and furrows perpendicular to the major axis of the diaphysis were evident and the proximal extreme presented scooping (Fig. 10.3). No pits or punctures were detected in this bone; after the removal of the soft tissue, fine parallel series of incisor furrows were observed in the greater trochanter, compatible with rodent activity (Fig. 10.4). The radiography revealed a piece of cortical bone inside the medullar channel.

Fig. 10.3: Posterior view of the left humerus. Detail of scoring and furrows at the distal end.

LEFT RADIUS

Only the diaphysis was represented, with scooping and splinting fractures on the borders of the fragment. Punctures were observed in the proximal extreme and, after removal the soft tissue, one pit smaller than 5 mm was observed on the radial tuberosity.

LEFT ULNA

This was represented by the diaphysis and the base of the olecranon which exhibited various punctures, all smaller

Fig.s 10.4: Rodent marks observed through the stereoscope after removing the softy tissue.

than 5 mm. The distal epiphysis presented splinting fractures. The cancellous bone was preserved in this bone, with no signs of scooping.

RIGHT TIBIA

Only the diaphysis was present, the proximal end exhibited irregular and sharp borders, with a staggered appearance. Major destruction was observed on the anterior surface. Scooping was observed in both extremes with small remnants of cancellous bone.

RIGHT FIBULA

Only a fragment of the diaphysis was recovered, with both extremes showing irregular borders, splintering and a staggered appearance. It also presented a spiral fracture of the diaphysis. After removal of the soft tissue no further marks were found.

Analysed together, the group of bones not exposed to fire exhibited damage consistent with canid and rodent consumption (Haglund 1991; Haglund and Sorg 1997). Meticulous examination of the bones before and after the removal of soft tissue did not reveal any marks that could be interpreted as peri-mortem or related to the cause of death.

Remains exposed to heat

INCOMPLETE FEMORAL HEAD

The side was not determined. It presented different colour changes due to the exposure to heat; calcined and charred on the head and burnt towards the diaphysis (Fig. 10.5). This is indicative of a greater heat focus from the proximal to distal end.

Approximately 150 charred and calcined bone fragments (Fig. 10.6) were evaluated. Among them a fragment of a humeral or femoral head, innominate, costal bodies, vertebral bodies, and two fragments of cranium and a patella were recognised. Two bone fragments of cortical long bone approximately 3 cm long presented a series of fine incisor furrows parallel marks consistent with

Fig. 10.5: Femoral head with different colour modification due to the action of heat. Arrow shows the direction of the burning process.

Fig. 10.6: Calcined and charred fragments.

rodent activity (Fig. 10.7). Around 150 fragments of dimensions smaller than 1 × 1 cm and ashes were also recovered (Figs 10.8 and 10.9).

When compared to the chart detailing directionality of burning preapred by Symes *et al.* (2008) there are major differences; for example hands, knees and elbows are shown in the chart as the first sites to burn in a body. The left upper limb does not have signs of exposure to heat and in the knee area there is a fragment of distal femur that is burnt but the tibia does not show the effects of heat damage. Another discrepancy is found in the mandible; the chart describes the angles and basilar border of the mandible as first sites to burn, however the mandible was found with remnants of soft tissues and an absolute lack of signs of exposure to heat. Also, according to the chart, the heads of the humerus and femur are areas that burn after the diaphysis. In this case, the heads were calcined, showing a direction of burn from the head to the diaphysis.

Table 10.1: Time since death based on macroscopic alteration remains on surface.

Stage	Bone surface	Appearance	Crack edges	Soft tissues	Possible time since death (yrs)
0	No cracking or flaking	Usually greasy		Marrow present. Muscles, ligaments and skin may cover part or all the surface	0–1
1	Cracking, parallel to the fibre structure. Articular surfaces might show mosaic cracking	Might be greasy.		Might present skin and other tissues	0–3
2	Flacking usually associated with cracks	Damage to the outermost layers of bone	Angular in cross section	Remnants of ligaments, muscle and skin might be present	2–6
3	Patches of rough, homogeneously weather compact bone. Damage does not penetrate deeper than 1–1.5 mm	Fibrous texture	Rounded in cross-section	Rarely present	4–15+
4	Coarsely fibrous and rough in texture	Large and small splinters occur. Weathering penetrates into cavities	Splintered or rounded edges		6–15+
5	Cancellous bone usually exposed	Bone is falling apart in situ with large splinters			6–15+

Adapted from Beherensmeyer (1978)

Taphonomic analysis

The material under analysis corresponded to incomplete human remains which were found in two different states of preservation. One group corresponded to partially skeletonised remains, which presented remnants of soft tissue and a greasy appearance.

Beherensmeyer (1978) defined six weathering stages (Table 10.1), and the remains not exposed to fire were compatible with stage 1, since the bones had a greasy appearance and there were small areas of damage (erosion) on the cortical bone.

The burnt material presented great fragmentation and not a single complete bone was found in this group. This can be interpreted as indicating a prolonged exposure to heat. Both groups of bones presented clear signs of having been consumed by canids and rodents.

Haglund *et al.* (1989) defined five stages for the canid scavenging/disarticulation sequence of human remains (Table 10.2). All the unburnt material, and some of the material exposed to fire, presented signs of post-mortem consumption by carnivores, specifically canids and rodents, compatible with stage 4. It is important to note that common taphonomic changes are still observable on burned remains.

Biological profile and MNI

The age estimation, due to complete radicular development of the third molars and the presence of attrition facets, was above 21 years of age. Although the patterns of

Table 10.2: Post-mortem interval based on scavenging.

Stage	Characteristics	Disarticulation	Observed post mortem interval
0	Removal of soft tissue , no bony involvement	No	4 hours–14 days
1	Destruction of the ventral thorax, absence of the sternum, damage to distal ribs, evisceration	Removal of one or both upper extremities, including scapulae and partial or complete removal of clavicles	22 days–2.5 months
2	Most muscle has been eaten from the thorax and pelvic region as well as from the thigh	Fully or partially separated and removed lower extremities	2–4.5 months
3	Only segments of vertebral column articulated	Nearly complete disarticulation	2–11 months
4	Total scattering, with only cranium and assorted skeletal elements or fragments recovered	Total disarticulation	5–52 months

Adapted from (Haglund 1989; Haglund1997)

Fig. 10.7: *Charred fragments with rodent consumption marks.*

attrition are variable among populations, when comparing the degree of attrition of the molars with the Miles System (Hillson 1996), a range of 35–40 years was estimated. When applying the Lamendin method for age on the lateral left incisor, a mean age of 42 years with a range of 32–52 years of age was calculated (Lamendin *et al.* 1992). Considering all these odontological parameters, a broad age range of 32–52 years was established.

The mandible displayed masculine features, with a wide ramus, gonial eversion, prominent and quadrangular

Fig. 10.8: *Calcined and charred fragments.*

mental eminence and overall robusticity. Stature and ancestry were not estimated due to the lack of complete features in these remains.

The minimum number of individuals was established as one due to lack of repetition of anatomical units and the absence of elements belonging to different stages of development.

Individualising traits

The individual had lost three inferior molars during life, one of which (the second inferior right molar) could have been extracted in a period less than a year before the moment of death (Whittaker 1989). No restorative dental treatment was observed in the mandible.

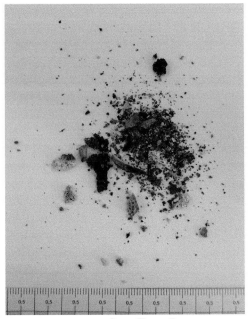

Fig. 10.9: Ashes of burnt bone.

Trauma analysis

All damage observed was categorised as post-mortem trauma. All the unburnt material as well as the burnt femoral head displayed signs of post-mortem disarticulation. Therefore, the timing of the burning event was after disarticulation of the remains. This is evident since two fragments of cranium were found in the fire pit and the mandible did not show any evidence of having being exposed to fire.

Partial charring and calcination of the remains was attributed to the action of a third party. The intentionality of the act of disposal of the remains through the deliberate act of burning the remains, in a specific fire pit, and for a prolonged time (or maybe with the aid of accelerants) is the main fact that gives this case the suggestion of homicide. Through the analysis of the burnt material, it was established that the remains were intentionally burnt after a considerable amount of time had passed from the moment of death. This behaviour could be interpreted as that of the murderer(s) going back to the crime scene with the intention of disposing of the remains through the action of fire. What the perpetrators did not consider was the activity of carnivores and rodents that had dispersed the remains in the area. Many cases studied in the Special Unit of Forensic Identification are cases where illegal exhumations have taken place, there is a pattern of elements recovered where most of the time the skull, hip bones and long bones are exhumed, leaving small bones such as vertebrae and hand and feet bones on the site. Taking this into consideration, if the skull was on the site at the time when the remains were burnt, it is acceptable to think that, in the case of the skull being there, it would have been added to the fire pit. It is also known that the skull is usually recovered from surface scavenged sites because it tends not to be transported by animals unless it is fragmented. Could it have been that the victim died of head trauma? It is curious that there was not a single tooth recovered from the fire pit. As teeth tend to survive the action of fire better than bone, it could be a possibility that the maxilla was never recovered by the perpetrators and added to the fire pit. All these are questions that are still unanswered, and ultimately the cause of death is still a mystery. The fact that there were two fragments of bone belonging to the cranium found in the pit, and nothing else (for example, teeth) supports the idea that there it could have been peri-mortem trauma to the cranium, and maybe the fragmented cranium was transported by scavengers, explaining why when the perpetrator/s returned to the scene the cranium was not accounted for. If the complete cranium had been burnt it could have been expected to find more fragments, particularly petrous portions and teeth, among the elements recovered.

Unfortunately our Unit was not in charge of the recovery of the remains, and therefore important contextual information might have been missed.

Time since death
Combining the systems of Behrensmeyer (1978) and Haglund and Sorg (1997), regarding damage patterns and carnivore consumption, it was established that the individual died in a period 3 years before the moment of the discovery of the remains. Behresmayer stage 1 considers a post-mortem interval of less than 3 years, however the range for total disarticulation is more extensive, being observed between 5 and 52 months. Considering that no studies of skeletonisation rates have been done in Chile, and that the contextual information was poor, we established a time since death of up to 3 years, based on the greasy appearance of the bone which, according to Behrensmeyer, can be observed between 0 and 3 years.

Discussion
One of the key limitations found in this case was the lack of information regarding the situation of the remains on the site prior to their recovery. An adequate evaluation of the site and the disposition of the remains is vital to establish the relationships amongst them, disturbance patterns, time since the deposition on the site and the factor or agents that have acted on the state of preservation or damage (Mayne-Correia 2002). Because of these restraints, and the lack of adequate registration, the results of the anthropological analysis must be broad and conservative, avoiding proving conclusions without testable bases.

Considering the above conditions, the meticulous analysis of the remains allowed, first of all, to estimate the MNI as one, based on the absence of repeated anatomical units. This conclusion, which might appear obvious, is not as simple as it might appear at first glance. For example, very different states of preservation were found among the remains, one group was subjected to the action of fire where the other presented rests of soft tissue and a greasy appearance. The other issue to consider was the number of elements recovered, this is rather a small number compared to the number of bones from an adult (McKinley 1994). Nevertheless, it was through the macro- and microscopic analyses that it was established that the burnt material was subjected to the action of the fire after the skeletonisation process, allowing the combining of the two different groups of bones as a single individual.

In fact, the most interesting aspect of this case is this differential preservation status. The group of bones that were not subjected to the action of fire allowed for estimating a time since death that was relatively accurate, considering that the remains were exposed to the outdoor elements. The incompleteness of the skeleton, the loss of tissue on the diaphysis, undulated borders, linear marks perpendicular to the major axis of the diaphysis, punctures, indentations and spiral fractures are all signs concordant with the carnivore consumption by canids (Haglund 1991; Haglund and Sorg 1997).

The literature about carnivore consumption of human remains (Haglund *et al.* 1988; 1989) describes a sequence that is only altered by specific conditions, such as difficulties in accessing the body. In standard conditions there is initial consumption and posterior disarticulation of the limbs, first the upper limbs and, usually, the last disarticulation corresponds to the pelvic femoral joint. It seems very likely that this was the sequence, which was of complete disarticulation, since two vertebral fragments were found completely separated from each other.

With respects to the bones exposed to heat it was possible to indicate that they were subjected to considerable damage by fire; this could have been over a long period of time of exposition, or a shorter period aided by accelerants, since most of the bones were calcined or charred (Thompson 2004; 2005). Although for many burned fragments it was impossible to determinate to which anatomical unit they belonged, it was possible with some of them to establish their human nature.

Another point of interest in the analysis of the burnt remains was the evaluation of the burning patterns to establish the form and situation of incineration (Pope and Smith 2004). There is abundant literature about the colour changes (Shipman *et al.* 1984; Mayne-Correia 1997; Nicholson 1993; Bennett 1999; Clark and Ligouis 2010) and their association with the direction of the fire, and that this shows constant patterns unless there are specific characteristics that alter this pattern. According to these patterns, the femoral head is normally preserved from the fire action because it is protected by an important bulk of muscle tissue. In the case of it being burned when still articulated and with plenty of soft tissue, the expected pattern of burning would be calcination in the diaphysis, charring towards the head and the head only burnt, in other words a progression from distal to proximal. Contrary to this pattern, a fragment of femoral head described on the remains exposed to heat presented the opposite, with calcination observed on the pole of the head and a gradual diminution of heat-altered changes towards the femoral neck area. This could have only happened if the femoral head was already disarticulated when exposed to the fire, which in the particular context of the case in study, is compatible with advanced disarticulation, a product of the time elapsed since death and the action of scavengers.

The burnt fragments that showed rodent furrows also sustain the idea that consumption by carnivores happened before the burning event. Rodent marks are parallel, perpendicular to the mayor axis of the bone, and clearly different to the canid marks by size, regularity and linear appearance (Haglund *et al.* 1988; Haglund and Sorg 1997). According to consumption sequence patterns, rodents usually access the remains after they have been consumed by larger animals, when there is still organic material available (Haglund and Sorg 1997). This, added to the observation that the borders of the indentations were calcined and the borders of the grooves were charred, is concordant with the fact that these fragments were consumed by rodents before the event of the fire, in other words it was considered very improbable that the marks were created after calcination,[2] and that it is probable that they occurred after the bone had been consumed by larger animals, which was clearly evident on the unburnt material.

With regards to the interpretation of the marks observed on the burnt material, it is important to mention that the literature indicates that incineration does not affect certain types of marks present on bone, especially those made by cutting elements, and that they retain the traits allowing posterior identification of the type of tool/ blade that caused them (Thompson 2004; 2005). In this case we extrapolated the characteristics of the rodent teeth as the cutting tool.

With respects to the biological profile, the scarcity of the remains due to the fire and scavenging action prevented a detailed profile, but it is important to mention that the mandible was of great utility in this respect, providing basically all the information for the biological profile. This shows the great relevance that sex dimorphism studies and age parameters derived from dental structures have in cases such as the one described here.

Conclusions

The anthropological and odontological analyses of this case lead us to conclude that the incomplete and altered human remains, belonged to a male in the age range 32–52 years. Ancestry and stature were not estimated due to the incomplete and fragmented nature of the remains. As an individualising trait, the dentition of the mandible showed that this person had lost three molars during life, of which one could have been extracted in a period less than a year from the moment of death. Also, the mandible showed no odontological restorative treatment.

The taphonomic characteristics of the remains showed an advanced state of disarticulation, scattering and consumption by carnivores (canids and rodents) and partial destruction by fire. The time since death was established as less than 3 years before the discovery in February of 2007. It was determined that the action of fire was posterior to the disarticulation of the body and performed intentionally by a third party.

Regarding the cause of death, no peri-mortem trauma was observed, so that the cause of death could not be determined. However, the intentionality behind the purpose of eliminating the remains through the action of fire might be interpreted to indicate that the manner of death was probably homicide.

The remains are still not identified and a genetic profile is available for further comparisons with missing persons.

Notes

1   The protocols of the Forensic Genetic Laboratories of the Chilean Forensic Service include the tibia as one of the preferred bones among the femur and humerus for sample selection. They also indicate that no treatment should be performed, such as removing soft tissue or subjecting the sample to the effects of cleaning solutions, dry or humid heat.
2   Luis Cabo, M. S., Applied Forensic Sciences Dept. Mercyhurst Collage, Erie, PA 16546. Personal comunication.

References

Bennett, J. L. 1999. Thermal alteration of buried bone. *Journal of Archaeological Science*, 26(1), 1–8.

Behrensmeyer, A. K. 1978. Taphonomic and ecologic information from bone weathering. *Paleobiology*, 4(2), 150–62.

Buikstra, J. E. and Ubelaker, D. H. 1994. *Standards for Data Collection from Human Skeletal Remains*. Arkansas: Arkansas Archaeological Survey Research Series 44.

Clark, J. L. and Ligouis, B. 2010. Burned bone in the Howieson's Poort and post-Howieson's Poort Middle Stone Age deposits at Sibudu (South Africa): Behavioral and taphonomic implications. *Journal of Archaeological Science* 37(10), 2650–61.

Dai, L. and Jia, L. 1996. Role of facet asymmetry in lumbar spine disorders. *Acta Orthopaedica Belgica* 62(2), 91–3.

Direccion General de Aeronautica Civil. 2008. Anuario climatológico 2007.Santiago, Chile. [Online] Available at http://164.77.222.61/climatologia/ Accessed, 07/06/13.

Elórtegui, S. and Moreira A. (eds). 2002. *Parque Nacional La Campana: Origen de una Reserva de la Biosfera en Chile Central*. Santiago: Taller La Era.

Garrido Varas, C. and Intriago Leiva, M. 2012. Managing commingled remains from mass graves: Considerations, implications and recommendations from a human rights case in Chile. *Forensic Science International* 219(1–3), 19–24.

Haglund, W. D. 1991. Applications of Taphonomic Models to Forensic Investigations. Applications of Taphonomic Models to Forensic Investigations, PhD. Dissertation in Anthropology, University of Washinton.

Haglund, W. D. 1997. Dogs and coyotes: postmortem involvement with human remains. In: Haglund, W. D. and Sorg, M. H. (eds), *Forensic Taphonomy: The Postmortem Fate of Human Remains*. Boca Raton FL: CRCPress, 367–81.

Haglund, W. D., Reay, D. T. and Swindler D. R. 1989. Canid scavenging/disarticulation sequence of human remains in the Pacific Northwest. *Journal of Forensic Sciences*, 34(3), 587–606.

Haglund, W. D., Reay, D. T. and Swindler, D. R. 1988. Tooth mark artifacts and survival of bones in animal scavenged human skeletons. *Journal of Forensic Sciences* 33(4), 985–97.

Hillson, S. 1996. Tooth wear and modification. In: Hillson, S. (ed.), *Dental Anthropology*. Cambridge: Cambridge University Press, 231–53.

Kingsmill, V. J. 1999. Post-extraction remodeling of the adult mandible. *Critical Reviews in Oral Biology and Medicine* 10(3), 384–404.

Lamendin, H., Baccino, E., Humbert, J. F., Tavernier, J. C., Nossintchouk, R. M. and Zerilli, A. 1992. A simple technique for age estimation in adult corpses: The two criteria dental method. *Journal of Forensic Sciences* 37(5), 1373–9.

Mayne-Correia P. 1997. Fire modification of bone: a review of the literature. In: Haglund W. D. and Sorg, M. H. (eds), *Forensic Taphonomy: Postmortem Fate of Human Remains*. Boca Raton, FL: CRC Press, 275–93.

Mayne-Correia P. and Battie, O. 1997. A critical look at methods for recovering, evaluating, and interpreting cremated human remains. In: Haglund W. D. and Sorg, M. H. (eds), *Forensic Taphonomy: Postmortem Fate of Human Remains*. Boca Raton, FL: CRC Press, 435–50.

McKinley, J. I. 1994. Bone fragment size in British cremation burials and its implications for pyre technology and ritual. *Journal of Archaeological Science* 21(3), 339–42.

Nicholson, R. A. 1993. A morphological investigation of burnt animal bone and an evaluation of its utility in archaeology. *Journal of Archaeological Science* 20(4), 411–28.

Ortner, D. J. 2003. *Identification of Pathological Conditions in Human Skeletal Remains*. New York: Elsevier.

Pope, E. J. and Smith, O. C. 2004. Identification of traumatic injury in burned cranial bone: An experimental approach. *Journal of forensic sciences* 49(3), 431–40.

Shipman, P., Foster, G. and Schoeninger, M. 1984. Burnt bones and teeth: an experimental study of color, morphology, crystal structure and shrinkage. *Journal of Archaeological Science* 11(4), 307–25.

Symes, S. A., Rainwater, C. W., Chapman, E. N., Gipson, D. R. and Piper, A. L. 2008. Patterned thermal destruction of human remains in a forensic setting. In: Schmidt, C. W. and Symes, S. A (eds), *The Analysis of Burned Human Remains*. New York: Elsevier, 15–54.

Thompson, T. J. U. 2004. Recent advances in the study of burned bone and their implications for forensic anthropology. *Forensic Science International* 146, 203–5.

Thompson, T. J. U. 2005. Heat-induced dimensional changes in bone and their consequences for forensic anthropology. *Journal of Forensic Sciences* 50(5), 1008–15.

Whittaker, D. K. and Macdonald, D. G. 1989. *A Colour Atlas of Forensic Dentistry*. New York: Wolfe .

Chapter 11

Conclusion

Tim Thompson

This book marks a significant step towards developing the archaeology of cremation that workers have discussed previously. It is not the first book to be published on burned bone, but it is the first to emphasise the archaeological context over methodologies, and the first to make an attempt at drawing together studies of cremation practice to better comment on this cultural phenomenon. A number of interesting conclusions can be drawn out.

Throughout this volume, the authors have made repeated claims that the focus on developing methods for studying burned and cremated bone are useful, but not sufficient on their own. The preceding case examples in this book have demonstrated that novel techniques can be useful when fully integrated with more traditional osteological analyses and the wider archaeological context. There are a number of examples in this volume of new interpretations being made of important archaeological sites and communities based on the application and considered integration of new methods of analysis.

Typically, cremation studies focus on Europe in their analysis. Partly this stems from the origins of cremation studies in Germany, but still, more recent work tends to focus on England, Italy, Spain and Portugal. It is clear that there is much to learn and assimilate from studies that focus on populations and individuals who died much further afield. By taking a more global approach to the subject, we can see the similarities and differences between practices from less well-documented contexts. One of the interesting directions for future work will be to explore these similarities more closely. For example, are they the result of similar views of the dead, or of the significance of fire, or could it be something external, such as similarities in the environment.

In a similar vein, it can be seen quite clearly that cremation is a common theme through time. That it is a constant theme of human funerary practice demonstrates that this is a subject worthy of greater attention, time and resources.

With this in mind, it has been noted that the published academic literature with regard to burned bone often splits between the forensic and archaeological contexts. This is understandable considering the differences in the conditions of the skeletal remains in each arena, but there is much that one discipline can teach the other. In our last two chapters in this volume we can see that approaches developed in the archaeology context can be applied successfully in modern, forensic case work, and the interpretation of this work can then be applied to studies of the past. Partly this is because in the modern context there is the real possibility of discovering what "actually" happened to the deceased, and this allows for the confirmation or refutation of ideas concerning fire and the body in a way that is not possible with ancient remains. This then gives us more certainty as anthropologists or bioarchaeologists when confronted with similar heat-induced features on archaeological remains.

The chapters presented here also suggest an exciting future for research in the study of burned bone. While we have more techniques available to us than ever before, many still need more thorough testing in the field. New technical developments will perhaps focus on biomolecular evidence or elemental and stable isotopic signatures within the cremated bone. New interpretive developments may focus on attempts to discover the currently undetectable aspects of the cremation rite as discussed in the Introduction.

In the Introduction it was argued that there are three key interpretive routes that archaeologists take when examining cremated human bone – that cremation is performed as a transformative event, that it marks a religious rite, or that it forms a public display for some reason. All three frameworks have been criticised, largely for being rather simplistic and one-dimensional. This is perhaps understandable considering cremated contexts lack the same understanding and theoretical frameworks that are present for inhumations. What has been presented in this volume shows how multi-dimensional such funerary rites can be.

Like a cremation itself, developing a new approach or approaches to the study of archaeological cremation contexts is not an event but a process. As such this volume is one step on that journey. It is hoped that others with cremated bone in their collections and archives will feel encouraged to bring it out and study it fully; that the adoption and integration of more advanced analytical methods will become increasingly desirable and commonplace, and; that cremation is viewed increasingly not as an aside or alternative to burial but as a distinct, intentional act with agency in its own right.